KB087314

THIS IS
GRAMMAR

THIS IS GRAMMAR 중급 2

지은이 넥서스영어교육연구소
펴낸이 임상진
펴낸곳 (주)넥서스

출판신고 1992년 4월 3일 제311-2002-2호 2-25
10880 경기도 파주시 지목로 5
Tel (02)330-5500 Fax (02)330-5555

ISBN 979-11-5752-366-5 54740
979-11-5752-362-7 (SET)

www.nexusEDU.kr

넥서스영어교육연구소 지음

NEXUS Edu

Preface

To Teachers and Students,

This brand new edition of *This Is Grammar* contains a wide range of engaging exercises designed to improve students' English grammar skills in the areas of speaking and writing. In Korea, middle and high school students have traditionally learned English grammar through rote memorization. We believe, however, that grammar learning is more effectively realized when explicit explanation is paired with practice. *This Is Grammar*(Updated version) provides Korean students with opportunities to practice using English while learning more about the world around them.

The exercises in the workbooks have been specially redesigned to give students more practice producing the target structures in a wide range of natural contexts. The teacher's guide includes additional grammar explanations and notes, comments on usage, and classroom presentation tips.

In sum, *This Is Grammar* provides teachers in Korea with a comprehensive set of materials to help them teach their students English grammar more effectively and with greater ease. It will help beginner to advanced level students improve their English skills in the areas of speaking and writing. We trust you will enjoy using *This Is Grammar* as a classroom textbook or by itself as a self-study aid.

- *Christopher Douloff*

This Is Grammar 최신개정판은 무조건 외우면서 학습하던 과거의 방법과는 달리, 현실에서 많이 쓰이는 진정성 있는 문장들을 토대로 핵심 문법을 체계적으로 설명하고 있다. 또한, 자연스러운 문맥 안에서 영어의 문장 구조가 습득될 수 있도록 단계별 연습문제와 활동들을 제공하고 있어 초급부터 고급까지의 학습자들이 문법 지식을 바탕으로 말하기와 쓰기 등의 영어 실력을 향상시키는 데 큰 도움을 줄 수 있으리라 기대한다. *This Is Grammar*(최신개정판)가 강의용뿐만 아니라 자습서로서도 훌륭히 그 역할을 해 낼 수 있으리라 믿으며, 학습자들의 영어 실력 향상에 큰 다리 역할을 할 수 있기를 기대한다.

- 집필진 Christopher Douloff, McKathy, Rachel S. L., Jenicia H., Jackie Kim

Series of features
시리즈의 특징

초급 1, 2

기초 문법 강화 + 내신 대비

영어의 기본 구조인 형태(form)와 의미(meaning), 용법(usage) 등을 설명하여 기초적인 문법 지식을 강화할 수 있도록 하였습니다. 다양한 유형의 연습문제를 단계별로 구성하였습니다. 또한, 시험에 자주 등장하는 문법 문제를 Review 및 Review Plus에서 다루고 있어 기본 실력을 강화하고 내신에 대비할 수 있도록 구성하였습니다.

중급 1, 2

문법 요약(Key Point) + 체계적인 문법 설명

Key Point 부분에 도식화 · 도표화하여 한눈에 보기 쉽게 문법을 요약해 놓았습니다. Key Point에는 문법의 기본적인 내용을, FOCUS에는 문법의 상세한 설명을 수록해 놓았습니다. 이를 통해 기초 문법부터 심화 문법까지 체계적으로 습득할 수 있습니다. 또한, 문법 오류 확인 문제부터 문장 완성하기와 문장 바꿔 쓰기 등의 다양한 유형의 연습문제들로 문법 지식을 확실히 다질 수 있도록 구성하였습니다.

고급 1, 2

핵심 문법 설명 + 각종 수험 대비

중 · 고급 영어 학습자들을 대상으로 수능, 텝스, 토플, 토익 등 각종 시험을 완벽하게 대비할 수 있도록 핵심적인 문법 포인트를 분석, 정리하였습니다. 다양하고 진정성 있는 지문들을 통해 풍부한 배경지식을 함께 쌓을 수 있도록 하였습니다. 고급 1권으로는 일목요연하게 정리된 문법으로 수험 완벽 대비를 할 수 있도록 하였고, 그리고 고급 2권으로는 문장 쓰기에서 에세이 쓰기까지의 영작 연습을 통해 기본적인 작문 실력을 향상시킬 수 있도록 구성하였습니다.

Workbook

초급 1, 2, 중급 1, 2, 고급 1 총 5권

별책으로 구성된 workbook은 원어민이 직접 집필하여 생생한 실생활 영어 표현으로 문장을 구성 하였으며, Unit별 2페이지씩 연습문제를 수록하여 학습한 내용을 다시 한 번 점검하고 확실한 본인의 실력을 쌓을 수 있도록 구성 하였습니다.

Composition and Features
구성과 특징

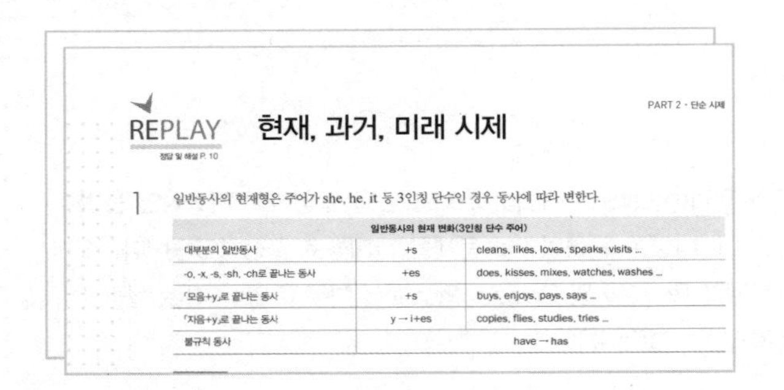

REPLAY 현재, 과거, 미래 시제

PART 2 · 단순 시제

정답 및 해설 P. 10

1 일반동사의 현재형은 주어가 she, he, it 등 3인칭 단수인 경우 동사에 따라 변한다.

일반동사의 현재 변화(3인칭 단수 주어)		
대부분의 일반동사	+s	cleans, likes, loves, speaks, visits ...
-o, -x, -s, -sh, -ch로 끝나는 동사	+es	does, kisses, mixes, watches, washes ...
「모음+y」로 끝나는 동사	+s	buys, enjoys, pays, says ...
「자음+y」로 끝나는 동사	y → i+es	copies, flies, studies, tries ...
불규칙 동사	have → has	

• REPLAY

문법의 기본 형태와 의미, 그리고 쓰임을 간단히 요약하였으며 Check-up을 통해 기초 문법을 다질 수 있습니다.

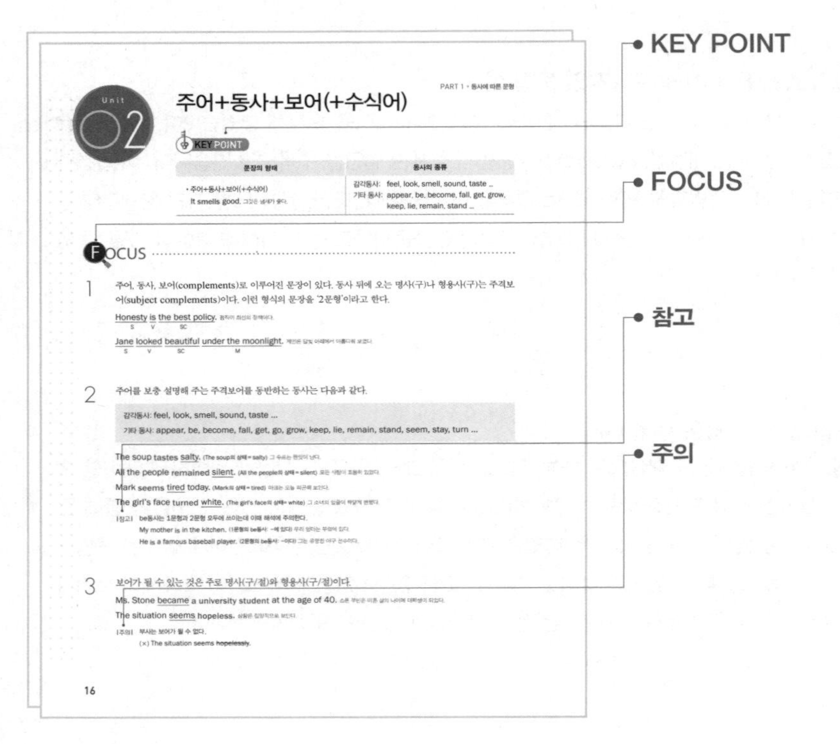

Unit 02 주어+동사+보어(+수식어)

PART 1 · 동사에 따른 문형

KEY POINT

문장의 형태	동사의 종류
• 주어+동사+보어(+수식어) It smells good.	감각동사: feel, look, smell, sound, taste ... 기타 동사: appear, be, become, fall, get, grow, keep, lie, remain, stand ...

FOCUS

1 주어, 동사, 보어(complements)로 이루어진 문장이 있다. 동사 뒤에 오는 명사(구)나 형용사(구)는 주격보어(subject complements)이다. 이런 형식의 문장을 '2문형'이라고 한다.

Honesty is the best policy.

Jane looked beautiful under the moonlight.

2 주어를 보충 설명해 주는 주격보어를 동반하는 동사는 다음과 같다.

감각동사: feel, look, smell, sound, taste ...
기타 동사: appear, be, become, fall, get, go, grow, keep, lie, remain, stand, seem, stay, turn ...

The soup tastes salty.
All the people remained silent.
Mark seems tired today.
The girl's face turned white.

3 보어가 될 수 있는 것은 주로 명사(구/절)와 형용사(구/절)이다.

Ms. Stone became a university student at the age of 40.
The situation seems hopeless.

16

• KEY POINT

도식화 · 도표화하여 한눈에 보기 쉽게 문법을 정리하였습니다.

• FOCUS

문법을 체계적으로 학습할 수 있도록 핵심 포인트를 예문과 함께 설명하였습니다.

• 참고

문법 포인트의 궁금한 점을 해결해 주고 개념 확장에 도움을 줄 수 있도록 하였습니다.

• 주의

시험에 자주 등장하는 문제 중에서 틀리기 쉬운 부분을 꼭 집어 설명하였습니다.

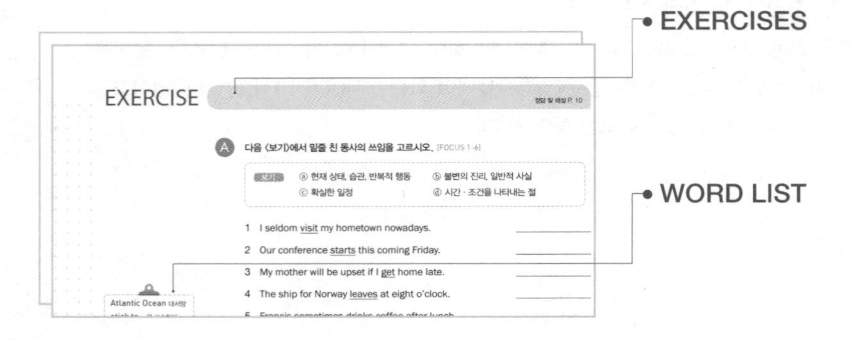

EXERCISE

정답 및 해설 P. 10

A 다음 〈보기〉에서 밑줄 친 동사의 쓰임을 고르시오. [FOCUS 1-6]

보기 ⓐ 현재 상태, 습관, 반복적 행동 ⓑ 불변의 진리, 일반적 사실 ⓒ 확실한 일정 ⓓ 시간 · 조건을 나타내는 절

1 I seldom visit my hometown nowadays.
2 Our conference starts this coming Friday.
3 My mother will be upset if I get home late.
4 The ship for Norway leaves at eight o'clock.

Atlantic Ocean 대서양

• EXERCISES

고르기, 빈칸 채우기, 문장 쓰기, 영작하기 등 다양한 유형의 연습문제들로 체계적인 학습을 할 수 있습니다.

• WORD LIST

문제에 나오는 단어들을 뜻과 함께 정리하여 제공함으로써 문법 학습에 집중할 수 있도록 도움을 줍니다.

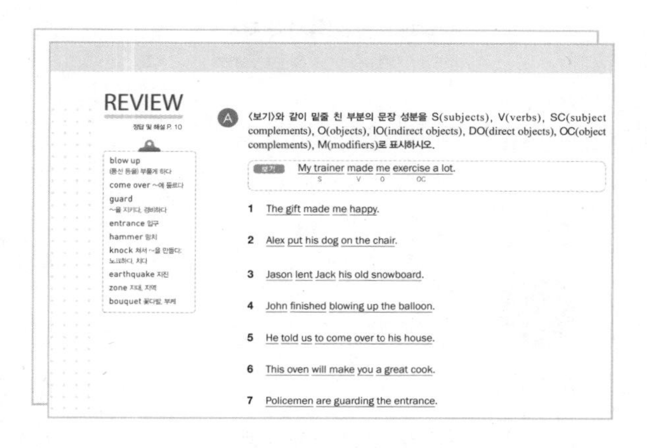

REVIEW

정답 및 해설 P. 10

blow up (풍선 등을) 부풀게 하다
come over ~에 들르다
guard ~을 지키다, 경비하다
entrance 입구
hammer 망치
knock 쳐서 ~을 만들다; 노크하다, 치다
earthquake 지진
zone 지대, 지역
bouquet 꽃다발, 부케

A 〈보기〉와 같이 밑줄 친 부분의 문장 성분을 S(subjects), V(verbs), SC(subject complements), O(objects), IO(indirect objects), DO(direct objects), OC(object complements), M(modifiers)로 표시하시오.

보기 My trainer made me exercise a lot.
S V O OC

1 The gift made me happy.
2 Alex put his dog on the chair.
3 Jason lent Jack his old snowboard.
4 John finished blowing up the balloon.
5 He told us to come over to his house.
6 This oven will make you a great cook.
7 Policemen are guarding the entrance.

- **REVIEW**

문장 완성하기, 문장 고쳐 쓰기, 문장 배열하기 등 PART에서 배운 문법을 통합하여 학습할 수 있습니다.

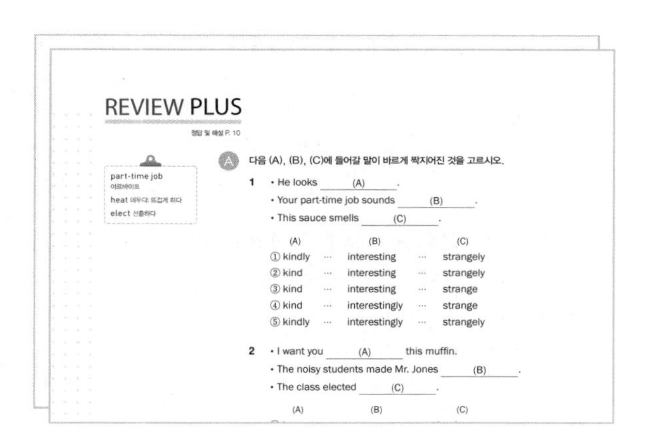

REVIEW PLUS

정답 및 해설 P. 10

part-time job 아르바이트
heat 데우다; 뜨겁게 하다
elect 선출하다

A 다음 (A), (B), (C)에 들어갈 말이 바르게 짝지어진 것을 고르시오.

1 • He looks ____(A)____.
• Your part-time job sounds ____(B)____.
• This sauce smells ____(C)____.

	(A)		(B)		(C)
①	kindly	…	interesting	…	strangely
②	kind	…	interesting	…	strangely
③	kind	…	interesting	…	strange
④	kind	…	interestingly	…	strange
⑤	kindly	…	interestingly	…	strangely

2 • I want you ____(A)____ this muffin.
• The noisy students made Mr. Jones ____(B)____.
• The class elected ____(C)____.

(A) (B) (C)

- **REVIEW PLUS**

어법상 올바른 문장 고르기, 어색한 대화 찾기, 지문에서 문법 오류 찾아 고치기 등의 활동으로 학습한 문법을 적용하여 응용력을 키울 수 있습니다.

Workbook

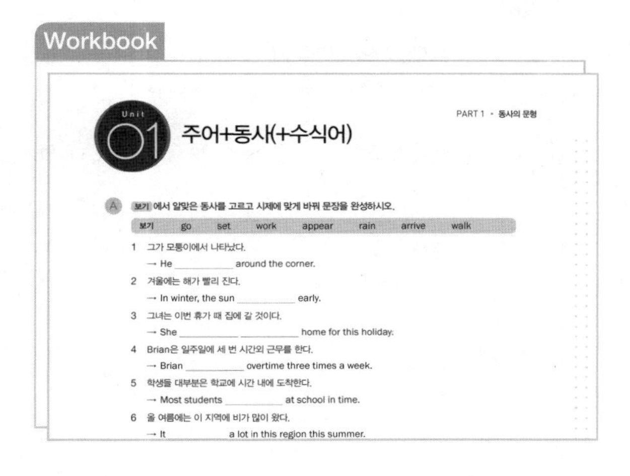

PART 1 • 동사의 문형

Unit 01 주어+동사(+수식어)

A 보기 에서 알맞은 동사를 고르고 시제에 맞게 바꿔 문장을 완성하시오.

보기 go set work appear rain arrive walk

1 그가 모퉁이에서 나타났다.
→ He ________ around the corner.
2 겨울에는 해가 빨리 진다.
→ In winter, the sun ________ early.
3 그녀는 이번 휴가 때 집에 갈 것이다.
→ She ________ ________ home for this holiday.
4 Brian은 일주일에 세 번 시간외 근무를 한다.
→ Brian ________ overtime three times a week.
5 학생들 대부분은 학교에 시간 내에 도착한다.
→ Most students ________ at school in time.
6 올 여름에는 이 지역에 비가 많이 왔다.
→ It ________ a lot in this region this summer.

- **UNIT EXERCISES**

UNIT별로 2페이지에 걸쳐 문장, 대화, 지문 등 다양한 유형의 연습문제를 수록하였습니다. 공부한 내용을 제대로 이해하였는지 Workbook을 통해 확인할 수 있습니다.

Contents 차례

중급 2

PART 16 접속사 Conjunctions

PART 17 관계사 Relatives

PART 18 가정법 Subjunctive Mood

PART 19 전치사 Prepositions

PART 20 화법, 일치, 도치 Reported Speech, Agreement & Inversion

Contents 차례

중급 1

PART 11

조동사 I
Helping Verbs I

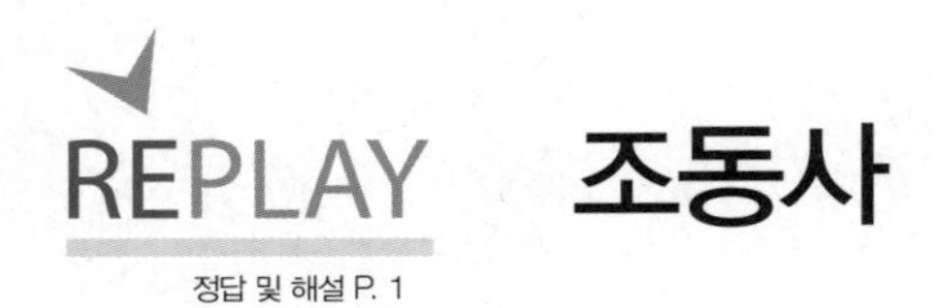

조동사

정답 및 해설 P. 1

1

조동사(helping verbs)는 본동사와 함께 쓰여 본동사의 의미를 보충해 주는 동사를 말한다. 조동사가 있는 문장의 긍정문은 「주어+조동사+동사원형 ~.」의 문장 형태를 갖는다.

I **can play** the piano. 나는 피아노를 칠 수 있다.

Jasmin **may stop by** today. 재스민이 오늘 들를지도 모른다.

You **should go** now. 너는 지금 가야 한다.

CHECK-UP

〈보기〉와 같이 주어진 조동사를 사용하여 문장을 다시 쓰시오.

보기	She swims very well. (can) → She can swim very well.

1 You take notes. (should)
→ ______________________

2 He gets up early. (must)
→ ______________________

3 My brother rides a bicycle. (will)
→ ______________________

4 She translates Latin into English. (can)
→ ______________________

5 Ben travels around South Africa. (might)
→ ______________________

6 The children go to bed early. (had better)
→ ______________________

7 I finish my homework by tonight. (must)
→ ______________________

8 You watch the film. (should) It's wonderful.
→ ______________________ It's wonderful.

9 Amy buys a new laptop computer today. (may)
→ ______________________

10 He jumps seven meters in the long jump. (can)
→ ______________________

2 조동사가 있는 문장의 부정문은 「주어+조동사+not+동사원형 ~.」의 문장 형태를 갖는다.

You **must not touch** the pictures at the art gallery. 미술관에서 그림을 만져서는 안 됩니다.

James **can not** [**can't** / **cannot**] **speak** German. 제임스는 독일어를 못한다.

It's freezing outside. You **had better not go out** today. 밖은 몹시 추워. 너는 오늘 밖에 나가지 않는 게 좋겠어.

CHECK-UP

주어진 문장을 부정문으로 바꿔 쓰시오.

1 I can find my cell phone.

→ ______________________________

2 You had better leave.

→ ______________________________

3 She should do it again.

→ ______________________________

4 He must take this bag.

→ ______________________________

3 조동사가 있는 문장의 의문문은 「조동사+주어+동사원형 ~?」의 문장 형태를 갖는다.

May I **have** a glass of water, please? 물 한 잔 마실 수 있을까요?

Can you **read** these Chinese characters? 너는 이 한자들을 읽을 수 있니?

Would you **help** me find my cell phone? 제 휴대 전화 찾는 것을 도와주시겠습니까?

CHECK-UP

주어진 문장을 의문문으로 바꿔 쓰시오.

1 I may have some sugar.

→ ______________________________

2 She can check out this book.

→ ______________________________

3 You would drink something cold.

→ ______________________________

4 He could spend time with you this weekend.

→ ______________________________

can, could, be able to

쓰임	예문
능력, 가능	I **can** swim, but I **can't** dive. 나는 수영은 할 수 있지만, 다이빙은 할 수 없다. I **am able to** jump high. 나는 높이 뛸 수 있다. I **could** dive when I was young. 나는 어렸을 때 다이빙을 할 수 있었다.
부탁, 허가	**Can** I have some water? 물 좀 줄래요? **Could** you help me, please? 저를 도와주시겠어요? You **can** eat this. 너는 이것을 먹어도 돼.
추측	It **can't** be true. 그것은 진실일 리가 없다. He **could** be in the bathroom. 그는 욕실에 있을 수도 있다.

1 can과 could는 능력(ability)이나 가능(possibility)을 나타내며, be able to로 바꿔 쓸 수 있다.

I **can** see the traffic sign from here.
→ I **am able to** see the traffic sign from here. 나는 여기서 교통 표지판을 볼 수 있다.

You **can** rent a guesthouse on the beach in Bali for a little money.
→ You **are able to** rent a guesthouse on the beach in Bali for a little money.
당신은 적은 돈으로 발리의 해변에 있는 숙소를 빌릴 수 있어요.

She **could** play the drums.
→ She **was able to** play the drums. 그녀는 드럼을 칠 수 있었다.

Can you speak a foreign language?
→ **Are** you **able to** speak a foreign language? 너는 외국어를 할 수 있니?

|주의| 조동사는 연달아 함께 쓸 수 없으므로, 다음의 경우 can은 be able to의 형태로 써야 한다.
Jennifer **might be able to** come tomorrow. (*NOT* might can) 제니퍼는 내일 올 수 있을지도 모른다.
Jennifer **will be able to** come tomorrow. (*NOT* will can) 제니퍼는 내일 올 수 있을 것이다.

|참고| 「Can ~?」은 강한 의심이나 놀람을 표현하여 '과연 ~일까?'라는 뜻으로 쓴다.
Can they arrive here on time? 과연 그들이 제시간에 도착할 수 있을까?

2 can과 could는 부탁(request)이나 허가(permission)를 나타내며, could는 can보다 정중한 표현이다.

Can you give me a hand? (부탁) 나 좀 도와줄 수 있니?
Could you please open the door? (부탁) 문을 좀 열어 주시겠습니까?

You **can** ask questions about the assignment. (허가) 너는 이 과제에 대해 질문할 수 있다.
Can my younger brother come with me to your exhibition? (허가) 내 남동생과 함께 너의 전시회에 가도 되니?

3 can의 부정은 can't(=cannot)로 '~할 수 없다'라는 불가능을 나타내거나, '~일 리가 없다'라는 강한 부정의 추측을 나타낸다. 과거에 대한 부정의 추측을 나타낼 때는 「cannot[could not]+have+p.p.」의 형태로 쓰면 되고 '~이었을 리가 없다'라는 의미가 된다.

I'm afraid I **can't** come to your birthday party on Saturday. (불가능) 미안하지만, 토요일에 너의 생일 파티에 갈 수 없어.

My hotel room wasn't good. I **couldn't** see the beach. (불가능) 내 호텔 방은 좋지 않았다. 나는 해변을 볼 수 없었다.

Jacob stayed with me last night. You **cannot[couldn't] have seen** him. (불가능)
제이콥은 어젯밤에 나와 함께 있었어. 너는 그를 봤을 리가 없어.

That **can't** be Anthony. He is in New York now. (추측) 저 사람이 앤서니일 리가 없어. 그는 지금 뉴욕에 있거든.

4 could는 현재나 미래에 대한 불확실한 추측을 나타낸다.

When you go to San Francisco next month, you **could** stay with Bruno.
다음 달에 네가 샌프란시스코에 가면, 브루노와 머물 수도 있어.

The phone is ringing. It **could** be Brandon.
전화가 울리고 있어. 브랜든일지도 몰라.

A: What would you like to do tonight? 오늘 밤에 뭐 하고 싶니?

B: We **could** go to the movies. 영화를 보러 갈 수도 있어.

|참고| 1. 불확실한 추측을 표현할 경우, could는 may나 might로 바꿔 쓸 수 있다.
The phone is ringing. It **may[might]** be Brandon. 전화가 울리고 있어. 브랜든일지도 몰라.

2. 과거의 불확실한 추측은 「could/may/might+have+p.p.」로 나타내며, '~했을 수도 있다/~했을지도 모른다'라고 해석한다.

5 「could+have+p.p.」는 '~할 수 있었는데 …하지 못했다'라는 의미로 과거에 하지 못한 일에 대한 유감을 표현할 때 사용한다.

Why didn't you call me? You **could have stayed** with us instead of at a hotel. (You didn't stay with us.)
왜 나에게 전화 안 했니? 호텔 대신 우리와 함께 머물 수도 있었잖아. (너는 우리와 함께 머무르지 않았다.)

|참고| 그 밖에도 「could+have+p.p.」는 과거에 대한 불확실한 추측을 나타낼 때 사용할 수 있다. 반면 「couldn't[can't]+have+p.p.」는 매우 확실한 추측을 나타내는데 사용된다.
She **could have been** absent from work. 그녀는 결근을 했을 수도 있다.
She **couldn't have been** absent from work. 그녀는 결근을 했을 리가 없다.

6 can을 이용한 관용 표현으로 「cannot+help+-ing」와 「cannot+but+동사원형」이 있으며, '~하지 않을 수 없다'라는 뜻이다.

I **cannot help studying** hard.

→ I **cannot but study** hard. 나는 열심히 공부하지 않을 수 없다.

I **could not help climbing** the mountain.

→ I **could not but climb** the mountain. 나는 그 산을 오르지 않을 수 없었다.

EXERCISES

정답 및 해설 P. 1

reach (전화 등으로) 연락하다; ~에 도착[도달]하다
envy 부러워하다
experienced 노련한; 경험 있는
outdoorsman 야외 스포츠 애호가, 야외에서 지내는 것을 좋아하는 사람
survive 살아남다
in the wild 야생에서

A 빈칸에 can이나 be able to 중 알맞은 것을 써넣으시오. [둘 다 가능한 것도 있음]

1 Our baby will ________________ walk in a few weeks.

2 We hope that you will ________________ join us on Saturday.

3 ________________ I buy bus tickets here? I want to travel into town.

4 I might ________________ reach her on the phone. I hope she's all right.

5 ________________ you mail this letter for me? I have a meeting right now.

6 My sister ________________ play the piano and the guitar. I really envy her.

7 Walter is an experienced outdoorsman. He ________________ survive alone in the wild.

relieve (불쾌감, 고통 등을) 없애 주다, 덜어 주다
mimic 흉내 내다
be over 끝나다

B 〈보기〉에서 알맞은 동사를 골라 can 또는 can't를 이용하여 문장을 완성하시오.

보기	travel	relieve	think	believe	play	mimic

1 I ________________ the violin for you if you want.

2 I ________________ of the name of that song, sorry.

3 Chocolate or a cup of coffee ________________ your stress. Try it!

4 Some birds ________________ humans, but they can't talk.

5 I ________________ that my summer vacation is already over!

6 We ________________ abroad this year. Flights are too expensive.

instructions (제품 등의) 사용 설명서
tease 놀리다, 괴롭히다
long-distance 장거리의
the environment 자연 환경

C 밑줄 친 단어의 의미를 〈보기〉에서 골라 쓰시오.

보기	ⓐ 능력, 가능	ⓑ 부탁, 허가	ⓒ 추측

1 Can you understand these instructions? ________

2 He can't be serious. He is just teasing you. ________

3 Can I have just a little more of that delicious cake? ________

4 Could you tell me how to make long-distance calls? ________

5 I couldn't go shopping after work today. I was too tired. ________

6 We can save the environment, but we can't do it alone. ________

7 She can't be a professor. She looks too young. ________

D 빈칸에 can이나 could, can't나 couldn't 중 알맞은 것을 써넣으시오. [중복 사용 가능]

concentrate 집중하다
turn up (라디오 등의) 소리를 크게 하다
communicate 의사소통하다

1 A: Excuse me, ______________ you hold the door for me?
B: Sure.

2 A: You look very tired. Didn't you get enough sleep last night?
B: No, I didn't. I ______________ sleep well.

3 A: You're home early. What happened?
B: It was too noisy in the library, so I ______________ concentrate.

4 A: ______________ you turn up the volume? We can't hear in the back.
B: OK, just a minute. Now, how's that?

5 A: Do you know the brand of the watch that woman is wearing?
B: I ______________ tell from here, but it looks expensive.

6 A: When Mina first moved to Canada, she ______________ speak a word of English.
B: That's amazing. ______________ she communicate now?

E 〈보기〉에서 알맞은 동사를 골라 「could+동사원형」 또는 「could+have+p.p.」로 바꿔 문장을 완성하시오.

warn 경고하다
come over (집을) 방문하다
how to + 동사원형 ~하는 방법
besides ~ 외에[밖에](도)
be in a bad mood 심기가 불편하다
be supposed to ~하기로 되어 있다

보기	ask	play	teach	warn	buy	come over

1 A: John and Kelly didn't do anything all weekend.
B: Really? They ______________________ with us.

2 A: What shall we do tomorrow? It's a holiday.
B: Well, I ______________________ to your house.

3 A: Why didn't she tell us about the sale this weekend?
B: We ______________________ things at lower prices.

4 A: I wish I knew how to cook something besides toast.
B: Well, I ______________________ you if you like.

5 A: You ______________________ me for help. I was free.
B: You're right. It was too much work for just one person.

6 A: Mary is in a bad mood today. You ______________________ me not to tease her.
B: I'm sorry I didn't tell you. But how am I supposed to know that you're going to tease her?

may, might

쓰임	예문
허가	**May** I borrow your pen, please? 펜 좀 빌려 주시겠어요? You **may** leave now. 너는 지금 떠나도 좋다.
추측	He **may** be in his office. 그는 아마도 사무실에 있을 것이다. She **might** be at school. 그녀는 아마도 학교에 있을 것이다.

FOCUS

1 may는 상대방에게 허가를 구하거나 허가를 해줄 때 사용한다.

A: **May** I come in? I need your advice. 들어가도 되나요? 나는 당신의 조언이 필요해요.

B: Yes, you **may**. 네, 들어오세요.

|참고| 일상생활에서는 may보다 can을 더 많이 사용한다.

2 may와 might는 '~일지도 모른다'라는 뜻으로 불확실한 추측이나 가능성을 나타낸다.

I haven't decided what I'm doing for spring break. I **may** go to Mexico. (= Perhaps I will go to Mexico.)
나는 봄 방학에 무엇을 할지 결정하지 못했어. 멕시코에 갈지도 몰라. (아마 나는 멕시코에 갈 것이다.)

She **might** be having lunch with Andy. (= Perhaps she is having lunch with Andy.)
그녀는 앤디와 점심을 먹고 있을지도 모른다. (아마도 그녀는 앤디와 점심을 먹고 있을 것이다.)

He **may** be in the cafeteria. (= Perhaps he is in the cafeteria.)
그는 카페테리아에 있을지도 몰라. (아마도 그는 카페테리아에 있을 것이다.)

|참고| might는 may의 과거형으로 쓰기도 하고, 「may[might]+have+p.p.」 '~이었을지도 모른다'라는 의미로 과거에 대한 추측을 나타내기도 한다.
He **thought** that she **might** accept his offer. (may의 과거형) 그는 그녀가 자신의 제안을 받아들일지도 모른다고 생각했다.
She **might have been** angry at you when you told her that. 네가 그녀에게 그렇게 말했을 때 그녀는 네게 화가 났을지도 몰라.

3 may의 부정은 may not, might의 부정은 might not이다.

Alex **may not** be coming to visit this weekend. He's a little busy.
알렉스는 이번 주말에 오지 않을지도 몰라. 그는 좀 바쁘거든.

There **might not** be enough food for the trip. Let's go shopping tonight.
여행하기에 음식이 충분하지 않을지도 몰라. 오늘 밤에 쇼핑하러 가자.

4 「may as well」 또는 「might as well」은 '(~하지 않을 이유가 없으니/어차피 해야 할 일이니) ~하는 것이 좋겠다'라는 뜻이다.

A: What should we do? Should we wait a little longer? 우리가 어떻게 해야 할까? 조금 더 기다려야 할까?

B: No, we **may[might] as well** leave. I don't think Brian is going to show up.
아니, 떠나는 게 좋겠어. 내 생각에 브라이언은 나타나지 않을 것 같아.

|주의| may well은 '~하는 게 당연하다'라는 뜻으로 쓰인다.
You **may well** feel confused. This is way too difficult. 네가 혼동하는 것은 당연해. 이것은 너무 어렵거든.

EXERCISES

정답 및 해설 P. 2

A 밑줄 친 조동사의 의미가 '허가'인지 '추측'인지 밝히시오.

1 I thought I <u>might</u> have to move to another city. ______

2 There <u>may</u> be some nice restaurants around the corner. ______

3 You <u>may</u> leave now. Please close the door on your way out. ______

4 Excuse me. <u>May</u> I get the interview on tape? ______

5 <u>May</u> I borrow your notebook after class? I couldn't concentrate today. ______

6 Sophia likes watching musicals, so she <u>might</u> want to come with us. ______

on one's way out 나가는 길에, 떠나는 길에
concentrate 집중하다

B 주어진 문장을 may[might]나 may[might] not을 이용하여 같은 뜻이 되도록 바꿔 쓰시오.

1 Perhaps he doesn't believe your story.
→ ______________________________

2 Perhaps Ken isn't feeling well right now.
→ ______________________________

3 Perhaps Ms. Kim is in the teachers' room.
→ ______________________________

4 Perhaps she is the girl who Tom told you about.
→ ______________________________

feel well 건강이 좋다; 기분이 좋다
teachers' room 교무실

C 〈보기〉에서 알맞은 동사를 골라 may[might] as well을 이용하여 글을 완성하시오.

보기	watch	go	walk	tell

1 You have just missed the bus. The bus comes only once an hour. You say: "I don't want to wait for an hour. I ______________."

2 Your friend told his girlfriend a lie. You want to give him advice. You say: "You ______________ her the truth. She'll find out soon."

3 You have no special plan, and you are bored. There's a movie on TV starting in a few minutes. You say: "We ______________ the movie. There is nothing else to do."

4 You have a ticket to a concert. You're not a fan of the band, but you will go because you have no other plans. You say: "I ______________ to the concert. I have nothing better to do."

lie 거짓말, 거짓말하다; 눕다
find out 알아내다, 찾아내다

must (not), have to, don't have to

쓰임	예문
강한 의무	You **must** stay at home tonight. 너는 오늘 밤에 집에 있어야 한다. You **have to** hand in your homework by six. 너는 여섯 시까지 숙제를 제출해야 한다.
금지	You **must not** open this box until Christmas. 크리스마스까지 이 상자를 열어서는 안 된다.
강한 추측	Jason went to school. He **must be** in class. 제이슨은 학교에 갔다. 그는 수업 중임이 틀림없다.
불필요	You **don't have to** eat it if you don't like it. 네가 먹기 싫으면 먹을 필요가 없다.

FOCUS

1 must와 have to는 '~해야 한다'라는 의미로, 강한 의무(obligation)와 규칙, 지시사항을 나타낸다.

must = have[has] to ~해야 한다

I **must** get to the bank before it closes.

→ I **have to** get to the bank before it closes.
나는 은행이 문을 닫기 전에 은행에 가야 해.

She **must** take an umbrella. It will rain tonight.

→ She **has to** take an umbrella. It will rain tonight.
그녀는 우산을 가져가야 해요. 오늘 밤에 비가 올 거예요.

When you visit Dennis in London next week, you **must** give him this file.
다음 주에 런던에서 데니스를 방문하면, 너는 그에게 이 서류를 전해 주어야 해.

Be careful with this medicine. You **must** keep it away from the children.
이 약을 주의하세요. 아이들이 가까이하지 못하게 보관해야 합니다.

Don't forget! You **have to** email me your final reports by next Friday afternoon.
잊지 마세요! 여러분은 다음 주 금요일 오후까지 최종 보고서를 이메일로 보내야 합니다.

|참고| 1. must의 과거는 had to(~해야 했다), 미래는 will have to(~해야 할 것이다)를 사용한다.

We ran out of bread this morning. I **had to** go to the market to buy some bread. (과거)
오늘 아침에 빵이 다 떨어졌다. 나는 빵을 사러 가게에 가야 했다.

You can borrow my car, but you'**ll have to** bring it back before nine. (미래)
너는 내 차를 빌려 가도 되지만, 9시까지는 돌려줘야 한다.

2. have to는 have got to로 바꿔 쓸 수 있다.

I **have to** clean my room. It's too messy.

→ I **have got to** clean my room. It's too messy. 나는 방을 치워야 한다. 너무 지저분하다.

2

must not[mustn't]은 '~해서는 안 된다'라는 금지(prohibition)를 나타내고, don't have to는 '~할 필요가 없다'라는 불필요(lack of necessity)를 나타낸다.

mustn't[must not] ~해서는 안 된다	vs.	don't have to ~할 필요가 없다

You **must not** shout in the library.
도서관에서 소리치면 안 된다.

Alana **must not** eat sesame seeds because of an allergy.
알래나는 알레르기 때문에 참깨를 먹으면 안 된다.

Sarah **doesn't have to** wake up early because today is a school holiday.
사라는 일찍 일어날 필요가 없다. 왜냐하면 오늘은 휴교일이기 때문이다.

|참고| don't have to는 need not과 바꿔 쓸 수 있다.

You **don't have to** finish it by yourself. I'll help you.
→ You **need not** finish it by yourself. I'll help you. 너는 그것을 혼자서 끝낼 필요가 없어. 내가 도와줄게.

3

must는 '~임이 틀림없다'라는 뜻으로, 강한 추측을 나타낸다. 추측의 의미를 나타내는 must의 부정형은 '~일 리가 없다'는 의미의 can't를 쓴다.

must ~임이 틀림없다	vs.	can't ~일 리가 없다

A: Look! It's Alain Robert! He's free-climbing another skyscraper.
저기 봐! 알랭 로베르야! 그는 도구 없이 또 다른 고층 건물을 등반하고 있어.

B: He **must** be very brave.
그는 대단히 용감한 게 틀림없어.

A: Will bought Jessy a diamond necklace with matching earrings.
윌이 제시에게 다이아몬드 목걸이랑 그에 어울리는 귀걸이를 사줬어.

B: He **must** be rich.
그는 부자인 게 틀림없어.

A: The door is ringing. It **must** be Jenny.
초인종이 울린다. 틀림없이 제니일 거야.

B: It **can't** be Jenny. I saw her doing homework upstairs a few minutes ago.
제니일 리가 없어. 내가 몇 분 전에 위층에서 숙제하고 있는 모습을 봤어.

4

「must have+p.p.」는 '~했음이 틀림없다'라는 뜻으로 과거에 대한 강한 추측을 나타낸다. 「must not have+p.p.」는 '~하지 않았음이 틀림없다'라는 뜻이다.

must have p.p. ~했음이 틀림없다	vs.	must not have p.p. ~하지 않았음이 틀림없다

I've lost one of my mittens. I **must have dropped** it somewhere.
나는 벙어리장갑 한 짝을 잃어버렸다. 어딘가에 떨어뜨린 게 틀림없다.

Nobody is answering the door. They **must have gone out**.
아무도 문을 열어 주지 않고 있다. 그들은 외출한 게 틀림없다.

Kathy walked right past me without saying a word. She **must not have seen** me.
캐시는 아무 말도 하지 않고 나를 지나쳐 갔다. 그녀가 나를 보지 못한 게 틀림없다.

EXERCISES

정답 및 해설 P. 2

sleep in 늦잠 자다
giggle 낄낄 웃다

( ) 안에서 가장 알맞은 것을 고르시오.

1 We aren't late, so we (don't have to / must) hurry.

2 Tomorrow is Sunday, so I (don't have to / mustn't) get up early.

3 You (don't have to / mustn't) ask foreigners their age. It isn't polite.

4 You (don't have to / mustn't) be handsome or smart to be successful.

5 Mary can sleep in because she (doesn't have to / mustn't) go to work.

6 Please be quiet. You (don't have to / mustn't) giggle here in the study room.

be on a diet 다이어트를 하다
signal 신호(기)
of good quality 품질이 좋은
Thai 타이의
pack (사람·물건으로) 가득 채우다
keep in mind 명심하다

B 빈칸에 must와 must not 중 알맞은 것을 써넣으시오.

1 I ______________ eat any more dessert. I'm on a diet.

2 That traffic sign means you ______________ drive faster than 80km/h.

3 Sandy didn't say a word to me all day. She ______________ still be angry.

4 We ______________ cross the street when the signal is red. It's dangerous.

5 You paid a lot of money for those boots. They ______________ be of good quality.

6 The new Thai restaurant is always packed. The food ______________ be good.

7 You ______________ keep in mind that this project is to be finished by the end of May.

hang up 걸다, 매달다; (전화를) 끊다
wrinkle 구겨지다, 주름지다
eye sight 시력

〈보기〉에서 알맞은 동사를 골라 must[have to]를 이용하여 문장을 완성하시오.

보기	hang up	be	repeat	wear	buy	study	remember

1 I ______________________ at the test center at 8:00 a.m. tomorrow.

2 You ______________________ the laundry right away, or it will wrinkle.

3 She ______________________ glasses because her eye sight is so bad.

4 We ______________________ Juhyuk and Jihye something for their wedding.

5 Jisup ______________________ English. Tomorrow is the day of the final test.

6 You ______________________ to call Mike and wish him happy birthday.

7 You ______________________ what you've learned so that you won't forget it.

D 〈보기〉에서 알맞은 것을 골라 mustn't 또는 don't have to를 이용하여 문장을 완성하시오.

[1-4] 보기 let wear shave open

1 You ____________ this box until your birthday.

2 You ____________ your children do as they please.

3 Jim ____________ a necktie to work, but he often does.

4 My grandfather is growing a beard, so he ____________.

[5-8] 보기 decide give up eat tell

5 You ____________ even though victory seems unlikely.

6 You ____________ raw shellfish. It contains harmful bacteria.

7 I don't want Dad to know I lost my wallet. You ____________ him.

8 You ____________ yet whether to study arts or science. You still have plenty of time to think about it.

shave (수염 등을) 면도하다
please ~하고 싶다, 원하다; 제발
beard 턱수염
even though 비록 ~일지라도
victory 승리
unlikely ~할 것 같지 않은
raw 날것의, 익히지 않은
shellfish 조개
contain ~이 들어 있다, 포함하다
harmful 해로운
bacteria 박테리아
plenty of 많은

E 주어진 동사와 must have p.p.를 사용하여 대화를 완성하시오.

1 A: I attended summer camp in Australia last year.
B: That ____________ (be) fun.

2 A: Daisy fell asleep on the bus this morning and missed her stop.
B: She ____________ (be) very tired.

3 A: I haven't seen that American teacher Louis around lately.
B: Neither have I. He ____________ (move) back to the States.

4 A: They were tearing down the apartment building across the street.
B: It ____________ (be) very noisy.

5 A: Excuse me, your name is Paul, isn't it?
B: I'm sorry, you ____________ (mistake) me for someone else.

6 A: What should I do with Susie? Should I watch James Cameron's new movie with her?
B: I don't think that's a good idea. She ____________ (see) it already.

7 A: I got all the questions wrong.
B: The quiz was really easy. You ____________ (be) dozing off during the class.

attend 참여하다, ~에 출석하다
fall asleep 잠들다
stop 정류장; 멈춤; 그만두다
tear down (건물 등을) 헐다, 부수다
mistake 혼동하다; 오해하다, 잘못 판단하다
doze off 졸다

should, ought to, had better

쓰임	예문
충고 ~해야 한다	You **should** go to bed early tonight. 너는 오늘 밤에 일찍 잠자리에 들어야 한다. You **ought to** prepare well for the quiz. 너는 시험 준비를 잘해야 한다.
경고 ~하는 편이 낫다	You **had better** ask him first before you make a reservation. 예약하기 전에 그에게 먼저 물어보는 것이 좋겠다.
추측 ~일 것이다	You studied hard. You **should** get a good score. 너는 열심히 공부했다. 너는 시험에서 반드시 좋은 점수를 받을 것이다. He left early. He **ought to** be there by now. 그는 일찍 떠났다. 그는 지금쯤 거기에 도착해 있을 것이다.

FOCUS

1 should는 '~해야 한다'라는 의미로, 상대방에게 조언이나 충고를 할 때 쓴다. 이때 should는 ought to로 바꿔 쓸 수 있다.

should = ought to ~해야 한다

should not = ought not to ~해서는 안 된다

You look very sick. You **should** see a doctor.

→ You look very sick. You **ought to** see a doctor. 너 많이 아파 보여. 병원에 가 보는 것이 좋겠어.

You **should** help your little brother with his homework. 너는 동생이 숙제하는 것을 도와줘야 한다.

You **should not [shouldn't]** talk with your mouth full. 입안에 음식이 가득한 채로 말해서는 안 된다.

A: **Should** I prepare to introduce myself in the first class? 첫 수업 때 자기소개를 준비해야 하나요?

B: Yes, you **should.** 네, 해야 합니다.

|참고| 1. ought to의 부정형은 ought not to이지만, to 없이 ought not으로 쓰기도 한다. oughtn't로 줄여 쓸 수 있지만, 잘 쓰지 않는다.

You **ought not to** eat so much fast food. 너는 패스트푸드를 너무 많이 먹어선 안 된다.

2. must와 have to는 규제성이 있는 강한 의무에, should와 ought to는 규제성은 없으나 도덕적으로 옳은 일에 대한 의무에 사용한다.

You **must** wear a school uniform when you go to school.

→ You **have to** wear a school uniform when you go to school.
너는 학교에 갈 때 반드시 교복을 입어야 한다.

You **should** wear a suit when you come to the party.

→ You **ought to** wear a suit when you come to the party.
너는 파티에 올 때 정장을 입어야 한다.

3. Should ~?는 '~해야 할까?'의 의미로 조언이나 충고를 구할 때 쓰인다.

Should I tell the teacher the truth? 선생님께 사실대로 말해야 할까?

2

should나 ought to는 '(당연히, 반드시) ~일 것이다'라는 의미로, 미래의 일에 대한 확실한 추측과 기대를 나타낼 때 쓴다.

Mike left for Busan about 6 hours ago. He **should** be there by now.
마이크는 6시간 전에 부산으로 떠났다. 그는 지금쯤 거기에 도착했을 것이다.

There are plenty of restaurants downtown. It **ought to** be easy to find a place to eat.
시내에는 많은 식당이 있어. 먹을 곳을 찾기는 쉬울 거야.

3

「should+have+p.p.」는 '~해야 했는데 (결국은) 그렇게 하지 못했다'라는 의미로, 과거에 있었던 일에 대한 후회나 유감을 나타낸다. 부정형인 「shouldn't+have+p.p.」는 '~하지 말았어야 했는데, (결국은) 그렇게 했다'라는 의미로 쓴다.

Oh, I missed the bus! I **should have left** home earlier! (I didn't leave home early enough.)
아, 버스를 놓쳤어! 집에서 더 빨리 나왔어야 했는데. (나는 충분히 일찍 나오지 않았다.)

I did poorly on the final exam. I **should have studied** harder. (I didn't study hard.)
나는 기말고사를 형편없이 봤다. 더 열심히 공부했어야 했는데. (나는 열심히 공부하지 않았다.)

I had a stomachache. I **shouldn't have eaten** so much at lunch. (I ate too much.)
나는 배가 아팠어. 점심때 그렇게 많이 먹지 말았어야 했는데. (나는 너무 많이 먹었다.)

|참고| that절에 사용되는 should의 쓰임: 이때 should는 생략 가능하다.

1. 주장, 요구, 제안 등의 의미를 갖는 동사의 목적어로 that절이 왔을 때:
   I suggested that we (**should**) stay one more night. 나는 하룻밤 더 머물 것을 제안했다.
2. 감정적, 이성적 판단을 나타내는 형용사 다음의 that절에서:
   I'm shocked that you (**should**) think I'm a liar. 내가 거짓말쟁이라고 생각하고 있다니 충격적이구나.
   It is urgent that they (**should**) act now to prevent war. 전쟁을 막기 위해서 그들이 지금 행동을 취하는 것이 시급하다.

4

「had better+동사원형」은 '~하는 것이 좋겠다'라는 의미로, 당연이나 강한 충고를 나타낼 때 쓴다. 부정은 「had better not+동사원형」으로, '~하지 않는 편이 낫다'라는 뜻이다.

I have to be there soon. I **had better** take a taxi.
나는 거기에 빨리 가야 해. 택시를 타는 게 좋겠어.

You'**d better** leave now. It is getting dark.
너는 지금 떠나는 게 좋겠어. 어두워지고 있어.

You **had better** put a bandage on your finger. Otherwise, it might get infected.
손가락에 반창고를 붙이는 게 좋겠어. 그렇지 않으면 감염될지도 몰라.

We **had better not** bother Mom right now because she's in a bad mood.
지금 엄마의 기분이 좋지 않으니 귀찮게 하지 않는 게 좋겠다.

A: I really ought to go and see Joseph one of these days. 정말 조만간 조셉을 만나 봐야겠어.
B: Well, you'**d better** do it soon. He is leaving for Europe at the end of this month.
빨리 만나는 게 좋을 거야. 그는 이번 달 말에 유럽으로 떠나거든.

|참고| should는 주로 일반적인 상황에서, had better는 경고성 있는 상황에서 조언이나 충고를 할 때 사용한다.
You **should** fasten your seat belt when you drive. 너는 운전할 때 안전벨트를 매야 한다.
You **had better** fasten your seat belt because I drive fast. 안전벨트를 매는 것이 좋을 거야. 나는 빨리 달리거든.

EXERCISES

정답 및 해설 P. 3

protect 보호하다
break the law 법을 어기다
respect 존경하다
trustworthy 신뢰할 수 있는, 믿을 수 있는
hesitate 망설이다
troublemaker 사고뭉치, 말썽꾸러기
cause trouble 문제를 일으키다

A 주어진 동사와 should[ought to] 또는 shouldn't[ought not to]를 이용하여 문장을 완성하시오.

1 We ____________________ (protect) nature.

2 People ____________________ (break) the law.

3 You ____________________ (respect) your parents.

4 I ____________________ (stay) any longer. My children are waiting for me.

5 I think you ____________________ (work) with him. He isn't trustworthy.

6 There's no time to hesitate. He ____________________ (make) a decision.

7 He's a troublemaker. He ____________________ (cause) so much trouble in class.

8 To improve your English, you ____________________ (read) more English books.

look back (과거를) 뒤돌아보다
go away (여행을) 떠나다
embarrass 당황하게 하다
complain 불평하다
positive 긍정적인; 명확한

B (　) 안에서 가장 알맞은 것을 고르시오.

1 I'm sorry for being late. I (should call / should have called) you.

2 Looking back now, I (should take / should have taken) your advice.

3 You need a break. You (should go / should have gone) away for a few days.

4 The party was a lot of fun last night. You (should come / should have come).

5 You (shouldn't say / shouldn't have said) that. He looked very embarrassed.

6 You (shouldn't complain / shouldn't have complained) so much. Try to be more positive.

invest 투자하다
stock market 주식 시장
crash 폭락하다; 파산하다; 충돌하다
in bulk 대량으로
discount 할인, 할인하다
referee 심판(원)
fair 공평한, 타당한
permission 허락, 승인

C 〈보기〉에서 알맞은 것을 골라 「should+동사원형」 또는 「should have+p.p.」를 이용하여 문장을 완성하시오.

보기	ask	invest	send	buy	get	win

1 I ____________________ in the stock market after it crashed.

2 Since the oranges were on sale, you ____________________ more.

3 When you buy something in bulk, you ____________________ for a discount.

4 Our team ____________________ the game. The referee wasn't fair.

5 I sent a letter, but he hasn't received it. I ____________________ it earlier.

6 If you want to stay overnight at your friend's place, you ____________________ your parents' permission.

D 〈보기〉에서 알맞은 것을 골라 had better (not)을 이용하여 문장을 완성하시오.

보기	stay	take	put on	go out	drive	put

1 Your friend has just cut her finger. You say to her:
→ You ________________ a bandage on your finger.

2 Your friend is going to the beach. It's sunny outside. You say to him:
→ You ________________ plenty of sunblock, or you might get burned.

3 You are going out for a walk with Tom. It is likely to rain. You say to Tom:
→ We ________________ an umbrella.

4 It's snowing a lot, but your father wants to drive to work. You say to him:
→ You ________________ to work today. It's snowing a lot.

5 Your younger brother has a bad cold, but he wants to go out. You say to him:
→ You ________________ inside until you get better.

6 Tom asked to go out with him, but you have a test tomorrow. You say to him:
→ I ________________________________.

put on ~을 바르다, ~을 입다
sunblock 자외선 차단제
get burned (피부가) 타다, 화상을 입다
be likely to ~할 것 같다
get better (병·상황이) 좋아지다, 호전되다

E ( ) 안에서 가장 알맞은 것을 고르시오.

1 A: When is the due date?
B: Applications (should / shouldn't) be sent before January 11th.

2 A: This cake is delicious. You (should / shouldn't) try a piece.
B: I'd love to. Is there a plate I can use?

3 A: Oh, no. I spilled spaghetti sauce on my pants.
B: You (had better / had better not) wash it off right away before it stains.

4 A: We (had better / had better not) wrap up the practice. It's getting late.
B: OK. Let's stop for today. But remember, the contest is only one week away.

5 A: Could you pass me my phone? I want to call Leo.
B: It's already past eleven. You (should / shouldn't) call him this late.

6 A: You (should / shouldn't) tease the dog like that. Just give him his food.
B: Sorry, Mom.

7 A: I have an appointment with Professor Park in a few minutes.
B: You (had better / had better not) be late. He's busy these days.

due date 마감일
application 지원서
wash off ~을 씻어내다
stain 얼룩지다
wrap up 마무리를 짓다
tease 괴롭히다, 놀리다
appointment 약속

will, would, used to

쓰임	예문
미래에 대한 의지·추측	I **will** study late tonight. 나는 오늘 밤에 늦게까지 공부할 것이다. His new movie **will** be fun. 그의 새 영화는 재미있을 것이다.
공손한 제안·요청	**Will** you help me, please? 나 좀 도와줄래요? **Would** you help me, please? 저 좀 도와주시겠어요?
관용 표현	I **would like to** watch that musical. 나는 저 뮤지컬을 보고 싶어요. I **would rather** drink water than Coke. 나는 콜라보다 물을 마시고 싶어요.
과거의 행동·습관	I **would** often go to see the movies. 나는 종종 영화를 보러 가곤 했다. She **used to** bite her fingernails, but now she doesn't. 그녀는 손톱을 물어뜯곤 했었는데 이제는 그러지 않는다.
과거의 상태·상황	There **used to** be a big tree on the hill, but now there is a school. 언덕에 큰 나무가 있었으나 지금은 학교가 있다.

FOCUS

1 조동사 will은 '~일 것이다'라는 의미로, 말하는 사람의 의지, 미래에 일어날 일, 확실한 추측을 나타낸다.

I **will** lend you some money. 내가 돈을 좀 빌려 줄게.

David **will** be fifteen next year. 데이비드는 내년에 열다섯 살이 될 것이다.

The baseball game **will** be finished soon. 야구 경기는 곧 끝날 것이다.

|참고| will의 부정은 will not[won't], would의 부정은 would not[wouldn't]이다.
I'm sorry for being late. I **won't** be late again. 늦어서 죄송해요. 다시는 늦지 않을게요.

2 will과 would는 '~해 줄래요(주시겠습니까)?'라는 의미로, 공손한 제안이나 요청을 할 때 쓴다. would가 will보다 좀 더 부드럽고 정중한 표현이다.

Will you please lend me your notebook for the test? 시험을 위해 너의 공책을 나에게 빌려 줄래?

Would you please lend me your notebook for the test? 시험을 위해 당신의 공책을 제게 빌려 주시겠습니까?

3 「would like to+동사원형」은 '~하고 싶다'라는 의미로, 공손한 표현이다.

I **would like to** travel to France. 나는 프랑스로 여행을 가고 싶다.

What **would** you **like to** have for dinner? 저녁으로 무엇을 드시겠어요?

|참고| would like 다음에 (대)명사가 오기도 한다.
A: **Would** you **like** something to drink? 마실 것 좀 드릴까요?
B: I'll just have some water, please. 그냥 물 주세요.

4

「would rather+동사원형」은 '차라리 ~하는 것이 낫겠다'라는 의미로, 말하는 사람의 선호도를 나타낸다. would rather의 부정형은 「would rather not+동사원형」이고, 의문문은 「Would+주어+rather+동사원형 ~?」이다.

We **would rather** stay home than go to the cinema. 극장에 가는 것보다 집에 있는 것이 낫겠다.

I **would rather not** tell you the secret. 너에게 비밀을 말하지 않는 것이 낫겠어.

|참고| would rather는 주로 축약된 형태인 'd rather로 쓰며, 종종 than과 함께 쓴다.
I'**d rather** stay home **than** go out with you. 너와 함께 외출하느니 집에 있는 게 낫겠다.

5

「would+동사원형」과 「used to+동사원형」은 '~하곤 했다'라는 의미로, 과거의 반복적인 행동이나 습관을 나타낼 때 쓴다. 반면 과거의 상태를 나타낼 때는 「used to+동사원형」만 쓸 수 있다.

I **would** practice speaking English in front of the mirror when I was in high school.

→ I **used to** practice speaking English in front of the mirror when I was in high school.
나는 고등학교 시절 거울 앞에서 영어 말하기를 연습하곤 했다.

We **would[used to]** swim in this river when we were kids. 우리가 어린아이였을 때 종종 이 강에서 수영을 하곤 했다.

My mom **would[used to]** sing to me before I went to bed. 우리 엄마는 내가 잠들기 전에 나에게 노래를 불러 주곤 했다.

There **used to** be a school here, but now there is a condo. (X) There ~~would~~ be a school here, but now there is a condo.
여기에는 학교가 있었다. 그러나 지금은 아파트가 있다.

|참고| used to의 부정은 「didn't use to+동사원형」 또는 「used not to+동사원형」을 쓴다.
I didn't use to [used not to] get up at six o'clock, but now I do. 나는 6시에 일어나지 않았으나 지금은 6시에 일어난다.

6

used to가 사용되는 관용 표현은 반드시 구분하여 알아두자.

「used to+동사원형」 ~하곤 했다

He **used to** drink cola. Now, he drinks orange juice. 그는 콜라를 마시곤 했지만, 이제는 오렌지주스를 마신다.

「be used to+동사원형」 ~하는 데 사용되다

Escalators **are used to** get from one floor to another. 에스컬레이터는 한 층에서 다른 층으로 가는 데 사용된다.

「be/get used to -ing」 ~하는 데 익숙하다/익숙해지다

I'm **used to** driving in London now, but it was hard at first. 나는 이제 런던에서 운전하는 데 익숙해. 하지만 처음에는 힘들었어.

You'll soon **get used to** living in the city. 너는 곧 도시에서 사는 데 익숙해질 거야.

7

일반동사 need와는 달리 조동사 need는 인칭과 수에 따라 형태가 변하지 않는다. 조동사 need의 부정은 need not이다.

He **need not** come that early. (조동사: (X) He ~~needs~~ not ~) 그가 그렇게 일찍 올 필요는 없어.

He doesn't **need** to come that early. (일반동사)

EXERCISES

정답 및 해설 P. 4

patient
참을성[인내심]이 있는

come over
(집을) 방문하다

A (　) 안에서 알맞은 것을 모두 고르시오.

1 The line (will / won't) move soon. Please be a little more patient.

2 I'm sorry I'm late, Mr. Kim. It (will / won't) happen again. I promise.

3 My dad is fifty-one this year. He (will / would) be fifty-two next year.

4 (Will / Would) you please come over and help me study for the test?

5 I'm going to the pop concert this Saturday. (Will / Would) you come with me?

6 Don't drink another cup of coffee. You (will / won't) be able to sleep tonight.

regularly 규칙적으로
go on a diet
다이어트를 하다
furious
몹시 화가 난, 격노한; 격렬한
sell out
매진되다, 다 팔리다
get involved in
~에 관여하다

B 〈보기〉에서 알맞은 것을 골라 would rather (not)을 이용하여 문장을 완성하시오.

보기	exercise	buy	come	stay	tell	get

1 I ______________________ the blue one. It's much nicer.

2 He ______________________ regularly than go on a diet.

3 I ______________________ Dad. He'll be furious with me.

4 I ______________________ at home. It's too cold to go outside.

5 The tickets are sold out. I ______________________ again tomorrow.

6 I ______________________ involved in that project. It's not an easy work.

tofu 두부
queue
줄을 서서 기다리다
assignment 과제, 할당
troublemaker
사고뭉치, 말썽꾸러기

C (　) 안에서 가장 알맞은 것을 고르시오.

1 Beans are used to (make / making) tofu.

2 We are used to (queue / queuing) for taxis.

3 My father used to (go / going) fishing every weekend.

4 I used to (drive / driving) an old Toyota, but now I drive a Lexus.

5 We (used to / were used to) play basketball here when we were young.

6 Jimin (used to working / was used to working) on difficult assignments.

7 Sam (used to be / is used to be) a troublemaker, but he has changed a lot.

8 He was nervous at first, but he soon (used to / got used to) speaking in front of many people.

D ( ) 안에서 알맞은 것을 모두 고르시오.

1 My sister (used to / would) have really long hair. She (used to / would) dye it a different color every week.

2 The river (used to / would) be very clean, so I (used to / would) swim in the river with my friends when I was young.

3 I (used to / would) be very quiet. Whenever visitors came to our house, I (used to / would) sit silently until they asked a question.

4 Clara (used to / would) spend all of her allowance buying music CDs. Every week, she (used to / would) rush down to the local music store.

5 When I was a kid, I never ate vegetables. I (used to / would) hide them in a napkin and feed them to my dog later. He (used to / would) love it.

6 Before she became a nurse, Nina (used to / would) have a lot of free time. She (used to / would) take long walks with her boyfriend in the park.

7 Dad and I (used to / would) spend a lot of time together on the weekends. He (used to / would) take me fishing or sometimes hunting with him.

dye 염색하다
silently 말없이; 조용히
allowance 용돈
rush 돌진하다, 서두르다
hide ~을 숨기다
feed ~에게 먹이를 주다

E 밑줄 친 부분을 어법에 맞게 고치시오.

1 Would you like have dessert? Maybe some ice cream?

2 I would better cook something at home than go out to eat.

3 You look bored. Would you like reading some comic books?

4 Karen is very shy. She is not used to make speeches in public.

5 There would be a convenience store on the corner, but now it's gone.

6 Dan said he would not rather have a big party this year for his birthday.

7 She is used to wear glasses. But after having surgery, she can see clearly without them.

8 I would rather to see the Eiffel Tower. How about you? What would you like to see?

9 Greg is used to travel quite a bit. Now he can't because he's too busy with work.

10 Jenny used to living in a small apartment in the city, but she moved to the countryside last year.

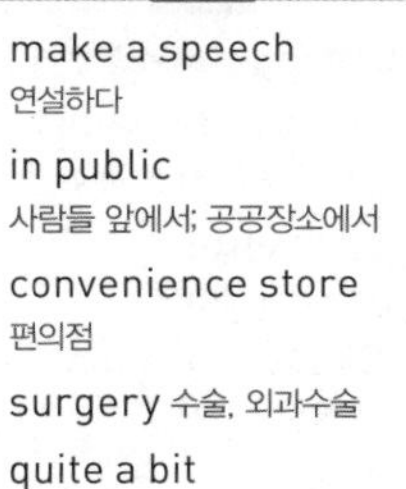

REVIEW

정답 및 해설 P. 4

come over
(집을) 방문하다
Big Dipper 북두칠성
inexpensive
비싸지 않은
souvenir 기념품
considerate
이해심이 많은, 사려 깊은
bounce (아래위로) 흔들다
be covered with
~으로 덮여있다
frost 서리
apologize 사과하다

A 밑줄 친 조동사의 의미를 〈보기〉에서 골라 그 기호를 쓰시오.

보기 ⓐ 능력 · 가능 ⓑ 부탁 · 허가 ⓒ 추측 ⓓ 과거의 행동 · 습관
ⓔ 불필요 ⓕ 후회 ⓖ 충고

1 You don't have to shout. I can hear you just fine. ______

2 I need some advice. Can I come over to chat? ______

3 I should have bought it last week when it was on sale. ______

4 On a clear night, you can see the Big Dipper in the sky. ______

5 Visitors to Seoul can buy inexpensive souvenirs in Itaewon. ______

6 You should be more considerate of other people's feelings. ______

7 We should have dropped by his office on our way home. ______

8 My father used to bounce me on his knee when I was a child. ______

9 It must have been cold last night. The car is covered with frost. ______

10 You had better apologize to Katie, or she will never forgive you. ______

11 This could be the right way to Wonderland, but I'm not 100% sure. ______

bathing suit 수영복
have a word (with)
(~와) 잠깐 이야기를 하다
hospitalize
입원시키다, 입원하다
ID(=identification)
신분증
clean out
깨끗이 정리하다
collection 수집(품)
performance 공연
lightning 번개
strike 치다, 부딪치다
fall down
쓰러지다, 넘어지다

B 밑줄 친 부분을 어법에 맞게 고치시오.

1 I might bake some cookies today. Would you like help me?

2 Jamie can make anyone laugh when he was in high school.

3 You have not better buy this bathing suit. It's too small for you.

4 You have better had a word with your teacher about the matter.

5 Do you think I ought buy this book for Liz? What if she doesn't like it?

6 My friend was hospitalized. I must visit my friend in the hospital yesterday.

7 You may have opened a bank account here, but you need two forms of ID.

8 All students must have cleaned out their lockers before the school ends.

9 I used to having a large CD collection, but now I just download MP3 files from the Internet.

10 My friend wants to see a movie, but I would rather to see live performances, like *Cats* or *Mamma Mia*.

11 There would be a big tree in front of my grandmother's house. But one day, lightning struck the tree, and it fell down.

C 〈보기〉에서 알맞은 말을 골라 빈칸에 써넣으시오. [한 번씩만 쓸 것]

보기	must	don't have to	could	be able to	had to	will

1 We ________________ be using e-books starting next year.

2 You ________________ turn off the heater before you go to bed.

3 Jay may ________________ help you out. Why don't you ask him?

4 I ________________ speak English better after studying in LA last year.

5 You ________________ ask me every time you want something from the fridge. Just help yourself.

6 I ________________ call home and ask my parents for some more money. They weren't happy.

help out (~을) 도와주다
fridge 냉장고
help oneself 마음껏 먹다

D ( ) 안에서 가장 알맞은 것을 고르시오.

1 He (will / won't) be able to play soccer again. He is recovering very fast.

2 I (may not / couldn't) meet Molly at the airport because I had to work late.

3 Dad (used to / would) be in good shape. He could do 220 push-ups easily!

4 Do you think we (should / ought) put our advertisement in a few more newspapers?

5 I (must / should) have gone to the party with you last night. It sounds like you had a blast.

6 My mother doesn't know how to use her new computer, so I (will able to / will have to) teach her.

7 I (have to / would like) get a job. I'm tired of asking my mom for money every week. It's so embarrassing.

8 If you have a bird, you (must / must not) cover it before you go to bed, or it will wake up singing with the sun.

9 Excuse me, Professor Kim? (May / Should) I have a moment of your time? I (used to / would like to) ask you a question about the final assignment.

10 A: We can't go to see the movie this evening. The tickets have all sold out.
B: Really? We (should / could) have made reservations earlier.

11 A: Will you study with me in the library after school?
B: Sorry, I (would like / would rather) go home early today.

recover 회복되다
in good shape (몸의) 상태가 좋은
push-up 팔 굽혀 펴기
advertisement 광고
blast 아주 즐거운 한 때; 돌풍
embarrassing 부끄러운, 창피한
assignment 과제; 할당
sell out 매진되다, 다 팔리다
reservation 예약

REVIEW PLUS

정답 및 해설 P. 6

get close to ~에 가까워지다
decoration 장식(품)

다음 (A), (B), (C)에 들어갈 말이 바르게 짝지어진 것을 고르시오.

- I'm sorry, but I ____(A)____ speak English. I need help.
- When I was in elementary school, the teacher ____(B)____ give us gold stars.
- It ____(C)____ be getting close to Christmas. Decorations are everywhere.

	(A)		(B)		(C)
①	can't	…	was used to	…	mustn't
②	can't	…	used to	…	must
③	can't	…	was used to	…	must
④	would rather	…	used to	…	must
⑤	would rather	…	was used to	…	mustn't

embarrassing 부끄러운, 창피한
accept (대학에) 입학시키다; 받아들이다
be proud of ~을 자랑으로 여기다

다음 ( ) 안에서 가장 알맞은 것을 고르시오.

1 A: Tell me your problem. I (would rather / may) be able to help you.
B: I would rather not. It's too embarrassing.

2 A: I've been accepted at one of the best law schools in the country.
B: Your family (must / had better) be very proud of you.

3 A: I (had better / may) write down your number. Otherwise, I'll forget it.
B: OK. Let me tell you again: 1457-9836.

intermediate 중간의, 중급의
currently 현재, 지금
attend (학교에) 다니다
enroll 등록하다
successfully 성공적으로
complete 끝마치다; 완성하다
how to + 동사원형 ~하는 방법
deliver (의견을) 말하다; 배달하다
coursework 교과 학습
participant 참가자
cooperatively 협동적으로
attendance 출석

C 다음 (A), (B), (C)에 들어갈 말이 바르게 짝지어진 것을 고르시오.

English 201 is an intermediate-level speaking skills course for ESL students who are currently attending Brown University. Before enrolling in this course, you ____(A)____ successfully complete English 101. In this course, students will learn how to prepare and deliver short speeches, which ____(B)____ be required of you in your coursework at the university. Participants ____(C)____ be prepared to work cooperatively with the other members of the class. Attendance is required, and all students must pass the final exam.

	(A)		(B)		(C)
①	must	…	may	…	could
②	must	…	may	…	should
③	must	…	may as well	…	should
④	could	…	may as well	…	should
⑤	could	…	may as well	…	could

PART 12

조동사 II
Helping Verbs II

추측의 정도

	추측의 정도	현재	과거
긍정	100% 확신	She **is** tired.	She **was** tired.
	↑	She **must be** tired.	She **must have been** tired.
	50% 미만	She **may be** tired.	She **may have been** tired.
		She **might be** tired.	She **might have been** tired.
	↓	She **could be** tired.	She **could have been** tired.
부정	100% 확신	She **isn't** tired.	She **wasn't** tired.
	↑	She **can't be** tired.	She **can't have been** tired.
	50% 미만	She **couldn't be** tired.	She **couldn't have been** tired.
		She **may not be** tired.	She **may not have been** tired.
	↓	She **might not be** tired.	She **might not have been** tired.

1 현재 사실(100%)이라면 조동사를 사용하지 않는다. must는 현재 사실에 대한 강한 추측에, may, might, could는 약한 추측에 쓴다.

I **am** so happy. I **am having** my birthday party now. (현재 사실) 나는 너무 행복하다. 나는 지금 생일 파티를 하고 있다.

「must+동사원형」 ~임이 틀림없다

Carol is smiling. She **must be** happy. 캐롤은 미소 짓고 있다. 그녀는 행복한 게 틀림없다.

My father **must be** at home. There's his car in front of the house. 우리 아버지는 집에 계심이 틀림없다. 집 앞에 아버지의 차가 있다.

「may/might/could+동사원형」 ~일지도 모른다, ~일 수도 있다

John isn't here. He **may be** home. 존은 여기 없다. 그는 집에 있을지도 모른다.

I heard the news, too. It **may be** true. 나도 그 소식을 들었다. 그것은 사실일지도 모른다.

|참고| maybe는 부사로 '아마'라는 뜻이며, may be는 「조동사+동사원형」의 형태로 '~일 수도 있다'라는 뜻이다.

Maybe he is sick. 아마 그는 아플 것이다.

He **may be** sick. 그는 아플지도 모른다.

2

과거 사실(100%)은 조동사를 사용하지 않고, 일반동사의 과거형만 사용하여 나타낸다. 과거 사실에 대한 추측은 「must/may/might/could+have+p.p.」로 표현한다.

I **was** very happy. I **got** a new digital camera for my birthday. (과거 사실) 나는 매우 행복했다. 생일에 새 디지털 카메라를 받았다.

「must+have+p.p.」 ~했음이 틀림없다

A: Where's Arnold? He was just here a minute ago. 아널드는 어디에 있지? 조금 전에 바로 여기에 있었는데.

B: He **must have stepped** outside. I'll go and find him. 그는 밖에 나간 게 틀림없어. 내가 가서 찾아볼게.

「may/might/could+have+p.p.」 ~했을지도 모른다

A: She was not at her desk after lunch. Where was she? 그녀는 점심 이후에 자리에 없었어. 어디에 있었지?

B: She **may [might/could] have had** a meeting. 그녀는 회의 중이었을지도 몰라.

3

현재 일에 대한 부정적인 추측은 「can/could/may/might+not+동사원형」으로 표현한다. can't, couldn't는 확실한 논리적인 근거를 바탕으로 판단했을 때 거의 불가능한 일에, may not, might not은 불확실한 추측에 쓴다.

「can't/couldn't+동사원형」 ~일 리가 없다

Mr. Brown likes hamburgers. He **can't be** a vegetarian. 브라운 씨는 햄버거를 좋아한다. 그는 채식주의자일 리가 없다.

「may not/might not+동사원형」 ~가 아닐지도 모른다

The water **may not be** warm enough to swim in. 물은 수영할 만큼 따뜻하지 않을지도 모른다.

4

과거 일에 대한 부정적인 추측은 「can/could/must/may/might+not+have+p.p.」로 표현한다.

「can't/couldn't+have+p.p.」 ~했을 리가 없다

He **can't [couldn't] have been** happy about losing the race.
그는 경주를 진 것이 기뻤을 리가 없다.

「must not+have+p.p.」 ~가 아니었음이 틀림없다 (can't/couldn't have p.p.보다 확신의 정도가 약함)

I don't think he pretended not to see you. He **must not have seen** you. He has bad eyesight.
나는 그가 너를 못 본 척했다고 생각하지 않아. 그가 너를 못 본 것이 틀림이 없어. 그는 시력이 좋지 않거든.

「may/might not+have+p.p.」 ~하지 않았을지도 모른다

Terry **may [might] not have bought** a new car. I often see him drive his old one.
테리는 새 자동차를 사지 않았을지도 모른다. 나는 그가 자기의 낡은 차를 운전하는 것을 자주 본다.

EXERCISES

정답 및 해설 P. 7

pack up 짐을 싸다
be over 끝나다
feel unwell 몸이 편치 않다
allow 허용하다, 용납하다
book 예약하다
as soon as possible 가능한 한 빨리

추측의 정도에 유의하여 (　　) 안에서 가장 알맞은 것을 고르시오.

1 Look! Everybody is packing up and leaving. Class (may / must) be over.

2 Sam isn't in class today. I'm not sure, but he (might / must) be feeling unwell.

3 Mike's team (may / must) be the strongest. They haven't lost a game this season.

4 You and your sister have just finished eating. You (can't / may not) possibly be hungry again!

5 We (may not / can't) wear jeans and T-shirts to school because we are not allowed to wear them.

6 Why don't you make a reservation for the restaurant? I'm not sure but it (may / must) be booked up quickly.

run over (사람을) 치다
hang out 시간을 보내다; 어울리다
someplace 어딘가에
apologize 사과하다
make up (~와) 화해하다
from now on 지금부터는, 앞으로는
hallway 복도
look right through ~을 못 알아보다; 못 본 체하다

B 〈보기〉에서 알맞은 것을 골라 주어진 조동사를 이용하여 어법에 맞게 대화를 완성하시오.

보기			
go	steal	run over	drop
see	leave	make up	hang out

1 A: What are you looking for?
B: I can't find my glasses. I ____________________ (must) them somewhere.

2 A: Hey, Charlie. What are you going to do on spring break?
B: I don't know. I ____________________ (may) on a beach in Mexico.

3 A: My bike is gone. Somebody ____________________ (must) it.
B: Are you sure? You ____________________ (may) it someplace else.

4 A: I heard Louise apologized to Jean, and they became friendly again.
B: They ____________________ (can't). They haven't talked to each other all day long.

5 A: You should have looked both ways before you crossed the road. The car ____________________ (could) you.
B: I'll be careful from now on.

6 A: Where's Mike? I have something to give him.
B: He ____________________ (may) home. He took his bag and went out half an hour ago.

7 A: What's wrong with Amy? I passed her in the hallway, and she looked right through me.
B: She ____________________ (can't) you. If she had seen you, she would have said hello.

C 주어진 단어와 must (not) 또는 may (not)를 이용하여 대화를 완성하시오.

million 100만
center 중심(지)
employ 고용하다

1 A: Where is Tom? I need to talk to him.
B: I'm not sure, but he ________________ (be) in the music room.

2 A: How much do I need for the trip to Japan? Will a million won be enough?
B: I'm not sure but that ________________ (be) enough. I heard things are very expensive there.

3 A: He ________________ (be) a successful man. He has a building in the center of the city, and a lot of workers are employed at his company.
B: I agree. His business is growing very fast.

4 A: He ________________ (be) very popular among the girls. He received a lot of boxes of chocolates from them.
B: You're right. He is the most handsome boy in my school.

D 주어진 단어와 「can't+동사원형」 또는 「can't+have+p.p.」를 이용하여 대화를 완성하시오.

canned 통조림으로 된
cupboard 찬장
chubby 통통한
complain 불평하다
make noise 떠들다, 떠들어대다
careful 세심한, 주의 깊은

1 A: Who took canned fruit out of the cupboard? Was it Mike?
B: It ________________ (be) him. He wasn't at home.

2 A: Peter must have stolen my tablet PC.
B: He ________________ (take) it. He was with me all day long.

3 A: Is that boy Mike, whom Jenny likes?
B: That ________________ (be) Mike. Jenny said he is slim, but that boy is chubby.

4 A: Have you seen Jake? He didn't answer my phone call.
B: He ________________ (hear) his phone ringing. I saw his phone in the living room, and he was sleeping in his room.

5 A: I have finished the question.
B: Already? That ________________ (be) possible. It takes at least five minutes just to read the question.

6 A: Excuse me, Ms. Brown? I'm sorry to be complaining, but I couldn't sleep again last night because of your dog. It was making too much noise.
B: It ________________ (be) my dog. Max is in the animal hospital.

7 A: Hey, did you check this report by yourself? It has a lot of mistakes in numbers.
B: No, Philip did. But he ________________ (make) such mistakes. He is a very careful person.

정중한 부탁이나 허가

쓰임	예문
허가를 구할 때 ~해도 될까요?	**Can I** use your eraser? 너의 지우개를 써도 되니? **Could I** come in? 제가 들어가도 될까요? **May I** borrow your pen? 당신의 펜을 좀 빌려도 될까요?
부탁할 때 ~해 주실래요?	**Can you** give me a napkin? 냅킨 좀 줄래? **Could you** help me, please? 저를 좀 도와주시겠어요? **Will you** pass me the pepper? 후추 좀 건네줄래? **Would you** take a photo? 사진 좀 찍어 주시겠어요?
부탁할 때 ~해 주시겠어요?	**Would you mind saying** that again? 다시 한 번 말씀해 주시겠어요?
허가를 구할 때 ~해도 될까요?	**Would you mind if I sat** here? 제가 여기에 앉아도 될까요?

FOCUS

1 「Can/Could/May I ~?」는 상대방의 허가를 구할 때 쓰는 표현이다. may/could I가 can I보다 공손한 표현이다.

A: **Can I** borrow your highlighter? 너의 형광펜을 빌릴 수 있을까?

B: Yes, of course. Here you are. 응, 물론이야. 여기 있어.

A: **Could I** have another cup of coffee? 커피 한 잔 더 마실 수 있을까요?

B: Okay. Wait a minute. 네. 잠시만 기다리세요.

A: **May I** borrow your car? 당신의 차를 빌려도 될까요?

B: No, you may not. I'm sorry. 아니요, 안 돼요. 죄송해요.

2 「Can/Could/Will/Would you ~?」는 상대방에게 부탁할 때 쓰는 표현이다. could/would you가 can you보다 공손한 표현이다.

A: **Can you** come to my birthday party? 내 생일 파티에 올 수 있니?

B: Of course, I'd be glad to. 물론이야. 기꺼이 그러고 싶어.

A: I need some help with the groceries. **Could you** help me carry them into the house, please?
식료품 때문에 도움이 필요해요. 이것들을 집 안으로 옮기도록 좀 도와주시겠어요?

B: Sure. Just a second. 물론이죠. 잠시만요.

A: **Will you** change my bike's flat tire? 내 자전거의 바람 빠진 타이어를 갈아 끼워줄래?

B: I'm sorry, but I don't have the right tools. 미안하지만, 적당한 도구가 없어.

A: **Would you** tell him that Emily phoned? 에밀리가 전화했다고 그에게 전해 주시겠어요?

B: I'm sorry, but I'm going out in five minutes. 미안하지만, 나는 5분 후에 나갈 거예요.

3 「Would you mind -ing ~?」는 '~해 주시겠어요?'라는 의미로, 상대방에게 정중하게 부탁할 때 쓴다.

A: **Would you mind taking** the laundry to the cleaner's?
세탁물을 세탁소에 가져다주시겠어요?

B: Not at all. 그럼요.

A: Excuse me, I didn't catch what you just said. **Would you mind speaking** a little louder?
죄송합니다만, 방금 말씀하신 것을 못 들었어요. 조금 더 크게 말씀해 주시겠어요?

B: Oh, of course not. I'm sorry. 아, 물론이죠. 죄송해요.

A: Excuse me, **would you mind dropping** me off at the next stop?
죄송합니다만, 다음 정류장에서 내려 주시겠어요?

B: No problem. Please be careful when you exit the bus. 물론이죠. 버스에서 내릴 때 조심하세요.

4 「Would you mind if+주어+동사의 과거형 ~?」은 '~해도 되겠습니까?'라는 의미로 정중하게 상대방의 허가를 구할 때 쓴다.

A: **Would you mind if I closed** the window? 제가 창문을 닫아도 되겠습니까?

B: No, not at all. 네, 괜찮아요.

A: **Would you mind if I came** with you? 제가 당신과 함께 가도 되겠습니까?

B: Of course not. 물론이죠.

A: **Would you mind if I asked** you a few questions? Our students are very curious about life in South Africa.
제가 당신에게 몇 가지 질문을 해도 되겠습니까? 우리 학생들이 남아프리카에서의 생활에 대해 매우 궁금해 해서요.

B: No, I don't mind. 네, 괜찮아요.

|참고| 1. 회화에서는 종종 과거 시제 대신 현재 시제를 사용하기도 한다.

A: **Would you mind** if I closed[close] the window?

B: No, not at all.

2. mind는 '꺼려하다'라는 뜻으로 응답에 유의해야 한다.

A: Would you **mind** if I opened the window? 제가 창문을 여는 것이 싫으세요?

B: **No, not at all.** 아니요, 전혀 안 싫어요.

A: Would you **mind** if I opened the window? 제가 창문을 여는 것이 싫으세요?

B: **I'm sorry, I'd rather you don't.** I'm kind of cold. 죄송하지만, 그렇게 하지 않았으면 좋겠어요. 저는 좀 추워요.

EXERCISES

정답 및 해설 P. 7

turn up (소리를) 높이다
recipe book 요리책
statistics 통계학

A 〈보기〉와 같이 주어진 단어를 이용하여 허가를 구하는 문장을 만드시오.

보기 You want to have a cup of coffee. You can ask: (may)
→ May I have a cup of coffee?

1 You want to turn on the radio. You can ask: (can)
→ ______________________

2 You want to turn up the volume. You can ask: (could)
→ ______________________

3 You want to use the recipe book. You can ask: (could)
→ ______________________

4 You want to get some help to move the heavy boxes. You can ask: (may)
→ ______________________

5 You want to borrow the notebook for the statistics exam. You can ask: (could)
→ ______________________

silent 조용한
hand 건네주다; 도움
lean 기대다
occupy (공간을) 차지하다, 점령하다

B 주어진 단어를 어법에 맞게 바꾸어 대화를 완성하시오.

1 A: Would you mind if I __________ (have) a window seat?
B: Of course not.

2 A: Would you mind if I __________ (turn) on the radio? It's too quiet here.
B: Not at all.

3 A: Would you mind __________ (hand) this document to the teacher?
B: No problem. Anything else?

4 A: Excuse me. Would you mind if I __________ (lean) my seat back a little?
B: No problem. Go ahead.

5 A: Would you mind __________ (give) me a hand to carry these bags upstairs?
B: No, I don't mind.

6 A: Would you mind if I __________ (call) you back a bit later? I can't talk to you right now.
B: No, that would be fine.

7 A: Would you mind __________ (wait) about twenty minutes more? The seats are all occupied at the moment.
B: Well, we'll come later.

C 〈보기〉에서 알맞은 것을 골라 Can I ~? 또는 Can you~?를 이용하여 대화를 완성하시오.

보기 ask look after hold get use help have

1 A: Excuse me. ____________ the elevator, please?
B: Yes, of course.

2 A: ____________ you for some directions?
B: Actually, I'm a stranger here myself.

3 A: It is too hot today. ____________ something cold to drink?
B: Sure. Is orange juice okay?

4 A: ____________ your cell phone for a minute? I left mine at home.
B: Yes, of course. Here you are.

5 A: ____________ my dog while I am away for a couple of days?
B: Of course. You know I love dogs.

6 A: Sue! ____________ the phone? I'm doing the dishes now.
B: OK.

7 A: ____________ me prepare for the school festival?
B: I'd love to, but I have something to do.

look after ~을 돌보다, ~을 맡다
direction 방향; 지시
get the phone 전화를 받다
festival 축제

D 〈보기〉에서 알맞은 것을 골라 어법에 맞게 바꿔 대화를 완성하시오.

보기 ask proofread keep ride use empty take

1 A: Would you mind ________ the recycling bins?
B: Not at all. Just point me in the right direction.

2 A: Would you mind if I ________ your bike to go to the store?
B: Of course not. But be careful. The brakes are a little worn out.

3 A: Would you mind ________ a picture of me and my friend together?
B: No problem at all. Just show me how to use your camera.

4 A: Would you mind if we ________ you a few questions?
B: No, I don't mind. What would you like to know?

5 A: Would you mind ________ my essay for me? It would be a big help.
B: I'd love to, but I'm busy right now. Can you wait until after the weekend?

6 A: Would you mind if I ________ this chair? I need a chair.
B: Of course not.

7 A: Would you mind ________ your dog in the yard? I'm allergic to dogs.
B: Not at all.

proofread 교정을 보다
recycling bin 재활용 통
point 알려주다; 가리키다
worn out 닳아 해진; 써서 낡은
allergic 알레르기가 있는

제안하기

표현	예문
Shall I/we ~? ~할까요?	**Shall I** turn down the radio? 라디오 소리를 줄일까요? **Shall we** meet at six? 여섯 시에 만날까요? Let's dance, **shall we**? 춤추자, 응?
Let's ~. ~하자 Let's not ~. ~하지 말자	**Let's** eat out tonight. 오늘 밤에는 외식하자. **Let's not** eat out tonight. 오늘 밤에 외식하지 말자.
Why don't you/we ~? ~하는 게 어때?	**Why don't you** call me at seven? 일곱 시에 나에게 전화하는 게 어때? **Why don't we** study together in the library? 도서관에서 함께 공부하는 게 어때?

FOCUS

1 「Shall I/we+동사원형 ~?」은 '~할까요?'라는 뜻으로, 상대방에게 제안할 때 쓴다.

Shall I call her now? 그녀에게 지금 전화할까요?

Shall we go on a picnic this weekend? 우리 이번 주말에 소풍 갈까요?

2 「Let's+동사원형 ~.」은 '~하자'라는 뜻으로, 상대방에게 제안할 때 쓴다. 이때 let's는 let us를 줄인 말이다. let's의 부정형은 let's not이다.

Let's look for your dog together. Don't worry! He'll turn up. 우리 함께 너의 개를 찾아보자. 걱정하지 마! 나타날 거야.

Let's not go to see a movie. I'd rather stay home and take a rest. 영화 보러 가지 말자. 나는 집에서 쉬고 싶어.

3 「Why don't you/we ~?」는 '~하는 게 어때?'라는 뜻으로, 상대방에게 제안할 때 쓴다. 「Why don't we ~?」는 「Let's ~.」와 「Shall we ~?」로 바꿔 쓸 수 있다.

Why don't we go on a picnic this weekend? 이번 주말에 소풍 가는 게 어때?

→ **Let's** go on a picnic this weekend. 이번 주말에 소풍 가자.

→ **Shall we** go on a picnic this weekend? 우리 이번 주말에 소풍 갈까?

A: **Why don't you** come over to my place this evening? 오늘 저녁에 우리 집에 놀러 올래?

B: Sure. What time shall I go? 좋아. 몇 시에 갈까?

A: **Why don't we** go out and have pizza? I'm not in the mood to cook tonight.
우리 나가서 피자 먹는 게 어때? 오늘 밤은 요리할 기분이 아니야.

B: That sounds great. **Let's** do that. 그거 좋겠다. 그렇게 하자.

|참고| Let's~는 부가의문문을 만들 때 문장 끝에 shall we~?를 쓴다.
Let's go to the movies tomorrow, **shall we**? 내일 영화 보러 가자, 그럴래?

EXERCISES

정답 및 해설 P. 8

 〈보기〉에서 알맞은 표현을 고르고, 주어진 동사를 이용하여 대화를 완성하시오.

보기	why don't you	why don't we	let's	let's not	shall I

A: The weather is gorgeous this morning. ____________________ (go) to the beach right after breakfast?

B: I would rather go downtown and browse through the shops.

A: Shopping already? It's our first day in Fiji. ____________________ (go) shopping.

B: You're right. ________________ (spend) the morning on the beach and then go shopping in the afternoon.

A: OK, let's have breakfast before we go out. Shall we go to a restaurant in the hotel?

B: Well, how about just ordering some meals from room service?

A: That sounds good. ____________________ (call) room service?

B: It's okay. I'll do it. What will you have? I'll order American Breakfast. ____________________ (have) the same one with me?

downtown 시내
browse through 대강 훑어보다
gorgeous 아주 멋진, 좋은

B 〈보기〉에서 알맞은 표현을 골라 대화를 완성하시오.

보기			
	why don't you order	shall we try	why don't you come over
	why don't we write	shall we go	let's start

1 A: __________________ camping when Sally visits us this summer?

B: Do you think she'll want to go camping? ________________ her a letter and ask?

A: No, I want it to be a surprise. It'll be so much fun! ________________ making plans now.

B: OK, if you think so.

2 A: This hotel room is beautiful! __________________ here and have a look out the window?

B: Wow! We have a great view of downtown.

A: And look! The brochure here says there's a spa on the first floor. __________________ it out?

B: OK. But first, I think I'll order something from room service.

A: Great. __________________ us something to eat while I unpack our luggage?

have a look out 밖을 내다보다
view 전망; 의견
brochure 팸플릿, 광고 전단
spa 온천
try something out 효과를 시험해 보다
unpack (가방에 든 것을) 꺼내다, (짐을) 풀다
luggage 소형 여행 가방, 수하물

REVIEW

정답 및 해설 P. 9

밑줄 친 부분의 의미를 〈보기〉에서 고르시오.

보기 ⓐ 부탁 · 허가 ⓑ 추측 ⓒ 제안

payday 급여일, 월급날
restroom 화장실
any minute 금방, 곧
get ready 준비하다
donate 기부하다
blood 피, 혈액
outfit 옷 한 벌
be absent from ~에 결석하다

1 Why don't we visit the Louvre? ______

2 Could I borrow a few dollars until payday? ______

3 Can you watch my bag while I go to the restroom? ______

4 May I see your passport and boarding pass, please? ______

5 Would you mind if I brought my dog into your coffee house? ______

6 Dennis might be here any minute, so hurry up and get ready. ______

7 Why don't we donate our blood? We can help save many lives. ______

8 Why don't you buy the other outfit? It looked much cuter on you. ______

9 Juliet didn't want to join us for sushi tonight. She must be busy. ______

10 Was Jane absent from school yesterday? She might have been sick. ______

B 〈보기〉에서 알맞은 것을 골라 may나 must를 이용하여 대화를 완성하시오. [중복 사용 가능]

보기 help be go have

knock 노크하다, (문 등을 똑똑) 두드리다
clerk 점원
depend on ~에 달려 있다
schedule 스케줄, 일정

1 A: Hello, ma'am. How ______ I ______ you?
B: I would like two kilos of beef, please.

2 A: Did you receive the book that I gave your brother yesterday?
B: No, not yet. But he ______ it.

3 A: It looks like it's going to rain this afternoon.
B: You ______ right. I guess we will have to wait and see.

4 A: Do you see the boy Chris is carrying?
B: Yes, I do. He looks just like Chris. He ______ his son.

5 A: This ______ the right apartment. Justin's name is on the door.
B: I guess you're right. Why don't you knock?

6 A: What should we have for lunch? The salad looks good, doesn't it?
B: I'm not sure. It ______ not ______ fresh. Let's ask the clerk when it was prepared.

7 A: We ______ hiking tomorrow, but it will depend on the weather. Would you like to come?
B: I would like to, but I ______ busy. Let me check my schedule.

C 상황을 읽고, 주어진 단어를 이용하여 허가, 부탁, 또는 제안하는 문장을 만드시오.

1 You want to eat out for lunch with your friend. You can say: (let)
→ ____________________ for lunch. I want to eat Thai food.

2 You want to have some pizza. You can ask: (I, can)
→ ____________________ some pizza? I'm a bit hungry.

3 You want to close the curtains. You can ask: (you, would, mind, if)
→ ____________________ the curtains? It's too bright in here.

4 You want your brother to help you set the table. You can ask: (you, can)
→ ____________________ me set the table?

5 You want to meet her in front of the bank at six. You can ask: (we, shall)
→ ____________________ in front of the bank at six?

6 You want your sister to pick up the laundry. You can ask: (you, would, mind)
→ ____________________ the laundry on your way home?

7 You want your friend to go to see a doctor. You can say: (why, you)
→ ____________________ to see a doctor? You'll get much better.

bright 밝은, 눈부신
set the table 식탁을 차리다
pick up ~을 찾아오다

D 우리말과 같은 뜻이 되도록 주어진 단어를 배열하시오.

1 그녀가 고양이 애호가일 리가 없어. 그녀는 고양이를 무서워해. (be, can't, a cat lover)
→ She ____________________. She is afraid of cats.

2 그는 그 시간에 카페테리아에서 점심을 먹었는지도 몰라. (may, lunch, he, had, have)
→ ____________________ at the cafeteria at that time.

3 차가 많이 막혀서 그는 집에 늦게 올 수도 있어. (late, could, he, home, be)
→ ____________________ because there is a lot of traffic.

4 티나는 지금 회의 중이야. 저 사람이 티나일 리가 없어. (be, Tina, can't, that)
→ Tina is in a meeting right now. ____________________

5 그녀는 도서관에 있는 게 틀림없어. 내일 시험이 있거든. (the library, must, she, be, in)
→ ____________________ because she has a test tomorrow.

6 그가 무례하게 행동했을 리 없어. 그는 항상 예의 바르게 행동해.
(behaved, have, can't, rudely)
→ He ____________________. He is always polite.

7 여기서 큰 행사가 있는지도 몰라. 줄 서서 기다리고 있는 사람들 좀 봐.
(might, there, event, be, a big)
→ ____________________ here. Look at the people waiting in line.

be afraid of ~을 두려워하다
traffic 교통(량)
behave 행동하다
rudely 무례하게
wait in line 줄을 서서 기다리다

REVIEW PLUS

정답 및 해설 P. 10

share ~을 함께 나누다, 공유하다; 몫
server 웨이터
attention 관심, 주의
go ahead (망설이지 않고) 진행시키다
bite 한 입

A 다음 대화를 읽고, (A), (B), (C)에 들어갈 말이 바르게 짝지어진 것을 고르시오.

1

A: This restaurant is fantastic! ___(A)___ try something new.
B: ___(B)___ order two different meals and share them?
A: OK. I'll have meatball spaghetti. ___(C)___ order the Beef Wellington?
B: Great. Get the server's attention and let's order.

	(A)		(B)		(C)
①	Let's	…	Shall we	…	Why don't you
②	Let's	…	Shall we	…	Why don't we
③	Let's	…	Can you	…	Why don't we
④	Let's not	…	Can you	…	Why don't you
⑤	Let's not	…	Could you	…	Would you mind

2

A: That was a fantastic meal. I'm full!
B: How about dessert? We ___(A)___ order a chocolate mousse.
A: No, thanks. I ___(B)___ eat any more. But go ahead if you want to.
B: I ___(C)___ trouble finishing it all by myself. Will you have a few bites?
A: OK, but just a bite.

	(A)		(B)		(C)
①	could	…	could	…	should have
②	could	…	can't	…	should have
③	could	…	can't	…	might have
④	should	…	can't	…	might have
⑤	should	…	could	…	should have

dinosaur 공룡
cold-blooded 냉혈의
reptile 파충류
opposite 반대, 반대의
evidence 증거
warm-blooded 온혈의
behave 행동하다
mammal 포유동물
conclusion 결론, 판단
draw (결론·생각을) 얻다
temperature 온도
hatch (알 등을) 까다, 부화하다

B 다음을 읽고, (   ) 안에서 어법상 알맞은 것을 고르시오.

In school, we all learned that dinosaurs were slow and cold-blooded reptiles. However, the opposite may be true. New scientific evidence shows dinosaurs ① (should / might) have been warm-blooded animals that behaved more like mammals than reptiles. Such a conclusion can be drawn from the following two facts. One is the growth patterns of dinosaurs, which are more like those of warm-blooded mammals. The other is that their body temperatures ② (have to / had to) be higher than the air to hatch eggs.

PART 13

형용사와 부사
Adjectives & Adverbs

형용사와 부사

정답 및 해설 P. 10

1

형용사(adjectives)는 사물의 성질이나 상태를 나타내 주는 말로써 명사를 수식하거나 주어, 목적어를 보충 설명해 준다.

명사 수식	주어 보충 설명	목적어 보충 설명
형용사+명사 small hands	주어+동사+형용사 The water was cold.	주어+동사+목적어+형용사 I found the game exciting.

CHECK-UP

밑줄 친 형용사가 수식 또는 설명하는 말을 찾아 표시하시오.

1 You look tired today.

2 The news made him sad.

3 The soup smells delicious.

4 My sister's bedroom is pink.

5 We saw many wild animals in the forest.

2

부사(adverbs)는 형용사, 다른 부사, 동사, 문장 전체 등을 수식하여 그 뜻을 분명하게 해준다.

	형용사+-ly	형용사=부사	불규칙
형태	quiet → quietly slow → slowly quick → quickly	long → long high → high fast → fast	good → well
부사의 쓰임	동사 수식	He really wants to see you.	
	형용사 수식	Daeseong is a very kind boy.	
	다른 부사 수식	My mother will come home very soon.	
	문장 전체 수식	Fortunately, Heymin quickly solved the problem.	

CHECK-UP

( ) 안에서 가장 알맞은 것을 고르시오.

1 You can do it (easy / easily).
This is an (easy / easily) project.

2 John is a (quiet / quietly) boy.
John speaks (quiet / quietly).

3 The little girl wore a (beautiful / beautifully) dress.
The little girl was (beautiful / beautifully) dressed.

4 My father speaks Japanese (fluent / fluently).
I hope to be a (fluent / fluently) French speaker one day.

5 He is an (honest / honestly) student.
He answers all of his teacher's questions (honest / honestly).

3 기수, 서수, 분수, 소수점은 다음과 같이 표현한다.

기수	서수	분수	소수점
one two three	first second third	2/3 two thirds 1/2 a half[one half] 3/4 three fourths [= three quarters]	1.2 one point two 0.34 (zero) point three four 3.14 three point one four

CHECK-UP

주어진 숫자 표현을 영어로 바꿔 쓰시오.

1 2/5 ______________________

2 1/3 ______________________

3 12.67 ______________________

4 1/4 ______________________

5 3/5 ______________________

6 5/9 ______________________

7 0.72 ______________________

8 11.88 ______________________

형용사의 종류와 어순

종류	'-ing' 형용사 (현재분사) 능동이나 진행을 의미	It is an **exciting** activity. 그것은 흥미진진한 활동이다.
	'-ed' 형용사 (과거분사) 수동이나 완료를 의미	She took care of the **injured** man. 그녀는 상처 입은 남자를 돌보았다.
	서술적으로 쓰이는 형용사	He is still **alive.** 그는 아직 살아 있다. I'm **afraid** of spiders. 나는 거미가 무서워요.
어순	opinion – size – age – color – origin – material – purpose 의견 크기 나이 색깔 기원 재료 목적	

FOCUS

1 '-ing' 형용사는 '~하고 있는, ~하는, ~시키는'이라는 의미로, 능동이나 진행을 나타내며, '-ed' 형용사는 '~된, ~되어진, ~당한'이라는 의미로, 수동이나 완료를 나타낸다.

Increasing weight can lead to health problems. 증가하는 몸무게는 건강 문제를 일으킬 수 있다.

How can I save this **dying** pine tree? 죽어 가는 이 소나무를 어떻게 살릴 수 있을까?

The goal of this foundation is to raise money for **wounded** soldiers.
이 재단의 목표는 부상당한 군인들을 위해 자금을 모으는 것이다.

A **fallen** tree blocked my path while I was riding my bike home.
내가 자전거를 타고 집에 오는데 쓰러진 나무가 나의 길을 막았다.

2 함께 쓴 명사가 어떤 감정을 느끼게 할 때 '-ing' 형용사를 쓰고, 함께 쓴 명사가 어떤 감정을 느낄 때 '-ed' 형용사를 쓴다.

amazing 놀라게 하는	amazed 놀란	boring 지루하게 하는	bored 지루한
depressing 우울하게 하는	depressed 우울한	disappointing 실망스럽게 하는	disappointed 실망스러운
embarrassing 당황케 하는	embarrassed 당황한	exciting 흥분시키는	excited 신나는
frightening 깜짝 놀라게 하는	frightened 무서워하는	interesting 흥미 있는	interested 흥미를 느낀
shocking 충격적인	shocked 충격받은	surprising 놀라게 하는	surprised 놀란
terrifying 무서운	terrified 무서워하는	tiring 피곤하게 하는	tired 피곤한
delighting 기쁘게 하는	delighted 기뻐하는	exhausting 지치게 하는	exhausted 지친
satisfying 만족스러운	satisfied 만족한	worrying 걱정스러운	worried 걱정하는

To go outside at night **frightened** the girl. 밤에 외출하는 것은 그 소녀를 무섭게 했다.

→ The girl was **frightened** to go outside at night. (소녀가 무서움을 느낌) 그 소녀는 밤에 외출을 해서 무서웠다.

→ To go outside at night was **frightening** for the girl. (밤에 밖에 나가는 것이 소녀를 무섭게 함) 밤에 외출하는 것이 소녀를 무섭게 했다.

Spiders terrify me. 거미가 나를 겁나게 한다.

→ Spiders are such **terrifying** creatures. 거미는 무서운 생물체이다.

→ I am **terrified** of spiders. 나는 거미가 무섭다.

Your joke amused me. 너의 농담이 나를 즐겁게 했다.

→ Your joke was **amusing**. 너의 농담은 재미있었다.

→ I was **amused** by your joke. 나는 너의 농담으로 즐거웠다.

3 명사를 앞에서 직접 수식(한정적)하지 않고 서술적으로만 쓰는 형용사에는 다음과 같은 것들이 있다.

afloat, afraid, alike, alive, alone, aware, asleep, awake ...

My parents are much **alike** in character. 우리 부모님의 성격은 매우 비슷하다.

A chimpanzee is **asleep** in the tree. 침팬지가 나무에서 자고 있다.

(×) an asleep chimpanzee (○) a **sleeping** chimpanzee

|참고| 1. 일시적인 건강 상태와 관련 있는 ill, well 등도 서술적 형용사로만 쓰인다.

Stephanie has been **ill** recently, but she is looking **well** now. 스테파니는 최근에 계속 아팠지만, 지금은 건강해 보인다.

2. 서술적으로 쓰지 않고 대개 한정적으로 쓰는 형용사에는 elder, live, little(잠시 동안의), mere, sheer 등이 있다.

They took a **little** break. 그들은 잠시 동안 휴식을 취했다.

He is my **elder** brother. 그는 나의 형이다.

(×) He is elder than me. (○) He is **older** than me. 그는 나보다 나이가 많다.

3. -thing, -one, -body, -where로 끝나는 명사의 경우, 형용사가 명사 뒤에서 명사를 수식한다.

I wanted to give you **something beautiful.** (beautiful something (×)) 나는 네게 무언가 아름다운 것을 주고 싶었어.

You'd better keep this document **somewhere safe.** (safe somewhere(×)) 이 서류를 안전한 곳에 보관하는 게 좋을 거야.

4 형용사는 주로 의견, 크기, 나이, 색깔, 기원, 재료, 목적 순서로 나열할 수 있지만, 절대적인 것은 아니다.

한정사	의견 (주관적 형용사)	크기	나이·신구(新舊)	색깔	기원·출신	재료	목적 (형용사적 명사)	명사
that		fat	young	black	African			gorilla
a(n)/the		small		red		leather		purse
two	expensive		antique			silver		mirrors
this	ugly	big		blue			sleeping	bag
several					Cuban		baseball	players

Look at **that fat young black African gorilla!** 저기 뚱뚱하고 어린 검은 아프리카 고릴라를 보세요!

The New York Mets have just signed **several Cuban baseball players.** 뉴욕 메츠가 몇 명의 쿠바 야구 선수들과 막 계약을 했다.

|참고| next, last와 서수(first) 등은 주로 기수 앞에 쓴다.

the **first** four weeks 첫 4주

his **last** two semesters 그의 지난 두 학기

EXERCISES

정답 및 해설 P. 11

motivate ~에게 동기를 부여하다
damage 훼손하다
discover ~을 발견하다
floodwater 홍수(의 물)
recede ~이 빠지다
argument 주장; 논쟁
against ~에 맞서
cloning 복제
not entirely 전적으로 ~한 것은 아닌
convince (~하도록) 설득하다
toddler 유아
acquire ~을 습득하다
seemingly 겉보기에는
effort 노력
lecture 강의, 강연
confuse ~을 혼동하다

주어진 단어를 '-ing' 또는 '-ed' 형용사로 바꿔 문장을 완성하시오.

1. Lisa always has a ____________ (welcome) smile.
2. We're looking for a highly ____________ (motivate) person for this position.
3. He was very ____________ (excite) about performing the play for the first time.
4. Several ____________ (damage) bridges were discovered after the floodwaters receded.
5. Your argument against cloning isn't entirely ____________ (convince). Let me explain why.
6. Toddlers are ____________ (amaze). They acquire new words seemingly without effort.
7. The last trip to India was a little ____________ (tire), but I have lots of happy memories of it.
8. I understood and enjoyed most of his lecture, but some part of it was a bit ____________ (confuse).

haunted 유령이 나오는
frighten ~을 깜짝 놀라게 하다
embarrass ~을 당황케 하다
silly 어리석은
answering machine 자동 응답기
encore (앙코르에 답하는) 노래, 연주
delight ~을 즐겁게 하다, ~을 기쁘게 하다
audience 관객, 청중, 관중
possible 가능성, 일어날 수 있는
spread 확장, 퍼짐
bird flu 조류 독감
alarm ~을 불안하게 하다

B **〈보기〉와 같이 문장을 완성하시오.**

보기 The haunted house frightened the children.
→ The children were __frightened__ at the haunted house.
→ The haunted house was __frightening__ for the children.

1. The silly mistakes embarrassed him.
   → He was ____________ by the silly mistakes.
   → The silly mistakes were ____________ to him.
2. The message on my answering machine confused me.
   → I was ____________ by the message on my answering machine.
   → The message on my answering machine was ____________ to me.
3. This evening's encore performance delighted the audience.
   → The audience was ____________ with this evening's encore performance.
   → This evening's encore performance was ____________ to the audience.
4. The possible spread of bird flu to that area alarmed us.
   → We were ____________ at the possible spread of bird flu to that area.
   → The possible spread of bird flu to that area was ____________ to us.

C 밑줄 친 부분이 어법상 맞지 않다면 바르게 고치시오.

1 He put a blanket over the asleep child.

2 This year's sales figures were very disappointed.

3 Oh, I didn't know you were Korean—that's interested.

4 Eunice looked up at him and gave him an ashamed smile.

5 I was afraid for my little dog, so I carried her home in my arms.

6 I'm very satisfied with the content of the magazine and its information.

7 Liz fell off while she was riding her bike. It was so embarrassed.

8 Newspapers have been reporting an astonished rumor about the president.

9 To be honest, I'm surprised to see you here. I didn't think you would show up.

10 We're very much aware of the problem, but unfortunately we don't have a solution.

asleep 잠든
sale 판매; 매상
figure 수치, 액수
disappoint ~을 실망시키다
interest ~에 흥미를 갖게 하다
ashamed ~을 부끄러워하는
satisfy ~을 만족시키다
content 내용(물)
fall off 떨어지다
report ~을 알리다
astonish ~을 놀라게 하다
rumor 소문
show up 나타나다
solution 해결책

D 주어진 단어를 알맞게 배열하여 문장을 완성하시오.

1 Please hand me (bowl, the, large, plastic) in the sink.
→ ______________________________

2 Hanbok is an example of (clothing, Korean, traditional).
→ ______________________________

3 I'm so jealous of Jackie's (black hair, long straight, beautiful).
→ ______________________________

4 Ben replaced (ugly, the, wooden, desk, big brown) with a new one.
→ ______________________________

5 They're (an, British, band, exciting, new). You should see them play.
→ ______________________ You should see them play.

6 I can't find (sleeping bag, red, small, my). Have you seen it?
→ ______________________ Have you seen it?

7 David received (new, interesting, two) video games for Christmas.
→ ______________________________

8 Serry and Yumi are wearing the same (cotton, blue, work) clothing.
→ ______________________________

hand ~을 건네주다
sink 싱크대, (~에) 가라앉다
example 예(시)
traditional 전통적인
be jealous of ~을 질투하다
replace ~을 교체하다
receive ~을 받다
cotton 솜의, 무명의
work 작업용의

부사의 종류와 위치

종류	시간	He became a professor two years **later**. 그는 2년 뒤에 교수가 되었다.
	장소	We hurried **down** to dinner. 우리는 저녁 식사를 하러 서둘러 내려갔다.
	빈도	She **always** wears miniskirts. 그녀는 항상 짧은 치마를 입는다.
순서	• 태도(manner) → 장소(place) → 방법(means) → 시간 부사(time) • 작은 시간, 작은 장소 단위 → 큰 시간, 큰 장소	

FOCUS

1 시간을 나타내는 부사는 다음과 같다.

ago, already, before, early, just, later, now, soon, still, then, today, yet ...

Brandon came to this island on vacation two years **ago**, and he is **still** here.
브랜던은 2년 전에 휴가차 이 섬에 와서, 아직도 여기에 있다.

The children were **already** asleep when their parents got home.
부모님이 집에 도착했을 때, 아이들은 이미 자고 있었다.

2 장소를 나타내는 부사는 다음과 같다.

away, back, down, here, out, there, up ...

We could go to my house and have dinner **there**. 우리 집에 가서 저녁을 먹을 수도 있어.

Where's my book? It was **here** just a minute ago. 내 책이 어디 있지? 방금 전에 여기에 있었는데.

3 횟수를 나타내는 부사를 빈도 부사라고 하고, 일반적으로 be동사나 조동사 뒤, 일반동사 앞에 쓰며, 문장 끝에 쓰기도 한다. 다음과 같은 빈도 부사가 있다.

always, frequently, never, often, seldom, sometimes, usually ...

The overworked actor missed his cues **frequently**. 과로한 그 배우는 자주 대사를 잊어버렸다.

I **often** attend my high school reunions. 나는 종종 고등학교 동창회에 참석한다.

4 정도를 나타내며, 일반적으로 문장 앞에 쓰지 않는 부사는 다음과 같다.

almost, badly, completely, enough, hard, much, terribly, very, well ...

I am **terribly** susceptible to colds. (*NOT* Terribly I am) 나는 굉장히 감기에 잘 걸린다.

My brother **almost** drowned in the river. (*NOT* Almost my brother) 내 남동생은 강에서 거의 익사할 뻔했다.

5

모양이나 태도를 나타내는 부사는 주로 동사 다음에 쓰지만, 목적어가 있을 때에는 목적어 뒤에 쓴다. 모양이나 태도를 나타내는 부사에는 다음과 같은 것들이 있다.

quickly, carefully, violently, slowly, politely, safely ...

Running out of energy, Jerry rowed the boat **slowly**.
제리는 기운이 떨어져서, 천천히 배를 저었다.

Many believe that children grow up too **quickly** these days.
많은 사람이 요즘에는 아이들이 너무 빨리 자란다고 생각한다.

6

부사는 주로 태도(manner), 장소(place), 방법(means), 시간(time) 순으로 쓴다.

태도	장소	방법	시간
enthusiastically	on the stage		last Friday
carefully	to the library		this morning
	on the street		yesterday
	to the East Sea	by car	tomorrow

Minho danced **enthusiastically on the stage last Friday.**
민호는 지난 금요일에 무대에서 정열적으로 춤을 추었다.

Karen drove **carefully to the library this morning.**
오늘 아침에 카렌은 조심스럽게 도서관을 향해 운전했다.

She scolded her son **on the street yesterday.**
그녀는 어제 길거리에서 아들을 꾸짖었다.

I'm going **to the East Sea by car tomorrow.**
나는 내일 차로 동해에 갈 것이다.

7

시간이나 장소를 나타내는 부사가 2개 이상 연이어 나올 때는 주로 작은 단위에서 큰 단위의 순으로 쓴다.

We were supposed to meet **at an Italian restaurant in Myeong-dong** yesterday.
우리는 어제 서울 명동에 있는 이탈리아 음식점에서 만나기로 했었다.

My boyfriend is arriving at Incheon airport **at 8:40 a.m. on December 3rd.**
내 남자 친구는 12월 3일 오전 8시 40분에 인천 공항에 도착한다.

The star arrived **at the convention center in Busan** to accept her award.
그 스타가 상을 받기 위해 부산에 있는 컨벤션 센터에 도착했다.

EXERCISES

정답 및 해설 P. 11

ahead of ~ 앞에
have a feeling ~한 예감이 들다
delivery 배달
pull over (길 한쪽으로) 차를 대다
be in the middle of 한창 (바쁘게) ~하는 중이다

〈보기〉에서 알맞은 것을 골라 문장을 완성하시오.

보기	this month	ahead of	before	later	there	almost

1 I have a feeling that I've been here ________________.

2 I'll be back in Korea sometime later ________________.

3 The pizza delivery driver pulled over ________________ the police car.

4 Jenny and I met at the King Street Grill and ate lunch ________________.

5 I'm in the middle of something, so can I call you back ________________?

6 My mother ________________ fell on the icy street on her way to work.

take the subway 지하철을 타다
work 직장, 일
Australia 호주
make trouble 말썽을 피우다

B 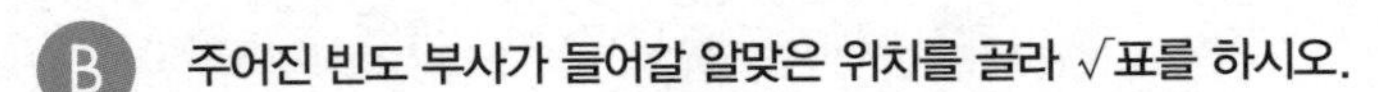

주어진 빈도 부사가 들어갈 알맞은 위치를 골라 √표를 하시오.

1 Do you take the subway to work? (usually)

2 Mr. and Ms. Kim have been to Australia. (never)

3 Gwen is a nice student, so she makes trouble in school. (seldom)

4 My friend and I have salad for lunch at the cafeteria these days. (often)

5 Tim and I do everything together. (always) We're the best of friends.

6 My mother drinks coffee, but my father drinks coffee. (sometimes, never)

hard 세차게; 단단하게; 열심히
aggressively 공격적으로; 적극적으로
embarrassingly 당혹스럽게도, 곤란할 정도로
how to + 동사원형 ~하는 방법
fall asleep 잠들다
final 최종의
draft 원고, 초안
hand in ~을 제출하다
beat ~을 이기다; ~을 치다
opposing team 상대팀

〈보기〉에서 알맞은 것을 골라 문장을 완성하시오.

보기	easily	already	yet	carefully
	hard	aggressively	embarrassingly	soon

1 It has been raining ________________ most of the day.

2 ________________, Liz didn't know how to ride a bicycle.

3 Susan fell asleep ________________ after getting into bed.

4 Sam hasn't heard anything back from UCLA ________________.

5 Please check your final draft ________________ before you hand it in.

6 The Korean soccer team beat the Japanese team ________________.

7 I guess she has ________________ arrived at the airport. Let's hurry.

8 Rudy played ________________. He hurt some players on the opposing team.

D 주어진 단어를 알맞게 배열하여 문장을 완성하시오.

1 I'll go (tomorrow, to the library, by bus) to return these books.

→ ______________________________

2 The concert tickets sold out (at the box office, quickly, this afternoon).

→ ______________________________

3 I saw someone running away from the jewelry shop (last night, at 11:30).

→ ______________________________

4 He expressed his opinion (yesterday, in front of many people, confidently).

→ ______________________________

5 Chris lived (for twelve years, happily, in Korea) before he moved back to Canada.

→ ______________________________

6 I bought a roll of film (yesterday, at a photography shop) to photograph the carnival.

→ ______________________________

7 We were all waiting (outside the studio, eagerly, at 7 o'clock) to catch a glimpse of Alex.

→ ______________________________

sell out 매진되다, 다 팔리다
run away from ~로 부터 도망치다
express ~을 말하다, 표현하다
opinion 의견, 생각
confidently 자신 있게
a roll of film 필름 한 통
photography shop 사진관
photograph ~을 촬영하다
carnival 축제, 행사
eagerly 간절히, 열망하여
glimpse 언뜻 봄

E 〈보기〉에서 알맞은 것을 골라 글을 완성하시오.

1 보기 excitedly always loudly at night

There was ________ something fun going on. ________, families would gather in the local park. Kids would run around ________ while adults gossiped, told jokes, and laughed ________. The atmosphere was always upbeat and lively.

2 보기 just ever quickly rarely

Hardly anything ________ happens! As soon as the sun goes down, everybody ________ runs inside and closes their doors. Walking silently down the street, I ________ see anybody—________ the flickering of television screens inside people's homes.

excitedly 흥분하여, 기를 쓰고
loudly 큰 소리로
go on 일어나다; 시작하다
gather 모이다
run around 뛰어다니다
adult 어른, 성인
gossip 잡담하다
joke 농담
laugh 웃다
atmosphere 분위기
upbeat 쾌활한, 명랑한
lively 생기 넘치는, 활기 넘치는
go down (해가) 지다
silently 조용히, 말없이
flicker 깜빡이다

주의해야 할 형용사와 부사

주의해야 할 형용사	-ly로 끝나는 형용사	chilly, costly, friendly, lonely, lovely ...
	쓰임에 따라 의미가 달라지는 형용사	**certain** 어떤; 확실한 **late** 작고한; 늦은; 후반의 **present** 현재의; 참석한
enough	「enough+명사」 「형용사/부사/동사+enough」	**enough** experience 충분한 경험 fair **enough** 충분히 공정한 We talked **enough**. 우리는 충분히 이야기 했다.
too, very	형용사, 부사를 강조	**too** heavy 너무 무거운 **too** far 지나치게 멀리 **very** tired 매우 피곤한 **very** seriously 아주 심각하게
so	「so+형용사/부사」	**so** quick 아주 빠른 **so** quickly 아주 빨리
such	「such+a(n)+형용사+명사」	**such** a good book 대단히 좋은 책

FOCUS

1 chilly, friendly, lovely 등 -ly로 끝나는 형용사는 부사로 혼동하기 쉽다.

Staff members at this hospital are very **friendly**. 이 병원의 직원들은 매우 친절하다.

It was such a **lovely** day yesterday. 어제는 날씨가 참 좋았다.

|참고| costly, likely, lonely, lovely, ugly는 –ly로 끝나지만 보통 형용사로 쓰이며, daily, weekly, monthly 등은 형용사와 부사로 모두 쓰인다.
She got the payment **weekly**. (부사) 그녀는 급여를 주급으로 받았다.
The employees at this company are paid on a **weekly** basis. (형용사) 이 회사의 직원들은 급여를 주 단위로 받는다.

2 certain, late, present는 한정적 용법으로 쓰였는지 서술적 용법으로 쓰였는지에 따라 그 뜻이 달라진다.

Certain types of chips contain trans fats. ('어떤'_한정적 용법) 어떤 종류의 과자는 트랜스 지방을 함유하고 있다.

I was not **certain** whether I should obey the order. ('확실한'_서술적 용법) 나는 그 명령에 따라야 할지 확신이 없었다.

Elliot received the house as an inheritance from his **late** father. ('작고한'_한정적 용법)
엘리엇은 작고하신 아버지로부터 집을 상속받았다.

My mother is in her **late** fifties. ('후반의, 말기의'_한정적 용법) 우리 어머니는 오십 대 후반이시다.

I promise not to be **late** next time. ('늦은'_서술적 용법) 다음에는 늦지 않는다고 약속할게.

Max is satisfied with his **present** position. ('현재의'_한정적 용법) 맥스는 현재의 지위에 만족한다.

Please let me know if you won't be **present** at the meeting. ('참석한'_서술적 용법)
만약 회의에 참석하지 못하신다면, 저에게 알려주세요.

3

enough는 '충분한'이란 뜻의 형용사와 '충분히'란 뜻의 부사로 쓰인다. enough는 명사 앞에 오고, 형용사와 부사 뒤에 온다.

Make sure you add **enough** salt to the *kimchi*. (명사 수식_형용사) 김치에 충분한 소금을 넣도록 해라.

Is this tea warm **enough** for you? (형용사 수식_부사) 이 차(茶)가 충분히 따뜻하니?

Jack is running fast **enough**. (부사 수식_부사) 잭은 충분히 빨리 달리고 있다.

You've played **enough** with your friends today. (동사 수식_부사) 너는 오늘 친구들과 충분히 놀았다.

4

too와 very는 형용사와 부사 앞에 놓여 이들을 강조하는 역할을 한다. too는 필요 이상으로 '~하기에 지나친' 또는 '너무 ~한'이라는 부정적인 의미가 있다.

The river was **very** cold, but we swam anyway.
강물이 아주 차가웠지만, 우리는 그래도 수영을 했다.

The water was **too** cold for swimming, so we played volleyball instead.
수영하기에는 물이 너무 차가워서, 대신에 우리는 배구를 했다.

5

such는 '그러한' 또는 '대단히'라는 의미로, 「such+a(n)+형용사+명사」 어순으로 쓴다.

She is **such** a lovely person. 그녀는 대단히 사랑스러운 사람이다.

He gave me **such** good advice. 그는 나에게 굉장히 좋은 충고를 해주었다.

|참고| such 다음에 셀 수 없는 명사가 오면 관사를 쓰지 않는다.

6

so는 '매우' 또는 '그만큼'이라는 의미로, 「so+형용사/부사」 어순으로 쓴다.

My younger sister is **so** friendly. 내 여동생은 매우 친절하다.

Why do you think **so** negatively? 당신은 왜 그렇게 부정적으로 생각해요?

7

early, fast, hard, high, late, long, near 등은 형용사와 부사로 쓰인다.

James is a **fast** pitcher. (형용사) 제임스는 속구 투수이다.

I don't like to eat **fast**. (부사) 나는 빨리 먹는 것을 좋아하지 않는다.

Mr. Kim has given his students a **hard** test. (형용사) 김 선생님이 학생들에게 어려운 시험을 내 주었다.

No wonder you failed. You didn't try very **hard**. (부사) 네가 실패한 것은 당연하다. 너는 아주 열심히 노력하지 않았다.

It's a **long** story. I'll tell you in person tomorrow. (형용사) 긴 이야기야. 내일 직접 만나서 이야기해 줄게.

Junsu hasn't been in the army **long**. (부사) 준수는 군대에 간 지 오래되지 않았다.

|주의| '-ly'가 붙어 전혀 다른 의미의 부사가 되기도 한다.

late 늦은, 늦게 — lately 최근에
high 높은, 높이 — highly 매우, 몹시
close 가까운, 가까이에 — closely 주의 깊게
hard 어려운, 열심히 — hardly 거의 ~ 않는
near 가까운, 가까이 — nearly 거의
most 대부분의, 가장 많이 — mostly 대체로

EXERCISES

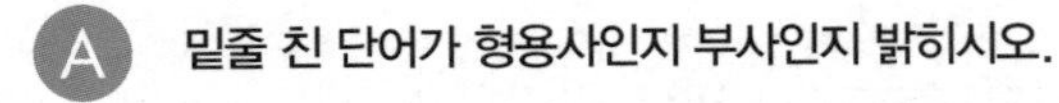

정답 및 해설 P. 12

silly 어리석은
lonely 외로운, 어리석은
grow up 자라다, 성장하다
gallery 갤러리, 미술관
daily 매일의
except ~을 제외하고
realize ~을 깨닫다, 이해하다
costly 비용이 많이 드는

A 밑줄 친 단어가 형용사인지 부사인지 밝히시오.

1 He made a lot of silly mistakes. ________

2 I live alone, but I never feel lonely. ________

3 Kids grow up so quickly these days. ________

4 The gallery is open daily except Tuesdays. ________

5 We have to listen carefully to other people. ________

6 He realized that it is a very costly business. ________

jury 배심원
refuse ~을 거절하다
defendant (법률) 피고인[측](의)
guilty 유죄, 유죄의
state 말하다, 진술하다
residence 거주지, 주소
occupation 직업
annoy ~을 화나게 하다
Forbidden City 자금성 (중국 베이징에 있는 명·청 시대의 궁전)
declare ~을 선언하다
World Heritage Site 세계 문화유산
council 협의회; 회의
serve ~에 봉사하다
be in trouble 곤경에 처하다

B 〈보기〉에서 밑줄 친 단어의 뜻이 같은 의미로 쓰인 문장을 고르시오.

보기
ⓐ Certain members of the jury refused to find the defendant guilty.
ⓑ It's certain that the kids will need counseling after the accident this morning.
ⓒ Please state your present country of residence and occupation.
ⓓ There were no children present, so the library was peaceful.
ⓔ My friend is always late. It really annoys me.
ⓕ The Forbidden City was declared a World Heritage Site in the late 20th century.

1 ① Our team looks almost certain to win the match. ____
② There are certain things we need to discuss immediately. ____

2 ① Will you be present at tomorrow's graduation ceremony? ____
② Unlike the present student council president, I believe in serving you. ____

3 ① Do you know how old James is? I guess he's in his late twenties. ____
② The train is late again. I'll be in big trouble if I miss the meeting. ____

come out 출시되다; 나타나다
stupid 어리석은
successful 성공한, 성공적인
age 나이

C 빈칸에 so와 such 중 알맞은 것을 써넣으시오.

1 They were ________ good shows. I can't wait for the DVDs to come out.

2 It's ________ a beautiful day! Let's go out to the park for a picnic.

3 I was ________ stupid! I should not have acted like that.

4 My teacher is hard to understand because he speaks ________ quickly.

5 I was surprised that he became successful at ________ a young age.

6 Why haven't you answered my phone all day long? I was ________ worried about you.

D ( ) 안에서 알맞은 것을 모두 고르시오.

handy 유용한, 편리한
upset 속상한,
fair 공평한; 정당한
intelligent 총명한, 똑똑한
distract (주의를) 딴 데로 돌리다
intently 열심히
catch ~을 따라잡다
laptop computer 노트북 컴퓨터
expensive 값이 비싼

1 She looks old (enough / too / very) to be a university student.

2 It's (too / very) handy that you live so close to the subway station.

3 Is there (enough / too) room for us? Maybe we should call a taxi van.

4 Tim was (enough / very) upset that Sue didn't come to the party yesterday.

5 I think we're close (enough / too / very) to the screen. Let's not move up.

6 It wasn't fair because Mr. Park didn't give us (enough / too / very) time to finish the test.

7 My brother was (enough / too) short to ride Kingda Ka, the world's tallest roller coaster.

8 Your son is a(n) (enough / too / very) intelligent child, but he's (enough / too / very) easily distracted by others.

9 I had to listen (enough / too / very) intently just to catch what she was saying. She was speaking (enough / too / very) softly.

10 I really wanted to buy my sister a laptop computer for her birthday, but it was (enough / too / very) expensive. So I gave her a beautiful dress instead.

E 〈보기〉와 같이 밑줄 친 단어의 품사와 역할을 밝히고 해석하시오.

cause ~의 원인이 되다
plant 식물
noticeably 눈에 띄게, 두드러지게
advanced 고급의
course 과정, 강좌
on time 제시간에, 정시에
marriage 결혼 생활, 결혼
donate 기부하다, 기증하다
charity 자선 단체; 자선기금; 자비
chemical 화학제품

보기 The accident was caused by people driving too fast.
부사, driving 수식, 빨리

1 Michael is a fast swimmer. ____________

2 I'm writing an email, but it won't take long. ____________

3 Plants grow noticeably in the early summer. ____________

4 Advanced Writing is a very hard course for you. ____________

5 Though I got up late, I could get to class on time. ____________

6 My parents have had a long and happy marriage. ____________

7 I need to study hard, so I can be a scientist later. ____________

8 Jay arrived early in the morning, so he is a bit tired. ____________

9 We'll donate our late grandma's furniture to charity. ____________

10 This chemical is highly dangerous, so you need to be careful.

____

REVIEW

정답 및 해설 P. 13

pretty 꽤, 상당한
endless 끝없는
complain 불평하다
robbery 강도 사건
frighten ~을 무서워하다
satisfy ~을 만족시키다
alarm ~을 놀라게 하다
depress ~을 우울하게 하다
delight ~을 기쁘게 하다
response 반응
advertisement광고
remove ~을 벗다; ~을 없애다
contacts 콘택트렌즈
embarrass ~을 당황케 하다

A ( ) 안에서 가장 알맞은 것을 고르시오.

1 I'm getting pretty (boring / bored) with his endless complaining.

2 Most people were (shocking / shocked) to learn about the robbery.

3 The animals felt (frightening / frightened) during the performance.

4 The meal I had last night at Lucky Gardens was (satisfying / satisfied).

5 Most teenagers find hip-hop music very (pleasing / pleased) to the ear.

6 Though the accident wasn't serious, people were (alarming / alarmed).

7 I try not to watch (depressed / depressing) movies when I'm home alone.

8 Workers at the company are (delighted / delighting) at the response to its advertisement.

9 Jenny had such a (tired / tiring) day that she went to bed without removing her contacts.

10 She kept talking about how great her new boyfriend was. It was really (embarrassed / embarrassing).

metal 금속의
rug 양탄자
woolen 양모의
on business 업무로, 상용으로
puppy 강아지
excitedly 신이 난; 흥분한
cotton 면직의
table cloth 식탁보
knock over 뒤엎다
flower pot 화분

B 주어진 단어를 알맞게 배열하여 문장을 완성하시오.

1 She gave me (metal, small, a, jewelry, box).
→ ______________________________

2 There was (a, rug, woolen, wonderful) on the floor.
→ ______________________________

3 I've just bought (coffee table, beautiful, a, wooden).
→ ______________________________

4 My father will be (next month, in Germany) on business.
→ ______________________________

5 The puppies played (in the park, all afternoon, excitedly, by the river).
→ ______________________________

6 I gave my mother (pink, these, cotton, beautiful, two) table cloths.
→ ______________________________

7 Who knocked over the (green, plastic, flower pot, big, new) in the living room?
→ ______________________________

C 두 문장의 뜻이 통하도록 ( ) 안에서 가장 알맞은 것을 고르시오.

usual 평상시의, 보통의
accept ~을 받아들이다
decision 결정
result 결과
competitive 경쟁심이 강한
soar 날아오르다
ground 땅, 육지
air 공중, 공기
close (~에) 아주 가까이
entrance 입구
employee 직원
mainly 주로, 대체로
against ~에 반대하여

1 ① She arrived after the usual time.
→ She arrived (late / lately).
② I haven't cleaned the house recently.
→ I haven't cleaned the house (late / lately).

2 ① It wasn't easy to accept her decision.
→ It was (hard / hardly) to accept her decision.
② They won, but the result wasn't at all surprising.
→ They won, but the result was (hard / hardly) surprising.

3 ① William is a very competitive player.
→ William is a (high / highly) competitive player.
② The eagle soared a long way from the ground into the air.
→ The eagle soared (high / highly) into the air.

4 ① It took almost six hours to download this software.
→ It took (near / nearly) six hours to download this software.
② A group of students was standing close to the entrance.
→ A group of students was standing (near / nearly) the entrance.

5 ① The employees in this company are mainly women.
→ The employees in this company are (most / mostly) women.
② Nearly all of the people in the meeting room were against his idea.
→ (Most / mostly) people in the meeting room were against his idea.

D 밑줄 친 부분이 어법상 맞지 않다면 바르게 고치시오.

niece (여자) 조카
remarkable 현저한, 주목할 만한
for one's age 나이에 비해서는
suitcase 여행 가방
hold ~을 담다
exhaust ~을 기진맥진하게 만들다
fall asleep 잠들다
comfortable 편안한
luxurious 화려한, 호화로운

1 He speaks <u>fluently five languages</u>.

2 Your niece has <u>such a love face</u>.

3 Make sure you eat <u>food enough</u> every day.

4 John <u>always sings</u> when he's in the shower.

5 My sister <u>never had been</u> to London before.

6 He plays the guitar <u>remarkable</u> well for his age.

7 The suitcase was <u>so</u> small to hold all of his clothes.

8 Kelly was <u>completely exhausting</u> and soon fell asleep.

9 The house was <u>enough comfortable</u>, but not luxurious.

10 The <u>present owner</u> of the restaurant is my grandmother.

REVIEW PLUS

정답 및 해설 P. 14

awful 지독한; 끔찍한
quite 꽤, 상당히
impossible 불가능한
annoy ~을 짜증나게 하다

1 다음 중 어법상 바르지 않은 문장을 고르시오.

① He is such a good player.
② I've never eaten such awful food.
③ I'm so tired. I wish I could go home.
④ It was quite impossible for me to finish it by then.
⑤ Are you still annoying with me? Please forgive me.

steel 철강의
attitude 태도
toward ~을 향한
chilly 냉담한, 차가운
curiously 이상하게, 기묘하게
time off 일이 없는 시간

2 다음 중 어법상 바른 문장을 고르시오.

① Where have you been late?
② I bought my mom a steel new knife.
③ Her attitude toward me has become a little chilly recently.
④ How many times have you seen this movie? I'm curiously.
⑤ I visit sometimes my brother in Seoul when I have time off work.

assignment 과제; 할당
word 말; 단어
graduation day 졸업식
agree 동의하다
inspiring 영감을 불러일으키는
bulb 전구

3 다음 대화가 자연스럽지 않은 것을 고르시오.

① A: Have you met Jenny before?
B: Yes, I met her six months ago.
② A: How often do you get your hair cut?
B: I get my hair cut once a month.
③ A: When did you complete the assignment?
B: I completed it yesterday.
④ A: I will never forget his words to us on graduation day.
B: I agree. Dr. King is a very inspiring speaker.
⑤ A: Why don't you get Jason a chair?
B: That's all right. He's too tall to change the bulb without one.

depart from ~에서 출발하다
loss 유실, 감소
realize ~을 깨닫다
spare ~을 남겨두다
experienced 노련한, 숙련된
steer ~을 조종하다
bring down ~을 낮추다, 내리다
passenger 승객
crew 승무원
rescue ~을 구조하다
alive 살아 있는
owe ~을 빚지다

4 다음을 읽고, ( ) 안에서 알맞은 것을 고르시오.

"Hero of the Hudson"

US Airways Flight 1549 had just departed from LaGuardia Airport in New York City when pilot Chesley Sullenberger reported a total loss of engine power. With no time to spare, the experienced pilot quickly realized that he wasn't going to be able to fly the damaged airplane back to the airport. So instead, he ① (successful / successfully) steered the jet toward the Hudson River and slowly brought it down on the water. All 155 passengers and crew were ② (safe / safely) rescued, and now the pilot is being called a hero. "We are all so lucky to be alive," said one ③ (frightening / frightened) passenger. "We owe Captain Sullenberger our lives," said another.

PART 14

비교
Comparisons

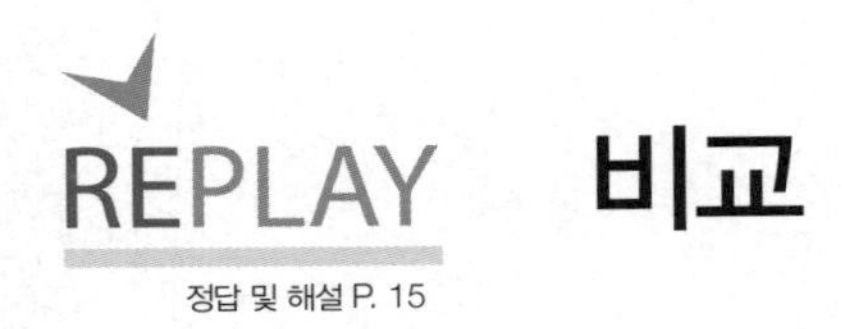

비교

정답 및 해설 P. 15

1 비교급과 최상급의 형태

	원급 (~한/~하게)	비교급 (더 ~한/~하게)	최상급 (가장 ~한/~하게)
규칙	원래 형태 그대로	• 형용사/부사+-(e)r • more+형용사/부사	• 형용사/부사+-(e)st • most+형용사/부사
	young beautiful fast carefully	younger more beautiful faster more carefully	youngest most beautiful fastest most carefully
불규칙	• good / well	better	best
	• many / much	more	most
	• little	less	least
	• bad / ill	worse	worst

CHECK-UP

주어진 형용사와 부사의 비교급과 최상급을 쓰시오.

		비교급	최상급
1	wise	______	______
2	much	______	______
3	cheap	______	______
4	pretty	______	______
5	young	______	______
6	well	______	______
7	hot	______	______
8	easy	______	______
9	warm	______	______
10	early	______	______
11	large	______	______
12	hard	______	______
13	big	______	______
14	little	______	______
15	heavy	______	______
16	popular	______	______
17	bad	______	______
18	weak	______	______
19	important	______	______
20	sad	______	______
21	long	______	______
22	difficult	______	______
23	slowly	______	______
24	ill	______	______
25	good	______	______
26	many	______	______

2 비교급

비교급	
• 비교급(-er) + than • 비교급(more + 원급) + than	~보다 더 …한 / ~보다 더 …하게

Australia is **bigger than** New Zealand. 호주는 뉴질랜드보다 더 크다.
Tim speaks **more softly than** Sunny. 팀은 써니보다 더 부드럽게 말한다.

CHECK-UP

주어진 단어를 사용하여 비교급 문장을 완성하시오.

1 (good) This book is ________________ than that one.

2 (heavy) My friend's bag is ________________ than mine.

3 (sweet) The pears are ________________ than the oranges.

4 (quietly) Michelle spoke ________________ than Samantha.

5 (big) My older sister's bed is ________________ than my younger sister's.

3 최상급

최상급	
• (the)+최상급(-est) • (the)+최상급(most+원급)	~ 중에(서) 가장 …한 / ~ 중에(서) 가장 …하게

Taipei 101 was **the tallest** building in the world. 타이베이 101은 세계에서 가장 높은 건물이었다.
These are **the most expensive** sneakers in the shop. 이 운동화는 그 가게에서 가장 비싸다.

CHECK-UP

주어진 단어를 사용하여 최상급 문장을 완성하시오.

1 (hot) Noon is the ________________ part of the day.

2 (busy) Tom is the ________________ boy in the room.

3 (beautiful) Kelly is the ________________ girl in the class.

4 (clean) Beth's room is the ________________ room in the dorm.

5 (slowly) My computer works the ________________ among my friends'.

원급을 이용한 비교 구문

A as+원급+as B A는 B만큼 ~하다	I work as hard as Jeffrey does. 나는 제프리만큼 열심히 일한다.
A not as(so)+원급+as B A는 B만큼 ~하지 않다	This question is not as difficult as that question. 이 문제는 저 문제만큼 어렵지 않다.
「A+동사+ ~ times+as+원급+as B」 A는 B의 ~ 배 …이다	Minho ate twice as much pizza as I did. 민호는 나보다 두 배나 많은 피자를 먹었다.

FOCUS

1

「A as+원급+as B」는 'A는 B만큼 ~하다'라는 의미로, 두 대상의 정도가 동등하다는 것을 나타낸다.

Lisa can swim **as** fast **as** Jaehee can. 리사는 재희만큼 빨리 수영할 수 있다.

The first volume is **as** thick **as** the second volume. 1권은 2권만큼 두껍다.

|참고| 양을 비교할 때에는 「as much[many]+(명사)+as ~」 형태로 표현할 수 있으며,
「as much[many] as+숫자」는 '~만큼이나 되는'이라는 뜻으로 쓰여 강조를 나타낸다.
You can see **as many** movies **as** you want with this membership card. 이 회원 카드로 여러분이 원하는 만큼 많은 영화를 볼 수 있습니다.
As many as 500 people were present at the event. 500명이나 되는 사람들이 행사에 참석했다.

2

「A not as[so]+원급+as B」는 'A는 B만큼 ~하지 않다'라는 의미로, 두 대상의 정도가 같지 않다는 것을 나타낸다. 「A less+원급+than B(A는 B보다 덜하다)」로 바꿔 쓸 수 있다.

This dog doesn't look **as** fierce **as** that one. 이 개는 저 개만큼 사나워 보이지 않는다.

→ This dog looks **less** fierce **than** that one.

It was **not so** easy **as** I thought. 그것은 내가 생각한 것만큼 쉽지 않았다.

→ It was **less** easy **than** I thought.

|참고| 비교 대상과 비교의 격을 일치시키는 것이 원칙이나, 주격 대신 목적격을 쓰기도 한다.
I'm not as good at English as **he is** [**him**]. 나는 그만큼 영어를 잘하지 못한다.

3

「A+~ times+as+원급+as B」는 'A는 B의 ~ 배 …이다[하다]'라는 의미이다.

Michelle has **five times as** many books **as** I do. 미셸은 나보다 다섯 배나 더 많은 책을 가지고 있다.

Their playground is **three times as** large **as** ours. 그들의 운동장은 우리 것보다 세 배 크다.

|참고| '~의 반'이란 의미로 ~ times 대신에 half를 사용한다.
This river is **half** as deep as the Nile in Egypt. 이 강의 깊이는 이집트의 나일 강의 깊이의 반이다.

4 「as+원급+as」 형식을 사용한 관용 표현은 다음과 같다.

「as+원급+as possible」 = 「as+원급+as one can」 가능한 한 ~하게

Please let me know the test results **as** soon **as possible.**

→ Please let me know the test results **as** soon **as you can.**
가능한 한 빨리 시험 결과를 알려 주세요.

Sue's mother read the story to her **as** clearly **as possible.**

→ Sue's mother read the story to her **as** clearly **as she could.**
수의 어머니는 수에게 가능한 한 명료하게 이야기를 읽어 주었다.

「as soon as+주어+동사」 = 「No sooner+동사+주어 ~ than」 ~하자마자

The pickpocket ran away **as soon as** he snatched the handbag.

→ **No sooner** had the pickpocket snatched the handbag **than** he ran away.
소매치기는 핸드백을 낚아채자마자 도망갔다.

「as long as+주어+동사」 ① ~하는 만큼 오래 ② ~하기만 하면

You may stay with us **as long as** you want. 당신이 원하는 만큼 오래 우리와 있어도 좋다.

You can stay here **as long as** you help pay the bills. 요금 내는 것을 도와주기만 하면, 여기 있어도 좋아.

「not so much+A+as+B」 = 「rather+B+than+A」 ~A라기 보다는 B

Surfing is **not so much** a science **as** a skill.

→ Surfing is **rather** a skill **than** a science.
서핑은 과학이라기보다는 기술이다.

***** 「as+원급+as」를 이용한 최상급 표현 *****

부정어+as[so]+원급+as A A만큼 ~한 것은 없다	**Nothing** is **as[so]** important **as** health. 건강만큼 중요한 것은 없다.
as+원급+as any+명사/절 어느 사람[것] 못지않게 ~하다	Bradley is **as** handsome **as any** man alive. 브래들리는 살아 있는 어느 남자 못지않게 잘생겼다. (브래들리는 어느 남자들보다도 더 잘생겼다.)
as+원급+as ever+동사 어느 사람[것] 못지않게 ~하다	She is **as** great a figure skater **as ever** lived. 그녀는 지금까지 산 어느 사람 못지않게 훌륭한 피겨 스케이팅 선수이다. (그녀는 지금까지 없었던 훌륭한 피겨스케이팅 선수이다.)
as+원급+as ever 여전히	Daniel's mother is **as** kind **as ever.** 대니얼의 어머니는 여전히 친절하다.

EXERCISES

정답 및 해설 P. 15

tough 질긴; 강인한
come out (얼룩 등이) 빠지다
long-distance 장거리의
add to 추가하다
topping 요리 위에 얹거나 치는 것
leather 가죽

A 〈보기〉에서 알맞은 것을 골라 as ~ as를 이용하여 문장을 완성하시오.

보기			
difficult	many	pretty	much
hard	strong	tough	white

1 Sujin studies English ________________ Minjin does.

2 The final exam was not ________________ I thought.

3 Will my white T-shirts come out ________________ snow?

4 Your daughter looks ________________ a princess in that dress.

5 Jenny is ____________ a long-distance runner __________ Beth.

6 Sarah has three times ____________ money __________ I have.

7 You can add ____________ toppings to your pizza __________ you like.

8 I couldn't eat the steak at all because it was ________________ leather.

doorbell 초인종
calorie 칼로리, 열량
come over (집에) 들르다
break through (햇빛 등이) ~ 사이에서 나타나다
memory (컴퓨터) 기억 장치

B 두 문장의 의미가 통하도록 문장을 완성하시오.

1 As soon as I went to bed, someone rang my doorbell.
→ __________ __________ had I gone to bed __________ someone rang my doorbell.

2 You ate 100 calories. You can eat 500 calories more.
→ You can eat __________ __________ __________ many calories __________ you did.

3 I need your help! Come over to my house as soon as you can.
→ I need your help! Come over to my house __________ __________ __________ __________.

4 No sooner had it stopped raining than the sun broke through the clouds.
→ __________ __________ __________ it stopped raining, the sun broke through the clouds.

5 We should practice speaking English as much as possible.
→ We should practice speaking English __________ __________ __________ __________ __________.

6 Her computer has 800GB of memory while mine has only 400GB of memory.
→ The memory of her computer is __________ __________ big __________ that of mine.

부정형과 긍정형에 주의하여 〈보기〉와 같이 문장을 완성하시오.

보기 Tasty Donut = Sweet Donut (get, many customers)

→ Tasty Donut gets as many customers as Sweet Donut on Saturdays.

Tasty Donut < Round Donut (get, many customers)

→ Tasty Donut doesn't get as many customers as Round Donut on weekends.

customer 고객
photocopy (복)사본
pearl 진주
rare 드문, 진기한
grizzly bear (동물) (북미 서부산(産)의) 큰 회색곰
superstitious 미신에 사로잡힌; 미신의

1 sugar = honey (be, sweet)

→ ______________________________

2 a lake < a sea (be, big)

→ ______________________________

3 my photocopy < hers (be, clear)

→ ______________________________

4 pearls < black diamonds (be, rare)

→ ______________________________

5 Jieun = you (have visited Europe, many times)

→ ______________________________

6 a koala < a grizzly bear (be, dangerous)

→ ______________________________

7 the Thompsons = the Browns (have, many children)

→ ______________________________

8 winter in Canada = winter in Russia (be, cold and bitter)

→ ______________________________

9 John < his brother Peter (eat, much junk food)

→ ______________________________

10 ice hockey players = basketball players (be, superstitious)

→ ______________________________

11 romantic comedies = horror movies (be, interesting)

→ ______________________________

12 the waiters at this restaurant < the waiters at that restaurant (be, kind)

→ ______________________________

비교급을 이용한 비교 구문

A 비교급 than B A가 B보다 ~하다	This dictionary is **more useful than** that one. 이 사전은 저것보다 더 유용하다.
even/much/far/still/a lot + 비교급 훨씬 ~하다	She looked **even prettier** than usual. 그녀는 평소보다 훨씬 더 예뻐 보였다.
the + 비교급, the + 비교급 ~하면 할수록 더 …하다	**The more** you smile, **the happier** you become. 더 많이 웃을수록 더 행복해진다.
비교급 + and + 비교급 점점 더, 더욱더	We've gotten **less and less** snow along with **warmer and warmer** winters. 겨울이 점점 더 따뜻해지고 있어서 눈이 점점 더 줄어들고 있다.

FOCUS

1

「A 비교급 than B」는 'A가 B보다 ~하다'라는 의미로, 두 대상을 비교할 때 쓴다.

Nancy is **happier than** before. 낸시는 전보다 더 행복하다.

Heejung cuts my hair **better than** Julia. 희정이가 줄리아보다 머리를 더 잘 자른다.

|참고| 앞서 언급한 말과 중복되는 than 이하의 주어 · 동사 등은 주로 생략한다.
Nancy is happier than (**she was**) before.
Heejung cuts my hair better than Julia (**cuts my hair**).

2

「less+원급+than」은 '~보다 덜 …하다, ~만큼 …않다'라는 의미이다.

You need to help people who are **less** fortunate **than** you. 너보다 불행한 사람들을 도와야 한다.

Soccer is **less** tough **than** rugby. 축구는 럭비보다 덜 거칠다.

|참고| 「less+원급+than」은 「not as[so]+원급+as(~만큼 ~하지 않다)」로 바꿔 쓸 수 있다.
Soccer is **not as[so]** tough **as** rugby. 축구는 럭비만큼 거칠지 않다.

3

비교급은 even, much, far, still, a lot 등을 사용하여 강조하고, '훨씬, 더욱 ~한'으로 해석한다.

Mr. Harrison is **a lot** taller than his wife. 해리슨 씨는 자기 아내보다 훨씬 키가 크다.

The movie was **much** more exciting than I had expected. 그 영화는 내가 기대했던 것보다 훨씬 더 재미있었다.

|주의| very는 비교급을 강조할 수 없다.
(×) Mr. Harrison is ~~very taller~~ than his wife.

4 「the+비교급, the+비교급」은 '~하면 할수록 더 …하다'라는 의미이다.

The longer I live in this country, **the more** I like it. 이 나라에 오래 살면 살수록 나는 더욱더 이곳이 좋아진다.

The higher you climb, **the colder** it gets. 높이 오르면 오를수록 더 추워진다.

5 「비교급+and+비교급」은 '점점 더, 더욱더'라는 의미이다.

It's getting **colder and colder** outside. 밖은 점점 더 추워지고 있다.

More and more people are moving back to the countryside. 점점 더 많은 사람들이 다시 시골로 이사를 가고 있다.

6 비교의 대상이 되는 것은 문법적으로 동등해야 하고, 앞서 언급된 명사와 동일한 명사가 나올 때는 that이나 those로 받는다.

The climate of Canada is colder than **that** of Korea. 캐나다의 기후는 한국의 기후보다 춥다.

(×) The climate of Canada is colder than ~~Korea~~. (캐나다의 기후와 한국을 비교하면 안 된다.)

The population of Busan is smaller than **that** of Seoul. 부산의 인구는 서울의 인구보다 적다.

(×) The population of Busan is smaller than ~~Seoul~~. (부산의 인구와 서울을 비교하면 안 된다.)

7 「the+비교급+of the two」는 '두 개 중 더 ~한'이라는 의미이다.

This is **the sweeter of the two** candies. 두 개의 사탕 중에서 이것이 더 달다.

That laptop computer is **the noisier of the two**. 두 개의 노트북 컴퓨터 중에서 저 노트북 컴퓨터가 더 시끄럽다.

8 라틴어에서 온 단어의 비교급에는 than 대신 to를 쓴다.

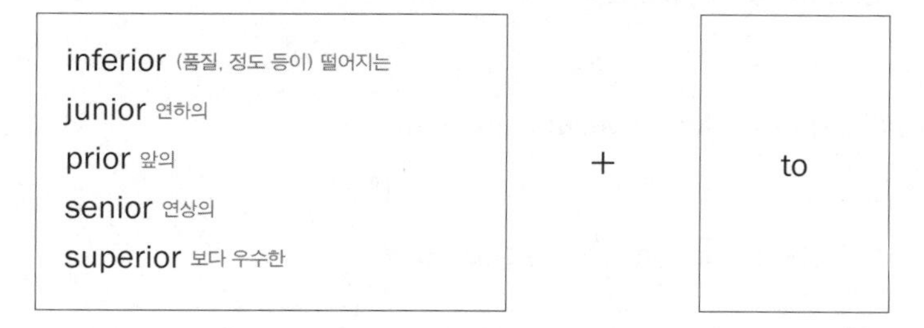

Major is an **inferior** rank **to** colonel. 소령은 대령보다 낮은 계급이다.

My graduation occurred **prior to** hers. 내 졸업식이 그녀의 졸업식보다 먼저이다.

My eldest brother is seven years **senior to** me. 큰형은 나보다 일곱 살 위다.

|참고| not more than (=at most) 기껏해야, 많아야
not less than(=at least) 최소한, 적어도

I guess she is **not more than** thirty. 내 생각에 그녀는 기껏해야 서른 살이다.

I decided to study **not less than** two hours a day. 나는 적어도 하루에 두 시간은 공부를 하기로 결심했다.

EXERCISES

정답 및 해설 P. 16

watermelon 수박
definitely 분명히, 확실히
brave 용감한
presentation 발표
light bulb 백열전구
efficient 효율적인, 능률적인
elm 느릅나무
Ethiopian 에티오피아(인)의
product 생산물[품], 제품
Leeds 리즈 (영국 요크셔주 중부의 도시)
Manchester 맨체스터 (영국 서북부주의 상공업 도시)

A 빈칸에 of, than, to 중 알맞은 것을 써넣으시오.

1 This watermelon is the sweeter ________ the two.

2 You are definitely a braver person ________ I am.

3 I need to talk to her prior ________ the presentation.

4 This light bulb is the more efficient ________ the two.

5 These are the cheaper ________ the two pairs of skis.

6 The elm in the backyard is taller ________ the house.

7 Peter is a less confident chess player ________ Joe is.

8 Ethiopian coffee is superior ________ Indonesian coffee.

9 Leeds is a smaller city ________ London or Manchester is.

10 These products are inferior ________ those we bought last year.

11 Michelle has watched many more horror movies ________ her sister has.

12 Pete is one year junior ________ me, but we've been friends for a long time.

fluent 유창한
wise 현명한
nervous 불안해하는
crowd 관객; 군중
leave ~을 떠나다
rise 뜨다
balloon 기구(氣球); 풍선
savanna 사바나, 대초원

B 〈보기〉와 같이 두 문장을 한 문장으로 만드시오.

보기 You practice speaking English for a **long** time. You'll become **fluent**.
→ The longer you practice speaking English, the more fluent you'll become.

1 We grow **old**, we get **wise**.
→ ________________________________

2 The taxi driver drove **fast**. I became **nervous**.
→ ________________________________

3 The band played **loud**. The crowd got **excited**.
→ ________________________________

4 We get the classroom clean **fast**. We can all leave **soon**.
→ ________________________________

5 Jeff rose **high** in the balloon. He could see **much** of the savanna.
→ ________________________________

6 You practice the piano **hard**. You will be a famous pianist **quickly**.
→ ________________________________

C 밑줄 친 부분이 어법상 맞지 않다면 바르게 고치시오.

1 His experiences are more various than you.

2 The quicker you eat, sooner I can clean up.

3 Mom bought more vegetables to fruit today.

4 This movie is the more interesting in the two.

5 I have exactly twice as much money as you do.

6 Michelle is less happier than Sue is about the trip.

7 Kevin owns very more expensive clothes than I do.

8 Surprisingly, the bus is less crowded of the subway.

9 The economists became more and more optimistic.

10 The climate of Singapore is much hotter than Russia.

11 Trollope's novels are more entertaining than that of Dickens.

12 People in the countryside are usually friendlier to those in big cities.

various 다양한
clean up 청소하다
trip 여행
economist 경제학자
optimistic 낙관적인
crowded 혼잡한, 붐비는
climate 기후
entertaining 재미있는

D 〈보기〉에서 알맞은 것을 골라 「비교급 and 비교급」을 이용하여 문장을 완성하시오.

보기				
tired	dark	good	fluently	anxious
dangerous	heavy	angry	expensive	cold

1 It is likely to rain soon. The sky is growing ______________________.

2 Jake's neighbor was making too much noise. He grew ______________.

3 I was skiing without wearing gloves. My hands became ______________.

4 Hitchhiking is no longer safe. It is becoming ______________________.

5 Beth joined the school choir. Her singing is getting ______________.

6 Mom is worried because things are getting ______________________.

7 The girl studies English these days. She speaks ______________.

8 As days went by, he became ______________________ of doing the same thing every day.

9 Sue was taking a test. It seemed that time was flying. She became ________ ______________________.

10 I had to carry all my luggage by myself. As time passed by, it seemed to grow ______________________.

anxious 걱정스러운
be likely to ~할 것 같다
neighbor 이웃
grow angry 화내다
hitchhike 히치하이크하다 (지나가는 자동차에 편승하다)
join 가입하다
choir 합창단, 성가대
things 물건
go by (시간이) 지나가다, 흐르다
fly (시간이) 쏜살같이 지나가다
luggage 여행 가방
pass by (시간이) 지나가다, 흐르다

최상급을 이용한 비교 구문

Peggy is tall. (161cm)	Ted is tall. (168cm)	Edward is tall. (177cm)

Edward is **the tallest of** the three. 에드워드는 세 사람 중에서 가장 키가 크다.

FOCUS

1

셋 이상을 비교하여 '~에서 가장 …한'이라는 의미를 나타낼 때는 주로 다음의 두 가지 표현을 쓴다.

the+최상급(+in+장소나 범위의 단수 명사)

This room is **the cleanest** in the house. 이 방이 이 집에서 가장 깨끗하다.

The Amazon is **the widest** and **longest** river in the world. 아마존 강이 세계에서 가장 넓고 긴 강이다.

the+최상급(+of+기간/비교의 대상이 되는 복수 명사)

This book is **the most interesting** one of the series. 이 책이 이 시리즈 중에서 가장 재미있다.

This photo is **the finest** of all. 이 사진이 모든 사진들 중에서 가장 훌륭하다.

|참고| 「the+최상급+(that)+주어+현재완료」는 '지금까지 ~한 것 중 가장 …한'이라는 뜻으로 쓰인다.
It was **the most touching movie (that) I have ever seen.** 그것은 지금까지 내가 본 영화들 중 가장 감동적인 영화였다.

2

「one of the+최상급+복수 명사」는 '가장 ~한 것 중 하나'라는 의미이다.

She is **one of the most famous actresses** in Korea. 그녀는 한국에서 가장 유명한 여배우 중 한 사람이다.

This is **one of the best sellers** in the shop. 이것이 이 가게에서 가장 잘 팔리는 것 중 하나이다.

3

비교급을 써서 최상급의 의미를 나타내기도 한다.

「비교급+than any other+단수 명사」 어떤 ~보다 더 …하다

The crime rate in this city is **lower than any other city's.** 이 도시의 범죄율은 다른 어떤 도시보다 낮다.

→ The crime rate in this city is **the lowest.** 이 도시의 범죄율이 가장 낮다.

「비교급+than all the other+복수 명사」 어떤 ~보다 더 …하다

The history teacher is **more handsome than all the other teachers** in my school.
역사 선생님이 우리 학교의 다른 어떤 선생님들보다 잘생겼다.

→ The history teacher is **the most handsome** in my school. 우리 학교에서 역사 선생님이 가장 잘 생겼다.

「부정어+비교급+than」 어떤 ~보다 더 …한 것은 없다

Nothing is **more important than** happiness. 행복보다 더 중요한 것은 없다.

→ Happiness is **the most important** thing. 행복이 가장 중요한 것이다.

「부정어+as[so]+원급+as」 ~만큼 …한 것은 없다

Nothing is **as[so] important as** working together cooperatively. 협동해서 함께 일하는 것만큼 중요한 것은 없다.

→ Working together cooperatively is **the most important thing.** 협동해서 함께 일하는 것이 가장 중요한 것이다.

|참고| 비교급을 이용한 최상급 표현 가장 ~하다

→ 비교급+than any other+단수 명사 어떤 ~보다 더 …하다

→ 비교급+than all the other+복수 명사 어떤 ~보다 더 …하다

→ 부정어+비교급+than 어떤 ~보다 더 …한 것은 없다

→ 부정어+as[so]+원급+as ~만큼 …한 것은 없다

4 단어의 뜻에 따라 비교급과 최상급의 형태가 달라지는 형용사, 부사가 있다.

원급	비교급	최상급
old	older 더 늙은, 더 오래된	oldest 가장 늙은, 가장 오래된
	elder 손위의	eldest 가장 손위의
late	later (시간) 후에, 나중에	latest 최근의
	latter (순서) 후자의	last 마지막의
far	farther (거리) 더 먼, 더 멀리	farthest 가장 먼
	further (시간, 정도) 더 먼, 더 멀리	furthest 가장 멀리

She is **older** than my **eldest** sister. 그녀는 나의 큰언니보다 나이가 많다.

A: Which planet is **farthest** away from the Sun? 어느 행성이 태양에서 가장 멀리 떨어져 있나요?

B: Neptune is the **farthest** planet. In the past, it was Pluto, but Pluto is no longer considered a planet.
해왕성이 가장 먼 행성입니다. 과거에는 명왕성이었으나, 명왕성은 더는 행성으로 간주되지 않습니다.

|참고| 1. farther, further는 거리, 시간, 정도에 거의 구분 없이 쓰기도 한다.

2. William would be **the last** student to cheat. 윌리엄은 결코 부정행위를 할 학생이 아니다.

***** 기타 최상급 표현 *****

1. 최상급에는 주로 the를 붙이지만 the를 붙이지 않는 경우도 있다.
   Julia gets up **earliest** in her family. (부사의 최상급) 줄리아가 식구들 중에서 가장 일찍 일어난다.
   Dennis is my **best** friend. (소유격+최상급) 데니스는 나의 가장 친한 친구이다.
   I have finished **most of** my homework. (most of = 대부분) 나는 숙제를 대부분 끝마쳤다.
2. 최상급 구문의 관용적 표현에는 다음과 같은 것들이 있다.
   We have ten minutes **at best** to finish up. 우리가 그것을 마무리할 수 있는 시간이 기껏해야 10분이다.
   The cherry blossoms will be **at their best** this weekend. 벚꽃은 이번 주말에 가장 한창일 것이다.
   Justin will **make the most of** that opportunity. 저스틴은 그 기회를 최대한으로 이용할 것이다.
   She did **not in the least** expect to see her ex-boyfriend there. 그녀는 전 남자 친구를 거기에서 만날 것이라고 전혀 예상하지 못했다.

EXERCISES

정답 및 해설 P. 17

bright 총명한, 영리한; 밝은
remind ~을 상기시키다
distance 거리
snowstorm 눈보라

〈보기〉에서 알맞은 것을 골라 최상급으로 바꿔 문장을 완성하시오.

보기	bright	late	bad	far

1 This is the ______________ time I'm going to remind you.

2 What's the ______________ distance you've ever swum?

3 Greg is the ______________ boy in the class. He got all A's.

4 That was the ______________ snowstorm we've had for many years.

Quebec
퀘벡(캐나다 동부의 주)
attractive 매력적인
crime 범죄
modern 현대의

B 주어진 단어를 사용하여 '가장 ~한 것 중 하나'라는 의미가 되도록 문장을 완성하시오.

1 Quebec is ______________________ in Canada. (attractive, city)

2 Crime is ______________________ in modern cities. (big, problem)

3 Manhattan is ______________________ in the USA. (famous, city)

4 Einstein was ______________________ in the world. (great, scientist)

route 길, 방법
downtown 시내

C 주어진 표현을 이용하여 최상급 의미가 되도록 문장을 완성하시오.

1 This is the shortest route downtown.
→ This is ______________________ downtown. (비교급, any other)
→ ________ other route downtown is ______________ this route. (no, 비교급)
→ ________ other route downtown is ______________ this route. (no, 원급)

2 Today is the hottest day of this summer.
→ Today is ______________________ of this summer. (비교급, any other)
→ ________ day this summer is ______________ today. (no, 비교급)
→ ________ day this summer is ______________ today. (no, 원급)

3 My room is the cleanest room in my house.
→ My room is ______________________ in my house. (비교급, any other)
→ ________ other room in my house is ______________ my room. (no, 비교급)
→ ________ other room in my house is ______________ my room. (no, 원급)

4 This is the most expensive car in the world.
→ This is ______________________ in the world. (비교급, all the other)
→ ________ other car in the world is ______________ this car. (no, 비교급)
→ ________ other car in the world is ______________ this car. (no, 원급)

D 주어진 단어와 「최상급+전치사」 구문을 이용하여 문장을 완성하시오.

respected 훌륭한, 높이 평가되는
influential 영향력이 큰
writer 작가
recording studio 녹음실
sound 음향
machine 기계
mystery novel 추리 소설
thrilling 스릴 만점의

1 It was ______________ (hard) day ________ my life.

2 Today is ______________ (cold) day ________ the year.

3 Who is ______________ (tall) student ________ your class?

4 That school is ______________ (old) building ________ the city.

5 He is ______________ (respected) scientist ________ the world.

6 Pepperoni is ______________ (delicious) pizza ________ this restaurant.

7 Ms. Brown is ______________ (influential) writer ________ the world.

8 Tom Smith is ______________ (famous) actor ________ his country.

9 This song is ______________ (popular) one ________ his more than 100 songs.

10 The recording studio has ______________ (new) sound machine ________ the country.

11 His recent mystery novel is ______________ (thrilling) ________ the books he has written.

E 우리말과 같은 뜻이 되도록 주어진 단어를 이용하여 문장을 완성하시오.

season 계절
wasteful 낭비의, 헛된
deceive ~을 속이다
depressing 우울한

1 건강보다 더 중요한 것은 없다. (important)
→ Nothing is ______________ than health.

2 그것은 내가 지금까지 본 것 중 최악의 콘서트였다. (bad)
→ It was ______________ concert I have ever seen.

3 가을 하늘은 다른 어떤 계절보다 맑아 보인다. (clear)
→ In fall, the sky looks ______________ than any other season.

4 공을 가장 멀리 던진 사람이 승자가 된다. (far)
→ The person who throws the ball ______________ will be the winner.

5 아무것도 안 하면서 시간을 보내는 것만큼 아까운 것은 없다. (wasteful)
→ Nothing is ______________ as spending time doing nothing.

6 내가 아는 한 브래드는 결코 사람을 속일 사람이 아니다. (late)
→ As far as I know, Brad would be ______________ person to deceive people.

7 생일을 혼자 보내는 것보다 우울한 것은 없다. (depressing)
→ Nothing is ______________ than spending your birthday alone.

형용사를 이용한 기타 비교 구문

the same as ~와 같은	This motorcycle is **the same as** that one. 이 오토바이는 저것과 같다.
similar to ~와 비슷한	This cushion is **similar to** that one. 이 쿠션은 저것과 비슷하다.
different from ~와 다른	This desk is **different from** that one. 이 책상은 저것과 다르다.
alike 서로 같은, 비슷한	These kids look **alike**. 이 아이들은 서로 닮아 보인다.

FOCUS

1 사물을 비교할 때 the same as, similar to, different from을 이용할 수 있다.

첫 번째 비교 대상 + 동사 + [**the same as** / **similar to** / **different from**] + 두 번째 비교 대상

Your shoes look **the same as** mine. 너의 신발이 내 것과 같아 보인다.
Peter's T-shirt is **the same as** James's. 피터의 티셔츠는 제임스의 티셔츠와 같다.

My bicycle looks **similar to** his. 내 자전거는 그의 것과 비슷해 보인다.
Her voice is **similar to** her mother's. 그녀의 목소리는 그녀의 어머니의 목소리와 비슷하다.

His dreams are **different from** hers. 그의 꿈은 그녀의 꿈과 다르다.
Their purpose was **different from** ours. 그들의 목적은 우리의 목적과 달랐다.

2 alike는 '서로 같은, 비슷한'이라는 의미를 지니는 형용사로 서술적으로 사용되므로 명사를 수식할 수 없다.

The size of the wheels is not **alike**. 이 바퀴들의 크기가 서로 같지 않다.
The little girls are dressed exactly **alike**. 그 어린 여자아이들은 똑같이 옷을 입었다.

|참고| like ~처럼, ~같이 vs. like ~을 좋아하다
My sister looks **like** my grandmother. (전치사) 우리 언니는 할머니를 닮았다.
He **likes** to watch movies. (동사) 그는 영화 보는 것을 좋아한다.

EXERCISES

정답 및 해설 P. 17

A 두 문장의 의미가 통하도록 문장을 완성하시오.

1 Humans and chimpanzees have similar DNA.
→ The human DNA is ________________ that of chimpanzees.

2 My handwriting and your handwriting are similar.
→ My handwriting is ________________ yours.

3 My new inline skates and Steve's inline skates look similar.
→ My new inline skates look ________________ Steve's.

4 The human brain and the chimpanzee's brain are different.
→ The human brain is ________________ that of the chimpanzee.

5 My final essay topic and your final essay topic are the same.
→ My final essay topic is ________________ yours.

6 Fish that live in the ocean and fish that live in lakes are different.
→ Fish that live in the ocean are ________________ those that live in lakes.

7 The date of the concert and the date of the final exam are the same.
→ The date of the concert is ________________ that of the final exam.

human 인간의, 사람의
chimpanzee (동물) 침팬지
handwriting (개인의) 필적, 서체(書體)
brain 뇌
essay 수필, 에세이
topic 주제, 화제
ocean 바다, 해양

B 빈칸에 alike, to, as, from 중 하나를 써넣으시오.

1 My sister doesn't look similar ____________ my brother.

2 The children all look very ____________ in their uniforms.

3 The movie was completely different ____________ the book.

4 This bread tastes exactly the same ____________ that bread.

5 My schedule is the same ____________ your schedule. Great!

6 I don't think his phone number is the same ____________ before.

7 The new software is not that different ____________ the old one.

8 Sally is very similar ____________ her mother in terms of characters.

9 My experiences traveling in Africa were different ____________ his.

10 That excuse sounds similar ____________ the one you told me yesterday.

11 The two sculptures look so ____________ that we can hardly distinguish them.

12 To the untrained eye, these two photos look ____________, but they're actually very different.

uniform 유니폼, 제복
schedule 일정
character 성격; 특징
excuse 변명; 해명
sculpture 조각품
distinguish ~을 구별하다
untrained 훈련받지 않은, 미숙한
actually 실제로, 사실은

REVIEW

정답 및 해설 P. 18

expect ~을 기대하다
fitness club 헬스클럽
currently 현재, 지금
available 이용할 수 있는; 유효한
modern 현대의
hippopotamus 하마
freshman (대학·고교의) 신입생, 1학년생
how to + 동사원형 ~하는 방법
French Riviera 프랑스령 리비에라(프랑스 지중해 연안의 남동쪽 해안에 위치)
Cairns 케언즈 (호주 동북부의 항구 도시)
coast 해안
be located in ~에 있다, ~에 위치하다

A ( ) 안에서 가장 알맞은 것을 고르시오.

1 I didn't eat as much for lunch as (she / her) did.

2 My brother's new sports car is as fast as (they / them / theirs).

3 That was fast! He has arrived (soon / sooner) than I'd expected.

4 You're the (last / latest) guy I expected to see here at the fitness club.

5 It's expensive because it's the (newer / newest) model currently available.

6 This building is older, but (most modern / more modern) than the one next to it.

7 The hippopotamus is more dangerous than any other (animal / animals) in Africa.

8 Freshmen will be taught how to make (better / the best) use of their time while studying at UCLA.

9 The French Riviera is a very beautiful, but expensive, place to live. In fact, it is one of the most expensive (place / places) in the world.

10 The city of Cairns on the east coast of Australia is hotter than Melbourne in the south. It is located in one of the (hotter / hottest) areas of Australia.

thin 마른; 얇은
densely 밀집하여, 빽빽하게
populated 거주하는; 입주한
attract (주의·흥미)를 끌다
tourist 관광객

B 문장을 읽고, 생략 가능한 부분을 모두 생략하여 문장을 다시 쓰시오.

1 Susan is much thinner now than she was last year.
→ ______

2 She speaks English as well as she speaks Spanish.
→ ______

3 It's much colder today than it was yesterday.
→ ______

4 Seoul is more densely populated than any other city in Korea is.
→ ______

5 Jonathan studies English and math as hard as his brother does.
→ ______

6 Beijing has not been as successful as Tokyo has at attracting tourists.
→ ______

7 Joe has risen to the top because he trains harder now than he did before.
→ ______

C 주어진 단어를 알맞게 배열하여 문장을 완성하시오.

1 We're sorry to be so late. We got here ______________________.
(as / as / could / fast / we)

2 I didn't find *Spiderman III* ______________________ the previous film in the *Spiderman* series. (entertaining / as / as)

3 I'm studying to be a vet, so I read ______________________ about animal anatomy. (as / as / books / many / possible)

4 Making online contacts is becoming ______________________ for job seekers these days. (and / more / more / important)

5 My father's favorite proverb is "______________________, ______________________."
(we become / we spend / less / richer / the / the)

previous 이전의, 앞선
series 시리즈, 연속물
vet(=veterinarian) 수의사
anatomy 해부학
contact 연락
job seeker 구직자
favorite 가장 좋아하는
proverb 속담, 격언

D 주어진 단어를 원급, 비교급, 최상급 중 가장 적절한 형태로 바꿔 대화를 완성하시오.

1 A: Is the *Mona Lisa* as __________ (small) as people say it is?
B: Yes, it's much __________ (small) than you'd think. But it's also __________ (stunning) than you could ever imagine. It gets more and more beautiful each time you see it.

2 A: Business this month has been twice as __________ (slow) as last month. In truth, it's shaping up to be the __________ (bad) month we've ever had.
B: That's terrible news, Joe. But I'm sure next month will be __________ (good). Stay positive!

3 A: What kind of pet would you like to have? I think it would be __________ (nice) to have a dog than a cat.
B: I disagree. Dogs may be __________ (playful) than cats, but cats make the __________ (good) house pets because they're clean and quiet.

4 A: Why does everyone think climbing Everest is such a feat? It may be the __________ (tall) mountain in the world, but it's not the __________ (hard) to climb. K2 is much more technically challenging than Everest.
B: I don't know. But to be honest, they're both well out of my league.

5 A: Your brother is by far the __________ (energetic) boy I've ever seen.
B: Maybe that's because he used to be a soccer player when he was in elementary school. He was __________ (fast) and __________ (strong) than any other player on his team.

stunning 놀랄 만큼 아름다운
imagine ~을 상상하다
shape up (어떤 방향으로) 되어 가다
terrible 끔찍한
positive 긍정적인
disagree (~와) 의견을 달리하다
feat (눈부신) 위업; 뛰어난 솜씨
technically 기술적으로
challenging 고된, 도전 의식을 북돋우는
to be honest 사실, 솔직히 말해서
out of one's league ~의 능력이 미치지 못하는
by far 훨씬
energetic 활동적인

REVIEW PLUS

정답 및 해설 P. 19

weather balloon 기상 관측기구
commercial 상업[무역]의
airliner 여객기
nearly 거의

다음 빈칸에 들어갈 알맞은 말을 고르시오.

1 Many weather balloons fly ______________ most commercial airliners.

① high than ② higher than ③ higher as
④ as high than ⑤ highly

2 The weather this summer has been ______________ the weather last summer.

① even bad than ② even worst than ③ even worse than
④ very worse than ⑤ much bad than

3 This spaghetti tastes nearly ___________ the pasta Susan made for us last weekend.

① as well as ② better ③ good than
④ as good as ⑤ the best

motorcycle 오토바이
the Alps 알프스 산맥
human 인간의
population 인구
Yangtze River 양쯔강 (중국 대륙 중부를 횡단하는 중국에서 가장 긴 강)

다음 중 어법상 바르지 않은 것을 고르시오.

① Motorcycles are faster than scooters.
② The Alps are the highest mountains in Europe.
③ John is younger than Peter by only two months.
④ China has the largest human population in the world.
⑤ The Yangtze River in China is shortest than the Amazon.

bright 총명한, 영리한, 밝은
decision 결정
attend ~(학교 등)에 가다
engineering 공학
desperately 필사적으로; 몹시
architect 건축가
hometown 고향
desire 욕망, 소망
succeed 성공하다

다음을 읽고, (   ) 안에서 가장 알맞은 것을 고르시오.

Sarah is one of the brightest ① (student / students) in New York State. Now she has an important decision to make: should she attend Dartmouth College in New Hampshire or Columbia University in New York? Dartmouth has one of the best engineering ② (program / programs) in the USA, and Sarah desperately wants to become an architect one day. But Columbia is much ③ (close / closer / closest) to Sarah's hometown than Dartmouth. Her wish to stay with her family is just as ④ (strong / stronger / the strongest) as her desire to succeed. So what would you do?

PART 15

분사와 분사 구문
Participles & Participle Phrases

현재분사와 과거분사

	현재분사	과거분사
형태	동사원형+ing	동사원형+ed[p.p.]
의미	능동, 진행	수동, 완료
쓰임	• 함께 쓴 명사가 동작을 하는 주체 a **sleeping** baby 잠자는 아기	• 함께 쓴 명사가 동작을 당하는 대상 **broken** glasses 부러진 안경
	• 함께 쓴 명사가 감정을 느끼게 하는 원인 an **amazing** story 놀라운 이야기(놀라게 하는 이야기)	• 함께 쓴 명사가 감정을 느끼는 주체 an **amazed** girl 놀란 소녀

1 분사는 동사원형에 '-ing'나 '-ed'를 붙여 형용사처럼 쓰는 말이다.

동사	현재분사	과거분사
study speak	a **studying** student 공부하는 학생 a **speaking** man 말하는 사람	a **studied** behavior 학습된 행동 **spoken** language 말해지는 언어

2 현재분사는 능동이나 진행의 의미를 나타낸다. 함께 쓴 명사가 동작을 하는 것이면 현재분사를 쓴다.

The **barking** dog makes me scared. (→ The dog is barking.)
짖는 개가 나를 무섭게 한다.

A **crying** baby can feel stressed. (→ The baby is crying.)
우는 아이는 스트레스를 받을 수 있다.

3 과거분사는 수동이나 완료의 의미를 나타낸다. 함께 쓴 명사가 동작을 당하는 것이면 과거분사를 쓴다.

Many children were injured by the **broken** glass. (→ Someone broke the glass.)
많은 아이들이 깨진 유리에 다쳤다.

I saw an **abandoned** car on the street last night. (→ Someone abandoned the car.)
나는 지난밤에 길에 버려진 자동차를 보았다.

4

감정을 나타내는 동사에 '-ing'나 '-ed'를 붙여 분사를 만든다. 함께 쓴 명사가 어떤 감정을 느끼게 하면 현재분사를, 함께 쓴 명사가 어떤 감정을 느끼면 과거분사를 쓴다.

감정을 느끼게 하는 원인	vs.	감정을 느끼는 주체
She told me the **shocking** news. 그녀가 나에게 충격적인 소식을 말해 주었다.		I was really **shocked**. 나는 정말 충격을 받았다.
The movie was very **exciting**. 영화가 매우 흥미로웠다.		We were so **excited**. 우리는 매우 신이 났다.
The lecture was **boring**. 강의가 지루했다.		The students were **bored**. 학생들은 지루해했다.

5

현재분사와 동명사는 형태는 같지만 역할이 다르다. 현재분사는 형용사의 역할을 하고, 동명사는 명사의 역할을 한다. 또한 현재분사는 명사를 수식하는 반면 동명사는 명사와 결합하여 하나의 합성어를 만든다.

현재분사 (~하는)	vs.	**동명사** (~하기 위한)
a **sleeping** baby 잠자는 아기		a **sleeping bag** 침낭(잠자기 위한 주머니)
waiting people 기다리는 사람들		a **waiting room** 대기실(기다리기 위한 방)
a **swimming** fish 헤엄치는 물고기		a **swimming pool** 수영장(수영하기 위한 풀)

|참고| 동명사는 문장에서 주어, 보어, 동사나 전치사의 목적어 역할을 한다.
Walking fast is good for your health. (주어) 빨리 걷는 것은 건강에 좋다.
My hobby is **collecting** sneakers. (보어: My hobby = collecting sneakers) 나의 취미는 운동화를 모으는 것이다.
I enjoy **swimming**. (동사의 목적어) 나는 수영을 즐긴다.
He is afraid of **going** out alone at night. (전치사의 목적어) 그는 밤에 혼자 밖에 나가는 것을 무서워한다.

***** 기타 감정을 나타내는 분사들 *****

alarming 불안하게 하는	alarmed 겁먹은	exciting 신나게 하는	excited 신이 난
amazing 놀라게 하는	amazed 놀란	exhausting 지치게 하는	exhausted 지친
amusing 즐겁게 하는	amused 즐거워하는	frightening 깜짝 놀라게 하는	frightened 깜짝 놀란
annoying 성가시게 하는	annoyed 짜증 난	inspiring 영감을 주는	inspired 영감을 받은
astonishing 놀라게 하는	astonished 놀란	interesting 흥미 있는	interested 흥미를 느낀
boring 지루하게 하는	bored 지루한	satisfying 만족하게 하는	satisfied 만족하는
confusing 혼란케 하는	confused 혼란스러운	shocking 충격을 주는	shocked 충격받은
convincing 이해시키는	convinced 확신한	surprising 놀라게 하는	surprised 놀란
delighting 기쁘게 하는	delighted 기뻐하는	terrifying 무섭게 하는	terrified 무서워하는
depressing 울적하게 하는	depressed 우울한	tiring 피곤하게 하는	tired 피곤한
disappointing 실망하게 하는	disappointed 실망한	troubling 걱정시키는	troubled 근심하는
embarrassing 창피하게 하는	embarrassed 창피한	worrying 걱정시키는	worried 걱정하는

EXERCISES

정답 및 해설 P. 19

sparrow 참새
nest 둥지
steal ~을 훔치다
hand ~을 건네주다
name ~라고 불리다
grow 커지다, 증가하다
abandon ~을 버리다, 포기하다
earthquake 지진
surround ~을 둘러싸다
admiring 찬미하는, 감탄하는
for a change 기분 전환으로; 가끔, 때때로

A ( ) 안에서 가장 알맞은 것을 고르시오.

1 I saw a sparrow (building / built) a nest.

2 He bought a new cell phone (making / made) in Korea.

3 Do you know the man (talking / talked) with Mike over there?

4 My father caught a boy (stealing / stolen) apples from the garden.

5 Please hand this document to the woman (naming / named) Tina Jeong.

6 There are a (growing / grown) number of abandoned dogs in our country.

7 A window and a glass vase were (breaking / broken) after the earthquake.

8 Kelly was (surrounding / surrounded) by a group of admiring photographers.

9 She heard somebody (singing / sung) in a loud voice in the middle of the night.

10 In these (troubling / troubled) times, it is great to hear a bit of good news for a change.

disappoint ~을 실망시키다
satisfy ~을 만족시키다
comment 의견; 비평
touch ~을 감동시키다
celebrity 유명 인사
divorce 이혼
complex 복잡한
instruction 지시 사항
short film 단편 영화
festival 축제
viewer 관객, 시청자

B 주어진 단어를 문맥에 맞게 현재분사나 과거분사로 바꿔 문장을 완성하시오.

1 (disappoint) The gift was ____________ to her.
She was ____________ with the gift.

2 (satisfy) Your comment was ____________ for us.
We were very ____________ by your comment.

3 (amaze) The size of their backyard was ____________ to me.
I was ____________ at the size of their backyard.

4 (touch) The movie I saw last weekend was ____________.
I was ____________ by the movie I saw last weekend.

5 (shock) People were ____________ by the celebrity couple's divorce.
The celebrity couple's divorce was ____________ to people.

6 (confuse) The readers were ____________ by the complex instructions.
The complex instructions were ____________ to the readers.

7 (amuse) Several short films shown at the film festival were ____________.
The viewers were ____________ by the short film shown at the short film festival.

C ( ) 안에서 가장 알맞은 것을 고르시오.

1 Minji became deeply (depressing / depressed) when her pet parrot died.

2 She has an (annoying / annoyed) habit of biting her nails while she talks.

3 The lecture was (inspiring / inspired). It totally changed my outlook on life.

4 There was an (interesting / interested) show about African monkeys on TV.

5 Amy was so (exciting / excited) on Christmas Eve. She couldn't get to sleep.

6 He eats junk food all day long, so it's not (surprising / surprised) that he is so unhealthy.

deeply 깊이, 매우
parrot 앵무새
habit 습관
bite ~을 물다
nail 손톱
lecture 강연, 강의
inspire ~에게 영감을 주다
outlook 시야, 견해
unhealthy 건강하지 못한

D 〈보기〉에서 알맞은 것을 골라 현재분사나 과거분사로 바꿔 문장을 완성하시오.

보기 worry surprise bore embarrass disappoint annoy satisfy

1 I was ___________ when I heard there had been an accident.

2 The students asked the new teacher lots of ___________ questions.

3 I was so ___________ during the principal's speech. I just fell asleep.

4 Suzie's making a squeaking noise with her chair. It's so ___________!

5 I was very ___________ that you left school early because of a stomachache.

6 Are you ___________ with the color? If not, we can change it to a lighter shade.

7 My trip to Hawaii was canceled. I'm very ___________ because I really wanted to go there.

principal 교장 선생님
speech 연설
fall asleep 잠들다
squeaking 삐걱거리는; 앙앙 우는
stomachache 복통
light (색이) 연한; 가벼운; 빛
shade 색조
cancel ~을 취소하다

E 밑줄 친 단어가 현재분사인지 동명사인지 밝히시오.

1 Look at the <u>sleeping</u> baby. How cute! ________

2 You can try the skirt on. The <u>fitting</u> room is over there. ________

3 I think you'd better buy a new <u>sleeping</u> bag. This one is ragged. ________

4 Poor Sam! His hand was badly injured by an <u>exploding</u> firecracker. ________

5 Please stay in the <u>waiting</u> room. The doctor will be with you soon. ________

6 Don't buy the kids any more <u>chewing</u> gum. Their teeth will rot out. ________

7 The little boy is hesitant to go into the house because he is afraid of the <u>barking</u> dog. ________

ragged 해어진, 찢어진
explode 폭발하다
firecracker 폭죽
rot 썩다
hesitate 머뭇거리는, 주저하는

분사의 쓰임

명사의 수식	Look at the **singing** boys. 노래하는 소년들을 봐라.
주격보어	She was thoroughly **exhausted.** 그녀는 완전히 지쳤다.
목적격보어	He found his wallet **gone.** 그는 자기의 지갑이 없어진 것을 알았다.
진행형	Steven **is learning** Italian so he can travel to Italy. 스티븐은 이탈리아로 여행을 가려고 이태리어를 배우고 있다.
완료형	I've already **finished** my assignment. 나는 이미 숙제를 끝마쳤다.
수동태	Writing **was invented** by the ancient Sumerians. 글은 고대 수메르인에 의해 발명되었다.

1 분사가 단독으로 쓰인 경우, 명사 앞에서 뒤에 나온 명사를 수식한다.

The **jumping** boy annoyed his neighbors. 뛰고 있는 소년이 그의 이웃을 화나게 했다.

A **used** car is much cheaper than a new one. 중고차는 새 차보다 훨씬 싸다.

2 분사가 수식어구를 동반하여 길어진 경우, 명사 뒤에서 앞에 나온 명사를 수식한다.

The woman **speaking** to Mike told me some shocking news.

마이크에게 말하고 있는 여자가 나에게 몇 가지 충격적인 소식을 전해 주었다.

The man **introduced** at the conference is a famous professor.

회의에서 소개된 그 남자는 유명한 교수이다.

3 분사는 주어의 상태를 보충 설명해 주는 주격보어로 쓰인다.

The audience became **bored.** 관객들은 지루해졌다.

The movie was **boring.** 그 영화는 지루했다.

The map was pretty **confusing.** 그 지도는 꽤 헷갈렸다.

4 분사는 목적어의 상태나 동작을 보충 설명해 주는 목적격보어로 쓰인다. 목적어와 목적격보어의 관계가 능동이나 진행이면 현재분사를, 수동이나 완료이면 과거분사를 쓴다.

I saw him **stealing** thousands of dollars.
나는 그가 수천 달러를 훔치는 것을 보았다.

Jane kept Ronald **waiting** for a long time.
제인은 로널드를 오래 기다리게 했다.

I heard my name **called**.
나는 내 이름이 불리는 것을 들었다.

I saw my father's car **parked** in the parking lot.
나는 아버지의 차가 주차장에 주차되어 있는 것을 보았다.

|주의| 지각동사(see, hear, feel 등)의 경우, 목적어와 목적격보어의 관계가 능동일 때, 목적격보어로 동사원형이나 현재분사를 쓸 수 있으나 의미상 차이가 있다.

I **saw** him **steal** thousands of dollars. (그가 수천 달러를 훔치는 것을 처음부터 끝까지 다 보았다는 의미)
→ I saw him. He stole thousands of dollars.

I **saw** him **stealing** thousands of dollars. (그가 수천 달러를 훔치고 있는데 내가 그 동작의 일부를 보았다는 의미)
→ I saw him. He was stealing thousands of dollars.

5 분사는 진행형, 완료형, 수동태에 쓰인다.

My mother **is watering** the plants in the garden. (진행형)
우리 어머니가 정원에서 나무에 물을 주고 있다.

The children **are playing** with robots in the kindergarten. (진행형)
그 아이들은 유치원에서 로봇을 가지고 놀고 있다.

Have you ever **been** to Paris? (완료형)
너는 파리에 가본 적 있니?

She **has studied** English since she was an elementary school student. (완료형)
그녀는 초등학생 때부터 영어 공부를 했다.

The trade center **was designed** in 1997 by a world-famous architect. (수동태)
그 무역 센터는 1997년에 세계적으로 유명한 건축가에 의해서 디자인되었다.

The package **will be delivered** tomorrow. (수동태)
그 소포는 내일 배달될 것이다.

EXERCISES

정답 및 해설 P. 20

artwork 예술 작품
recover ~을 되찾다; 복구하다
by chance 우연히
fry ~을 튀기다
renovate ~을 수리하다; ~을 새것으로 만들다
mansion 대저택
originally 원래
assignment 과제; 할당
challenging 고된, 도전 의식을 북돋우는
cancelation 취소
shopper 손님
rush 돌진하다
grand opening 개장, 개점

A 주어진 분사(구)가 밑줄 친 단어를 수식하도록 문장을 다시 쓰시오.

1 The <u>artwork</u> was recovered by chance. (stolen)

→ ______________________

2 Some <u>potatoes and onions</u> would taste good. (fried)

→ ______________________

3 The <u>boy</u> is her new boyfriend, John. (sitting next to Ally)

→ ______________________

4 They live in a renovated <u>mansion</u>. (originally built in 1890)

→ ______________________

5 The teacher gave us an <u>assignment</u> for homework. (challenging)

→ ______________________

6 The cancelation of the school trip was <u>news</u> to the students. (disappointing)

→ ______________________

7 A lot of <u>shoppers</u> rushed to the grand opening of the new shopping mall. (excited)

→ ______________________

to be honest 솔직히 말해서
cheat ~을 속이다
offer 제안
argument 논쟁
explain ~을 설명하다
exhaust ~을 기진맥진하게 하다
beat (심장이) 뛰다
wildly 거칠게; 난폭하게
final stretch (육상 등의) 최후의 직선 코스

B ( ) 안에서 가장 알맞은 것을 고르시오.

1 To be honest, I felt (cheating / cheated) by his offer.

2 I'm sorry to have kept you (waiting / waited) so long.

3 He said he wanted the report (doing / done) by 6 p.m.

4 My father had breakfast (reading / read) a newspaper.

5 Peggy was sitting in the café and looking at people (walking / walk) down the street.

6 I will not have you (saying / said) such things about my family!

7 Did you hear some people (having / had) an argument last night?

8 You seem (confusing / confused). Would you like me to explain it again?

9 We were (amazing / amazed) to see lots of delicious food at the wedding.

10 He got very (exhausted / exhausting) after working more than ten hours.

11 I felt my heart (beating / beaten) wildly when the runners entered the final stretch.

12 He seemed a little (annoying / annoyed) when his students asked too many questions.

C 주어진 동사를 어법에 맞게 바꿔 문장을 완성하시오.

1 Were you __________ (have) a bad dream?

2 The kids are __________ (swim) in the sea.

3 We have already __________ (see) that movie.

4 The meeting was __________ (delay) until the next day.

5 The building was __________ (destroy) by fire in 1886.

6 Have you ever __________ (think) about traveling abroad?

7 The *New York Times* was first __________ (publish) in 1851.

8 I have __________ (write) my diary in English since high school.

9 All the paintings in my house were __________ (do) by my mother.

10 The students are __________ (have) a discussion about school rules.

11 Eric was __________ (run) as quickly as he could not to be late for school.

12 The bus has just __________ (arrive), but it's very crowded. Let's take the next one.

delay ~을 연기하다
destroy ~을 파괴하다
publish ~을 발행하다
painting 그림; 작품
discussion 토론, 토의
crowded 붐비는, 혼잡한

D 두 문장의 의미가 통하도록 〈보기〉와 같이 문장을 완성하시오.

보기 She is reading an essay. It is written by her daughter.
→ She is reading an essay written by her daughter.

1 He found the wallet. It was stolen on the subway.
→ He found the wallet ______________________________.

2 I saw a monkey. It was performing in front of people.
→ I saw a monkey ______________________________.

3 Do you see that girl? She is talking on the phone over there.
→ Do you see that girl ______________________________?

4 The baby made me smile. He was singing and dancing in the video.
→ ______________________________ made me smile.

5 He opened all the windows of the room. The room was filled with bad odor.
→ He opened all the windows of the room ______________________________.

6 I watched a man. He was climbing a cliff without any safety equipment.
→ I watched a man ______________________________.

be filled with ~으로 가득 차다
odor 냄새
cliff 절벽, 벼랑
equipment 장비

분사 구문

분사 구문 만들기

He hurt his ankle when he rode a horse.
주절 부사절

→ **He** hurt his ankle ~~when he~~ rode a horse.
→ He hurt his ankle **riding** a horse.
그는 말을 타다가 발목을 다쳤다.

① 부사절의 접속사를 생략한다.
② 주절의 주어와 부사절의 주어가 같을 때 부사절의 주어를 생략한다.
③ 부사절에 남은 동사를 '-ing' 형태로 바꾼다.

1 부사절은 분사 구문으로 바꿔 쓸 수 있다. 분사 구문은 부사절의 접속사와 주어를 없애고, 남은 동사를 '-ing'으로 바꿔서 만든다. 이때, 부사절의 주어와 주절의 주어가 같아야 생략이 가능하며, 의미를 명확히 하기 위해 접속사를 생략하지 않을 수도 있다. 분사 구문은 문맥에 따라 시간(~할 때), 이유(~이므로), 조건(~라면), 양보(~라도), 동시동작(~하면서), 연속동작(~하고 나서 바로) 등의 여러 가지 의미로 쓰인다.

시간의 부사절을 이끄는 접속사: after, before, while, when, since 등

이유나 원인의 부사절을 이끄는 접속사: because, since, as 등

조건이나 양보의 부사절을 이끄는 접속사: if, even though, although, though 등

After Jennifer read the article three times, she finally understood it.
→ **(After) Reading** the article three times, Jennifer finally understood it. (시간)
제니퍼는 그 기사를 세 번 읽고 난 후에야, 마침내 그것을 이해했다.

As Jude had no money, he couldn't buy her a present.
→ **(As) Having** no money, Jude couldn't buy her a present. (이유)
주드는 돈이 없었기 때문에, 그녀의 선물을 살 수 없었다.

If you turn to the left, you will find the bakery.
→ **(If) Turning** to the left, you will find the bakery. (조건)
왼쪽으로 돌면, 빵집을 발견할 것이다.

Though I admit what he says, I still don't agree with him.
→ **(Though) Admitting** what he says, I still don't agree with him. (양보)
그가 말하는 것을 인정은 하지만, 나는 여전히 그의 말에 동의하지 않는다.

He was talking on the phone while he was taking notes.
→ He was talking on the phone, **(while) taking** notes. (동시동작)
그는 메모를 하면서 전화 통화를 하고 있었다.

|참고| 분사 구문은 문어체 표현으로 구어체에서는 잘 사용하지 않는다.

2 분사 구문의 부정은 분사 앞에 not을 붙인다.

As I didn't know what to do, I just stood there.

→ **Not** knowing what to do, I just stood there.
나는 무엇을 해야 할지 몰라서, 그냥 거기 서 있었다.

3 부사절이 주절보다 먼저 일어난 일을 나타낼 때 「Having+p.p.」를 사용하고, 이러한 형태의 분사 구문은 '완료 분사 구문'이라고 부른다.

After he had finished his homework, he went out to play basketball.

→ **Having finished** his homework, he **went out** to play basketball.
그는 숙제를 마치고 나서, 농구하러 나갔다.

Because Mary had read the book more than ten times, she didn't want to read it again.

→ **Having read** the book more than ten times, Mary **didn't want** to read it again.
메리는 그 책을 열 번 넘게 읽었기 때문에, 더는 읽고 싶지 않았다.

|참고| 일어난 일의 전후 관계가 분명한 경우 단순 분사 구문을 사용하기도 한다.
After I had had breakfast, I left for school.
→ After **having** breakfast, I left for school. 나는 아침을 먹고, 학교로 출발했다.

4 부사절이 수동태이면, 과거분사 구문으로 바꿔 쓸 수 있다. 이때 being이나 having been은 대부분 생략한다.

Because he was burned by the sun, he applied some ointment to his face.

→ **(Being) Burned** by the sun, he **applied** some ointment to his face.
그는 햇볕에 데어 얼굴에 연고를 발랐다.

As he was accepted by the university he had applied to, he is happy.

→ **(Having been) Accepted** by the university he had applied to, he **is** happy.
그는 자신이 지원한 대학에 합격해서 행복하다.

|주의| 1. 주절의 주어와 부사절의 주어가 다를 경우 주어를 생략하여 분사 구문을 만들 수 없다. 이때에는 분사의 주어를 분사 앞에 써 준다.
Mike petted the dog as it barked. (Mike≠it) 개가 짖어서, 마이크가 그 개를 쓰다듬었다.
(×) ~~Mike petted the dog as barking.~~
While I was walking home, a truck nearly hit me. (I≠a truck) 내가 집에 걸어가는데 트럭 한 대가 나를 거의 칠 뻔했다.
(×) ~~While walking home, a truck nearly hit me.~~

2 「there+be동사」 구문의 경우 분사 구문을 만들 때 there을 문장 앞에 써 준다.
As there was a big festival yesterday, I left work early. 어제 큰 축제가 있어서 나는 일찍 퇴근했다.
→ **There being** a big festival yesterday, I left work early.

|참고| 「with+명사+분사」는 '~한 채로'라는 뜻으로 분사 구문의 일종이다. 이때 명사와 분사의 관계가 능동이면 현재분사를, 수동이면 과거분사를 쓴다.
The boss was sitting on the sofa, **with his legs crossed.** (다리가 꼬아짐=수동, 과거분사) 사장은 다리를 꼰 채로 소파에 앉아 있었다.
We had to spend the night **with the roof leaking.** (지붕이 샘= 능동, 현재분사) 우리는 지붕이 새는 채로 하루를 보내야만 했다.

EXERCISES

정답 및 해설 P. 21

give up ~을 포기하다
sprain (발목, 손목 따위를) 삐다
ankle 발목
badly 심하게, 크게
footstep 발소리
reach (손을 뻗어서) ~을 잡다
discover ~을 발견하다; ~을 깨닫다
celebrity 유명인
throughout 처음부터 끝까지, ~동안 내내

A 〈보기〉와 같이 부사절을 분사 구문으로 바꿔 문장을 완성하시오.

보기 As she received a scholarship, she could go to college.
→ (As) Receiving a scholarship, she could go college.

1 Although she was born into a poor family, she never gave up her dream.
→ ________________, she never gave up her dream.

2 After John listened to the song several times, he was able to sing it perfectly.
→ ________________, John was able to sing it perfectly.

3 While Alex was playing baseball with his friends, he sprained his ankle badly.
→ ________________, Alex sprained his ankle badly.

4 While I was trying to sleep last night, I heard footsteps outside.
→ ________________, I heard footsteps outside.

5 When I reached into my bag for my wallet, I discovered that it had been stolen.
→ ________________, I discovered that it had been stolen.

6 As he won first place in the contest, he became a celebrity.
→ ________________, he became a celebrity.

7 As I lived in the USA as a child, I can speak English.
→ ________________, I can speak English.

stick (~에 끼여) 꼼짝하지 않다
recover (~에서) 회복하다
flu(=influenza) 독감, 유행성 감기
overseas 해외로, 외국으로
cost ~을 소비하게 하다
rescue ~을 구조하다
rush ~을 급히 나르다
appreciate ~의 진가를 알다; 감사하다
simplicity 소박함; 검소한
scold ~을 꾸짖다
shame 수치심, 부끄러움

B 밑줄 친 부분이 맞지 않다면 바르게 고치시오.

1 Been very hungry, Chelsea made herself spaghetti.

2 Stuck in traffic, he couldn't arrive at the meeting on time.

3 Recovered from the flu, Aram didn't need to go to the clinic.

4 Studying overseas, Hana was still unable to find a job back home.

5 Doing by a famous artist, this drawing will cost you a lot of money.

6 Rescued, the injured woman was rushed immediately to the hospital.

7 Raised in the city, Mark doesn't appreciate the simplicity of country life.

8 Scolding in front of his classmates, Jason was unable to hide his shame.

C 〈보기〉와 같이 주어진 접속사를 이용해서 분사 구문을 절로 바꿔 쓰시오.

> **보기** Hearing my name called, I was startled. (when)
> → When I heard my name called, I was startled.

1 Paying a bill, you need to check if it is correct. (when)
→ ______________________

2 Having had an operation, he began to recover. (after)
→ ______________________

3 Being hungry, I ate some bread between meals. (because)
→ ______________________

4 Getting up in the morning, he drinks a cup of water. (as soon as)
→ ______________________

5 Not having booked tickets, we still could see the musical. (though)
→ ______________________

6 Being promoted next year, I will treat you to a gorgeous dinner. (if)
→ ______________________

startle ~을 깜짝 놀라게 하다
correct 올바른, 틀림없는; 정확한
operation 수술; 운영
meal 식사
book ~을 예약하다
promote ~으로 승진시키다
treat ~에게 한턱내다
gorgeous 멋진; 훌륭한, 호화로운

D 우리말과 같은 뜻이 되도록 주어진 단어를 배열하시오.

1 라디오를 들으면서 그녀는 설거지를 했다. (the radio, to, listening)
→ She washed the dishes, ______________________.

2 그녀는 시험에 떨어져서, 시험을 다시 봐야만 했다. (failed, the exam, having)
→ ______________________, she had to take the exam again.

3 나는 점심을 너무 많이 먹어서, 밤늦게까지 배가 고프지 않았다. (having, a big lunch, had)
→ ______________________, I didn't feel hungry until late night.

4 할 일이 너무 많아서, 나는 친구들을 만날 시간이 없었다. (to do, having, work, so much)
→ ______________________, I didn't have time to meet friends.

5 감기에 걸려서 나는 일주일 동안 아무것도 할 수 없었다. (the flu, do, I, having, couldn't)
→ ______________________ anything for a week.

6 내일 비가 온다면, 우리는 행사를 취소해야 할 것이다.
(tomorrow, cancel, it, we'll, raining, have to)
→ ______________________ the event.

7 도로에 차가 너무 많아서 나는 제시간에 갈 수 없었다.
(on the road, there, cars, so many, being)
→ ______________________, I couldn't make it on time.

fail ~에 떨어지다; 실패하다
cancel ~을 취소하다

REVIEW

정답 및 해설 P. 22

behavior 행동
charm 매력이 있다
cottage 오두막집; 시골집
corner ~을 구석[궁지]에 몰아넣다
ambulance 구급차
litter ~를 어지르다, 흐트러뜨리다
neighborhood 근처
disapprove ~을 좋지 않게 생각하다
stare 시선, 응시
on one's feet 일어서서
cheer ~에게 환호하다
tempt ~의 마음을 끌다
convince ~을 설득시키다
argument 주장; 논쟁
whimper (개 따위가) 킹킹거리다

( ) 안에서 가장 알맞은 것을 고르시오.

1 His behavior was (embarrassing / embarrassed).

2 The car (parking / parked) over by the van is mine.

3 My parents now live in a (charming / charmed) old cottage.

4 A (cornering / cornered) animal is the most dangerous of all.

5 The ambulance took the (injuring / injured) man to the hospital.

6 (Falling / Fallen) trees littered the neighborhood after the storm.

7 The teacher gave the class a (disapproving / disapproved) stare.

8 She looked (interesting / interested) in the story he was telling her.

9 The (exciting / excited) fans were all on their feet yelling and cheering.

10 Your offer is (tempting / tempted), but I need some time to consider it.

11 She made a very (convincing / convinced) argument during the debate.

12 The (frightening / frightened) dogs whimpered in their cages during the storm.

scream (아이가) 울다, 소리 지르다
annoy ~을 짜증나게 하다
road sign 도로 표지판
confuse ~을 혼란시키다
get through ~을 통과하다
referee 심판; 중재자
decision 결정, 판단
disgust ~을 역겹게 하다, 정떨어지게 하다
habit 습관
quit ~을 그만두다
clown 광대
awesome 멋있는
conference 회의
receive 맞아들이다, 환영하다
fascinate ~을 매혹하다
spinning 돌아가는

B 주어진 동사를 '-ing'형이나 '-ed'형으로 바꿔 문장을 완성하시오.

1 Screaming babies can be __________ (annoy) to other passengers.

2 The road signs around here are so __________ (confuse).

3 The robot couldn't get through the __________ (close) door.

4 That Mark failed his driving test was quite __________ (shock).

5 I'm __________ (bore) with playing this game. Let's go outside.

6 The referee's decision was not that __________ (surprise) at all.

7 Smoking is such a __________ (disgust) habit! I wish you would quit.

8 The clown was __________ (entertain), and the magician was awesome.

9 The speaker __________ (introduce) at the conference was well received.

10 Jack's story about traveling to the Himalayas was __________ (fascinate).

11 The spinning wheel in this amusement park is really __________ (excite).

12 Mr. Jefferson looked __________ (interest) in the theory Professor Lee was explaining to him.

C 밑줄 친 부분이 맞지 않다면 바르게 고치시오.

1 She had her car repairing.

2 John is terrified of losing his job.

3 That noise is irritated. Please stop!

4 I heard my name calling by Mr. Lee.

5 She left his letter unopening in a box.

6 You shouldn't keep him waited so long.

7 I'm delighted to see you again so soon.

8 I was disappointing to hear about your decision.

9 I find modern art very confusing and boring.

10 Jessica left her food untouched on the plate.

11 I was surprising at the long line at the bank today.

12 Didn't know what to do, the little girl started to cry.

terrify ~을 두려워하게 하다
irritate ~을 짜증나게 하다
delight ~을 기쁘게 하다
disappoint ~을 실망시키다
modern 현대의
untouched 손을 대지 않은

D 부사절을 분사 구문으로 바꿔 문장을 완성하시오.

1 Because New York is an international city, it has many ethnic restaurants.
→ ______________________, New York has many ethnic restaurants.

2 When the image is seen upside down, it looks like a smiling face.
→ ______________________, the image looks like a smiling face.

3 As the sign was written in French, I wasn't able to understand it.
→ ______________________, I wasn't able to understand it.

4 As I had met him many times before, I recognized him immediately.
→ ______________________, I recognized him immediately.

5 Because I didn't have enough money to take a taxi, I walked home.
→ ______________________, I walked home.

6 Before Jason comes to class, he usually gulps down a cup of coffee.
→ ______________________, Jason usually gulps down a cup of coffee.

7 While Jini was waiting for her nails to dry, she was reading a magazine.
→ ______________________, Jini was reading a magazine.

8 Because the boy didn't know what to do, he burst into tears.
→ ______________________, the boy burst into tears.

burst into ~을 터뜨리다
recognize ~을 알아보다, 인지하다
immediately 즉시, 곧
gulp down (마실 것을) 벌컥벌컥 마시다
international 국제적인
ethnic (소수) 민족의, 민족적인

REVIEW PLUS

정답 및 해설 P. 23

confuse ~을 혼란시키다
truly 정말, 아주
upset ~을 속상하게 하다
Victoria Falls 빅토리아 폭포
sight 경치, 경관

다음 중 어법상 바르지 <u>않은</u> 문장을 고르시오.

① Today's puzzle is confusing.
② *Saw II* was truly a frightening movie.
③ Sarah was disappointed that she lost the game.
④ The news about Ms. Choi's accident was upsetting.
⑤ Victoria Falls is the most amazed sight you'll ever see.

rush 서두르다
paper 보고서
break ~을 부수다
leak (물이) 새다, 누출하다
tub 욕조

다음 밑줄 친 부분이 어법상 바르지 <u>않은</u> 것을 고르시오.

① <u>While I was watching TV last night</u>, the phone rang.
② <u>Had a big dinner already</u>, I don't want to eat anymore.
③ <u>Rushing to finish the paper</u>, Kelly accidentally turned off the computer.
④ <u>Having been thrown in the air</u>, the stick was caught by the dog.
⑤ <u>While I was having a bath</u>, water leaked over the sides of the tub.

lecture 강의, 강연
look up 쳐다보다
ride 탈것
layover 도중하차, 중단
exhaust ~을 지치게 만들다
direct 직행의

다음 중 대화가 자연스럽지 <u>않은</u> 것을 고르시오.

① A: I missed today's class. Was the lecture interesting?
B: Yes. It was great.
② A: Falling in front of Jisun was really embarrassing today.
B: Tell me about it. I was embarrassing for you.
③ A: Do you think Alex is interested in me?
B: He could be. He always looks up and smiles when you walk by.
④ A: That was a really exciting ride. Do you want to go again?
B: Well, I didn't find it that exciting. Let's try another one instead.
⑤ A: How was your flight? I heard you had a four-hour layover in Hong Kong.
B: I did, and it was exhausting. Next time, I will fly direct.

passport 여권
citizen 시민
diplomat 외교관
naturally 자연적으로
dumpling 만두
native country 본국, 고국

다음을 읽고, 밑줄 친 분사 구문을 이유의 부사절이 포함된 문장으로 바꿔 쓰시오.

Jiwoo has a Korean passport, but she likes to think of herself as a citizen of the world. Her father is a diplomat, so she has lived and studied in many different countries over the years. Naturally, <u>having grown up overseas, Jiwoo enjoys eating foods from other countries</u>. Among her favorite foods are Mexican tacos, Chinese dumplings, and Italian pizza. Of course, she loves her native country's food, too, especially *japchae*.

PART 16

접속사
Conjunctions

등위 접속사

등위 접속사	연결 성분	예문
and, but, or	단어+단어	I bought a pen **and** a notebook. 나는 펜과 공책을 샀다.
	구+구	Will you come on Saturday **or** on Sunday? 너는 토요일에 올 거니, 아니면 일요일에 올 거니?
	절+절	Kevin is diligent, **but** his brother is lazy. 케빈은 부지런하지만, 그의 남동생은 게으르다.
so, for, nor, yet	절+절	There weren't enough chairs, **so** I had to keep standing. 의자가 충분하지 않아서 나는 계속 서 있어야 했다.

1

and, but, or는 단어나 구, 절 등을 모두 대등하게 연결하는 등위 접속사이다.

This car is small **but** convenient. (단어 - 단어) 이 차는 작지만 편리하다.

Do you want me to leave **or** (to) stay? (구 - 구) 너는 내가 떠나길 바라니, 아니면 머무르길 바라니?

Her grandfather entered the room, **and** we all bowed to him. (절 - 절)
그녀의 할아버지께서 방에 들어오시자 우리 모두는 할아버지께 인사를 드렸다.

|참고| 1. 세 개 이상의 항목을 연결할 때는 마지막에 접속사를 쓰고, 나머지는 콤마(, : comma)로 연결한다.
You need eggs, flour, butter(,) **and** some sugar to make cookies. 쿠키를 만들려면 계란과 밀가루, 버터, 약간의 설탕이 필요하다.

2. 「명령문+and」는 '~해라, 그러면 …'의 뜻으로 쓰이고, 「명령문+or」은 '~해라, 그렇지 않으면 …'의 의미로 쓰인다.
Try your best **and** you will succeed some day.
→ **If** you try your best, you will succeed some day. 최선을 다해라, 그러면 언젠가 성공할 것이다.
Have a good night's sleep **or** you will be tired.
→ **If** you **don't** have a good night's sleep, you will be tired. 잠을 푹 자라, 그렇지 않으면 피곤할 것이다.

2

so, for, nor, yet은 주로 절을 연결하는 등위 접속사이다. 이때 접속사 앞에 콤마를 쓰지만, 앞에 나온 절이 짧으면 콤마를 생략하기도 한다.

William missed Jennifer, **so** he drove ten hours to see her. 윌리엄은 제니퍼가 그리워서, 그녀를 보려고 열 시간을 운전해서 왔다.

I want to stay home, **for** I have a headache. 나는 머리가 아파서 집에서 쉬고 싶어.

He didn't go to the party, **nor** did I. 그는 파티에 가지 않았고, 나도 가지 않았다.

The sun was shining brightly, **yet** it was still quite cold. 태양이 밝게 빛나고 있었지만, 여전히 꽤 추웠다.

|주의| nor 뒤에 오는 절은 「nor+be동사+주어」, 「nor+do/does/did/조동사+주어+동사원형」의 어순이다.
My sister isn't home, **nor** is my brother. 우리 언니도 집에 없고, 우리 오빠도 집에 없다.
Jun doesn't like singing, **nor** does he like dancing. 준은 노래하는 것도 춤추는 것도 좋아하지 않는다.

EXERCISES

정답 및 해설 P. 24

A 빈칸에 and, but, or 중 알맞은 것을 골라 써넣으시오. [각각 두 번씩만 쓸 것]

1 Were you born in June '97 ________ June '98?

2 The kids built a giant snow fort ________ threw snowballs.

3 I worked all night, ________ I couldn't finish the assignment.

4 Hanna's father ________ my uncle were best friends in college.

5 Electronic dictionaries are handy, ________ they are expensive.

6 She didn't answer the phone. She was probably sleeping ________ taking a shower.

be born 태어나다
giant 거대한
fort 요새
assignment 과제; 할당
in college 대학 시절에
handy 편리한

B 〈보기〉에서 알맞은 것을 골라 문장을 완성하시오.

보기	so	for	yet	nor

1 The sun is quite warm, ________ the air is cool.

2 I didn't go to the conference, ________ did they.

3 It was raining hard, ________ I got up to close the window.

4 I really wanted to go swimming, ________ it was an extremely hot day.

conference 회의
hard 세차게; 어려운; 열심히
extremely 대단히, 몹시; 극도로

C 두 문장을 주어진 접속사를 사용하여 한 문장으로 만드시오.

1 Jim stayed home all day. He was feeling quite ill. (for)
→ ________________________________

2 My knee started hurting again. I stopped running. (so)
→ ________________________________

3 John has a Ph.D. in engineering. He continues to work as a waiter. (yet)
→ ________________________________

4 Susan wasn't answering her phone. She wasn't answering her email. (nor)
→ ________________________________

5 The customers didn't like its new product. They didn't like its services. (nor)
→ ________________________________

6 Erick was good at singing and dancing. He didn't want to be a singer. (yet)
→ ________________________________

ill 아픈
Ph.D(=Doctor of Philosophy) 박사 학위
engineering 공학
continue 계속하다
product 제품

상관 접속사

both A and B A와 B 둘 다	**Both** Alice **and** John came to the party. 앨리스와 존 둘 다 파티에 왔다.
either A or B A나 B 둘 중 하나	Jim decided **either** to watch TV **or** to listen to the radio. 짐은 TV를 보거나 라디오를 듣기로 결정했다.
neither A nor B A와 B 둘 다 아니다	John **neither** sings **nor** dances very well. 존은 노래도 잘 못하고 춤도 잘 못 춘다.
not only A but also B **= B as well as A** A 뿐만 아니라 B도	This sofa is **not only** comfortable **but also** practical. → This sofa is practical **as well as** comfortable. 이 소파는 편안할 뿐만 아니라 실용적이다.

FOCUS

1 떨어져 있는 두 개의 어구가 짝을 이루어 접속사 역할을 하는 것을 '상관 접속사'라고 한다. 상관 접속사는 강조, 첨가 등의 의미를 갖는다.

Both my friend **and** I love chocolate milk. 내 친구와 나는 둘 다 초콜릿 우유를 좋아한다.

She is **not** my girlfriend **but** just a female friend. 그녀는 나의 여자 친구가 아니라 단지 여성 친구일 뿐이다.

2 상관 접속사에 따른 동사의 수 일치에 주의해야 한다.

동사와 가까운 대상에 수 일치

Usually, **either** Mike's big brother **or** his parents pay the bills. 대개 마이크의 큰형이나 그의 부모님이 요금을 지불한다.

Neither you **nor** she was late for the meeting. 당신도 그녀도 회의에 늦지 않았다.

both A and B+복수 동사

Both she **and** her sister now live in France. 그녀와 그녀의 여동생은 지금 프랑스에 산다.

not only A but also B = B as well as A: B에 수 일치

Not only the students **but also** the teacher looks forward to vacations.

→ The teacher **as well as** the students looks forward to vacations. 학생들뿐만 아니라 선생님도 방학을 기다린다.

3 등위 접속사나 상관 접속사는 단어, 구, 절 등 주로 문법적으로 같은 역할을 하는 것을 연결한다. 이를 병렬구조(parallel structure)라고 한다.

My dog enjoys **chasing squirrels** and **chewing bones.** (구-구) 나의 개는 다람쥐를 쫓고 뼈를 씹는 것을 좋아한다.

Where you live, or **what you do** is not important. (절-절) 네가 어디 살든 무엇을 하든 중요하지 않다.

|주의| 단어, 구, 절뿐만 아니라, 동명사, to부정사, 형용사, 시제 등의 문장 성분도 일치시키는 것이 원칙이다.

She enjoys **cooking** and **baking.** (동명사-동명사) 그녀는 요리와 제빵을 좋아한다.

Adam Sandler's movies are **funny** but **silly.** (형용사-형용사) 아담 샌들러의 영화들은 재미있지만 유치하다.

EXERCISES

정답 및 해설 P. 24

A 두 문장을 주어진 접속사를 사용하여 한 문장으로 만드시오.

clever 영리한, 총명한
hard-working 열심히 공부(일)하는
crowd 관중, 청중
enthusiastic 열광적인

1 Tracy is clever. She is hard-working, too. (not only A but also B)
→ ______________________________

2 We should walk quickly. Or we should take a taxi. (either A or B)
→ ______________________________

3 Mike doesn't like fast food. His sisters don't like it, either. (neither A nor B)
→ ______________________________

4 The crowd at the stadium was large. It was enthusiastic, too. (both A and B)
→ ______________________________

5 I was not invited to the party. She was not invited to the party, either.
(B as well as A)
→ ______________________________

B ( ) 안에서 가장 알맞은 것을 고르시오.

community 공동체; 지역 사회
effort 노력
meal 식사

1 Not only Cathy but also Debbie (enjoy / enjoys) listening to music.
2 Both the kitchen and the dining room (need / needs) to be painted.
3 Either my sister or my brothers (are / is) going to teach me how to drive.
4 San Francisco as well as LA (have / has) a large Chinese community.
5 Neither time nor effort (are / is) required to prepare this simple meal.
6 Both Tim and James (are / is) planning to visit Angkor Wat this summer.
7 Not only Lisa but also her sisters (has / have) lived in LA since last year.

C 밑줄 친 부분이 어법상 맞지 않다면 바르게 고치시오.

British 영국의
pick up ~을 데리러 가다
security guard 안전 요원
wave 흔들다

1 My father likes to ski, skating and swimming.
2 Neither Kelly or you will be able to join the club.
3 You should turn neither right nor left. Go straight.
4 My British friends will leave either today nor tomorrow.
5 Either Tom or I am going to pick up Sam at the airport.
6 The security guard was waving his arms and shouted at me.
7 Both my parents and my brother wants to spend a vacation in the mountains.

Unit 59 명사절을 이끄는 종속 접속사

that ~하는 것	**That** she is popular is true. → It is true that she is popular. 그녀가 유명한 것은 사실이다.
whether/if ~인지 아닌지	I wonder **whether** he is a student (or not). → I wonder **if** he is a student (or not). 나는 그가 학생인지 아닌지 궁금하다.

FOCUS

1 독립적으로 쓰이지 않고 문장의 일부로 쓰이는 절을 종속절이라고 한다.
종속 접속사 that, whether, if는 문장에서 명사절을 이끈다.

I heard **that** he is allergic to peanuts. 나는 그가 땅콩에 알레르기가 있다고 들었다.
(I heard: 주절 / that he is allergic to peanuts: 종속절)

Whether he likes it or not is unimportant to me. 그가 그것을 좋아하는지 아닌지는 내게 중요하지 않다.

My friends wonder **if** I'll join the club (or not). 나의 친구들은 내가 그 모임에 가입할 것인지 아닌지를 궁금해 한다.

2 that은 문장에서 '~하는 것'이라는 의미로, 명사절(주어절, 목적어절, 보어절)을 이끈다.
목적어절을 이끄는 that은 생략할 수 있다.

That he is falling in love with her is true. (주어) 그가 그녀와 사랑에 빠진 것은 사실이다.

I found **(that)** my wallet was no longer with me. (목적어) 나는 지갑이 더 이상 나에게 없다는 것을 알게 되었다.

The important thing is **that** you did your best. (보어) 중요한 것은 네가 최선을 다했다는 것이다.

3 주어로 사용되는 that절 대신에 「It(가주어) ~ that(진주어)」 구문이나 「The fact that ~」 구문을 주로 사용한다.

That he is a big-hearted man is obvious.

→ **It** is obvious **that** he is a big-hearted man.

→ **The fact that** he is a big-hearted man is obvious.

그가 관대한 사람이라는 사실은 명백하다.

4 if, whether는 문장에서 '~인지 아닌지'라는 의미로, 명사절을 이끈다.

I wonder **whether** James will come **(or not).** 나는 제임스가 올지 안 올지 궁금하다.

→ I wonder **if** James will come **(or not)**.

|주의| 1. if는 주어절을 이끌지 않는다.

Whether he will come or not is up to you. ((×) ~~If~~ he will come is up to you.) 그가 올지 안 올지는 너에게 달려 있다.

2. 보어절에는 주로 whether를 쓴다.

The question is **whether** the man can be trusted. 문제는 그 남자를 믿을 수 있는지 없는지이다.

3. 전치사 뒤와 to부정사 앞에는 whether를 쓴다. if를 쓸 수 없다.

I can't decide **whether** to sell the house or not. ((×) I can't decide ~~if to sell~~ ~.)
나는 그 집을 팔아야 할지 말아야 할지 결정할 수가 없다.

There was an argument about **whether** we should sell the house or not. ((×) There was an argument ~~about if~~ we sell ~.)
우리가 그 집을 팔아야 할지 말아야 할지에 대해 논쟁이 있었다.

|참고| 1. or not은 일반적으로 문장 맨 끝에 오지만, whether 바로 뒤에 쓰기도 한다.

I wonder **whether** Simon will come **or not.** 나는 사이먼이 올지 안 올지 궁금하다.

→ I wonder **whether or not** Simon will come.

(×) I wonder ~~if or not~~ Simon will come. (if 바로 뒤에는 쓸 수 없다.)

2. 명사절에는 미래 시제를 사용할 수 있지만, 조건 부사절에는 미래 시제를 사용할 수 없다.

My friend wonders **if I'll go** to the party. (명사절_목적어절) 내 친구는 내가 파티에 갈 것인지 아닌지 궁금해한다.

My friend will go to the party **if I go** there. (부사절_조건) 만약 내가 파티에 간다면 내 친구도 갈 것이다.

3. whether가 부사절을 이끄는 경우 if로 바꿔 쓰지 않는다.

Whether you arrive late or not, we will begin the meeting as scheduled. 네가 늦게 도착하든 안 하든 우리는 예정대로 회의를 시작할 거야.

5 의문문이 종속절처럼 주절에 포함된 것을 간접의문문이라고 한다. 주절에 포함된 간접의문문의 어순은 「의문사+주어+동사」이다.

Tell me. + What did she say?

→ Tell me **what she said.** 그녀가 뭐라고 했는지 나에게 말해 줘.

Do you know? + Where is the coffee shop?

→ Do you know **where the coffee shop is?** 너는 커피숍이 어디 있는지 알고 있니?

|참고| 간접의문문은 「의문사+주어+동사」의 어순으로 쓴다. 의문사 자체가 주어인 경우 의문문을 그대로 쓴다.

의문문	간접의문문
Who is(V) she(S)? 그녀는 누구니?	Do you know? + Who is she? → Do you know who she(S) is(V)? 너는 그녀가 누군지 아니?
Who(S) built(V) that house? 누가 저 집을 지었니?	Do you know? + Who built that house? → Do you know who(S) built(V) that house? 너는 누가 저 집을 지었는지 아니?

|주의| 주절이 do you think [believe, guess, suppose, say, imagine] ~?일 때는 「의문사+do you think+주어+동사」의 어순이 된다.

Do you **think**? + What does she want?

→ What do you **think** she wants? 너는 그녀가 무엇을 원한다고 생각하니?

EXERCISES

정답 및 해설 P. 24

lawn 잔디
trim ~을 손질하다
obvious 명백한, 분명한
convenient 편리한
impossible 불가능한
try one's best 최선을 다하다

문장을 읽고, 명사절을 이끄는 접속사 that의 자리에 √표시를 하시오.

1 Did you hear he'll be leaving soon?

2 It was quite surprising he passed the exam.

3 I think the lawn in your backyard needs trimming.

4 The problem is you aren't being honest enough with me.

5 It is obvious computers make our lives far more convenient.

6 The most important point is nothing is impossible if you try your best.

mathematics 수학
depend on ~에 의지하다, 의존하다
condition 컨디션, 상태
unpleasant 불쾌한; 불편한
litter 쓰레기

B 빈칸에 that과 whether 중 알맞은 것을 써넣으시오.

1 I think __________ mathematics is quite interesting.

2 It all depends on __________ she's got enough time or not.

3 I wonder __________ Jihoon finished his part of our project.

4 May asked __________ John was going to come to the festival.

5 __________ we win or not depends on the star player's condition.

6 It's quite unpleasant __________ there is so much litter in the streets.

miracle 기적
go up (값이) 오르다
currently 최근에는
blame 탓하다
audience 청중, 관객

주어진 문장을 「It(가주어) ~ that(진주어)」 구문을 사용하여 다시 쓰시오.

1 That you weren't hurt in the accident is a miracle.
→ ______________________________

2 That prices are currently going up is a big problem.
→ ______________________________

3 That you blame others for your own mistakes is wrong.
→ ______________________________

4 That Robert was late for school today is not surprising at all.
→ ______________________________

5 That your audience didn't understand you well enough is clear.
→ ______________________________

D 두 문장을 〈보기〉와 같이 한 문장으로 만드시오.

> 보기 Do you know? + Where is my schoolbag?
> → Do you know where my schoolbag is?

wonder ~을 궁금해하다, 호기심을 갖다
show up 나타나다

1 I don't know. + What did the man say?
→ ____________________

2 Tell me. + What did you have for dinner?
→ ____________________

3 We wonder. + When will Yunho show up?
→ ____________________

4 I'd like to know. + What did the teacher say?
→ ____________________

5 I wonder. + Where did Sara and James go last night?
→ ____________________

6 Do you know? + What did Sam give his best friend, Mike?
→ ____________________

7 Could you please tell me? + Where is the nearest music shop?
→ ____________________

8 Do you know? + When will Jin's parents arrive from Melbourne?
→ ____________________

9 Could you tell me? + What were you doing in front of my house?
→ ____________________

E 우리말과 같은 뜻이 되도록 주어진 단어를 알맞게 배열하시오.

react 반응하다
criticism 비판, 비평
fit in ~에 맞다, 어울리다
overcome ~을 극복하다
difficulty 어려움
in the end 결국에는, 마침내

1 그녀가 그들의 비판에 어떻게 반응할 것 같니? (she, think, will, how, react, do you)
→ ____________________ to their criticisms?

2 나는 내가 새 학교에서 잘 적응할지 궁금하다. (I, I, if, will, wonder, fit in)
→ ____________________ at the new school.

3 너는 어제 야구 경기에서 누가 이겼는지 아니?
(the baseball game, who, won, do you know)
→ ____________________ yesterday?

4 그는 그녀가 결국 어려움을 극복해낼 것이라는 것을 알았다.
(her difficulties, knew, would overcome, that, he, she)
→ ____________________ in the end.

부사절을 이끄는 종속 접속사 I

부사절	접속사	예문
시간	when ~할 때 while ~하는 동안 before ~ 전에 after ~ 후에 until ~할 때까지 since ~ 이래로 as ~할 때, ~하는 동안, ~함에 따라 as soon as ~하자마자	**When** I called her name, she looked at me. 내가 그녀의 이름을 불렀을 때, 그녀가 나를 보았다. **As** people get older, they get wiser. 사람들은 나이가 들어감에 따라, 더 현명해진다.
이유	because ~ 때문에 as ~ 때문에 since ~ 이니까 now (that) 이제 ~이니까	I can't buy the car **because** it's too expensive. 나는 그 차가 너무 비싸서 살 수 없다. **Now (that)** it's vacation, I'll spend more time with my family. 방학이니까 나는 가족과 더 많은 시간을 보낼 것이다.
목적	so that ~ can[could] = in order that ~하기 위해서, 하려고	I study hard **so (that)** I **can** get a good grade. → I study hard **in order that** I **can** get a good grade. 나는 좋은 성적을 받으려고 열심히 공부한다.

1 부사절은 문장에서 부사의 역할을 하기 때문에 주절이 필요하다. 시간, 이유, 목적, 조건, 양보, 결과 등을 의미하는 접속사가 이러한 부사절을 이끈다. 부사절이 주절보다 앞에 올 경우, 주절과 구분하기 위해 부사절 뒤에 콤마(, comma)를 붙인다.

Jessica fell asleep **while** she was reading the book.

→ **While** Jessica was reading the book, she fell asleep. 제시카는 책을 읽다가 잠이 들었다.

2 when, while, before, after, until, since, as, as soon as 등은 시간을 나타내는 접속사이다.

When I called her, Laura didn't answer her phone. 내가 전화했을 때, 로라는 전화를 받지 않았다.

While I was sleeping, John called three times. 내가 자는 동안, 존이 세 번 전화했다.

You should brush your teeth **before** you go to bed. 너는 자기 전에 이를 닦아야 한다.

After he exercises, James feels stronger. 운동을 하고 난 후, 제임스는 더 건강해짐을 느낀다.

The taxi driver waited **until** the traffic light changed. 그 택시 운전사는 신호등이 바뀔 때까지 기다렸다.

They have been in love **since** they first met ten years ago. 그들은 10년 전에 처음 만난 이래로 계속 서로 사랑하고 있다.

Peter likes to listen to music **as** he rests. 피터는 쉬는 동안 음악 듣는 것을 좋아한다.

As soon as I came home, I washed my hands. 나는 집에 오자마자 손을 씻었다.

|참고| until은 동작이나 상태의 지속을 나타내며 by the time은 동작이나 상태가 그 기한까지 완료됨을 나타낸다.

She will wait here **until** he comes. [그가 올 때까지 기다림이 계속됨을 나타냄]
그녀는 그가 올 때까지 여기서 기다릴 것이다.

I will have arrived **by the time** you get this letter. [편지가 도착하는 시점이 완료되는 시점을 나타냄]
네가 이 편지를 받을 때쯤 나는 도착해 있을 것이다.

|주의| 시간을 나타내는 부사절에서는 현재 시제가 미래를 대신한다.

I'll tell him the truth **when** he **comes** back. ((×) I'll tell him the truth when he ~~will come~~ back.)
나는 그가 돌아오면 진실을 말할 것이다.

3 because, as, since, now (that) 등은 이유를 나타내는 접속사이다.

Gina was thrilled **because** she got the lead in the school play.
지나는 학교 연극에서 주인공을 맡았기 때문에 신이 났다.

As it was getting dark, we decided to go home.
어두워지고 있었기 때문에, 우리는 집에 가기로 결정했다.

Since you are drunk, you shouldn't drive.
너는 술 취했기 때문에, 운전을 해서는 안 된다.

Now (that) you are a grown-up, you should behave more responsibly.
이제 너는 어른이니까, 좀 더 책임감 있게 행동해야 한다.

|참고| because는 접속사로 뒤에 절이 오고, because of는 전치사구로 뒤에 구가 온다.

The flight was canceled **because** the weather was bad. 날씨가 안 좋아서 비행기가 취소되었다.

The flight was canceled **because of** bad weather.

4 so (that) ~ can[could], in order that ~ 등은 목적을 나타내는 접속사이다.

She drank a glass of warm milk **so (that)** she **could** fall asleep easily.
그녀는 쉽게 잠들 수 있도록 따뜻한 우유 한 잔을 마셨다.

She turned off the radio **so (that)** she **could** concentrate better.
그녀는 더 집중하기 위해서 라디오를 껐다.

Alice is saving her earnings **in order that** she **can** buy a new dress.
앨리스는 새 드레스를 사려고 돈을 모으는 중이다.

|참고| in order that은 격식을 차린 표현이므로, 일반적으로 so that을 더 많이 쓴다.

EXERCISES

정답 및 해설 P. 25

as usual 늘 그렇듯이, 평소처럼
rise (해·달이) 뜨다
set (해·달이) 지다
hum 콧노래를 부르다
shave 면도하다
demand 요구하다
refund 환불하다
defective 결함이 있는
go by (시간이) 지나가다, 흐르다
culture 문화
possible 가능한

( ) 안에서 가장 알맞은 것을 고르시오.

1 As usual, the moon will rise (as soon as / so that) the sun sets.

2 My father likes to hum to himself (as soon as / while) he shaves.

3 I had to demand a refund (because / while) the TV was defective.

4 Cindy has been very busy (now that / since) she came back from Africa.

5 (When / While) Jack arrived, Jacob and Sarah were already having coffee.

6 I've known Tim (because / since) we were kids. He's one of my best friends.

7 (As / As soon as) time goes by, I find that I understand Korean culture better.

8 He told me to help him (so that / when) he could finish the work as soon as possible.

insist on 주장하다, 고집하다
explain 설명하다
hang up (전화를) 끊다
light 전등; 빛; 가벼운
deep 깊은
knock 노크하다, (문 등을 똑똑) 두드리다
rush 급히 가다

<보기>와 같이 두 문장을 주어진 접속사를 사용하여 한 문장으로 만드시오.

보기 Susan and Alex visited London. They saw several plays. (when)
→ When Susan and Alex visited London, they saw several plays.

1 You paid for the concert tickets. I insist on paying for dinner. (since)
→ ____________________

2 She was older than him. Greg let the lady take the taxi first. (as)
→ ____________________

3 Jihu was living in Melbourne. He made several new Australian friends. (when)
→ ____________________

4 I had a chance to explain. He just angrily hung up the phone. (before)
→ ____________________

5 I turned the lights off. He could have a deep sleep. (in order that)
→ ____________________

6 I have to leave home early tomorrow. I can catch the first train. (so that)
→ ____________________

7 Nicole heard someone knocking at the door. She rushed to answer it. (as soon as)
→ ____________________

C 〈보기〉에서 알맞은 접속사를 골라 빈칸에 써넣으시오.

보기	before	because	when	so that	until	after

1 I think we had better wait __________ the rest of the team arrives.

2 __________ you sit down, please bring me another glass of water.

3 I saw my parents sleeping __________ I returned home yesterday.

4 He got a job at a bank right __________ he graduated from college.

5 __________ it was so cold last night, we let the dog sleep inside.

6 Ice hockey players wear a lot of protective gear __________ they don't get hurt.

protective 보호하는, 보호용의
gear 장비, 도구

D 주어진 동사를 알맞은 시제로 바꿔 문장을 완성하시오.

1 I'm not sure if he can make it before the train __________ (leave).

2 I'm going to visit you in Sydney when I __________ (finish) my contract.

3 While I __________ (be) in Greece, I went to see the Parthenon in Athens.

4 After she finishes her MBA, she __________ (look for) a job in the USA.

5 As soon as it __________ (start) raining, we will pack up and head for home.

6 I won't forgive him until he __________ (apologize) to me from the bottom of his heart.

contract 계약
Parthenon 파르테논(기원전 438년경에 아테네의 Acropolis 언덕에 세워진 아테네신의 신전)
Athens 아테네(그리스의 수도)
MBA(=Master of Business Administration) 경영학 석사
pack up 짐을 싸다
head for ~로 향하다
bottom of one's heart 진심으로

E 〈보기〉와 같이 두 문장을 so that ~ can[could]을 이용하여 한 문장으로 만드시오.

보기 I gave you twenty dollars. I wanted you to buy books.
→ I gave you twenty dollars so that you could buy books.

1 Rock climbers use talc. They want to grasp slippery rocks.
→ ____________________

2 I gave Sally my phone number. I wanted her to contact me.
→ ____________________

3 Please arrive early. We want to have lunch together before the meeting.
→ ____________________

4 She took an English course. She wanted to talk with her foreign friends.
→ ____________________

talc (광물) 활석(滑石); 탤크
grasp ~을 붙잡다, 쥐다
slippery 미끄러운
contact ~와 연락하다

부사절을 이끄는 종속 접속사 II

부사절	접속사	예문
양보	even though, although, though, even if 비록 ~임에도 while, whereas 반면에	**Even though** I was tired, I went to the show with my friends. 나는 피곤했는데도 친구들과 쇼를 보러 갔다. My sister enjoys going out **while** I enjoy staying home. 우리 언니는 밖에 나가는 것을 즐기는 반면에 나는 집에 머무르는 것을 즐긴다.
조건	if 만약 ~라면 unless [if~not] 만약 ~이 아니라면 as long as ~하는 한, ~하기만 하면 in case ~일 경우에 대비하여	**If** it rains tomorrow, I will cancel my trip. 만약 내일 비가 온다면 나는 여행을 취소할 거야. **Unless** you have an ID card, you are not allowed to enter the library. ID 카드가 없다면, 너는 도서관에 들어올 수가 없다.
결과	such … that ~ so … that ~ 너무 …해서 그 결과 ~하다	Karen is **such** a nice person **(that)** everyone likes her. 카렌은 너무나 좋은 사람이어서 모두가 그녀를 좋아한다. I was **so** thirsty **(that)** I gulped down three cups of water. 나는 너무 목이 말라 물 세 잔을 벌컥벌컥 마셨다.

1 even though, although, though, even if는 '비록 ~임에도 (불구하고), 비록 ~일지라도'라는 의미이고, while, whereas는 '반면에'라는 의미로 양보절을 이끄는 접속사이다.

Even though the weather was horrible, we went for a walk.
날씨가 몹시 좋지 않았는데도, 우리는 산책하러 나갔다.

Although the vacuum cleaner was very noisy, the baby didn't wake up.
청소기가 매우 시끄러웠지만, 아기는 깨지 않았다.

Jason is tall **while** Mark is short.
마크는 키가 작은 반면에, 제이슨은 키가 크다.

The old computer was very slow **whereas** the new computer is quite fast.
오래된 컴퓨터는 매우 느리지만, 새 컴퓨터는 꽤 빠르다.

|참고| 1. '비록 ~임에도'라는 의미가 있는 부사절을 '양보절'이라고 한다.

2. even though, although, though, even if 등은 예상치 못한 결과를 나타낼 때 쓰며, while, whereas는 직접적인 대조를 나타낼 때 쓴다.

3. though가 문장 끝에 쓰이면 'however(하지만)'와 같은 뜻이 된다.
This apartment is rather small. It has a very nice view **though**. → However, it has a very nice view.
이 아파트는 다소 작다. 하지만 전망은 매우 좋다.

2 if, unless[if ~ not], as long as, in case 등의 접속사는 조건절을 이끄는 접속사이다.

If you have any questions, just raise your hand.
질문 있으시면 손만 들어주세요.

Unless it rains, we'll go on a picnic tomorrow.

→ **If** it does **not** rain, we'll go on a picnic tomorrow.
비가 오지 않는다면, 우리는 내일 소풍을 갈 것이다.

As long as he is happy, I'm happy.
그가 행복하기만 하면, 나는 행복해.

I'll give you my phone number **in case** you need help.
도움이 필요할 경우에 대비해서 내 전화번호를 줄게.

|주의| 조건을 나타내는 부사절에서는 현재 시제가 미래 시제를 대신하며, 주절에는 미래 시제를 사용한다.

If it rains tomorrow, I will just stay home. 내일 비가 오면, 나는 그냥 집에 있을게.

3 「such … (that) ~」, 「so … (that) ~」은 원인과 결과를 나타내는 접속사이며, 「such(+a/an)+형용사+명사+that」, 「so+형용사/부사+that」의 어순으로 쓴다.

He has **such a beautiful car (that)** his friends are jealous.
그는 매우 좋은 차를 가지고 있어서 친구들이 그를 부러워한다.

It was **such good wine (that)** all of the guests were content.
그것은 아주 좋은 포도주여서 모든 손님이 만족스러워했다.

The professor spoke **so fast (that)** no one understood his lecture.
그 교수님이 말을 너무 빨리해서 아무도 그의 강의를 이해하지 못했다.

The car was **so expensive (that)** he couldn't buy it.
그 차는 너무 비싸서 그는 그 차를 살 수 없었다.

|참고| so는 many, much, few, little 등을 수식하기도 한다. 이때 so many, so much, so few, so little 등은 '매우 많은, 매우 적은'이라는 의미로 마치 한 단어처럼 명사를 수식한다.

Anne ate so much ice cream **that** she got a stomachache. 앤은 아이스크림을 너무 많이 먹어서 배탈이 났다.

There were so few people at the meeting **that** it got canceled. 사람들이 거의 없어서 회의가 취소되었다.

EXERCISES

정답 및 해설 P. 26

borrow ~을 빌리다
muscular 근육질의; 힘이 센
make oneself understand 자신의 말을 남에게 이해시키다
fridge 냉장고
reach (전화 등으로) 연락하다; ~에 도착[도달]하다
pirate 해적
threaten 위협하다, 협박하다
sink 가라앉(히)다
crowd 관객, 구경꾼
assignment 과제; 할당

A (　) 안에서 가장 알맞은 것을 고르시오.

1 (If / In case) the weather is warm enough, I'm not going to wear my jacket.

2 It was (so / such) an expensive suit that Ron had to borrow money to buy it.

3 Jason is tall and muscular, (whereas / if) his brother Sam is short and skinny.

4 (Because / Though) it rained almost every day, we enjoyed our holiday in Bali.

5 Kim walked home by herself, (although / whereas) she knew it was dangerous.

6 (Even though / Because) Sue's Spanish isn't perfect, she can make herself understood.

7 I left my number on the fridge (in case / whereas) you need to reach me.

8 The pirates threatened to sink the ship (unless / if) the owner did what they asked him to do.

9 The Smiths will join us this evening (as long as / even though) they find a babysitter for Jane.

10 (While / As long as) some people enjoy singing in front of a crowd, others find it quite embarrassing.

11 (In case / Unless) any of you have questions about the assignment, I'll be in my office all day tomorrow afternoon.

protect ~을 보호하다
endangered species 멸종 위기의 생물[종(種)]
disappear 사라지다
correct 정확한; 올바른
postage 우편 요금, 우송료
in advance 사전에
apply ~을 신청하다
driver's license 운전면허
book ~을 예약하다

B 주어진 문장을 unless를 이용하여 같은 뜻의 문장으로 바꿔 쓰시오.

1 We'll both be late for the concert if you don't hurry up.
→ ______________________________

2 If we don't protect endangered species, many of them will soon disappear.
→ ______________________________

3 If you don't pay the correct postage in advance, your letter will not be mailed.
→ ______________________________

4 You cannot apply for a driver's license if you are not eighteen or older.
→ ______________________________

5 You won't be able to enter the museum if you don't book the tickets in advance.
→ ______________________________

C 부사절과 주절을 자연스러운 하나의 문장이 되도록 연결하시오.

1	Although he walks with a cane,	•	• ⓐ I respect your ideas.
2	Whereas I prefer staying in,	•	• ⓑ my girlfriend enjoys going out.
3	Even though Ms. Kim is still sick,	•	• ⓒ he is still quite active.
4	Even though I don't agree with you,	•	• ⓓ she'll teach her classes today.
5	Even if you try hard	•	• ⓔ you won't be able to solve the problem in a short time.

cane 지팡이
respect ~을 존중하다, 존경하다
stay in 집에 머무르다
active 활동적인
agree with ~에 동의하다

D 〈보기〉에서 빈칸에 알맞은 접속사를 골라 문장을 완성하시오.

보기 although if unless whereas in case

1 Why don't you save some money ______________ you need it later?

2 ______________ it rains tomorrow, we will just stay inside watching TV.

3 ______________ some people don't often complain, others do constantly.

4 You can't get a decent job these days ______________ you've tried hard enough.

5 ______________ Mina was still very thirsty, she was too shy to ask Ms. Smith for another drink.

complain 불평하다
constantly 변함없이; 끊임없이
decent 적당한, 알맞은

E 문장을 「such … that ~」 또는 「so … that ~」을 이용하여 한 문장으로 만드시오.

1 The leather jacket was very expensive. I couldn't buy it.
→ ______________________________

2 It was very cold. I didn't want to go out without my car.
→ ______________________________

3 She is a very good student. All the teachers in her school like her.
→ ______________________________

4 He has very high marks. He has applied for a full scholarship to Oxford.
→ ______________________________

5 The weather was very beautiful. We decided to go for a swim after dinner.
→ ______________________________

6 There was a very strong wind. We decided to stay indoors and play cards.
→ ______________________________

leather 가죽 제품의
mark 점수; 흔적
apply for ~에 지원하다
scholarship 장학금
indoors 실내에(서)

REVIEW

정답 및 해설 P. 27

burst out 터트리다, 폭발하다
laugh 웃다
make sure 반드시 ~하다
conductor (버스·열차의) 차장
blow ~을 불다
whistle 기적, 호루라기
hand ~을 제출하다
fall off ~에서 떨어지다
set (해·달이) 지다
approach ~에 접근하다
treat ~을 대접하다
allowance 용돈

( ) 안에서 가장 알맞은 것을 고르시오.

1 He got wiser (as soon as / as) he got older.

2 (While / As soon as) Michael heard the news, he burst out laughing.

3 Jenny closed her eyes (after / until) the scary movie scene passed.

4 Make sure your hands are clean (before / after) you sit down to dinner.

5 (When / As) it's getting late, let's leave the dish washing until tomorrow.

6 (Until / As soon as) the conductor blows the whistle, the train will leave.

7 Always check your work carefully (before / after) you hand it in for a grade.

8 (When / While) Mark was eight years old, he broke his leg in a bicycle accident.

9 Carol stayed on the beach (as soon as / until) the sun set.

10 I've known Ann (when / since) she was a kid. She's my friend's daughter.

11 (As / As soon as) we approached the upstairs, the noise became louder and louder.

12 I'm sorry, but I can't treat you to dinner (when / until) I get my allowance next month.

bright 눈부신, 밝은
dirtiness 더러움
drop out 낙제하다, 중퇴하다
manage to ~을 잘 해내다
now that ~이므로, ~이기 때문에
vote 투표하다, 선거하다
assignment 과제; 할당
debate 토론
hesitate 망설이다
stand for ~을 나타내다, 의미하다
insult 모욕

B 밑줄 친 부분을 바르게 고치시오.

1 I will wait until I'll hear from you.

2 Neither Jiho nor Seho live with their parents anymore.

3 Suha doesn't enjoy painting, nor does she enjoys singing.

4 Although we're early for the train, let's have a cup of coffee.

5 The sun was so bright that we have to wear dark sunglasses.

6 You'll get hungry during volleyball practice if you have a snack.

7 The hotel room we stayed in last week was both cold and dirtiness.

8 Because he dropped out of college, he still managed to become rich.

9 Now that you are over 18, you can vote, get married, and drove a car.

10 I can't go to the show with you tonight so I have an assignment to do.

11 Sam asked Carrie to join the debate club, when she hesitated to do so.

12 In some countries, the "V" sign stands for "victory," so in others it's used as an insult.

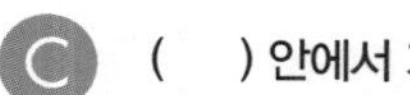

C ( ) 안에서 가장 알맞은 것을 고르시오.

1 Either study or work (are / is) what Josh must do.

2 I (stay in / will stay in) tonight if Sarah doesn't invite me over.

3 Neither Spanish nor German (are / is) studied much in Korea now.

4 Not only baseball players but also soccer players (are / is) paid a lot.

5 Neither my father nor I (eat / eats) raw fish. We'll have steak, thanks.

6 If you (won't / don't) make it by 2, your reservations will be canceled.

7 Either John or his brothers (are / is) supposed to use this room.

8 Tim as well as his friends (look / looks) forward to the ski camp each year.

9 Unless you (don't wear / wear) a warmer coat, you'll feel cold this evening.

10 Both Canberra and Ottawa (are / is) names of capital cities.

11 Not only the coach but also the team members (is / are) satisfied with the game result.

12 Your lettuce will stay crisp if you (keep / will keep) it in an airtight container in the refrigerator.

raw 날것의, 익히지 않은
reservation 예약
cancel 취소하다
look forward to ~을 기대하다
capital 수도
be satisfied with ~에 만족하다
result 결과
lettuce 상추
crisp 아삭아삭한, 바삭바삭한
airtight container 밀폐 용기
refrigerator 냉장고

D 밑줄 친 부분을 어법에 맞게 고치시오.

1 I wonder when will Gary arrive.

2 He doesn't like either swimming or ride a boat.

3 I was surprised that he had so a pretty daughter.

4 My father enjoys both fishing and to sail in his free time.

5 My homeroom teacher this year is not only kind but also patience.

6 Neither the children nor their mother are at home at the moment.

7 Either Sally or Henry are supposed to prepare dinner this evening.

8 Unless you don't have money to pay for the trip, I'll lend you some.

9 Neither the coach nor his star player doesn't attend press conferences.

10 Don't bother making dessert since neither Pamela or Sal enjoys sweets.

11 If the weather will be nice tomorrow, I'll take you and your brother fishing.

12 Jeff was such busy that he had to hire an assistant to help him last week.

homeroom teacher 담임 선생님
patience 인내심, 참을성
be supposed to ~하기로 되어있다
lend ~을 빌려주다
attend ~에 참석하다
press conference 기자 회견
hire ~을 고용하다
assistant 조수, 보조자

REVIEW PLUS

정답 및 해설 P. 29

baffle 당황하게 하다
patiently
참을성 있게, 끈기 있게
explain ~을 설명하다

A 다음 밑줄 친 부분 중 어법상 바르지 않은 것을 고르시오.

1

① Strangely, neither the boy ② nor his sister would tell the police officer ③ what had happened to them. The baffled officer patiently explained ④ that ⑤ unless they wouldn't tell him the truth, he would have to take them back to the police station.

2

① Both Jeff and his sister ② are coming to the movies with us on Saturday. ③ Because neither Jeff nor his sister ④ like horror movies, we'll have to watch ⑤ either a romantic comedy, like *Runaway Bride*, or a drama, like *Gladiator*.

be familiar with
~와 친숙하다
inflation
(경제) 인플레이션, 통화 팽창
rise 오르다
goods 상품
deflation
(경제) 디플레이션, 통화 수축
refer to ~을 가리키다
gradual 점진적인
fall
(가격의) 하락; 강하, 떨어지다
drop 떨어지다
lay off ~을 해고하다
in truth
사실대로 이야기하면
excessive 과도한
harmful to ~에 해로운
economy 경제

B 다음 (A), (B), (C)에 들어갈 말이 바르게 짝지어진 것을 고르시오.

Everyone is familiar with inflation—the rising cost of goods and services, but what about "deflation"? Deflation refers to a gradual fall in the price of goods. (A) (Even though / Because) this might sound great, actually it isn't. (B) (When / As long as) prices start to fall, people stop buying things like TVs, cars, and clothes because they think that prices will drop even further in the future. Prices drop so fast that companies close down or lay off workers. In truth, both excessive inflation and deflation (C) (are / is) harmful to an economy.

	(A)		(B)		(C)
①	Even though	…	As long as	…	are
②	Even though	…	As long as	…	is
③	Even though	…	When	…	are
④	Because	…	When	…	is
⑤	Because	…	As long as	…	are

PART 17

관계사
Relatives

관계대명사 I

주격 관계대명사	Anyone **who** is interested must apply before this Friday. 관심이 있는 사람은 누구나 이번 금요일 전에 신청해야 한다.
목적격 관계대명사	The support staff member **that** I talked to was very knowledgeable. 내가 이야기했던 보조 스태프는 아는 것이 매우 많았다.
소유격 관계대명사	That's the woman **whose** picture was in today's newspaper. 저 사람이 오늘 신문에 사진이 실린 여자이다.

FOCUS

1 주격 관계대명사 who는 관계대명사절에서 주어 역할을 하며, 사람을 선행사로 받는다.

I like the English teacher **who** has the British accent. 나는 영국식 억양을 가진 영어 선생님을 좋아한다.

She was the one **who** first suggested the idea. 그녀가 그 의견을 처음 제안했던 사람이었다.

| 참고 | 1. 주어와 동사가 있는 절이 형용사처럼 명사를 수식하는 것을 '형용사절'이라고 한다. 대부분의 관계대명사절이 형용사절이다.

2. 주격 관계대명사가 이끄는 형용사절을 형용사구로 바꿀 수 있다.

(1) [주격 관계대명사+be동사]의 형태로 되어 있는 경우: [주격 관계대명사+be동사]를 생략할 수 있다.

The woman **(who is) playing** the piano in the orchestra is my cousin.
오케스트라에서 피아노를 연주하고 있는 여자는 내 사촌이다.

(2) [주격 관계대명사+일반동사]의 형태로 되어 있는 경우: [주격 관계대명사]를 생략하고 동사를 -ing 형태로 바꾸어 쓸 수 있다.

I found a wallet **which contains** ten dollars.
→ I found a wallet **containing** ten dollars.
나는 10달러가 들어 있는 지갑을 주웠다.

| 주의 | 주어와 동사 사이에 관계대명사절이 삽입되어 주어와 동사가 멀어진 경우, 바로 앞의 명사를 주어로 착각하지 않도록 주의한다.

People [**who** don't cover their mouths while they are yawning] make me feel embarrassed.
하품을 하면서 입을 가리지 않는 사람들은 나를 당황하게 한다.

2 목적격 관계대명사 whom은 관계대명사절에서 목적어 역할을 하며, 사람을 선행사로 받는다. 목적격 관계대명사는 생략할 수 있다.

We easily tend to believe those **(whom)** we don't know.
우리는 모르는 사람을 쉽게 믿는 경향이 있다.

The math teacher **(whom)** I wanted to see wasn't in the teachers' room.
내가 만나고자 했던 수학 선생님께서는 교무실에 안 계셨다.

| 참고 | 목적격 관계대명사 whom 대신 who를 쓸 수 있다.
We easily tend to believe those **who** we don't know.

3 관계대명사 which는 사람 이외의 것을 선행사로 받으며, 주격과 목적격에 쓴다.

Most people like stories **which** have happy endings. (주격) 대부분의 사람들은 행복하게 끝나는 이야기를 좋아한다.

My sister told me about her hobby, **which** she's just started. (목적격) 내 여동생은 새로 시작한 취미에 대해 나에게 이야기해 주었다.

|참고| which는 앞 문장 전체 혹은 일부를 선행사로 받는다. 이때 which는 계속적 용법의 관계대명사로, 관계대명사 앞에 꼭 콤마(, : comma)가 와야 한다.

She stood me up last night, **which** really upset me. 그녀가 어젯밤에 나를 바람 맞혀서 마음이 상했다.

4 관계대명사 that은 사람뿐만 아니라 그 이외의 것도 선행사로 받으며, 주격과 목적격에 쓴다.

The woman **that** lives next door is very sensitive. (주격) 옆집에 사는 여자는 매우 예민하다.

Where is the milk **that** was in the refrigerator? (주격) 냉장고에 있던 우유 어디 있어요?

Ian asked for the book **that** Jane was reading. (목적격) 이안이 제인이 읽고 있던 책을 달라고 했다.

5 소유격 관계대명사 whose는 사람뿐만 아니라 그 외에 것도 선행사로 받는다. whose 다음에 명사가 온다.

I'm the one **whose** invention was awarded first prize.
일등상을 받은 발명품의 주인이 나다.

We have a writing lab for students **whose** native language isn't English.
우리는 영어가 모국어가 아닌 학생들을 위한 작문 실습실을 보유하고 있다.

|참고| 소유격 관계대명사 whose 대신 of which를 쓸 수 있으나 일상 회화에서는 of which를 잘 쓰지 않는다.

6 「전치사+관계대명사」에서 관계대명사는 전치사의 목적어이다. 전치사를 관계대명사절 뒤로 보내면 관계대명사를 생략할 수 있다.

The boy **with whom** Mr. Park is talking is my best friend.

→ The boy **(whom)** Mr. Park is talking **with** is my best friend. (Mr. Park is talking with the boy.)
박 선생님과 대화하고 있는 소년이 나의 가장 친한 친구이다.

The postcard **at which** he was looking was sent from Switzerland.

→ The postcard **(which)** he was looking **at** was sent from Switzerland. (He was looking at the postcard.)
그가 보고 있던 엽서는 스위스에서 온 것이었다.

|주의| 1. 아래 예문처럼 전치사를 생략하지 않도록 주의한다.
(○) The boy Mr. Park is **talking with** is my best friend.
(×) The boy Mr. Park is talking ~~with~~ is my best friend.

2. 관계대명사 who는 전치사의 목적어로 쓰지 않는다.
(×) The boy ~~with who~~ Mr. Park is talking is my best friend.

7 관계대명사의 쓰임은 선행사를 수식해 주는 한정적 용법과 선행사에 추가적인 정보를 제공해 주는 계속적 용법으로 나눌 수 있다.

People who come from Spain are said to be passionate. (한정적 용법) 스페인 출신 사람들은 매우 열정적이라고들 한다.

Celina, who comes from Spain, is a very passionate person. (계속적 용법) 셀리나는 스페인 출신인데, 매우 열정적이다.

EXERCISES

정답 및 해설 P. 29

trust with ~을 맡기다
savings 저금, 저축
criminal 범죄자, 범인
extremely 대단히, 몹시
well-behaved 예의 바른
spoil ~을 상하게 하다
literature 문학
lecturer 강연자, 강사
fridge 냉장고
equipment 장치, 장비
preserve ~을 보관하다, 보존하다
temperature 온도
cave 동굴
bat 박쥐; (야구) 배트
discover ~을 발견하다

A ( ) 안에서 가장 알맞은 것을 고르시오.

1 The man whom we trusted with our savings (was / were) a criminal.

2 The couple who invited us to this party (are / is) standing behind you.

3 The children who live next door to us (are / is) extremely well-behaved.

4 The milk (who / which / whom) they drank was spoiled, so they all got sick.

5 The gentleman (who / whose / whom) name you just called left an hour ago.

6 The people who are asking the way to the bus stop (are / is) from Norway.

7 The professor (that / which / whom) teaches Modern English Literature is an excellent lecturer.

8 A fridge is a piece of kitchen equipment (which / who) is used to preserve food at low temperatures.

9 The cave in (that / which / whom) hundreds of bats were discovered is only a few kilometers away from the village.

unlock (열쇠로) ~을 열다
in charge of ~을 책임하에
especially 특히
barista 바리스타(커피 만드는 전문가)
curator (박물관·미술관 등의) 큐레이터, 전시 책임자[관리자]
racket (테니스 등의) 라켓
celebrity 유명 인사

B 〈보기〉에서 알맞은 것을 골라 which나 who를 넣어 문장을 완성하시오.

보기
ⓐ ____ shops at a store
ⓑ ____ you use to play tennis
ⓒ ____ works in a coffee shop
ⓓ ____ you use to unlock a door
ⓔ ____ help you see better
ⓕ ____ you use to pick up and eat food
ⓖ ____ is in charge of a museum, art gallery, or library
ⓗ ____ is famous, especially in the entertainment business

1 A key is the thing ______________________________.

2 A barista is a person ______________________________.

3 A curator is a person ______________________________.

4 A racket is the thing ______________________________.

5 A celebrity is someone ______________________________.

6 A customer is someone ______________________________.

7 Glasses are the things ______________________________.

8 A fork is the thing ______________________________.

C 〈보기〉와 같이 관계대명사 who나 which를 이용한 문장으로 바꿔 쓰시오.

보기 The student will receive a prize. She finishes the quiz first.
→ The student who finishes the quiz first will receive a prize.

1 Did you see the postcard? It came this morning.
→ ______

2 The books are my favorite. They were written by Jane Austen.
→ ______

3 The people talk very loudly in the mornings. They live upstairs.
→ ______

4 Do you remember the girl? She showed us the way to the mall.
→ ______

5 She changed her mind. It made us all pleased.
→ ______

6 I was introduced to Mark's sister Jenny. She is a famous actress.
→ ______

receive ~을 받다
prize 상
postcard 엽서
favorite 가장 좋아하는 (것)
introduce ~을 소개하다
actress 여배우

D 〈보기〉와 같이 관계대명사 whom이나 which를 이용한 문장으로 바꿔 쓰시오.

보기 This is the Korean exchange student. I told you about her.
→ This is the Korean exchange student whom I told you about.

1 Where's the can of cola? I bought it yesterday.
→ ______

2 Here's the magazine. I told you about it earlier.
→ ______

3 The teacher was away on her honeymoon. I wanted to consult with her.
→ ______

4 The pictures were very impressive. Jim took them on his trip to Australia.
→ ______

5 The man has become one of my closest friends. I worked with him last week.
→ ______

6 The book was found in the first drawer of my desk. I misplaced it last week.
→ ______

exchange student 교환 학생
honeymoon 신혼여행
consult with ~와 의논하다
impressive 인상적인
close 친(밀)한
drawer 서랍
misplace ~의 놓는 장소를 틀리다

관계대명사 II - that, what

관계대명사 that vs. what	
that (선행사를 포함하지 않음)	It's the book that my mom used to read to me when I was young. 이것은 내가 어렸을 때 우리 엄마가 나에게 읽어 주던 책이다.
what (선행사 포함)	Please show me what you brought. 당신이 가져온 것을 나에게 보여 주세요.

접속사 that vs. 관계대명사 that	
관계대명사 that (that+불완전한 문장)	I like the idea that you suggested. 나는 당신이 제안한 의견이 마음에 듭니다. 선행사
접속사 that (that+완전한 문장)	I hope that she will visit me this weekend. 목적어절을 이끄는 접속사 나는 이번 주말에 그녀가 나를 방문하기를 바란다. I was aware of the fact that she graduated from Harvard. 동격절을 이끄는 접속사 나는 그녀가 하버드 대학교를 졸업했다는 사실을 알고 있었다.

1 관계대명사 that은 who, whom, which 대신 쓴다.

I saw a woman **that[who]** was carrying a puppy in her bag.
나는 강아지를 가방에 넣고 가는 여자를 보았다.

The phone call was from a friend **that[whom]** I went to high school with.
그 전화는 고등학교를 같이 다닌 친구에게서 온 전화였다.

Do you have a book **that[which]** will teach me how to use this new program?
너는 내가 이 새 프로그램의 사용법을 배울 수 있는 책을 가지고 있니?

Please give me the book **that[which]** you borrowed from me last month.
지난달에 나에게 빌려간 책을 주세요.

| 참고 | 1. 주로 관계대명사 that을 쓰는 경우

① 최상급, 서수, the very, the only, the same, all, every(thing), some(thing), any(thing), no(thing), none, little, few, much 등이 선행사에 포함되는 경우

Picasso was the greatest painter **that** has ever lived. 피카소는 전대미문의 가장 위대한 화가였다.

He did something **that** really bothered others. 그는 다른 사람들에게 정말 거슬리는 행동을 했다.

② 선행사가 「사람+동물」, 「사람+사물」인 경우

2. 하지만 선행사가 사람인 경우는 선행사가 ①번에 해당하더라도 who를 더 많이 쓴다.

Picasso was the greatest painter **who** has ever lived.

3. 선행사가 this, that 등의 대명사인 경우 관계대명사 that을 쓰지 않고 which를 쓴다.

2 관계대명사 that은 계속적 용법으로 쓸 수 없고, 전치사 바로 뒤에 전치사의 목적어로도 쓸 수 없다.

Our school, **which** has about 1,800 students, was built in 1920. (계속적 용법)
우리 학교는 1,800명 정도의 학생이 있고, 1920년에 지어졌다.

(×) Our school~~, that~~ has about 1,800 students, was built in 1920.

The man **to whom** I spoke was a bit rude. (전치사의 목적어) 내가 말을 건 남자는 약간 무례했다.

→ The man **(that)** I spoke **to** was a bit rude.

(×) The man ~~to that~~ I spoke was a bit rude.

|참고| 1. 관계대명사 that 바로 앞에는 콤마(,)나 전치사가 올 수 없다.
관계대명사 that이 전치사의 목적어로 쓰일 경우, 전치사는 관계대명사절 뒤에 와야 한다.
The man **that** I spoke **to** was a bit rude.

2. in that '~라는 점에서'라는 뜻의 접속사와 헷갈리지 않도록 주의하자.
The research was wrong **in that** it was based on bad information.
잘못된 정보를 바탕으로 했다는 점에서 그 조사는 잘못되었다.

3 관계대명사 that은 불완전한 문장을 이끌고, 접속사 that은 완전한 문장을 이끈다.

The detail **that** I wanted to know was on the company's website. (목적격 관계대명사, 목적어가 없는 불완전한 문장을 이끎)
내가 알고 싶었던 세부 사항은 그 회사의 웹사이트에 있었다.

I expect **that** you will finish the work in time. (접속사, 완전한 문장을 이끎)
나는 네가 시간 내에 그 일을 끝낼 것이라고 기대한다.

I like the idea **that** we should divide up the work. (동격의 접속사, 완전한 문장을 이끎, the idea = we should divide up the work)
나는 우리가 그 일을 나눠야 한다는 의견이 마음에 든다.

4 선행사를 포함하는 관계대명사 what은 the thing(s) that[which]으로 바꿔 쓸 수 있다. 이때 what이 이끄는 절은 문장 내에서 주어, 목적어, 보어 역할을 하는 명사절이다.

What I don't understand is why I can't go camping when final exams end. (주어)
내가 이해할 수 없는 것은 기말고사가 끝나도 왜 캠핑에 갈 수 없는 지이다.

Few people appreciate **what** they already have. (목적어)
이미 가지고 있는 것에 대해 감사하는 사람은 거의 없다.

Advice is **what** we ask for when we already know the answer. (보어)
조언은 자신이 답을 이미 알고 있으면서 부탁하는 것이다.

|정리| 1. 선행사를 포함한 what절은 문장 전체에서 주어, 목적어, 보어 역할을 하지만, 다른 관계대명사절은 선행사를 수식하는 형용사절의 역할을 한다.

2. 관계대명사 that이 관계대명사절 내에서 주어, 목적어, 보어 등의 역할을 대신하기 때문에 관계대명사 that 다음에는 주어나 목적어, 보어 중 하나가 빠진 불완전한 문장이 온다.

3. 접속사 that은 문장 내에서 주어, 목적어, 보어의 역할을 하지 않기 때문에 접속사 that 다음에는 완벽한 문장이 온다.

4. 접속사 that이 동격절을 이끄는 경우, 접속사 앞에 동격의 명사가 와서 선행사처럼 보이기도 하지만, that뒤에 완벽한 문장이 나오므로 동격절을 이끄는 접속사 that임을 알 수 있다. 동격절을 이끄는 that 앞에는 주로 the fact, the news, the idea, the information, the promise, the rumor, the opinion 등이 온다.

EXERCISES

정답 및 해설 P. 30

osteoporosis (의학) 골다공증(骨多孔症)
disease 병, 질병
affect ~에 영향을 미치다, 발생하다
mainly 주로
deny ~을 부인하다, 부정하다
circulate (소문 정보가) 퍼지다, 유포되다
recommend 추천하다
hillside 언덕, 산중턱
weaken ~을 약하게 하다, 약화시키다
due to ~때문에
episode 1회분의 이야기

( ) 안에서 알맞은 것을 모두 고르시오.

1 My brother works for a company (that / which) designs websites.

2 I showed Mom the shoes (that / which) I bought online last week.

3 Osteoporosis is a disease (that / which) affects mainly older people.

4 The pop star denied all the rumors (that / who) have been circulating.

5 The building, (that / which) was built in the 1950s, is now used as a museum.

6 The band played their latest hit, (that / which) had everyone sing along.

7 We stayed at the Paradise Hotel, (that / which) my friend recommended.

8 The picture at (that / which) he was looking was painted by a famous artist.

9 The hillside on (that / which) the houses are has been weakened due to the rain.

10 The latest episode of *24*, (that / which) I downloaded from the Internet, was really exciting.

11 The winter coat (that / which) you bought yesterday at Big Mart is on sale today for 50% off.

concern ~을 걱정스럽게 만들다
order 주문한 물건
illness 병, 질병
comfort 위로, 안락
importance 중요성
environmental 환경의
protection 보호, 보존

( ) 안에서 가장 알맞은 것을 고르시오.

1 Did you just hear (that / what) the teacher said?

2 I'm sorry, but I don't understand (that / what) you are trying to say.

3 The grades (that / what) he got this year were better than those from last year.

4 My friends (that / what) are visiting London will be back here next month.

5 I didn't know any of the people (that / what) had been invited to the party.

6 (That / What) really concerned us was how unhealthy the children looked.

7 The basketball game (that / what) we watched yesterday was very exciting.

8 (That / What) I wanted to know was how long it will take to receive my order.

9 The letters (that / what) you wrote during my illness gave me lots of comfort.

10 Though I asked her several times, she wouldn't tell me (that / what) he said.

11 I'm reading a book (that / what) is written about the importance of environmental protection.

C 밑줄 친 that을 관계대명사는 R(relative pronouns), 접속사는 C(conjunctions)로 나타내시오.

1 I heard that she may be living in Paris now. ______
2 Where can I get the bus that goes to COEX Mall? ______
3 She is the woman that I'd like to introduce you to. ______
4 Everybody firmly believed that they would make a difference. ______
5 That nobody was hurt in the explosion is indeed a miracle. ______
6 I promised my mother that I would be home by eight o'clock. ______
7 I found the information that I was looking for on the Internet. ______
8 The man was sent to prison for a crime that he didn't commit. ______
9 The man that told me how to get to the airport was very friendly. ______
10 Have you tried the Mexican restaurant that just opened in town? ______
11 Do you know that Teflon is the most slippery substance in the world? ______
12 I heard the news that Sue was chosen to be the valedictorian this year. ______

introduce ~을 소개하다
firmly 굳게
difference 차이
explosion 폭발
indeed 참으로, 정말로
miracle 기적
prison 감옥, 교도소
crime 죄, 범죄
commit (죄·과실 따위를) 범하다
Teflon (상표명) 테플론(열에 강한 합성수지)
slippery 미끄러운
substance 물질
valedictorian (고별 연설을 하는) 졸업생 대표

D 빈칸에 that 또는 what을 써넣으시오.

1 Honestly, I just can't decide ____________ I have to do next.
2 All the food ____________ was left out overnight has gone bad.
3 Tell Jennifer exactly ____________ you saw on your way to school.
4 Sam's story of ____________ happened that night is unbelievable.
5 I forgot the name of the little town ____________ we visited in France.
6 ____________ our team was going to win the game was never in doubt.
7 The chair ____________ you are sitting on was handcrafted by my father.
8 The weather forecast says ____________ a typhoon is approaching Japan.
9 He got me wrong. He just believed I did ____________ I never actually did.
10 The fact ____________ Richard already knows about his surprise party is disappointing.
11 I didn't like him because he ordered me to do ____________ he didn't want to do.
12 I'm reading a book by Douglas Kennedy ____________ has been translated into Korean.

decide ~을 결정하다
go bad (음식이) 상하다
unbelievable 믿기 어려운, 믿을 수 없는
in doubt 의심하여
handcrafted 손으로 만든, 수제품의
weather forecast 일기예보
typhoon 태풍
approach ~에 접근하다
get wrong ~을 오해하다
order ~에게 명령하다
translate into ~으로 번역[통역]하다

관계부사와 복합관계사

관계부사	
선행사(시간)+when	I remember the day **when** I first went to elementary school. 나는 처음 초등학교에 갔던 날을 기억한다.
선행사(장소)+where	Look around the place **where** you're going to live. 네가 살 곳을 한 번 둘러보아라.
선행사(이유)+why	I'd like to know the reason **why** she didn't finish her homework. 나는 그녀가 숙제를 끝내지 않은 이유를 알고 싶다.

복합관계사	
복합 관계대명사 (선행사 포함)	• whichever, whoever, whatever, whomever You can do **whatever** you want. 너는 원하는 것은 무엇이든 할 수 있다.
복합 관계부사 (선행사 포함)	• whenever, wherever, however **Wherever** you go, you will see this sign. 너는 어디를 가더라도 이 표시를 보게 될 거야.

FOCUS

1 선행사가 시간을 의미할 때 관계부사 when을 쓰고, 관계부사는 「전치사+관계대명사」로 바꿔 쓸 수 있다.

I can't forget **the day.**

\+ I first met my wife **on that day.**

→ I can't forget the day **when [on which]** I first met my wife. 나는 아내를 처음 만난 날을 잊을 수가 없다.

|참고| 1. 관계부사절 안에서 관계부사는 부사의 역할을 하므로, 관계부사가 이끄는 절은 완전한 문장이 된다.

2. 관계부사가 이끄는 절은 앞에 나오는 선행사를 수식하는 형용사절이다.
There was a time **when** dinosaurs roamed around the earth. 공룡이 지구를 돌아다녔던 시절이 있었다.

3. 관계부사 when은 일상 회화에서 생략하는 경우가 많고, that으로 대체해서 쓰기도 한다.
I will never forget the time **(when)** I went abroad for the first time.
→ I will never forget the time **that** I went abroad for the first time. 나는 처음으로 해외에 나갔던 때를 잊지 못할 것이다.

2 선행사가 장소를 의미할 때 관계부사 where를 쓰고, 관계부사는 「전치사+관계대명사」로 바꿔 쓸 수 있다.

Traditional classrooms are **the places.**

\+ Students work with a teacher face-to-face **in that place.**

→ Traditional classrooms are the places **where [in which]** students work with a teacher face-to-face.
전통적인 교실은 학생들이 선생님과 얼굴을 마주하고 공부하는 공간이다.

3

선행사가 이유를 의미할 때 관계부사 why를 쓰고, 관계부사는 「전치사+관계대명사」로 바꿔 쓸 수 있다.

Experts insist that this is **the reason**.

+ Dinosaurs vanished **for that reason**.

→ Experts insist that this is the reason **why[for which]** dinosaurs vanished.
전문가들은 이것이 공룡이 사라진 이유라고 주장한다.

|참고| 선행사가 time, place, reason일 때 관계부사 또는 선행사를 생략할 수 있다. 회화에서 관계부사 when은 주로 생략하고, where나 why는 잘 생략하지 않는다. 관계부사 when, where, why는 that으로 바꿔 쓸 수 있다.

4

선행사가 방식(the way)을 의미할 때 관계부사 how를 쓰고, 관계부사는 「전치사+관계대명사」로 바꿔 쓸 수 있다. 하지만 the way와 how는 같이 쓸 수 없다.

She taught us **the way**.

+ We could persuade others effectively **in that way**.

→ She taught us the way **in which** we could persuade others effectively.

→ She taught us **the way** we could persuade others effectively.

→ She taught us **how** we could persuade others effectively.
그녀가 사람들을 효과적으로 설득할 수 있는 방법을 가르쳐 주었다.

(×) She taught us ~~the way how~~ we could persuade others effectively.

5

whoever, whomever, whatever, whichever는 선행사를 포함하는 복합 관계대명사이다. 복합 관계대명사는 관계사절 내에서 주어, 목적어, 보어 역할을 한다.

Give this to **whoever[anyone who]** wants to keep it. 간직하고 싶어 하는 사람이 누구든지 이것을 주어라.

Give this to **whomever[anyone whom]** you like. 네가 좋아하는 사람이 누구든지 이것을 주어라.

|참고| 1. whoever ~하는 사람은 누구든지(anyone who), 누가 ~해도(no matter who)
whichever/whatever ~하는 것은 무엇이든지(anything which, anything that), 무엇이(무엇을) ~해도(no matter which, no matter what)
2. who(m)ever, whatever, whichever는 양보의 부사절(~하더라도)을 이끌 수 있다.
Whoever[No matter who] gets it, no one will be satisfied. 누가 그것을 갖게 되더라도, 아무도 만족하지 못할 것이다.
Whatever[No matter what] happens, I'll be there for you. 무슨 일이 있더라도, 내가 너를 위해 거기 있을 게.
Whichever[No matter which] you choose, I'll buy it for you. 네가 어떤 것을 선택하든지 간에, 내가 너를 위해 그것을 사 줄게.

6

whenever, wherever, however는 '복합 관계부사'라고 하며, 관계부사절 내에서 부사 역할을 한다. 복합 관계부사는 시간, 장소, 양보의 부사절을 이끈다.

Whenever[Every time] I study, I turn off the TV. 나는 공부할 때면 언제나 TV를 끈다.

Please sit **wherever[at any place that]** you want. 앉고 싶은 곳 어디든지 앉으세요.

However[No matter how] bitter it tastes, it is good for your health. 아무리 그것이 쓰더라도, 그것은 너의 건강에 좋다.

|참고| whenever ~할 때마다, ~할 때는 언제라도(at any time when, every time), 언제 ~해도(no matter when)
wherever ~하는 곳은 어디든지(at any place where), 어디로 ~하더라도(no matter where)
however 아무리 ~하더라도(no matter how)

EXERCISES

정답 및 해설 P. 31

refuse 거절하다
expert 전문가
form 형성되다
reach ~에 닿다
propose to ~에게 청혼하다
fiancée (여자) 약혼녀
cf. fiancé (남자) 약혼자
immediately 즉시, 곧
terrorist 테러리스트
attack 공격하다, 습격하다

A

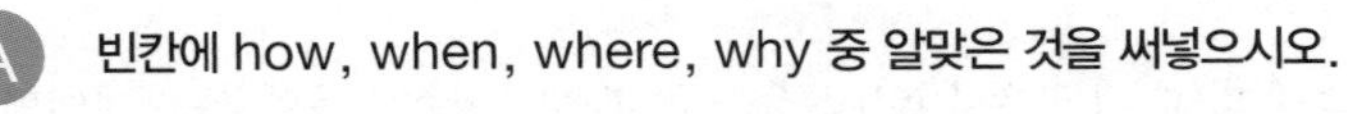

빈칸에 how, when, where, why 중 알맞은 것을 써넣으시오.

1 I don't know the reason ______ my dog keeps refusing to eat.

2 Experts still don't know exactly ______ the universe was formed.

3 Nineteen-sixty nine is the year ______ man reached the moon for the first time.

4 The star chef showed on TV ______ he makes bread without butter.

5 This is the restaurant ______ Greg proposed to his fiancée last week.

6 Do you know the reason ______ many Koreans learn English?

7 The police immediately arrived at the place ______ the car accident happened.

8 September 11, 2001, was the day ______ terrorists attacked the World Trade Center in New York.

plant 공장; 식물
produce ~을 생산하다
air craft 항공기
be born in ~에서 태어나다
pronunciation 발음
look forward to ~을 기대하다
Thanksgiving Day 추수 감사절
celebrate 축하하다
harvest 추수

B

〈보기〉와 같이 관계부사를 이용한 문장으로 바꿔 쓰시오.

보기 This is the plant. Air Fast produces its popular aircraft in that plant.
→ The is the plant where Air Fast produces its popular aircraft.

1 I really like the way. She dresses in that way.
→ ______

2 Do you know the reason? Jay isn't in class today for that reason.
→ ______

3 Edinburgh is the town. Alexander Graham Bell was born in that town.
→ ______

4 She didn't want to tell me the reason. She missed the class for that reason.
→ ______

5 Jim asked his teacher the way. He could improve his pronunciation in that way.
→ ______

6 All the students look forward to the day. Summer vacation begins on that day.
→ ______

7 Thanksgiving Day is the day. All the family members gather to celebrate the harvest on that day.
→ ______

C 밑줄 친 부분을 바르게 고치시오.

1 This is the exact spot <u>why</u> the car collided with the bus.

2 Can you tell me <u>the way how</u> you plan to spend your time?

3 Two thousand five was the year <u>where</u> Jisu got her MBA from Princeton.

4 Tokyo has lots of small restaurants <u>how</u> you can eat cheaply.

5 I will explain the reason <u>when</u> you failed to get a passing grade.

6 My father taught me <u>the way how</u> I can assemble the model plane.

7 The day <u>which</u> your mother and I got married was cold and rainy.

8 The part of town <u>which</u> I grew up has been completely redeveloped.

9 Next Thursday is the day <u>who</u> the repairman will come to the house.

10 Nineteen-eighty eight was the year <u>where</u> Korea hosted the Olympic Games in Seoul.

11 We were upset to hear <u>whom</u> she had been treated by the security staff.

12 I will show you three easy <u>ways how</u> you can quickly improve your English.

exact 정확한
spot 지점
collide with ~와 충돌하다, 부딪치다
MBA(=Master of Business Administration) 경영학 석사
passing grade 합격점
assemble ~을 조립하다
completely 완전히
redevelop ~을 재개발하다, 재건하다
repairman 수리공
host ~을 주최하다
treat 대우를 받다
security staff 안전 요원

D ( ) 안에서 가장 알맞은 것을 고르시오.

1 (However / Whichever) tired you are, you must do it.

2 (Whatever / Wherever) you decide to do, your parents will support you.

3 Try to use olive oil instead of butter (whenever / whoever) it is possible.

4 We can go (wherever / however) you like on vacation. The sky's the limit!

5 There's a reward for (whoever / however) finds and returns Haily's poodle.

6 I'm here to support you (whatever / however) happens, so just do your best.

7 Feel free to give the extra concert ticket to (wherever / whomever) you please.

8 Commander Graham has to go (wherever / whoever) the Royal Navy sends him.

9 We're going to play volleyball on the beach tomorrow (whatever / whenever) the weather is like.

10 (However / Whoever) smart you think you are, you'll find Professor Kim's class a challenge.

11 (Whatever / Whoever) spilled cola on my desk and didn't clean it up is a really bad guy.

support ~을 지지하다
possible 가능한
The sky's the limit. (구어) 제한 없다, 한도가 없다
reward 현상금, 사례금
poodle 푸들
do one's best 최선을 다하다
feel free to 마음대로 ~해도 좋다
extra 여분의
commander (해군) (군함의) 부함장, 해군 중령
Royal Navy 영국 해군
challenge 도전
spill ~을 엎지르다
clean up 치우다

REVIEW

정답 및 해설 P. 31

check out 확인하다
face (사실 등에) 직면하다
consequence 결과; 귀추
run across ~을 뛰어서 건너다
be born 태어나다
chore 집안일

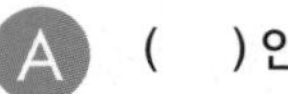

A (　) 안에서 가장 알맞은 것을 고르시오.

1 There's no reason (how / why) our plan shouldn't succeed.

2 The man (with whom / whom) I did the last project was quite helpful.

3 The hat (that / whom) you are wearing is rather large for your head.

4 The woman (which / who) checked out your condition is a nurse.

5 (Whatever / Why) the reason is, fewer people are shopping these days.

6 Mr. Smith or just Steve, you can call me (whatever / whoever) you like.

7 The computer (that / who) I use for work is too old.

8 (What / That) Tim did was wrong. Now he has to face the consequences.

9 The child (who / whom) runs across the field fastest will receive a prize.

10 The place (where / which) I was born is so small that you can't even find it on a map.

11 You have to do your chores today, (however / whatever) much you don't feel like doing them.

12 The boy (for whom / whom) we saw waiting outside the school this morning is Jenny's brother.

clerk 점원
right 옳은, 올바른
subject 주제; 과목
apologize 사과하다
valuable 가치 있는
ATM(=automatic teller machine) 현금 자동 입출금기
withdraw ~을 인출하다

B 〈보기〉에서 어법과 문맥에 알맞은 것을 골라 문장을 완성하시오.

보기	whose	that	what	whenever	which
	however	whatever	when	whom	

1 If I really like something, I'll buy it ___________ much it costs.

2 July is the month ___________ most Americans go on holiday.

3 Is this the sales clerk to ___________ you spoke the other day?

4 ___________ you decide to do, I'm sure it will be the right choice.

5 Sports is a subject about ___________ my father can talk for hours.

6 This is the man ___________ window you broke. Now please apologize.

7 ___________ I find the most valuable now is happiness.

8 We have a 24 hour ATM. You can withdraw money ___________ you wish.

9 This is the only picture ___________ the artist ever sold before his death.

C 〈보기〉에서 알맞은 것을 골라 빈칸에 that이나 what을 넣어 문장을 완성하시오.

보기
ⓐ ____ he told me
ⓑ ____ you can offer
ⓒ ____ she has to do next
ⓓ ____ you saw at the museum
ⓔ ____ gave a performance last night
ⓕ ____ I borrowed from the library yesterday
ⓖ ____ I need to plug in the notebook computer
ⓗ ____ I want to wear to the graduation ceremony

1 I can't believe ______________________. He tends to exaggerate.

2 I can't find the books ______________________.

3 She isn't quite sure ______________________. She needs advice.

4 Where's the adapter ______________________?

5 How was the museum? Tell me ______________________.

6 This is the outfit ______________________.

7 The hip-hop band ______________________ was fantastic.

8 Is this the best price ______________________?

offer ~을 제공하다
performance 공연
plug in (기구에) 플러그를 꽂아 접속하다
graduation ceremony 졸업식
tend to ~하는 경향이 있다
exaggerate 과장하다
adapter (전기·기계) 어댑터
outfit 의복

D 밑줄 친 부분을 어법에 맞게 고치시오.

1 The brown boots who are by the front door are mine.

2 The engineers which designed that building received an award.

3 The book what you are reading is the best book by that author.

4 The rumors what are being spread about Cindy are totally untrue.

5 I lost my address book in that I had all of my important contacts.

6 That I want to know is how long it will take to fix the broken heater.

7 I cry whoever I think about the day I left Holland to come to the USA.

8 This jacket will look great and make you stand out what the occasion is.

9 The camp counselor taught the kids the way how they could catch fish for dinner.

engineer 기술자
design ~을 설계하다
author 저자, 작가
spread ~을 퍼뜨리다
untrue 사실이 아닌
address book 주소록
contact 연락처
Holland 네덜란드
stand out 눈에 띄는, 훌륭한
occasion (특정한) 때, 경우
counselor 카운슬러, 상담사

REVIEW PLUS

정답 및 해설 P. 33

be born 태어나다
feature ~을 볼거리로 삼다
musical instrument 악기
common 흔히 있는
work on 작업하다

A 다음 (A), (B)에 들어갈 말이 바르게 짝지어진 것을 고르시오.

1

- This is the town ___(A)___ your grandfather was born and raised.
- The street performances, ___(B)___ feature singing and playing musical instruments, are common in Europe.

	(A)	(B)
①	which	which
②	where	which
③	where	that
④	which	that
⑤	which	who

2

- What happened to the file ___(A)___ you were working on?
- My best friend, ___(B)___ I see every day at school, always has something new and interesting to tell me.

	(A)	(B)
①	that	whom
②	that	that
③	which	whose
④	that	that
⑤	who	who

do something for a living 직업으로 ~을 하다
describe 묘사하다, 설명하다
jury 배심원

B 다음 밑줄 친 단어의 쓰임이 다른 하나를 고르시오.

① What he wants to know is your name.
② What does your father do for a living?
③ Describe to the jury exactly what you saw.
④ This letter shows clearly what they are planning.
⑤ I didn't have much money, but I gave him what I had.

early adopter 얼리어댑터, 앞선사용자
rush out 급하게 ~하다
electronic 전자의
gadget 작고 편리한 기계
queue 줄을 서다
picky 까다로운, (사소한 일에) 법석을 떠는
recommend ~을 추천하다
drop (가격이) 떨어지다
afford ~을 살 여유가 있다

C 다음을 읽고, (　) 안에서 가장 알맞은 것을 고르시오.

Early adopters are people ① (who / whom) rush out to buy new electronic gadgets before anyone else does. They can be found in shopping malls where they will queue for hours to buy the latest products. Early adopters are a little picky, but when they like something ② (what / that) they have bought, they will recommend it to others. Over time, prices for these gadgets drop to a point ③ (which / where) general consumers can afford them, too.

PART 18

가정법
Subjunctive Mood

가정법 과거

가정법 과거 ~라면 …할 텐데	**If** I **were** Superman, I **could fly**. 내가 슈퍼맨이라면 날 수 있을 텐데. → As I'm not Superman, I can't fly. 나는 슈퍼맨이 아니라서 날 수 없다. **If** I **had** enough money, I **would buy** a new computer. 내가 돈이 충분히 있다면, 새 컴퓨터를 살 텐데. → As I don't have enough money, I won't buy a new computer. 나는 돈이 충분하지 않기 때문에, 새 컴퓨터를 사지 않을 것이다.
조건절 ~한다면 …할 것이다	**If** I **win** this game, my mom **will buy** me a new computer. 만약 내가 이 게임에서 이긴다면, 우리 엄마가 나에게 새 컴퓨터를 사줄 것이다.

FOCUS

1

가정법 과거는 현재 사실을 반대로 가정하거나, 실현 가능성이 낮은 일을 가정할 때 쓴다.

「If+주어+동사의 과거형 ~, 주어+조동사의 과거형+동사원형 ~.」 ~라면 …할 텐데

If I **were** rich, I **could buy** a yacht. 내가 부자라면 요트를 살 텐데.

→ As I'**m not** rich, I **can't buy** a yacht. 나는 부자가 아니라서 요트를 살 수 없다.

If I **had** enough time, I **could help** you. 내가 시간이 충분하다면, 너를 도와 줄 텐데.

→ As I **don't have** enough time, I **can't help** you. 나는 시간이 없어서 너를 도와 줄 수 없다.

|참고| 가정법의 if절에서 be동사는 주어의 인칭이나 수에 관계없이 were를 쓰지만, 구어체에서는 was를 쓰기도 한다.

If the student **were** wise enough, he would not skip classes.

→ If the student **was** wise enough, he would not skip classes. 그 학생이 충분히 현명하다면 수업에 빠지지 않을 텐데.

2

if가 쓰였다고 해서 모두 가정법은 아니다. 단순 조건과 가정법 과거의 문장을 구별해야 한다. 단순 조건은 실현 가능성이 있을 때 쓰고, 가정법 과거는 실현 가능성이 거의 없을 때 쓴다.

If I'**m** free tomorrow, I **will join** you. (조건, 내일 시간이 날 수 있음)
내가 내일 시간이 있으면 너와 함께 할게.

If I **were** free today, I **would join** you. (가정법 과거, 나는 오늘 시간이 없음)
내가 오늘 시간이 있으면 너와 함께 할 텐데.

|참고| if를 쓰지 않고 조동사만으로 가정법의 뉘앙스를 살릴 수 있다. 이때 조동사는 항상 과거형으로 쓴다.

Couldn't be better. (이보다 더 좋을 순 없다.) 정말 잘 지내고 있어.

I'm so tired. I **could** sleep a week. 나는 정말 피곤해. 일주일도 잘 수 있겠어.

A wise student **would** not cheat on the test. 현명한 학생이라면 시험에서 부정행위를 하지는 않을 텐데.

EXERCISES

정답 및 해설 P. 33

A ( ) 안에서 알맞은 것을 고르시오.

1 If Boeun (goes / went) to Japan, she will learn Japanese.

2 If Wilson (doesn't arrive / didn't arrive) soon, he will miss the train.

3 If Suji (speaks / spoke) Chinese, she could travel more easily in Beijing.

4 If Miriam's eyesight (is / were) better, she would not need to wear glasses.

5 If Amy studies hard, she (could / can) enter the school she wants to go to.

B 〈보기〉와 같이 가정법 과거 문장을 완성하시오.

proposed 계획된
trans-Korea 한국을 가로지르는
railroad 철도
complete 완성하다
rail 기차

보기 As I don't have time, I can't spend a week at the beach.
→ If I had time, I could spend a week at the beach.

1 As we are not in Paris, we can't see the Eiffel Tower.
→ ______________________________

2 As the weather isn't good, Jason won't take his dogs for a walk.
→ ______________________________

3 As they don't have enough money, they can't build the proposed tower.
→ ______________________________

4 As the trans-Korea railroad isn't completed, we can't travel by rail to Europe.
→ ______________________________

C 주어진 동사를 알맞은 형태로 바꿔 조건 또는 가정법 과거 문장을 완성하시오.

global warming 지구 온난화
sea level 해수면
economy 경제
pocket money 용돈
Antarctic 남극
decrease 감소하다
have difficulty -ing ~하는 데 어려움을 겪다
greenhouse gas 온실 가스
reduce ~을 감소시키다
emission 배출(물)

1 If it __________ (snow) a lot, we would go out and make a snowman.

2 If global warming __________ (continue), the sea levels may rise seriously.

3 If the economy __________ (be) better, my parents could give me more pocket money.

4 There are too many cars in Seoul. If there __________ (be) fewer cars, the traffic wouldn't be so heavy.

5 If the number of fish in the Antarctic __________ (decrease) much more, the penguins will have difficulty finding food.

6 Many countries produce a lot of greenhouse gases. If we __________ (want) to control global warming, we must reduce greenhouse gas emissions.

가정법 과거완료 & 혼합 가정법

가정법 과거완료 ~했더라면 … 했을 텐데	**If I had known** you were sick, I **would have gone** to see you. 나는 네가 아픈 걸 알았다면 너를 보러 갔을 텐데. → As I didn't know you were sick, I didn't go to see you. 나는 네가 아픈 것을 몰랐기 때문에 너를 보러 가지 않았다.
혼합 가정법 (과거에) ~했더라면 (지금) …할 텐데	**If I had had** enough sleep, I **wouldn't be** tired now. 잠을 충분히 잤더라면, 지금 피곤하지 않을 텐데. → As I didn't have enough sleep, I am tired now. 나는 잠을 충분히 자지 못했기 때문에, 지금 피곤하다.

1

가정법 과거완료는 과거 사실을 반대로 가정할 때 쓴다.

「If+주어+had+p.p. ~, 주어+조동사의 과거형+have+p.p. ~」 ~했다면 …했을 텐데

If I had known the truth, I **would have told** you. 내가 진실을 알았더라면, 너에게 말해 줬을 텐데.

→ As I **didn't know** the truth, I **didn't tell** you. 나는 진실을 몰랐기 때문에 너에게 말하지 않았다.

If Pinocchio **hadn't lied**, his nose **wouldn't have grown**. 피노키오가 거짓말을 하지 않았다면, 그의 코는 자라지 않았을 텐데.

→ As Pinocchio **lied**, his nose **grew**. 피노키오가 거짓말을 했기 때문에, 그의 코가 자랐다.

2

혼합 가정법은 과거 사실에 반대되는 가정의 결과가 현재에 영향을 줄 때 쓴다. 조건절에서는 가정법 과거완료를, 주절에서는 가정법 과거를 쓴다.

「If+주어+had+p.p. ~, 주어+조동사의 과거형+동사원형 ~」 (과거에) ~했다면 (지금) …할 텐데

If Woojin **had gone** to Canada to study, he **could speak** English and French now.
우진이가 캐나다로 공부를 하러 갔었다면, 지금 영어와 불어를 할 수 있을 텐데.

→ As Woojin **didn't go** to Canada to study, he **can't speak** English and French now.
우진이는 캐나다로 공부하러 가지 않았기 때문에, 지금 불어와 영어를 할 수 없다.

If Harry **had paid** more attention in class, he **wouldn't worry** about the test now.
해리가 수업 중에 더 집중을 했더라면, 지금 시험에 대해 걱정하지 않을 텐데.

→ As Harry **didn't pay** more attention in class, he **worries** about the test now.
해리가 수업에 더 집중을 하지 않아서, 지금 시험에 대해 걱정한다.

3

「should have+p.p.」 '~했어야 했는데, 그러지 못해서 후회된다'라는 의미로 과거에 하지 않은 일에 대한 후회나 유감을 나타낼 때 쓴다.

I **should have taken** the doctor's advice. (의사의 충고를 따르지 않았다.) 나는 의사의 충고를 따랐어야 했는데.

It was a great party last night. You **should have come**. (너는 파티에 오지 않았다.) 어젯밤 파티는 정말 재미있었어. 너도 왔어야 했는데.

기타 should 관련 용법

1

요구, 주장, 제안 등을 나타내는 동사 뒤에 나온 that절에 should를 쓴다. 이때 should는 생략 가능하다.

advise ~을 조언하다	ask ~을 요청하다	command ~을 명령하다	demand ~을 요구하다
desire ~을 요구하다	insist ~을 주장하다	order ~을 명령하다	propose ~을 제안하다
recommend ~을 권하다	request ~을 요청하다	require ~을 필요로 하다	suggest ~을 제안하다

He **demanded (that)** she **(should) apologize** to him. 그는 그녀가 그에게 사과할 것을 요구했다.

They **insisted (that)** he **(should) not bring** them a present. 그들은 그에게 선물을 절대 가져오지 말라고 고집했다.

2

요구, 주장, 제안 등을 나타내는 동사라도 that절 이하가 어떤 일이 이루어지기를 바라는 것이 아니라, 사실을 있는 그대로 전달하는 내용이라면 should를 쓰지 않고 동사를 인칭, 수, 시제에 맞춰 쓴다.

His behavior **suggested that** he **wasn't** satisfied with my work. 그의 행동은 그가 나의 일에 만족하지 못했다는 것을 암시했다.

He **insisted that** he **didn't take** bribes. 그는 뇌물을 받지 않았다고 주장했다.

3

요구, 당연, 필요 등의 주관적 감정을 나타내는 형용사 뒤에 나온 that절에 should를 쓴다.
이때 should를 생략하고 동사원형만 쓰기도 한다.

desirable 바람직한	essential 필수적인	imperative 긴급한, 필수적인	important 중요한
natural 당연한	necessary 필요한	vital 필수적인	urgent 긴급한

It's **important that** he **(should) understand** how serious the situation is.
그가 상황이 얼마나 심각한지 이해하는 것이 중요하다.

It's **essential that** she **(should) not fail** any courses.
그녀에게는 어느 한 과정이라도 낙제하지 않는 것이 매우 중요하다.

4

영국식 영어에서는 요구, 주장, 제안을 나타내는 동사나 형용사 뒤의 that절에서도 should를 쓰지 않고 인칭이나 수에 따라 동사를 변형시켜 쓰기도 한다.

I **suggest that** he **should join** us.

→ I **suggest that** he **joins** us. 나는 그에게 우리와 함께할 것을 제안한다.

5

조건절에 were to나 should를 쓰면 일어날 가능성이 희박한 일을 의미한다.

If the sun **were to** rise in the west, I would believe him. 해가 서쪽에서 뜬다면 나는 그를 믿겠다.

If it **should** rain tomorrow, I would not go on a picnic. 내일 혹시라도 비가 온다면 나는 소풍을 가지 않을 것이다.

EXCERCISES

정답 및 해설 P. 34

judge 심판, 심사원
fair 공평한, 공정한
match 시합, 경기; 성냥
radar (전자) 레이더, 전파 탐지기
available 사용할 수 있는
strike ~에 부딪히다
iceberg 빙산
sink ~에 가라앉다
bald eagle 흰머리 독수리
endangered (동·식물이) 멸종 위기에 처해 있는
scholarship 장학금
apply for ~에 지원하다

A 주어진 문장을 〈보기〉와 같이 가정법 과거완료 문장으로 바꿔 쓰시오.

보기 As Sam made so many mistakes, he didn't get a good score.
→ If Sam hadn't made so many mistakes, he would have gotten a good score.

1 As the judges weren't fair, our team couldn't win the gold medal.
→ ______________________________

2 As our teammate Jinho was sick, we didn't win the volleyball match.
→ ______________________________

3 As radar wasn't available, the Titanic struck the iceberg and sank.
→ ______________________________

4 As we cut down so many trees, the bald eagle became endangered.
→ ______________________________

5 As he didn't save enough money, he couldn't buy a car.
→ ______________________________

6 As I didn't know there were various kinds of scholarships, I didn't apply for them.
→ ______________________________

spill ~을 엎지르다
invent ~을 발명하다
how to + 동사원형 ~하는 방법
knit ~을 짜다, 뜨다

B 주어진 문장을 〈보기〉와 같이 혼합 가정법 문장으로 바꿔 쓰시오.

보기 As Joshua didn't wear a coat yesterday, he feels sick now.
→ If Joshua had worn a coat yesterday, he wouldn't feel sick now.

1 As I didn't study French, I have a difficult time traveling in Africa now.
→ ______________________________

2 As my brother spilled milk over my computer, I need to buy a new one.
→ ______________________________

3 As Bell invented the telephone, we can live a comfortable life.
→ ______________________________

4 As Mom went out to meet her friend, she can't teach you how to knit.
→ ______________________________

5 As we didn't leave home earlier, we can't enter the musical theater now.
→ ______________________________

6 As I didn't turn on the alarm last night, I am not on the school bus now.
→ ______________________________

C 주어진 동사를 알맞은 형태로 바꿔 가정법 문장을 완성하시오.

1 If you hadn't insisted on taking this shortcut, we wouldn't ________________ (be) lost now.

2 If he hadn't spent so much money on clothes, he would ________________ (have) some money now.

3 I can't finish my homework. If I ________________ (not, go) to the party, I wouldn't need to worry now.

4 I didn't know you were coming for a visit. If I ________________ (know), I would ________________ (clean) the house.

5 If I ________________ (sing) better at the party last night, I wouldn't ________________ (embarrass) myself in front of my friends.

6 The dinosaurs were killed by a giant asteroid collision. If the dinosaurs ________________ (not, become) extinct, humans might never have come to rule the planet.

7 The Romans defeated the great Carthaginian general Hannibal at the battle of Zama. If Hannibal ________________ (defeat) the Romans, European history would have been very different.

shortcut 지름길
dinosaur 공룡
asteroid 소행성
collision 충돌
extinct 멸종된, 사라진
rule ~을 통치하다
the planet 지구
defeat ~을 패배시키다
general 장군; 대장; 일반의
battle 전쟁

D 주어진 동사와 후회, 유감을 나타내는 표현을 이용하여 문장을 완성하시오.

1 Everything went wrong. I ________________ (listen) to your advice.

2 We've missed our stop. We ________________ (get off) at the last stop.

3 Fred got poor scores on his finals. He ________________ (study) harder.

4 It is colder than I thought today. I'm freezing. I ________________ (wear) a heavier coat.

5 Sandra is a great actress. She ________________ (win) an Emmy for her role in *Grey's Anatomy*.

6 The natural beauty of Victoria is spectacular. We ________________ (take) more pictures while we were there.

7 We missed Jessica's concert because we couldn't get tickets. We ________________ (buy) tickets when they first went on sale.

go wrong 잘못되다
stop 정거장
final 결승전
actress 여배우
role 역할
natural beauty 자연미
spectacular 장관인, 굉장한
go on sale 판매를 시작하다

기타 가정법

I wish+가정법 과거 ~라면 좋을 텐데	**I wish I had** a cell phone like that. 저런 휴대 전화를 가지면 좋을 텐데. → I'm sorry I don't have a cell phone like that. 저런 휴대 전화를 가지지 못해서 유감이다.
I wish+가정법 과거완료 ~했더라면 좋을 텐데	**I wish I had brought** my lunch. 점심을 가져왔으면 좋을 텐데. → I'm sorry I didn't bring my lunch. 점심을 가져오지 않아 유감이다.
as if+가정법 과거 마치 ~인 것처럼 …한다/했다	She acts **as if** she **knew** nothing about it. 그녀는 마치 그것에 대해 아무것도 모르는 것처럼 행동한다. → In fact, she knows about it. 사실, 그녀는 그것에 대해 안다.
as if+가정법 과거완료 마치 ~였던 것처럼 …한다/했다	She talks **as if** she **had heard** the story before. 그녀는 마치 그 이야기를 전에 들었던 것처럼 말한다. → In fact, she didn't hear the story before. 사실 그녀는 전에 그 이야기를 듣지 못했다.

FOCUS

1

「I wish+가정법 과거」는 '~라면 좋을 텐데'라는 의미로 현재 사실에 대한 유감이나 이루기 힘든 소망 등을 표현할 때 쓴다. 「I wish+가정법 과거」는 wish의 시제와 동일한 시점에서 사실을 반대로 가정한다.

I wish I knew why he is upset with me. 그 사람이 왜 화가 난 건지 알면 좋겠는데.

→ I'm sorry I don't know why he is upset with me. 나는 왜 그가 나에게 화가 난 건지 몰라서 유감이다.

I wish I could speak English fluently. 영어를 유창하게 할 수 있으면 좋겠는데.

→ I'm sorry I can't speak English fluently. 나는 영어를 유창하게 할 수 없어서 유감이다.

|참고| 「I wish+주어+would」는 '~가 …하면 좋을 텐데'라는 뜻으로 실현되지 않을 것 같은 일에 대한 불만을 표현할 때 쓴다.
「I wish+주어+wouldn't」는 '~가 …하지 않으면 좋을 텐데'라는 뜻으로 누군가의 반복된 행동이나 미래에 일어날 것 같은 일에 대한 불만을 표현할 때 쓴다.

I wish he **would** listen to my advice. 그가 내 충고를 들으면 좋을 텐데.

I wish people **wouldn't** throw trash anywhere. 사람들이 아무데나 쓰레기를 버리지 않으면 좋을 텐데.

2

「I wish+가정법 과거완료」는 '~했다면 좋을 텐데'라는 의미로 과거에 이루지 못한 소망이나 유감 등을 표현할 때 쓴다. 「I wish+가정법 과거완료」는 wish의 시제보다 한 시제 앞서는 시점에서 사실을 반대로 가정한다.

I wish your company **had been** successful. 당신의 회사가 성공했으면 좋을 텐데요.

→ I'm sorry your company wasn't successful. 당신의 회사가 성공하지 못해서 유감입니다.

I wish I had taken some pictures of the beautiful scenery. 아름다운 풍경 사진을 찍었다면 좋을 텐데.

→ I'm sorry I didn't take some pictures of the beautiful scenery. 아름다운 풍경 사진을 찍지 않았던 것이 유감이다.

3

「as if[as though]+가정법 과거」는 '마치 ~인 것처럼 …한다/했다'라는 의미로 현재 사실에 반대되는 내용을 가정하는 것으로 실제 그렇지 않지만, 마치 그런 것처럼 한다는 의미이다. 단, 주절의 시제에 따라 가정법 과거는 주절의 시제와 같은 시점을 일을 가정한다.

Tom **talks as if** he **were** an expert. 톰은 마치 자신이 전문가인 것처럼 말한다.

→ In fact, Tom isn't an expert. 사실, 톰은 전문가가 아니다.

Tom **talked as if** he **were** an expert. 톰은 마치 자신이 전문가인 것처럼 말했다.

→ In fact, Tom wasn't an expert. 사실, 톰은 전문가가 아니었다.

4

「as if[as though]+가정법 과거완료」는 '마치 ~였던 것처럼 …한다/했다'라는 의미로 과거 사실에 반대되는 내용을 가정하는 것으로 실제 그렇지 않았지만, 마치 그랬던 것처럼 한다는 의미이다. 단, 주절의 시제에 따라 가정법 과거완료는 주절의 시제보다 한 시제 앞서는 시점의 일을 가정한다.

Tom **talks as if** he **had been** a professional photographer. 톰은 전문 사진작가였던 것처럼 말한다.

→ In fact, Tom wasn't a professional photographer. 사실, 톰은 전문 사진작가가 아니었다.

Tom **talked as if** he **had been** a professional photographer. 톰은 자신이 전문 사진작가였던 것처럼 말했다.

→ In fact, Tom hadn't been a professional photographer. 사실, 톰은 전문 사진작가가 아니었다.

|참고| as if, as though가 '마치 ~인 것처럼'이라는 의미의 부사절을 이끄는 접속사로 사용할 때는 직설법을 사용할 수 있다. 이때는 as if절에 현재 시제를 쓸 수 있다.

He looks **as if** he **is** very tired. (직설법) 그는 아주 피곤해 보인다.

→ I don't know whether he is very tired or not. 나는 그가 아주 피곤한지 아닌지 모른다.

He acts **as if** he **were** very tired. (가정법) 그는 아주 피곤한 것처럼 행동한다.

→ In fact, he isn't very tired. 사실, 그는 아주 피곤하지 않다.

5

가정문에서 if를 생략할 경우, 주어와 동사를 도치 시킨다.

If I were in your place, I would think one more time before I acted.

→ **Were I** in your place, I would think one more time before I acted.
내가 너의 입장이라면 행동으로 옮기기 전에 한 번 더 생각해 볼 텐데.

If you hadn't stayed up playing games all night, you wouldn't have fallen asleep during class.

→ **Had you not stayed up** playing games all night, you wouldn't have fallen asleep during class.
네가 게임을 하느라고 밤새 깨어 있지 않았다면, 수업 중에 잠들지 않았을 텐데.

|참고| 1. 「If it were not for ~」, 「If it had not been for ~」는 But for 또는 Without으로 바꿔 쓸 수 있다. '~가 없다면/없었다면 ~할 텐데/했을 텐데'라는 의미를 나타낸다.

If it were not for the assignment, we could go to the party this weekend.

→ **But for** the assignment, we could go to the party this weekend.

→ **Without** the assignment, we could go to the party this weekend. 과제가 없다면 이번 주말에 파티에 갈 수 있을 텐데.

If it had not been for your help, I could not have finished my project.

→ **But for** your help, I could not have finished my project.

→ **Without** your help, I could not have finished my project. 너의 도움이 없었다면 나의 프로젝트를 끝내지 못했을 텐데.

2. 「It's time+가정법 과거」는 '이제 ~할 시간이다'라는 의미로 진작했어야 하는데 하지 않았다는 유감의 의미를 내포할 때 사용한다. 「It's time+to부정사」의 형태로 쓰는 경우에는 유감의 뉘앙스가 없이 '~할 시간이다'라는 의미를 나타낸다.

It's time you **went** to bed. ('진작 잤어야 하는데 그러지 않았다'라는 내용을 내포) 너는 잠을 자야 할 시간이다.

It's time to go to bed. 잠 잘 시간이다.

EXERCISES

정답 및 해설 P. 35

final 결승전
grade 점수
quality time 귀중한 시간

A 주어진 상황을 읽고, 〈보기〉와 같이 가정법 문장을 완성하시오.

보기 I'm sorry my grandmother is sick.
→ I wish ___my grandmother weren't sick___.

1 I'm sorry I don't live closer to school.
→ I wish ______________________.

2 I'm sorry our team didn't make it to the final.
→ I wish ______________________.

3 I'm sorry English is so difficult for me to learn.
→ I wish ______________________.

4 I'm sorry I didn't study enough to get a good grade on the science exam.
→ I wish ______________________.

5 I'm sorry that my family is not here with me.
→ I wish ______________________.

6 I'm sorry my mother cannot spend enough quality time with me.
→ I wish ______________________.

care for ~을 좋아하다; 돌보다
subject 주제; 과목
expert 전문가
pretend ~인 체하다
try one's best 최선을 다하다
career 생애, 경력; 직업

B 〈보기〉와 같이 주어진 상황에 맞도록 문장을 완성하시오.

보기 He acts as if he ___hadn't cared for___ me. In fact, he cared for me very much.

1 He talks as if he ____________ my father. In fact, he isn't.

2 He speaks as if he ____________ a ghost. In fact, he didn't.

3 She acts as if she ____________ last night. In fact, she did.

4 She looks at me as if I ____________ a famous star. In fact, I'm not.

5 He speaks about the subject as if he ____________ an expert. In fact, he is not.

6 He speaks as if the actress ____________ his close friend. In fact, she is not.

7 He pretends as if he ____________ his mother every day. In fact, he never helps her.

8 The player tried his best as if it ____________ the last game of his career. In fact, it was not.

C 주어진 문장을 If를 생략한 가정법 문장으로 바꿔 쓰시오.

convenient 편리한
creature 생물, 사람
exist 살아있다, 존재하다
bravery 용기
patriot 애국자
independent 독립한

1 If it were not for the Internet, our lives would be less convenient.
→ ______________________________

2 If it were not for the sun and water, no creature would exist on the earth.
→ ______________________________

3 If it had not been for the bad weather, the event would have been more successful.
→ ______________________________

4 If it had not been for the bravery of the firefighters, many lives might have been lost.
→ ______________________________

5 If it had not been for my mother's love, I wouldn't have become a successful business person.
→ ______________________________

6 If it had not been for great patriots like Ahn Junggeun, Korea might never have become independent.
→ ______________________________

D 주어진 단어를 이용하여 문장을 완성하시오.

go on a diet 다이어트 하다
archeologist 고고학자
tomb 무덤, 묘
era 시대

1 ______________ (be) it not for music and art, our lives would be boring.

2 It's time you ______________ (go) on a diet. You put on too much weight.

3 I want to buy the coat. I wish I ______________ (have) money to buy it.

4 He talks as if he ______________ (finish) the project by himself. In fact, many people helped him.

5 I had an exam yesterday, and I did terribly on it. I wish I ______________ (have) enough time to study for it.

6 She talks as if she ______________ (know) everything about him. In fact, she doesn't know anything about him.

7 She talks as if she ______________ (spend) her summer vacation in Italy. In fact, she didn't.

8 Howard Carter was the archeologist who discovered King Tutankhamun's tomb. If it ______________ (not, be) for him, we might have never known of Tutankhamun's era.

REVIEW

정답 및 해설 P. 36

wet 젖은
earthquake 지진
in ruins 폐허가 되어, 황폐하여
deadline 최종 기한
stomach 위, 배, 복부
upset (위장이) 불편한

( ) 안에서 가장 알맞은 것을 고르시오.

1 If it (is / were) sunny tomorrow, we will go for a picnic.

2 If you (exercise / exercised) more, you would have more energy for life.

3 If Jen had taken the medicine, she would (feel / have felt) better by now.

4 If Suhee (goes / went) to New Zealand to study, I will miss her very much.

5 If Amy (didn't go / had not gone) outside with wet hair, she wouldn't be sick now.

6 If the earthquake had not happened, the city would not (be / have been) in ruins now.

7 If it (were not / had not been) for some help, we could not have finished this work before the deadline.

8 I wish I (didn't eat / hadn't eaten) a snack before going to bed. My stomach is very upset this morning.

sunburn 햇볕에 심하게 탐
admiral 해군 대장, 제독
invent ~을 발명하다
turtle ship 거북선
naval 바다의
battle 전투
stay up all night 밤을 꼬박 새다

B 주어진 상황을 읽고, 문장을 완성하시오.

1 I'm sorry I didn't get a new bicycle for my birthday.
→ I wish I ________________ a new bicycle for my birthday.

2 He doesn't practice the violin enough. So he doesn't play it well.
→ If he practiced the violin enough, he ________________ it well.

3 Joseph spent a long time playing in the ocean. He might have sunburn.
→ Joseph looks as if he ________________ sunburn.

4 Admiral Yi Sunsin invented the turtle ship. He won many naval battles in the Imjin War.
→ If Admiral Yi Sunsin ________________ the turtle ship, he wouldn't ________________ many naval battles in the Imjin War.

5 I stayed up all night studying for the exam, so I missed the bus to school.
→ If I ________________ all night studying for the exam, I wouldn't ________________ the bus to school.

6 Joe practiced basketball from an early age. He is a famous player now.
→ If Joe ________________ basketball from an early age, he wouldn't ________________ a famous player now.

7 Christine broke her laptop computer. So she has to buy a new one now.
→ If Christine ________________ her laptop computer, she would not ________________ a new one now.

C 주어진 동사를 알맞은 형태로 바꿔 문장을 완성하시오.

1 If he hadn't learned to swim, he would ____________ (drown).

2 If you ____________ (run) fast, you will still make it to the train.

3 I don't have pets. If I had pets, I wouldn't ____________ (feel) lonely.

4 If Kelly practiced harder, she would ____________ (be) a better pianist.

5 If it weren't for friends, life would ____________ (be) very lonely indeed.

6 My mother always treats me as if I ____________ (be) still ten years old.

7 If I ____________ (have) talent, I would have become a soccer player.

8 I wish I ____________ (have) the money to go to Hawaii. I'm sorry I don't.

9 If the storm ____________ going on, more sand will be washed away from the beaches.

10 If it had not been for my teacher, I wouldn't ____________ (attend) such a good university now.

11 If we ____________ (go) to New York City, we could have visited Ellis Island and the Statue of Liberty.

drown 익사하다
indeed 정말로
treat ~으로 여기다
talent 재능, 소질
storm 폭풍
sand 모래
be washed away ~을 씻겨 내려가다
Statue of Liberty 자유의 여신상

D 밑줄 친 부분을 어법에 맞게 고치시오.

1 If I were you, I would never have taken the exam.

2 If it hadn't been so foggy, the plane could take off.

3 If Bonnie had slept well, she would have feel refreshed now.

4 If Suzie had continued to study, she will become a great lawyer.

5 Had I not skipped breakfast, I wouldn't have been hungry now.

6 If that river were frozen, they would have gone ice fishing there.

7 If I knew your mother was in the hospital, I would have visited her.

8 If Daniel didn't come to Korea, he wouldn't have met his lovely wife.

9 If the world's population kept growing, we may experience severe food shortages.

10 If the last Ice Age had not ended, most of the northern hemisphere would still have been buried under ice.

11 If she did well on the exam, she would have applied to the university she wanted to attend.

foggy 안개가 낀
take off 이륙하다
refreshed 상쾌한
lawyer 변호사
skip (식사 등을) 거르다
population 인구
severe 격심한
shortage 부족, 결핍
Ice Age 빙하 시대
northern 북쪽의
hemisphere 반구
bury ~을 묻다, 매장하다
apply 지원하다

REVIEW PLUS

정답 및 해설 P. 38

A 다음 빈칸에 들어갈 알맞은 것을 고르시오.

deadline 마감기한
form 형성하다
volcano 화산; 분화구
erupt (화산이) 폭발하다, 분화하다
exist 존재하다

1 We only have a few more hours before the deadline. I wish we __________ more time to finish our project.

① have ② had ③ had had
④ will have ⑤ don't have

2 The Hawaiian Islands were formed by volcanoes. If the volcanoes hadn't erupted, the Hawaiian Islands __________ today.

① would have existed ② won't exist ③ would exist
④ wouldn't have existed ⑤ wouldn't exist

B 다음 중 어법상 바르지 않은 문장을 고르시오.

donate 기부하다
charity 자선 단체; 자선기금; 자비
intelligent 총명한, 똑똑한
engineer 기술자

① If I were you, I would try to read a book every day.
② If I were a rich man, I would donate more money to charity.
③ If he were tall enough, he would play basketball for our team.
④ If Jim were more intelligent, he could become an engineer.
⑤ If we went to the museum, we could have seen many beautiful paintings.

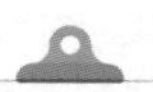

C 다음 (A), (B), (C)에 들어갈 말이 바르게 짝지어진 것을 고르시오.

tsunami 해일(海溢)
cause ~의 원인이 되다
earthquake 지진
predict ~을 예언하다
discovery 발견
prediction 예보, 예언
beyond ~을 넘어서는, ~할 수 없는
warning 경고, 경보
affect ~에 영향을 미치다

For centuries, we have known that tsunamis are caused by earthquakes, but we still don't understand them well. If scientists (A) (understand / understood) more about how earthquakes work, they could predict them. Were they able to build some kind of early warning system, the discovery could (B) (save / have saved) many lives. Unfortunately, a prediction system is still beyond our knowledge. If a tsunami were precisely predicted, a warning would (C) (be / have been) sent to all the areas that might be affected.

	(A)		(B)		(C)
①	understand	…	have saved	…	have been
②	understand	…	save	…	be
③	understood	…	save	…	have been
④	understood	…	save	…	be
⑤	understood	…	have saved	…	have been

PART 19

전치사
Prepositions

REPLAY 전치사

정답 및 해설 P. 38

1 시간 관련 전치사 at, on, in

- **AT**: at 3:30, at night, at Christmas, at the beginning of May, at that time
- **ON**: on Friday, on Christmas Day, on Friday evening, on the evening of May 1st
- **IN**: in the evening, in May, in winter, in 2015, in the 1970s, in the future

CHECK-UP

at, on, in 중 알맞은 시간 전치사를 골라 빈칸에 써넣으시오.

1 We had a party ___________ Christmas Day.

2 I was born ___________ May 28th ___________ 1994.

3 Carol called me ___________ 10:00 ___________ the morning.

4 Science class starts ___________ 11:00 and ends ___________ 12:30.

5 The plane left ___________ noon, so I should be on time for the meeting.

2 시간 관련 전치사 during/for, by/until

~ 동안	during+특정 기간	I will take ski lessons **during** the winter vacation.
	for+숫자 표현	I will take ski lessons **for** three months.
~까지	by	I have to finish the project **by** 1:00. (일회성의 동작이나 상태가 완료되는 것을 나타냄)
	until	Let's wait here **until** 6:00. (계속되던 동작이나 상태가 완료되는 것을 나타냄)

CHECK-UP

( ) 안에서 가장 알맞은 것을 고르시오.

1 I'll wait for you here (by / until) 9:00 p.m.

2 He has been reading the book (during / for) four hours.

3 You must pay attention (during / for) the class.

4 Jenny will finish her assignment (by / until) three o'clock.

5 She hasn't seen her mother (during / for) over three years.

3 장소·방향 관련 전치사 at, on, in, over, in front of ...

in	~ 안에	Tokyo is **in** Japan.
at	~에	He was standing **at** the bus stop.
on	~ (접촉하여) 위에	My picture is **on** the desk.
over	~ 위에	The clock is **over** the window.
under	~ 아래에	The window is **under** the clock.
in front of	~ 앞에	The bookstore is right **in front of** the building.
behind	~ 뒤에	The mouse hid **behind** the rock.
between A and B	A와 B 사이에	The train runs **between** Seoul **and** Gwangju.
among	~ 사이에	The small cottage was hidden **among** the trees.
by	~ 옆에	A woman is sitting **by** the tree.
next to		John sat **next to** me on the couch.
beside		The bicycle is **beside** the fence.
from A to B	A에서 B까지	It takes nine hours **from** Seoul **to** LA by plane.
into	~ 안으로	My dog came **into** my room.
out of	~ 밖으로	Let's get **out of** the house.
through	~ 통과하여	Our car is going **through** the tunnel.
up	~ 위로	A boy goes **up** the stairs.
down	~ 아래로	A girl goes **down** the stairs.

CHECK-UP

(　) 안에서 가장 알맞은 것을 고르시오.

1 I am going to pick you up (at / on) the airport.

2 The children put their paintings (in / on) the wall.

3 Victoria will be (in / on) London over the holiday.

4 We took the train (next / from) London to Oxford.

5 The woman sitting (at / on) the chair is my grandmother.

6 My cat ran (into / out of) the house to get away from the rain.

7 It's so dark! I can't see anything! We're going (over / through) a tunnel now.

전치사의 역할

형태	전치사+명사(상당어구)
전치사구	All of the students are anxious **about** their teacher's health. 모든 학생이 선생님의 건강을 걱정하고 있다.

역할	예문
형용사	The man **with the black baseball cap** is my uncle. 검은색 야구 모자를 쓴 남자가 우리 삼촌이다.
부사	We have to leave early **in the morning**. 우리는 아침 일찍 떠나야 한다.

1

전치사 뒤에는 명사, 대명사, 동명사 등 명사 상당어구가 목적어로 온다.

I looked **for** the remote control everywhere, but I still can't find it.
나는 리모컨을 여기저기 찾아봤지만, 여전히 찾을 수가 없다.

Lisu yelled **at** him. I don't know why she got so upset.
리수가 그에게 소리쳤다. 나는 그녀가 왜 그렇게 화가 났는지 모른다.

They all studied hard **without** complaining.
그들은 불평 없이 열심히 공부했다.

|주의| 전치사 뒤에는 동사원형을 쓸 수 없다.
I'm afraid **of** speaking in public. 나는 대중 앞에서 말하는 것이 두렵다.
(×) ~~of speak~~

2

전치사는 명사(구)와 결합하여 형용사나 부사 역할을 한다. 전치사구는 주로 부사 역할을 하지만, 명사를 수식하는 전치사구는 형용사 역할을 하는 것이다.

The lady **in** the yellow raincoat is going to get splashed. (명사 수식_형용사)
노란 비옷을 입은 저 숙녀에게 물이 튈 것 같아.

Jane is standing **next to** the principal. (동사 수식_장소 부사)
제인은 교장 선생님 옆에 서 있다.

As a matter of fact, I thought he would get first place in his class. (문장 전체 수식_부사)
사실 나는 그가 반에서 1등을 할 것이라고 생각했어.

3 하나 이상의 단어가 결합되어 전치사로 쓰이기도 한다.

according to ~에 의하면	due to ~때문에	for the sake of ~을 위하여
in addition to ~에 덧붙여서	in case of ~인 경우에는	in front of ~의 앞에
in spite of ~에도 불구하고	instead of ~의 대신에	on account of ~때문에
owing to ~때문에	thanks to ~의 덕택에	because of ~때문에

Owing to the storm, the airport has temporarily closed.
폭풍 때문에, 공항이 일시적으로 폐쇄되었다.

Henry gets very nervous whenever he has to deliver a speech **in front of** an audience.
헨리는 청중 앞에서 발표해야 할 때면 언제나 매우 긴장한다.

4 전치사 뒤에는 명사 상당어구가 오지만, 종속 접속사 뒤에는 절이 온다.

전치사+명사(구)			종속 접속사+절(주어+동사)	
because of ~때문에 despite[in spite of] ~에도 불구하고 during ~하는 동안 without ~하지 않고 in case of ~인 경우에는 except/but ~을 제외하고 after ~ 후에 before ~ 전에 until ~까지	+명사(구)	VS.	because ~때문에 although ~에도 불구하고 while ~하는 동안 unless ~하지 않는다면 in case ~인 경우에는 except (that)/but ~을 제외하고 after ~ 후에 before ~ 전에 until ~까지	+절[주어+동사]

My teacher scolded me **because of my lateness** this morning. (전치사)

My teacher scolded me **because I was late** this morning. (접속사) 내가 오늘 아침에 지각을 해서 선생님께서 나를 꾸짖으셨다.

The boys in my class usually play soccer **after lunch**. (전치사)

The boys in my class usually play soccer **after they have lunch**. (접속사) 우리 반 남학생들은 점심 식사 후에 대개 축구를 한다.

| 참고 | 1. 전치사 of는 '~이라고 하는, ~인'이라는 의미의 동격 관계에 사용한다.
Jihun has a bad habit **of** exaggerating the facts. (동격) 지훈이는 사실을 과장하는 나쁜 버릇이 있다.

2. 전치사 of는 '~에 속하는, ~의'라는 의미의 소유 관계에 사용한다.
The band met the Queen **of** England during their recent tour. (소유격) 그 밴드는 최근 투어 중에 영국의 여왕을 만났다.

3. 전치사 of는 형용사와 함께 목적격 관계(~을/를)를 나타낼 때 사용한다.
I'm proud **of** being Korean. (목적격) 나는 한국인이라는 것을 자랑스러워한다.

be fond of ~을 좋아하다	be afraid of ~을 두려워하다	be aware of ~을 알다
be capable of ~을 할 수 있다	be ashamed of ~을 부끄러워하다	be doubtful of ~을 의심하다

EXERCISES

정답 및 해설 P. 38

lay (알을) 낳다
be away 부재중이다
pass away 돌아가시다, 사망하다
birth 생일; 출생
inconvenience 불편

밑줄 친 단어가 전치사면 'P(prepositions)', 접속사면 'C(conjunctions)'로 나타내시오.

1 (1) Christine wanted to get to the party <u>before</u> six o'clock. ______

(2) Salmon swim up river <u>before</u> they lay their eggs. ______

2 (1) I think I will be away on business <u>until</u> Wednesday. ______

(2) We can't start eating dinner <u>until</u> your father comes home. ______

3 (1) Amy's grandmother passed away <u>after</u> her birth. ______

(2) She's going to go abroad <u>after</u> she graduates from college. ______

4 (1) He is the fastest runner in his class <u>although</u> he is the shortest. ______

(2) He went to work by bus <u>in spite of</u> the inconvenience. ______

security guard 안전요원
cheerful 쾌활한
participant 참가자

〈보기〉에서 밑줄 친 전치사구의 역할을 골라 쓰시오.

1 The security guard <u>in my building</u> is very cheerful. ______

2 My parents lived <u>on a small island</u> before I was born. ______

3 Free gifts for the participants are ready <u>in the main lobby</u>. ______

4 The picture <u>on the wall</u> in the living room is what I painted. ______

delay 지체시키다; 연기하다
sign up 등록하다
in advance 사전에
thoughtless 생각 없는
remark 비평, 논평; 의견
emergency 비상사태
earthquake 지진
drill 훈련

( ) 안에서 가장 알맞은 것을 고르시오.

1 I made lots of friends (during / while) my stay in New York.

2 She took a shower (during / while) her baby was sleeping.

3 We were upset (because / because of) our flight was delayed.

4 You can't take this course (without / unless) you sign up in advance.

5 He seemed deeply hurt (because / because of) my thoughtless remark.

6 Humans cannot survive (without / unless) water and air even for one day.

7 The teacher gave us his phone number (in case / in case of) emergencies.

8 The students regularly perform earthquake drills (in case / in case of) an earthquake happens.

D 〈보기〉에서 알맞은 말을 골라 빈칸에 써넣으시오.

[1-5] 보기 to for except opposite on

1 Nobody complained about his decision __________ me.

2 I wanted to read the diary __________ Jenny's desk, but I didn't.

3 You should exercise regularly __________ the sake of your health.

4 The houses __________ the station were built many decades ago.

5 Sophia went __________ the aquarium to see the dolphins yesterday.

[6-10] 보기 at for with in of

6 He sang along __________ the song on the radio while cooking.

7 Almost all the houses in this town were built __________ brick.

8 He apologized __________ his thoughtless behavior in the hospital.

9 Some violent soccer fans __________ the crowd totally spoiled the game.

10 The man __________ the bus stop asked me how to get to the subway station.

decision 결정
decade 10년
brick 벽돌
behavior 행동
violent 난폭한
crowd 관중, 청중
how to + 동사원형 ~하는 방법

E 빈칸에 알맞은 전치사를 써넣으시오.

1 He wasn't able to sleep well at night due __________ jet lag.

2 I smiled at my friends __________ front of the statue of David.

3 It is natural that you should be afraid __________ big changes.

4 Thanks __________ his advice, we could overcome the difficulties.

5 Doctors suggest people eat more fish instead __________ red meat.

6 In addition __________ English, she is learning French and Japanese.

7 According __________ my three-year-old niece, aliens indeed exist.

8 She said she was capable __________ solving the problem on her own.

9 I couldn't concentrate on my studies because __________ too much noise.

10 __________ the sake of the children, education should be our top priority.

11 In spite __________ her success, she isn't satisfied with her achievements.

12 The outdoor badminton competition was canceled __________ account of strong winds.

jet lag 시차
overcome 극복하다
difficulty 고난, 어려움
niece (여자) 조카
indeed 정말로
exist 존재하다
concentrate 집중하다
education 교육
priority 우선(권)
achievement 성취
competition 시합; 경쟁

전치사의 활용

동사 뒤에 전치사가 필요 없는 경우	We hoped to **reach the cottage** before dark. 우리는 어두워지기 전에 오두막에 도착하기를 바랐다.
to(전치사)+명사/동명사	He was not accustomed **to being** treated so poorly. 그는 그렇게 형편없이 대우를 받는 데 익숙하지 않았다.
시간 부사 앞에 전치사를 생략하는 경우	I've been waiting for her phone call **all day long**. 나는 온종일 그녀의 전화를 기다리고 있었다.

FOCUS

1 목적어가 '~을, ~를'로 해석되지 않아서 필요 없는 전치사를 덧붙이기 쉬운 동사가 있다.

동사	예문	NOT
discuss ~에 대해 토론하다	We will **discuss** Darwin's theory. 우리는 다윈 이론에 대해 토론할 것이다.	discuss ~~about~~
enter ~에 들어가다	Everybody stopped talking when the teacher **entered** the classroom. 선생님이 교실에 들어오자 모두가 이야기하는 것을 멈추었다.	enter ~~in(to)~~
marry ~와 결혼하다	My sister is going to **marry** Ann's uncle. 우리 언니는 앤의 삼촌과 결혼할 예정이다.	marry ~~with~~
lack ~이 부족하다	Julie is a smart girl, but she **lacks** common sense. 줄리는 똑똑한 학생이지만, 일반 상식이 부족하다.	lack ~~of~~
approach ~에 접근하다	A luxurious yacht was **approaching** the harbor. 호화로운 요트 한 대가 항구에 접근하고 있었다.	approach ~~to~~
answer ~에 대답하다	You didn't **answer** my question. 너는 내 질문에 대답하지 않았다.	answer ~~to~~
explain ~에 대해 설명하다	Could you **explain** the rules of the game? 이 경기의 규칙에 대해 설명해 주시겠어요?	explain ~~about~~
resemble ~와 닮다	The two brothers don't **resemble** each other. 그 형제는 서로 닮지 않았다.	resemble ~~with~~

|주의| 동사 marry가 be married 또는 get married로 쓰이면 '~와 결혼하다'라는 의미로, 뒤에 전치사 to를 동반한다.
My sister got married to Peter. 우리 언니는 피터와 결혼했다.

|참고| 1. 전치사가 필요 없는 경우

attend a party 파티에 참석하다 (*NOT* attend to a party)
reach the destination 목적지에 도착하다 (*NOT* reach to the destination)
mention it 그것에 대해 언급하다 (*NOT* mention about it)
consider his opinion 그의 의견에 대해 잘 생각하다 (*NOT* consider about his opinion)

2. leave의 쓰임

leave Korea 한국을 떠나다 (*NOT* leave from Korea)
leave from the ABC Hotel ABC호텔에서 출발하다
leave for Korea 한국을 향해 떠나다

2 to가 전치사로 쓰였을 때, 뒤에 명사 또는 동명사가 온다.

be accustomed to -ing ~하는 데 익숙하다
contribute to -ing ~하는 데 공헌하다
in addition to -ing ~하는 것에 덧붙여
be opposed to -ing ~하는 데 반대하다
be used to -ing ~하는 데 익숙하다
be dedicated to -ing ~하는 데 헌신하다
look forward to -ing ~하기를 기대하다
object to -ing ~하는 것을 반대하다

Taejin **isn't accustomed to** playing the violin in front of people yet.
태진이는 사람들 앞에서 바이올린을 연주하는 데 아직 익숙하지 않다.

I'**m used to** staying up late at night.
나는 밤늦게까지 깨어 있는 데 익숙하다.

I will be **looking forward to** hearing from you soon.
당신으로부터 곧 연락 받기를 기대하고 있겠습니다.

|참고| 「동사+전치사」 표현

think about ~에 대해 생각하다 / think of ~을 생각하다
be accused of ~로 기소하다 / specialize in ~을 특성화하다

3 다음과 같이 시간과 관련된 어구 앞의 전치사는 주로 생략된다.

last, next, this, that, one, every, each, all, yesterday, today, tomorrow, these days ...

I will see you **next Saturday.** 다음 주 토요일에 봐요.

I ran into an old friend **this morning.** 나는 오늘 아침에 오랜 친구를 우연히 만났다.

Please come and see me **any day** you like. 언제든지 좋으실 때 저를 보러 오세요.

EXERCISES

정답 및 해설 P. 39

lack
~이 부족하다, 부족, 결핍
approach ~에 접근하다
international 국제적인
short cut 지름길
illness 병, 질병
partnership 동업; 협력

A 빈칸에 전치사가 꼭 필요하면 알맞은 전치사를, 그렇지 않으면 ×표를 써넣으시오.

1 Britney and I are planning to go swimming ___________ Monday.

2 Ashley is going to get married ___________ a famous movie star.

3 I try not to waste water because Korea lacks ___________ water.

4 The airplane is now approaching ___________ JFK International Airport.

5 We will have a soccer match with ABC College ___________ next Saturday.

6 My teacher explained ___________ a short cut to solve the math problem.

7 The nurse entered ___________ the doctor's office to discuss ___________ Tommy's illness.

8 We are really looking forward ___________ meeting you and discussing ___________ our partnership.

patience 인내심, 참을성
overcome ~을 극복하다
disabled 장애를 가진
dinosaur 공룡
disappear 사라지다
praise ~을 칭찬하다
asteroid 소행성
be opposed to
~에 반대하다
carry out ~을 실행하다
policy 정책
resemble ~와 닮다
enthusiastic
열렬한, 열광적인
welcome 환영

B 밑줄 친 부분을 바르게 고치시오.

1 I used to going jogging early in the morning these days.

2 He lacks of patience, but he tries to overcome his weakness.

3 For today, students will be learning how to help disabled people.

4 My aunt is getting married with her long-time boyfriend next week.

5 We will discuss about when and how we will choose a class leader.

6 The science teacher explained about how dinosaurs disappeared.

7 Lily answered to all the questions correctly and was praised by her teacher.

8 Most children learn to use computers easily and quickly on these days.

9 The reporter said a huge asteroid will be approaching to the earth next year.

10 A great number of students and their parents are opposed to carry out the new policy.

11 My sister and I so closely resemble with each other that people often ask us if we are twins.

12 When the popular comedian entered into their classroom, he was given an enthusiastic welcome by the students.

C 〈보기〉에서 알맞은 단어를 골라 문장을 완성하시오.

보기	preserve	turn	study	go	develop

1 Most of the students objected to ________ on a school trip to Japan.

2 The students are accustomed to ________ until late at night.

3 The old man was dedicated to ________ nature for the next generations.

4 My dream is to contribute to ________ technology by creating great inventions.

5 In addition to ________ all the lights off, don't forget to check if the stove is off before you leave.

preserve 보존하다
object to ~에 반대하다
be accustomed to ~에 익숙하다
be dedicated to ~에 헌신하다
generation 세대
contribute to ~에 공헌하다
invention 발명(품)

D 우리말과 같은 뜻이 되도록 주어진 단어를 이용하여 문장을 완성하시오.

1 그녀는 자신의 삶을 가난한 사람들을 돕는 데 바쳤다. (dedicate, help)
→ She ________ her life ________ ________ the poor.

2 이 제안을 받아들이는 것을 반대하는 사람이 있나요? (object, accept)
→ Does anyone ________ ________ ________ the proposal?

3 우리는 모두 그 경기를 볼 것을 몹시 기대하고 있다. (forward, watch)
→ We are all ________ ________ ________ ________ the game.

4 그 지역의 몇몇 사람은 초고층 건물을 건축하는 것에 대해 반대했다. (oppose, build)
→ Some people in the community were ________ ________ ________ a skyscraper.

5 제시카는 아침에 일찍 일어나는 것에 익숙하다. (accustom, get up)
→ Jessica ________ ________ ________ ________ ________ early in the morning.

6 니콜은 도로의 왼편으로 운전하는 데 익숙하지 않다. (be, use, drive)
→ Nicole ________ not ________ ________ ________ on the left-hand side of the road.

7 장영실은 조선의 과학과 기술을 발전시키는 데 공헌했다. (contribute, develop)
→ Jang Young-sil ________ ________ ________ science and technology during the Joseon Dynasty.

8 오늘 아이들은 선물을 받는 것 외에도 다양한 행사를 즐길 수 있다. (addition, receive)
→ ________ ________ ________ ________ gifts, children can enjoy various events today.

proposal 제안
look forward to ~을 기대하다
community 지역 사회
skyscraper 고층 건물
left-hand 왼편[왼쪽]의
technology 기술
dynasty 왕조

전치사와 기타 관용 표현

1 at

aim[target] at / be aimed[targeted] at ~을 목표로 삼다, ~을 겨냥하다	be angry at ~에 화나다
get at 이해하다, 찾아내다	jump at ~에 덤벼들다; 기다렸다는 듯이 초대에 응하다
laugh at ~을 비웃다	smile at ~에게 미소 짓다
stare at ~을 노려보다, 응시하다, 빤히 보다	yell at ~을 향해 소리 지르다

This advertisement **is aimed at** teenagers.
이 광고는 10대를 겨냥한 것이다.

The other children **laughed at** his hair style.
다른 아이들은 그의 머리 모양을 비웃었다.

All of a sudden, the president stopped and **stared at** someone in the crowd.
대통령이 갑자기 멈춰 서서 군중 속의 한 사람을 빤히 보았다.

2 into

change into ~으로 변하다, 바꾸다	divide into ~으로 나누다
get into ~에 들어가다, 차에 타다	look into ~을 조사하다
run into ~와 우연히 마주치다	rush into ~을 서둘러 하다, 성급하게 행동으로 옮기다

I **changed into** a pair of sneakers before going out to play tennis. 나는 테니스를 치러 가기 전에 운동화로 갈아 신었다.

She **divided** up the profits **into** equal shares. 그녀는 이윤을 균등하게 분배했다.

The detective decided to **look into** the crime further. 형사는 그 범죄를 더 깊이 조사하기로 결정했다.

3 for

apply for ~에 지원하다	apologize for ~에 대해 사과하다
look for ~을 찾다	pay for ~을 지불하다
search for ~을 찾다	wait for ~를 기다리다

Why don't you **look for** a part-time job? 아르바이트를 찾아보는 것이 어때?

I **paid** twenty dollars **for** this bag. 나는 이 가방 값으로 20달러를 지불했다.

What are you **waiting for**? 너는 무엇을 기다리고 있니?

4 on

catch on ~을 이해하다, 알아듣다	concentrate on ~에 집중하다
depend on ~에 의존하다	focus on ~에 집중하다
go on ~을 계속하다	insist on ~에 대해 주장하다
put emphasis on ~에 중점을 두다	rely on ~에 의지하다

Although Jamie had never swum before, she was able to **catch on** quickly.
제이미는 전에 수영해 본 적이 없었는데도 수영을 빨리 배웠다.

Poorer nations **depend on** richer nations for aid.
가난한 나라일수록 부유한 나라의 원조에 의존한다.

He **insisted on** coming with me.
그는 나와 함께 가겠다고 고집했다.

5 of

be afraid of ~을 두려워하다	be ashamed of ~을 부끄러워하다
be proud of ~을 자랑스러워하다	consist of ~로 구성되어 있다
die of[from] ~로 죽다	dream of ~을 꿈꾸다, 상상하다

Although he lost the game, but his friends **were proud of** him.
그는 비록 경기에서 졌지만 그의 친구들은 그를 자랑스럽게 여겼다.

The country **consists of** a large mainland and many small islands.
그 나라는 큰 본토와 작은 섬들로 구성되어 있다.

My daughter **dreams of** becoming a famous violinist.
내 딸은 유명한 바이올린 연주자가 되는 것을 꿈꾸고 있다.

6 out

clean out 쫓아내다; 빼내다	figure out 이해하다; 합계를 내다; 해결하다
let out ~을 밖으로 내보내다; 비밀을 누설하다; 해방하다	rule out 제외하다, 배제하다
wear out 닳아 없어지게 하다; 닳다; 지치게 하다	

We all **let out** a deep sigh of relief when the exam was all over. 우리는 시험이 모두 끝났을 때 깊은 안도의 한숨을 쉬었다.

His shirts are **worn out**. 그의 셔츠가 낡았다.

EXERCISES

정답 및 해설 P. 40

separate 분리된, 구분된
opinion 의견
lawyer 변호사
question 심문하다
replace 바꾸다
senior (4년제 대학의) 최고 학년의
semester 학기

A 〈보기〉에서 알맞은 것을 골라 빈칸에 써넣으시오. [중복 사용 가능]

보기	out	at	into	for	on	of

1 He said nothing but just went ________ studying.

2 Mr. Kim divided the class ________ five separate groups.

3 The magazine *World News* is aimed ________ Korean teenagers.

4 Michael and James spent all day searching ________ their lost puppy.

5 Who is that handsome boy smiling ________ you? I think he likes you!

6 Let's not rule ________ anything yet. John, please give us your opinion.

7 The man insisted ________ seeing his lawyer before being questioned.

8 Mr. Lee's students have always relied ________ him for good advice.

9 I don't want to rush ________ anything. I'll wait and see what happens.

10 Those sneakers look a little worn ________. Why don't you replace them?

11 Leo did surprisingly well in his senior year. He even got ________ Oxford.

12 After each semester, students are asked to clean ________ their lockers.

13 I applied ________ a scholarship to study hotel management in the USA.

14 I've been afraid ________ water since I fell into a river when I was young.

nation 국가, 나라
treat ~을 다루다, 대우하다
give up 포기하다
advertisement 광고

B 〈보기〉에서 알맞은 동사를 골라 적절한 전치사를 함께 이용하여 문장을 완성하시오.

보기	figure	apologize	target	divide
	wear	search	concentrate	run

1 Korea is ________ two nations.

2 I can't ________ my work while you're making all that noise.

3 The heels of my old shoes were ________, so I got them repaired.

4 I ________ Cindy yesterday. She asked me to say hello to you.

5 You should ________ treating Jenny so badly in class last week.

6 After 10 hours, she gave up. She couldn't ________ the puzzle.

7 I often ________ the information I need by using the Internet.

8 This advertisement is ________ elementary school students.

C 두 문장에 공통으로 들어갈 전치사를 쓰시오.

1 (1) I didn't know why the man was staring __________ me.
(2) She said she didn't understand what I was getting __________.

2 (1) He ran __________ an old friend in the movie theater yesterday.
(2) When the princess kissed the frog, he changed __________ a prince.

3 (1) He doubted that I had let __________ the secret.
(2) The actor has not ruled __________ the possibility of retirement.

4 (1) On Christmas Eve, children wait __________ "real" Santa Claus.
(2) The manager apologized __________ sending the wrong item to me.

5 (1) At first, I wasn't good, but as I played it, I caught __________ quickly.
(2) The students in the classroom were concentrating __________ the exam.

6 (1) Many children are dying __________ hunger all over the world.
(2) You should be ashamed __________ your behavior because it's wrong.

7 (1) He put more emphasis __________ the process than the result.
(2) Teenagers tend to rely __________ their peers rather than their parents.

doubt ~을 의심하다
secret 비밀
actor 남자배우
possibility 가능성
retirement 은퇴
hunger 굶주림
behavior 행동
emphasis 강조
process 과정
result 결과
tend to ~하는 경향이 있다
peer 또래, 친구

D 우리말과 같은 뜻이 되도록 문장을 완성하시오.

1 그녀는 외출을 하겠다고 고집을 부렸다. (insist, go out)
→ She __________ __________ __________ __________.

2 나는 책을 잃어버렸고, 이제는 책값을 지불을 해야 한다. (pay)
→ I lost the book, and now I have to __________ __________ it.

3 내가 거짓말을 했기 때문에 그녀는 내게 화가 났다. (angry)
→ She __________ __________ __________ me because I lied to her.

4 그는 그 일자리에 지원했으나 받아들여지지 않았다. (apply)
→ He __________ __________ the job, but he wasn't accepted.

5 모두가 그가 광대 복장을 한 것을 보고 웃었다. (laugh)
→ Everybody __________ __________ the way he dressed up as a clown.

6 그는 열심히 공부했고, 그 대학에 쉽게 들어갔다. (get)
→ He studied hard, and he __________ __________ the university easily.

lie 거짓말 하다; 눕다
accept ~을 받다
dress up 옷을 입다
clown 광대

REVIEW

정답 및 해설 P. 40

be up 깨어 있다
achievement 성취
opportunity 기회
ceremony 예식, 식

( ) 안에서 가장 알맞은 것을 고르시오.

1 Jeff started working here (in / ×) 1991.

2 I was up (by / until) three o'clock last night.

3 How much did you pay (for / ×) the concert tickets?

4 Mark's mother was very proud (in / of) his achievements.

5 I'm looking (out / for) my car keys. Would you help me find them?

6 I look forward (on / to) hearing from you again in the near future.

7 My grandfather looks very healthy and strong (on / ×) these days.

8 He jumped (at / up) the opportunity to work at World Best last year.

9 Bill got married (to / ×) my sister yesterday in a beautiful garden.

10 Leo, who has just been to Japan, complained (for / about) the high prices.

drill 훈련
regularly 정기적으로
unusual 별난; 예외적인
difference 차이
opinion 의견
take a nap 낮잠 자다
construction 공사; 건설
cranky 짜증을 내는
mosquito 모기
degree 학위; (온)도
sign up for ~에 등록하다
in charge of ~을 맡아서, 담당해서
renowned 저명한
author 작가

B ( ) 안에서 가장 알맞은 것을 고르시오.

1 We should practice fire drills regularly (in case / in case of) a fire.

2 Did you hear any strange or unusual noises (during / while) the night?

3 They managed to work together (although / in spite of) their differences of opinion.

4 We went to buy Dad a Father's Day gift (during / while) he took a nap on the couch.

5 They went downtown to see a movie (although / despite) having a test the next day.

6 Please wait for me (during / while) I change out of my uniform and into a pair of jeans.

7 I couldn't concentrate on my homework (because / because of) there was construction outside.

8 The campers all felt tired and cranky (because / because of) the hot weather and mosquitoes.

9 You can't apply for the job (without / unless) you've got a university degree and two years' experience.

10 I signed up for the course mainly (because / because of) the professor who is in charge of it. He is a renowned author, and I am a big fan of his.

C 문장을 읽고, 밑줄 친 부분을 바르게 고치시오.

1 He got used to live alone after he left home.

2 We decided to eat out instead of eat at home.

3 My mother and I go to church on every Sunday.

4 My aunt got married with a famous basketball player.

5 The game had to be stopped because sudden heavy rain.

6 A stranger approached to her and introduced himself to her.

7 My sister resembles with my mother, and I resemble with my father.

8 Maggie practiced the piano during her mother was preparing dinner.

9 We should not learn English just for the sake of get good scores on tests.

10 My family got together to discuss about how to throw a 70th birthday party for my grandfather.

11 We were supposed to go on a picnic on next Friday, but it was canceled because a typhoon was coming.

eat out 외식하다
how to + 동사원형 ~하는 방법
for the sake of ~을 위해서
cancel 취소하다
typhoon 태풍

D 〈보기〉에서 알맞은 동사를 골라 적절한 전치사를 함께 이용하여 문장을 완성하시오.

보기				
figure	wear	jump	yell	divide
rush	look	wait	depend	go

1 He was very angry, and he ______________ me.

2 She ______________ why the microwave oven didn't work.

3 The policeman ______________ the suspect and arrested him.

4 I ______________ my lost wallet, but I couldn't find it anywhere.

5 Dad's shoes are ______________, so I decided to buy him new ones.

6 Whether we will go fishing this weekend ______________ the weather.

7 She ______________ working although she was busy caring for her baby.

8 The drought has lasted several months, and we are ______________ rainy days.

9 The firefighters ______________ the burning building and rescued the people in it.

10 The students are ______________ four groups according to their proficiency levels in English.

microwave oven 전자레인지
suspect 혐의
arrest ~을 체포하다
care for ~을 돌보다
drought 가뭄
rescue ~을 구조하다
according to ~에 의하면
proficiency level 능숙도

REVIEW PLUS

정답 및 해설 P. 42

attack ~을 공격하다
provoke ~을 화나게 하다, 약 올리다

A 다음 빈칸에 들어갈 알맞은 것을 고르시오.

1 Most wild animals won't attack ________ they are provoked.

① with ② if ③ without
④ × ⑤ unless

2 Alex had a car accident on his way to school ________ this morning.

① at ② for ③ from
④ × ⑤ on

3 Mina is good ________ figure skating because she practices every day.

① for ② with ③ by
④ on ⑤ at

sweetheart 남자[여자] 친구, 연인
be jealous of ~을 질투하다
lean against a wall 벽에 기대다
step on ~을 밟다

B 다음 중 어법상 바르지 않은 문장을 고르시오.

1 ① Robert needs to concentrate on his job.
② Sara married her sweetheart last year.
③ Yunha was jealous of Lea's beauty and great sense of humor.
④ I leaned my bicycle carefully against the wall.
⑤ Most people say that I resemble with my mother.

2 ① Mr. Brown owns the building on the corner.
② I'm used to take care of my baby sister.
③ Minjun apologized to Hana for stepping on her foot.
④ We could improve our English by using the Internet.
⑤ We're going to have a party at Eunhye's house this evening.

council 의회
announce ~을 발표하다
community 지역사회
marina (해안의) 산책길
Blvd.(=Boulevard) 대로, 넓은 가로수길
feature ~을 특징으로 하다
regulation 표준의, 정규의
arts and crafts 공예, 미술 공예
opportunity 기회

C 다음을 읽고, ( ) 안에서 가장 알맞은 것을 고르시오.

Glen Grove City Council is proud ① (to / of) announce the opening of our new community recreation center. The center is located ② (next to / ×) the marina on Lakeshore Blvd., and it features two regulation size basketball courts, a skateboard park, and an arts and crafts room ③ (for / in) kids under twelve. Much thought and care went into planning the center, so we hope that everyone in Glen Grove jumps ④ (at / with) the opportunity to visit us in the near future. See you all there soon!

PART 20

화법, 일치, 도치
Reported Speech, Agreement & Inversion

화법

문장의 종류	직접 화법 → 간접 화법
평서문	Ryan said, "I am very hungry." "나는 배가 매우 고파요."라고 라이언이 말했다. → Ryan **said (that) he was** very hungry. 라이언이 배가 매우 고프다고 말했다.
의문사가 있는 의문문	He said to me "Where are you going?" "어디 가니?"라고 그가 나에게 말했다. → He **asked** me **where I was going**. 그가 나에게 어디 가느냐고 물었다.
의문사가 없는 의문문	He said to me, "Are you happy now?" "넌 지금 행복하니?"라고 그가 나에게 말했다. → He **asked** me **if[whether] I was** happy **then**. 그가 그때 나에게 행복하냐고 물었다.
명령문	He said to me, "Do it yourself." "당신 스스로 하세요."라고 그가 나에게 말했다. → He **told** me **to do** it **myself**. 그가 나에게 스스로 하라고 말했다.

FOCUS

1 화법에는 직접 화법(direct speech)과 간접 화법(indirect[reported] speech)이 있다. 직접 화법은 큰따옴표를 사용하여 다른 사람이 말한 내용을 그대로 전달하는 것이고, 간접 화법은 전달하는 사람의 입장에서 바꿔 말하는 것이다.

"I'm very pleased," said Jisup. (직접 화법)

"I'm very pleased," he said. (직접 화법)

Jisup said, "I'm very pleased." (직접 화법) "나는 정말 기뻐."라고 지섭이가 말했다.

→ Jisup **said (that) he was** very pleased. (간접 화법) 지섭이가 정말 기쁘다고 말했다.

2 평서문의 경우, 직접 화법을 간접 화법으로 바꾸는 방법은 다음과 같다.

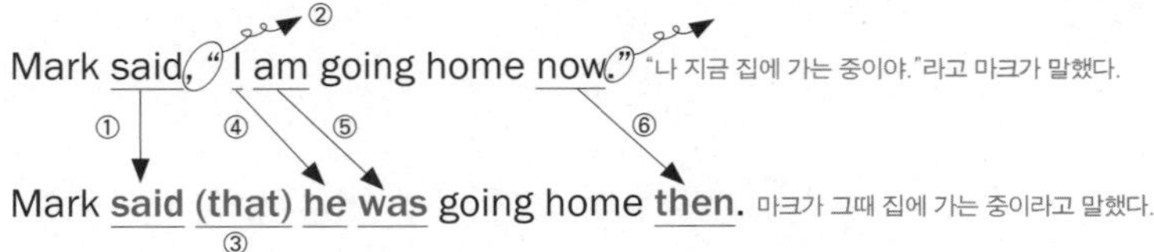

① 전달 동사를 쓴다. said → said, said to → said to 또는 told

② 쉼표와 큰따옴표를 삭제한다.

③ 접속사 that을 쓴다. 이때 접속사 that은 said의 목적어절을 이끄는 것으로 생략 가능하다.

④ that절의 주어를 알맞은 (대)명사로 바꾼다.

⑤ that절의 동사를 전달 동사(said)의 시제에 맞춰 알맞게 바꾼다.

⑥ that절의 부사를 상황에 맞춰 알맞게 바꾼다.

3 간접 화법의 경우, 시제에 주의해야 한다. 전달 동사가 현재 시제일 경우 that절의 동사를 그대로 써 주고, 과거 시제일 경우 that절의 동사를 과거나 과거완료로 쓴다.

He **says**, "Everything is all right." "모든 게 잘 될 거야."라고 그가 말한다.

→ He **says (that)** everything **is** all right. 그가 모든 게 잘 될 거라고 말한다.

He **said**, "Everything is all right." "모든 게 잘 될 거야."라고 그가 말했다.

→ He **said (that)** everything **was** all right. 그가 모든 게 잘 될 거라고 말했다.

He **said**, "I wanted to stay home yesterday." "나는 어제 집에 있고 싶었어."라고 그가 말했다.

→ He **said (that)** he **had wanted** to stay home the day before. 그가 그 전날에 집에 있고 싶었다고 말했다.

→ He **said (that)** he **wanted** to stay home the day before.

| 참고 | 전달 동사가 과거 시제이더라도 전달 내용이 현재에도 유효할 경우 that절의 시제는 현재, 과거 둘 다 가능하다.
화법의 변환은 절대적인 규칙이 아니다. 말하는 시점과 전달하는 시점에 따라 얼마든지 다양한 문장을 만들 수 있다.
다만, 보편적인 규칙을 이해하는 것이 필요하다.

My mother said, "This town is the best place to live in." 우리 엄마는 "이 마을이 가장 살기 좋은 곳이야."라고 말했다.

→ My mother said (that) this town is[was] the best place to live in. 우리 엄마는 이 마을이 가장 살기 좋은 곳이라고 말했다.

4 직접 화법을 간접 화법으로 전환할 때, 지시형용사와 시간, 장소 부사구도 다음과 같이 바꾼다.

직접 화법		간접 화법
this	→	that
these	→	those
here	→	there
ago	→	before
now	→	then
last week [year / Monday ...]	→	the previous week [year / Monday ...]
next week [year / Tuesday ...]	→	the following week [year / Tuesday ...]
today	→	that day
tonight	→	that night
yesterday	→	the day before, the previous day
tomorrow	→	the next [following] day

Ben said, "I am going to start taking guitar lessons **tomorrow**."
"나는 내일 기타를 배우기 시작할거야."라고 벤이 말했다.

→ Ben said (that) he was going to start taking guitar lessons **the next day**.
벤은 그 다음 날부터 기타를 배우기 시작할 것이라고 말했다.

Julia said, "I met Martin by chance **last weekend**."
"나는 지난 주말 우연히 마틴을 만났어."라고 줄리아가 말했다.

→ Julia said (that) she had met Martin by chance **the previous weekend**.
줄리아는 그 전 주말 우연히 마틴을 만났다고 말했다.

My parents said to me, "We will come back home **next Sunday**."
"우리는 다음 주 일요일에 집에 돌아올 거야."라고 부모님께서 말씀하셨다.

→ My parents told me (that) they would come back home **the following Sunday**.
부모님께서는 그 다음 일요일에 집에 돌아오실 것이라고 말씀하셨다.

5 의문문의 경우, 직접 화법을 간접 화법으로 바꾸는 방법은 다음과 같다.

의문사가 있는 경우

He said to her, "What can I do for you?" "무엇을 해 드릴까요?"라고 그가 그녀에게 말했다.

① ②

→ He **asked** her **what he could do for her.** 그는 그녀에게 그가 그녀를 위해 해 줄 수 있는 일이 무엇이냐고 물었다.

① 전달 동사를 ask, wonder, inquire 등으로 바꾼다.

② 「의문사+주어+동사」의 어순으로 쓰고 주어와 동사의 시제를 알맞게 바꾼다.

의문사가 없는 경우

He said to me, "Do you need something?" "필요한 것이 있나요?"라고 그가 내게 말했다.

① ②

→ He **asked** me **if/whether I needed something.** 그는 내게 뭔가 필요한 것이 있느냐고 물었다.

① 전달 동사를 ask, wonder, inquire 등으로 바꾼다.

② 「if/whether+주어+동사」의 어순으로 쓰고, 주어와 동사의 시제를 알맞게 바꾼다.

|참고| 1. 명령문의 경우, 직접 화법을 간접 화법으로 바꾸는 방법은 다음과 같다.

My mother said to me, "Clean your room." "네 방을 청소해라."라고 우리 어머니가 나에게 말했다.

→ My mother **told me to clean** my room. 우리 어머니가 나에게 내 방을 청소하라고 말했다.

① 전달 동사를 tell, ask, advise, beg, command, order, forbid 등으로 바꾼다.

② 동사를 to부정사로 바꾼다.

2. 주장, 요구, 명령, 제안의 뜻을 갖는 문장의 경우, 「that+주어+should ~.」 구문으로 바꿀 수 있다.

He said, "Let's play baseball." "우리 야구하자."라고 그가 말했다.

→ He suggested **that we (should)** play baseball. 그는 우리에게 야구를 할 것을 제안했다.

EXERCISES

정답 및 해설 P. 42

A 〈보기〉와 같이 직접 화법 문장을 간접 화법 문장으로 바꿔 쓰시오.

보기 James said to me, "You look great."
→ James told me that ____I looked great____.

1 Julia said, "I'm taking Biology 101 this week."
→ Julia said that ______________________.

2 She said to me, "I moved to Tokyo last year."
→ She told me that ______________________.

3 Justin said to me, "You are the most attractive girl in the class."
→ Justin told me that ______________________.

4 Cathy said to me, "I'm sharing my room with my sister now."
→ Cathy told me that ______________________.

5 My father said, "I'm proud of you because you always try your best."
→ My father said that ______________________.

6 He said to me, "We will have a party for the new student tonight."
→ He told me that ______________________.

biology 생물학
attractive 매력 있는
share 같이 쓰다, 공유하다
try one's best 최선을 다하다

B 〈보기〉와 같이 직접 화법 문장을 간접 화법 문장으로 바꿔 쓰시오.

보기 She said to him, "What is your name?"
→ She asked him ____what his name was____.

1 My friend said to me, "What do you want to eat?"
→ My friend asked me ______________________.

2 Jia said to me, "Do you really like studying English?"
→ Jia asked me ______________________.

3 The security guard said to us, "What are you doing here?"
→ The security guard asked us ______________________.

4 He said to me, "Do you know why she skipped the class today?"
→ He asked me ______________________.

5 He said to her, "Are you going to come to my photo exhibition?"
→ He asked her ______________________.

6 She said to me, "What time are you going to the English academy?"
→ She asked me ______________________.

security guard 안전요원
skip 건너뛰다, 빼다, 생략하다
exhibition 전람회, 전시회
academy 학원

일치

<table>
<tr><td rowspan="3">시제</td><td>일치</td><td>I know that you have a good memory. 나는 네가 좋은 기억력을 가지고 있다는 것을 안다.
I heard that she was coming. 나는 그녀가 오는 중이라고 들었다.</td></tr>
<tr><td rowspan="2">예외</td><td>I heard that she sometimes goes to the library to read English magazines.
나는 그녀가 영문 잡지를 읽으려고 가끔 도서관에 간다고 들었다.</td></tr>
<tr><td>I know that General Yi made a turtle ship.
나는 이순신 장군이 거북선을 만들었다는 것을 안다.</td></tr>
<tr><td colspan="2">주어-동사 일치</td><td>The hair pins on the dresser are my sister's.
화장대 위에 있는 머리핀은 우리 언니 것이다.
The people who are interested in the script seem to be actors.
대본에 관심이 있는 그 사람들은 배우들인 것 같다.</td></tr>
</table>

FOCUS

1

주절이 현재 시제일 경우, 종속절에는 현재, 과거, 미래 모두가 올 수 있으나, 주절이 과거 시제일 경우에는 주로 과거나 과거완료가 온다.

I **know** that he **is preparing** for the final test. 나는 그가 기말고사 준비를 하는 중이라는 것을 안다.

I **know** that he **was preparing** for the final test. 나는 그가 기말고사 준비를 하고 있었다는 것을 안다.

I **know** that he **will prepare** for the final test. 나는 그가 기말고사 준비를 할 거라는 것을 안다.

I **thought** that you **ate** the rest of the chocolate cake. 나는 네가 남은 초콜릿 케이크를 먹었다고 생각했다.

I **thought** that you **had eaten** the rest of the chocolate cake.

2

주절의 시제가 종속절에 영향을 주지 않을 때도 있다. 주절의 시제에 관계없이 일반적, 과학적 진리, 현재의 습관 등 현재에도 사실이면 현재 시제를, 역사적 사실이면 과거 시제를 쓴다.

She **said** that she **is** a computer programmer. (현재에도 계속되는 상황, 현재도 프로그래머임) 그녀는 자신이 컴퓨터 프로그래머라고 말했다.

I **learned** that a triangle **has** three sides. (일반적인 진리) 나는 삼각형은 세 면을 가지고 있다고 배웠다.

He **told** me that he **takes** walks after dinner. (현재의 습관) 그는 저녁 후 산책을 하는 습관이 있다고 나에게 말했다.

We **know** that the Korean War **broke out** in 1950. (역사적 사실) 우리는 한국 전쟁이 1950년에 일어났다는 것을 안다.

|참고| 주절이 과거인 경우, 현재 시제를 썼다면 현재에도 사실이지만, 과거 시제를 쓴 경우 그것이 현재에도 사실인지는 알 수 없다.
She **said** that she **was** a computer programmer. (현재는 프로그래머인지 알 수 없음)
She **said** that she **is** a computer programmer. (현재도 프로그래머임)

3

삽입구[절] 등 때문에 주어가 길어진 경우와 동명사 주어의 경우, 주어 · 동사 수의 일치에 주의해야 한다.

Eating apples is good for your health. 사과를 먹는 것은 너의 건강에 좋다.

The markers in the drawer **are** dried out. 서랍에 있던 마커 펜들이 말랐다.

The women who helped me yesterday **are** not here today. 어제 나를 도와준 그 여자들은 오늘은 여기 없다.

EXERCISES

정답 및 해설 P. 43

A 밑줄 친 부분이 어법상 맞지 않다면 바르게 고치시오.

1 He said that he is very happy to meet me.

2 James believed that he sees Carol here earlier.

3 She told me that she usually had dinner at seven.

4 My mom said that she does the laundry every Monday.

5 He thought that his school record improves a lot.

6 She told me that she bit her nails when she feels nervous.

7 Oil floats on water because it has a lower density than water.

8 He said that he usually comes to this restaurant to eat lunch.

9 We will learn that the Korean War divides our nation into two countries.

10 We learned that blood accounts for seven percent of the human body weight.

11 He believed that his son would get over his difficulties and succeed at last.

12 I know the USA enter WWII shortly after the attack on Pearl Harbor in 1941.

laundry 세탁물
improve ~을 향상시키다
bite ~을 물다
float 뜨다, 떠오르다
density 밀도; 농도
account for ~의 비율을 차지하다
get over ~을 극복 하다
difficulty 고난, 어려움
attack ~을 공격하다
Pearl Harbor 진주만 (미국 하와이주 오아후섬 군항)

B ( ) 안에서 가장 알맞은 것을 고르시오.

1 Crying (are / is) a natural response to stress.

2 The girl who is wearing leather gloves (are / is) my sister.

3 Taking too many vitamins (are / is) not good for your health.

4 The player with the most goals (are / is) going to be the MVP.

5 The clothes in the box (belong / belongs) to my sister and me.

6 He said that the teachers at his school (was / were) very nice.

7 Peter and Roman, who are brothers, (go / goes) to the same school.

8 The boys who are playing basketball over there (are / is) my classmates.

9 Juggling five bowling pins (require / requires) good hand-eye coordination.

10 Sue and Clara, who play on the volleyball team, (have / has) practice today.

11 Statistics, which is taught by Mr. Smith, (are / is) not offered this semester.

12 All the people who were selected for jury duty (seem / seems) to have good characters.

response 대답; 반응
MVP(=Most Valuable Player) 최우수 선수
juggling (공 등을 던지며 부리는) 곡예
hand-eye coordination 손과 눈의 협응력
statistics 통계학
select 선발하다

도치

부정어(구), 부사(구) 강조	Never **did I** think of him. ← I never **thought** of him. 나는 결코 그의 생각을 하지 않았다. Only this way **can you** solve the problem. ← You **can** solve the problem only this way. 너는 오직 이 방법으로 그 문제를 해결할 수 있다.
so neither nor	A: I like playing the drums. 나는 드럼 치는 것이 좋아. B: **So do I.** 나도 그래. A: I didn't watch that movie. 나는 그 영화를 보지 않았어. B: **Neither did I.** 나도 안 봤어. A: Can you and your brother ride a motorcycle? 너와 네 동생은 오토바이를 탈 수 있니? B: I can't ride a motorcycle, **nor can my brother.** 나는 오토바이를 못 타고 내 동생도 못 타.

1

부정어(구)나 부사(구)가 강조되어 문장의 앞에 오면 주어와 동사의 어순이 바뀌게 된다. 이렇게 동사가 주어 앞에 오는 것을 도치라고 한다. 주어 앞으로 나가는 동사는 be동사와 조동사, do[does, did], have[has, had]이다. do동사가 앞으로 나갔을 경우 뒤에는 동사원형이 온다.

Hardly **could I** breathe after I finished the 400-meter swim.

← I could hardly breathe after I finished the 400-meter swim. 400미터 수영을 끝낸 후 나는 거의 숨을 쉴 수 없었다.

Under no circumstance **would I** do such a thing.

← I would do such a thing under no circumstance. 어떤 일이 있더라도 결코 나는 그런 짓을 하지 않을 것이다.

|주의| 1. 주어가 일반명사인 경우 자동사가 주어 앞으로 나온다.

There **goes the pickpocket.** 저기 소매치기가 달아난다. / Here **comes the bus.** 여기 버스가 온다.

2. 주어가 대명사인 경우 도치되지 않는다.

Here you go. 여기 있어. → (×) Here ~~go you~~.

|참고| no sooner A than B = hardly[scarcely] A when[before] B 'A하자마자 B하다'

He had **no sooner** gone out **than** it began to rain.

→ He had **hardly[scarcely]** gone out **when[before]** it began to rain.

→ **No sooner** had **he** gone out **than** it began to rain.

→ **Hardly[Scarcely]** had he gone out **when[before]** it began to rain. 그가 밖에 나가자마자 비가 오기 시작했다.

2

so, neither, nor 구문에서 주어 동사가 도치된다.

A: I hate traveling by bus. 나는 버스로 여행하는 것을 싫어해.

B: **So do I.** 나도 그래.

A: I am not interested in that rumor. 나는 그 소문에 관심 없어.

B: **Neither am I.** 나도 그래.

A: Did Kerry and Jerry come to the party? 케리와 제리가 파티에 왔니?

B: No. Kerry didn't come to the party, **nor did Jerry.** 아니. 케리는 파티에 오지 않았고, 제리도 오지 않았어.

EXERCISES

정답 및 해설 P. 43

A 〈보기〉와 같이 밑줄 친 단어를 강조하는 문장으로 바꿔 쓰시오.

보기 He had never seen so many mysterious-looking people.
→ Never had he seen so many mysterious-looking people.

1 A beautiful maple tree was in his garden.
→ In his garden ______.

2 A lost child stood next to a big tree crying.
→ Next to a big tree ______.

3 A second had hardly passed before the lights turned on.
→ Hardly ______.

4 You can scarcely blame him for being absent from work today.
→ Scarcely ______.

5 I will never forget the foreign friends I met during my trip to London.
→ Never ______.

6 I had no sooner reached the door than I realized I had forgotten my keys.
→ No sooner ______.

mysterious 신비로운, 수상한
maple tree 단풍나무
blame [잘못]의 책임을 지우다, 전가하다
absent from ~에 결근[결석]하다
realize 깨닫다, 자각하다

B 빈칸에 알맞은 대답을 써넣어 대화를 완성하시오.

1 A: I'm from Sweden.
B: So ______. It's very nice to meet you.

2 A: Can you and your brother ski?
B: No. I can't ski and neither ______.

3 A: I don't like horror films.
B: Neither ______. Let's watch something else.

4 A: Are you and your sister going to music camp?
B: No. I'm not going to music camp, nor ______.

5 A: Are you and your brother going abroad to study?
B: No. I am not going abroad to study, nor ______.

6 A: We may have been walking too long. I've got a blister on my foot.
B: So ______. It hurts, doesn't it?

7 A: I like English best.
B: So ______. That's why I spend lots of time studying English.

blister (피부의) 물집, 수포(水疱)

it의 특별 용법

가주어	That I have to wake up one hour early is not easy. → It is not easy **that I have to wake up one hour early.** 나에게 있어 한 시간 일찍 일어나야 한다는 것은 쉬운 일이 아니다.
가목적어	I found **it** unpleasant **to watch the film.** 나는 그 영화를 보는 것이 불쾌하다는 것을 깨달았다.
It ~ that 강조	Rachel studied history at Columbia University last year. 레이첼은 작년에 콜롬비아 대학에서 역사를 공부했다. → **It was** Rachel **that** studied history at Columbia University last year. 콜롬비아 대학에서 작년에 역사를 공부한 것은 바로 레이첼이었다. → **It was** history **that** Rachel studied at Columbia University last year. 레이첼이 작년에 콜롬비아 대학에서 공부한 것은 바로 역사였다. → **It was** at Columbia University **that** Rachel studied history last year. 레이첼이 작년에 역사를 공부한 곳은 바로 콜롬비아 대학이었다. → **It was** last year **that** Rachel studied history at Columbia University. 레이첼이 콜롬비아 대학에서 역사를 공부한 것은 바로 작년이었다.

FOCUS

1 주어가 that절, 의문사절, to부정사구 등이 되어 길어질 경우, 가주어 it을 사용한 구문으로 바꿔 쓸 수 있다.

That he wasn't hurt in the accident was a miracle.

→ **It** was a miracle **that he wasn't hurt in the accident.** 그가 그 사고에서 다치지 않은 것은 기적이었다.

Why he rejected my offer is unclear.

→ **It**'s unclear **why he rejected my offer.** 그가 나의 제안을 거절한 이유가 분명하지 않다.

To sing in a church choir is enjoyable.

→ **It**'s enjoyable **to sing in a church choir.** 교회 성가대에서 노래하는 것은 즐겁다.

2 5형식 「주어+동사+목적어+목적격보어」에서 목적어가 to부정사(구)일 경우, to부정사(구)를 뒤로 보내고 그 자리에 가목적어 it을 쓴다.

I make **it** a rule **to keep a diary every day.** 나는 매일 일기 쓰는 것을 원칙으로 한다.

(×) I make ~~to keep a diary every day~~ a rule.

I think **it** a waste of money **to throw away food.** 나는 음식을 버리는 것은 돈 낭비라고 생각한다.

(×) I think ~~to throw away food~~ a waste of money.

3 주어, 목적어, 부사구 등을 강조하기 위해 「It is/was ~ that …」 강조 구문을 사용한다. 이때 강조하고자 하는 말을 It과 that 사이에 쓰고, '~한 것은 바로 …였다'라고 해석한다. 강조하는 말이 사람일 때는 that 대신 who/whom을, 사물일 때는 which를, 장소일 때는 where, 시간일 때는 when을 쓰기도 한다.

She met Jeff in the park last Sunday. 그녀는 지난 일요일 공원에서 제프를 만났다.

→ **It was** she **that [who]** met Jeff in the park last Sunday. (주어 강조)
지난 일요일 공원에서 제프를 만난 것은 바로 그녀였다.

→ **It was** Jeff **that [whom]** she met in the park last Sunday. (목적어 강조)
그녀가 지난 일요일에 만난 사람은 바로 제프였다.

→ **It was** last Sunday **that [when]** she met Jeff in the park. (시간 부사구 강조)
그녀가 제프를 공원에서 만난 때는 바로 지난 일요일이었다.

→ **It was** in the park **that [where]** she met Jeff last Sunday. (장소 부사구 강조)
그녀가 지난 일요일에 제프를 만난 곳은 바로 공원이었다.

|참고| 1. 동사를 강조할 때는 「do/does/did+동사원형」을 사용한다.
I promise not to tell a lie again. 다시는 거짓말하지 않겠다고 약속할게.
→ I **do promise** not to tell a lie again. 다시는 거짓말하지 않겠다고 정말로 약속해.

2. 의문사를 강조할 때는 「의문사+be동사+it+that」의 형태를 사용한다.
When did you see him in the library? 도서관에서 언제 그를 봤니?
→ **When was it that** you saw him in the library? 도서관에서 그를 본 게 도대체 언제였니?

3. 부정어와 의문문을 강조할 때는 뒤에 at all을 붙일 수 있다.
My parents didn't care for my school grades **at all**. 우리 부모님은 내 학교 성적에 전혀 관심이 없었다.
Why do we have to learn math **at all**? 도대체 우리가 왜 수학을 배워야 하는 거지?

4. on earth와 in the world는 의문사를 강조하는 어구이다. the very는 명사를 강조한다.
Why on earth are there many people in front of the theater? 극장 앞에 도대체 왜 많은 사람들이 몰려 있는 거지?
There was the famous poem at **the very** end of the book. 그 책의 맨 마지막에 그 유명한 시가 쓰여 있었다.

5. 「It takes(+목적격)+시간+to+동사원형」은 '(~가) …하는 데 ~의 시간이 걸리다'라는 의미이다.
It took me an hour **to finish** the homework. 나는 그 숙제를 마치는 데 한 시간이 걸렸다.
It takes a lot of effort **to master** English. 영어에 정통하는 데 많은 노력이 든다.

「It takes+시간+for+목적격+to+동사원형」으로 쓰기도 한다.
It took the man an hour **to restore** our network service.
→ **It took** an hour **for** the man **to restore** our network service. 그 남자가 우리의 네트워크 서비스를 복구시키는 데 한 시간이 걸렸다.

EXERCISES

정답 및 해설 P. 44

reward 보상하다
unclear 불분명한
education 교육
qualified 자격이 되는
representative 대표
questionable 의심스러운
influence 영향

〈보기〉와 같이 가주어 it을 이용한 문장으로 바꿔 쓰시오.

보기 To be rewarded like this is surprising.
→ It is surprising to be rewarded like this.

1 To prepare for the final exam is important for me.
→ ______________________

2 Where Nick will live next year is still unclear.
→ ______________________

3 What Jerry said to Mary yesterday was completely untrue.
→ ______________________

4 That you grew up and got an education in Israel is interesting.
→ ______________________

5 When the Hollywood star will visit Korea is not decided yet.
→ ______________________

6 That she is qualified to be the student representative is not questionable.
→ ______________________

7 That some computer games can have a bad influence on children is clear.
→ ______________________

in need 어려움에 처한
spank (손바닥 등으로) 엉덩이 등을 찰싹 때리다; ~을 심하게 꾸짖다
in public 공개적으로
habit 습관
consider ~라고 여기다
odd 이상한
wander 어슬렁거리다, 배회하다
application 애플리케이션, 응용 프로그램

B 밑줄 친 it의 내용에 해당하는 말을 찾아 밑줄을 그으시오.

1 They believe it right to help people in need.
2 I found it very hard to get up early every day.
3 Many believe it wrong to spank children in public.
4 I think it a waste of time to explain myself repeatedly.
5 Nicole made it a rule not to eat anything after 6:00 p.m.
6 I will make it a habit to keep a diary in English every day.
7 My mother considers it wise for me to go to bed early before exams.
8 He thought it odd to see an old man wandering alone around the park.
9 This application makes it possible to exchange text messages, images, and videos with people in different countries.

C 〈보기〉와 같이 밑줄 친 부분을 강조하는 문장으로 바꿔 쓰시오.

보기 I saw *Pirates of the Caribbean* last night with my father.
→ It was *Pirates of the Caribbean* that I saw last night with my father.

1 Mary called you this morning.
→ ______________________

2 Yunju wanted a new mobile phone.
→ ______________________

3 The plants on the balcony need watering.
→ ______________________

4 Jenny spends most of her allowance on shoes.
→ ______________________

5 Alex met his current girlfriend in London in 2004.
→ ______________________

6 Our class visited an animal shelter for volunteering.
→ ______________________

7 A fallen branch lying across the road caused the accident.
→ ______________________

8 Michael crashed his new motorcycle on Elm Street last night.
→ ______________________

plant 식물
water ~에 물을 주다
allowance 용돈
current 현재의
shelter 보호소
volunteer 자원 봉사하다
lie 놓여있다; 눕다; 거짓말 하다
cause ~의 원인이 되다
crash (차 등이) 충돌하다

D 우리말과 같은 뜻이 되도록 주어진 단어를 배열하시오.

1 그는 정말로 집에 일찍 올 거라고 말했다. (did, me, he, tell)
→ ______________ that he would come home early.

2 다양한 문화에 대해 배우는 것은 재미있다. (fun, to, it, learn about, is)
→ ______________ many different cultures.

3 나는 학교까지 가는 데 20분이 걸린다. (to go, takes, it, for me, twenty minutes)
→ ______________ to school.

4 나는 지하철역까지 걸어가는 데 30분 걸렸다. (took, to walk, it, half an hour, me)
→ ______________ to the subway station.

5 Jeff가 숙제를 도와달라고 내게 부탁한 것은 바로 어제였다. (yesterday, was, that, it)
→ ______________ Jeff asked me to help him with his assignment.

6 그는 라이언을 고용한 것을 실수라고 여겼다. (considered, to hire Ryan, it, a mistake)
→ He ______________.

assignment 과제; 할당
consider ~으로 여기다

REVIEW

정답 및 해설 P. 44

accept
(학설 등을) 인정하다, 용인하다
cookbook 요리책
refrigerator 냉장고
at no time
결코 ~하지 않다
allow ~을 허용하다
argue 논쟁하다
referee 심판
decorated 장식된
planet 행성
stress out
스트레스로 지친

( ) 안에서 가장 알맞은 것을 고르시오.

1 The CDs in this container (are / is) my brother's.

2 My friend asked me (if / that) Bridget invited Kevin.

3 (It / That) is strange that the stores are all closed today.

4 It was not always accepted that the world (is / was) round.

5 The cookbooks above the refrigerator (are / is) my mother's.

6 At no time (are / is) players allowed to argue with a referee.

7 The two cartons of milk in the fridge (has / have) gone bad.

8 Nowhere (I had / had I) seen a more beautifully decorated room.

9 We learned that the earth (is / was) the third planet from the sun.

10 I don't like Chinese food, nor (my brother does / does my brother).

11 She did (promise / promised) not to make the same mistake again.

12 She told me that she (is / was) going to start a study group that day.

13 Washing your hands often (are / is) the best way to avoid catching a cold.

14 Michael said that he (listens / listened) to music when he gets stressed out.

try one's best
최선을 다하다
result 결과
subject 과목; 주제
with honors 우등으로

B 〈보기〉와 같이 밑줄 친 부분을 강조하는 문장으로 바꿔 쓰시오.

보기 I have never seen a shooting star so far.
→ Never have I seen a shooting star so far.

1 A box of candy was on the top shelf.
→ On the top shelf ______________________.

2 The window in the kitchen was broken yesterday.
→ It was ______________________.

3 She won the gold medal at the Olympics last year.
→ It was ______________________.

4 He tried his best to get excellent results in all subjects.
→ He ______________________.

5 My brother graduated from high school with honors last year.
→ It was ______________________.

6 He rarely has breakfast because he has to go to school very early.
→ Rarely ______________________.

C 밑줄 친 부분이 어법상 맞지 않으면 바르게 고치시오.

1 Here the train comes!

2 He asked me where did I see the car.

3 She said me she doesn't speak Korean.

4 The CEO and his brother is going to jail.

5 He asked me if I still live in South London.

6 It was her who told us that she didn't need any help.

7 Little I did know that Mark was not telling me the truth.

8 She said that she usually sleeps with a doll in her arms.

9 Rarely I have seen such an exciting game of cricket on TV.

10 The kids who are playing next to the swing are my children.

11 I learned that the Rockies stretched from Canada to the USA.

12 It is Mr. Kim who coordinates the after-school sports program.

13 I think to wait in a long line to see the concert a waste of time.

14 I like to eat hot, spicy soup on cold days, and so does all of my friends.

CEO(=Chief Executive Officer) 최고 경영자
swing 그네
stretch (토지 등이) ~에 퍼지다, 이르다
coordinate ~을 조정하다
wait in line 줄을 서서 기다리다

D 〈보기〉와 같이 가주어 it을 이용한 문장으로 바꿔 쓰시오.

보기 To pronounce some English words is difficult.
→ It is difficult to pronounce some English words.

1 How this great pyramid was built is a mystery.
→ ____________________

2 To do outdoor activities on a sunny day is exciting.
→ ____________________

3 To see an old couple walking hand in hand is pleasant.
→ ____________________

4 To swim in the sea on a cold day like this is dangerous.
→ ____________________

5 That such a young kid can communicate with foreigners without difficulties is surprising.
→ ____________________

pronounce ~을 발음하다
hand in hand 서로 손을 잡고
communicate with ~와 연락하다
difficulty 어려움

REVIEW PLUS

정답 및 해설 P. 46

on time 제시간에
do one's best 최선을 다하다
nutritious 영양분이 많은
hold one's breath 숨을 참다

다음 중 어법상 바르지 않은 것을 고르시오.

1 ① She wants to know where the petting zoo is.
② It takes time to master a new sport like skiing.
③ It is important to be on time and do your best.
④ Billy said that he doesn't know where his shoes were.
⑤ It takes me only a few seconds to find something on the Internet.

2 ① It doesn't take long to make a nutritious salad.
② My neighbors who are on holiday has two dogs.
③ I can hold my breath for over three minutes. So can Jeff.
④ The store clerk asked if she could help me find my size.
⑤ I had to show him my ticket, and only then did he let me in.

come in 참여하다
extra 추가의

다음 중 대화가 자연스럽지 않은 것을 고르시오.

① A: Sorry? What did you just say?
B: I said, "I will call you tomorrow."
② A: He asked you if you could speak English.
B: Oh. Yes, I can, but just a little.
③ A: What did she say? I couldn't hear her.
B: She asked you that you wanted something to drink.
④ A: Mr. Kim advised me to come in for extra practice.
B: So what are you going to do?
⑤ A: Who just called?
B: It was Lily. She asked me if I had invited Leslie to the party.

riddle 수수께끼
inn 여인숙
reply 대답하다, 응답하다

다음을 읽고, ①~⑤에서 어법상 바르지 않은 것을 고르시오.

"I'm going to tell you a riddle, OK?" said Mark. "See ① if you can solve it for me," he continued. "A cowboy rode to an inn on Friday, stayed two nights, and left on Friday. How can that be?" Yunho asked Mark, "Did you say the cowboy left on Saturday?" "No, I said that the cowboy ② had left on Friday," replied Mark. "On Sunday?" asked Yunho again. "No! It was on Friday ③ that the cowboy left!" shouted Mark. "I'm lost," said Hyesu. "So ④ am I," complained Sohee. "Excuse me, Mark? When you say "on," do you mean on a horse or on that day?" asked Bada. "You've solved it! Friday is the name of the cowboy's horse," said Mark. "Never ⑤ we have heard such a silly riddle!" complained the class.

MEMO

MEMO

THIS IS GRAMMAR

Workbook

넥서스영어교육연구소 지음

내신·토익·토플·텝스 등 각종 시험 완벽 대비, 이것이 **현대 영문법의 결정판**이다!

★원어민이 사용하는 생생한 문장들로 구성된 예문

★단계별, 유형별로 구성된 연습문제와 리뷰문제

2

중급

NEXUS Edu

can, could, be able to

A 빈칸에 can이나 be able to 중 알맞은 것을 써넣으시오. [둘 다 가능하면 can을 쓸 것]

1 I'm afraid I ____________ not keep the promise.

2 I ____________ leave home after my mother gets home.

3 I'm in a hurry. ____________ you please drive a little faster?

4 Jennifer will ____________ make it to the meeting on time.

5 Albert might ____________ help you if you ask him for help.

B 두 문장이 의미가 통하도록 문장을 완성하시오.

1 She said she could handle the problem by herself.
→ She said she ______________________________ by herself.

2 We have a bad connection. I can't hear you clearly.
→ We have a bad connection. I ______________________________ you clearly.

3 Now I am able to drive skillfully because I practiced very hard.
→ Now ______________________________ skillfully because I practiced very hard.

4 He wasn't able to concentrate on his work because it was too noisy.
→ He ______________________________ because it was too noisy.

5 I couldn't see the mountains because they were covered with thick mist.
→ I ______________________________ because they were covered with thick mist.

C 밑줄 친 부분에 유의하여 해석을 완성하시오.

1 This is too expensive. Can I get a little discount?
→ 너무 비싸네요. 할인을 좀 ____________?

2 This is too heavy. Could you help me to carry it?
→ 이것은 너무 무거워. 나르는 것을 좀 ____________?

3 Mark will be able to finish the assignment by this Thursday.
→ Mark는 이번 주 목요일까지 과제를 ____________.

4 She can't be Emily because I was watching a movie with her that time.
→ 그녀가 Emily____________. 그 시간에 내가 그녀와 함께 영화를 보고 있었거든.

5 I'm so worried about her because I haven't been able to reach her on the phone.
→ 그녀와 전화 연결을 ____________ 너무 걱정이 돼.

D **우리말과 같은 뜻이 되도록 주어진 단어를 이용하여 문장을 완성하시오.**

1 너는 강을 가로질러서 수영할 수 있니? (swim)

→ ________ ________ ________ across the river?

2 결과를 듣고, 나는 울지 않을 수 없었다. (help, cry)

→ After I heard the result, I ________ ________ ________ ________.

3 급한 일이면 내가 네게 돈을 좀 빌려줄 수도 있어. (lend)

→ I ________ ________ you some money if it is an emergency.

4 왜 이렇게 늦었니? 좀 더 일찍 출발할 수도 있었잖아. (leave)

→ Why are you so late? You ________ ________ ________ earlier.

5 나가고 싶지 않으면 음식을 배달시켜도 돼. (have)

→ If you don't want to go out, we ________ ________ some food delivered.

6 그걸 왜 지금 얘기하는 거야? 좀 더 일찍 내게 이야기해 줄 수도 있었잖아. (tell)

→ Why are you telling me about it now? You ________ ________ ________ me earlier.

7 우리가 언제 도착할지 잘 모르겠지만, 네가 생각한 것보다 빨리 도착할 수도 있어. (get)

→ I'm not sure when we'll get there, but we ________ ________ there sooner than you expected.

E **우리말과 같은 뜻이 되도록 주어진 단어를 알맞게 배열하시오.**

1 그가 우리의 우정을 배신했다니, 사실일 리 없어! (be, it, true, can't)

→ ________________________ that he betrayed our friendship!

2 잠깐만 제 가방 좀 봐주실 수 있어요? (keep, my bag, could, an eye, you, on)

→ ________________________ for a moment?

3 누군가 초인종을 울리고 있어. 내 친구 Lily일 수도 있어. (be, my friend, could)

→ Somebody is ringing the doorbell. It ________________________ Lily.

4 내 귀여운 강아지를 보고 있으면 미소를 짓지 않을 수 없다. (help, I, smiling, cannot)

→ When I see my cute puppy, ________________________.

5 그는 엄청난 노력을 통해 금메달을 획득할 수 있었다. (win, able, was, the gold medal, to)

→ He ________________________ by making a lot of effort.

6 이번에는 당신의 부탁을 들어줄 수 없을 것 같아요. (your request, can't, this time, comply with)

→ I'm afraid I ________________________.

7 네가 외출하기 전에 한 번 더 확인할 수도 있었잖아. (once again, checked, you, it, have, could)

→ ________________________ before you went out.

A 보기 에서 알맞은 것을 골라 may 또는 might를 이용하여 대화를 완성하시오.

보기	let	drop by	reject	be

1 A Do you think Ann will take our offer?
  B I'm not sure. She ______________ it.

2 A Who is the guy next to Sarah?
  B I don't know. He ______________ her boyfriend.

3 A Will you go to the amusement park with me this weekend?
  B I'm not sure. My mother ______________ not ______________ me go.

4 A When are you going to meet her?
  B I'm not sure. I ______________ her house next Saturday.

B may[might] 또는 may[might] not을 이용하여 문장을 바꿔 쓰시오.

1 Perhaps they are stuck in a traffic jam.
  → ______________________________

2 Perhaps he doesn't know how to solve this problem.
  → ______________________________

3 Perhaps he is playing basketball with his friends.
  → ______________________________

4 Perhaps she doesn't want to participate in this project.
  → ______________________________

C 밑줄 친 부분에 유의하여 우리말 해석을 완성하시오.

1 You may well think he is a bit rude.
  → 그가 좀 무례하다고 ______________.

2 Sandy might not come to the party today.
  → Sandy는 오늘 파티에 ______________.

3 She's just stepped out. May I take a message?
  → 그녀는 방금 나갔어요. 메모를 ______________?

4 The shopping mall is too crowded. We may as well go back home.
  → 쇼핑몰이 너무 붐빈다. 우리는 집으로 ______________.

D 우리말과 같은 뜻이 되도록 주어진 단어를 이용하여 문장을 완성하시오.

1 실례합니다. 제가 성함을 물어봐도 될까요? (ask)
→ Excuse me. ___________ ___________ ___________ your name, please?

2 오늘 그녀는 별로 안 좋아 보여. 아픈지도 모르지. (be sick)
→ She doesn't look good today. She ___________ ___________ ___________.

3 그녀에게 전화하지 마. 지금 자고 있을지도 몰라. (be asleep)
→ Don't call her. She ___________ ___________ ___________ now.

4 태풍이 오고 있다고 하던데. 비행기가 취소될지도 몰라. (cancel)
→ I heard that a typhoon is coming. The flight ___________ ___________ ___________.

5 그의 제안을 받아들이는 것이 좋겠어. 우리가 그 기회를 날려버릴 수는 없잖아. (accept)
→ We ___________ ___________ ___________ ___________ his offer. We can't blow a chance.

6 그가 화를 내는 것도 당연하지. 그는 사람들이 약속 어기는 것을 싫어하거든. (be upset)
→ He ___________ ___________ ___________ ___________ about it. He hates it when people break promises.

7 리모컨 좀 줄래? 지금 다른 채널에서 더 재미있는 게 할지도 몰라. (be)
→ Can you pass me the remote control? More fun programs ___________ ___________ on other channels now.

E 우리말과 같은 뜻이 되도록 주어진 단어를 배열하시오.

1 제가 창문 좀 닫아도 될까요? 여기 좀 추워서요. (the windows, I, may, close)
→ ______________________________ It's a bit cold in here.

2 네가 지루하게 느끼는 것도 당연해. 이 주제는 네게 쉽지 않거든. (feel, you, bored, well, may)
→ ______________________________ This topic is not easy for you.

3 조금 더 기다려보는 게 좋겠어. 그가 곧 나타날 것 같아. (may, a little more, we, wait, as well)
→ ______________________________ I think he will show up soon.

4 사무실에서 기다리세요. 그는 지금 고객을 만나고 있을 거예요. (a client, may, meeting, he, be)
→ Please wait in his office. ______________________________ now.

5 그녀는 어제 괜찮아 보이지 않았다. 그녀는 지금 병원에 있을지도 모른다. (might, in the hospital, be, she)
→ She didn't look good yesterday. ______________________________ now.

6 그는 기차를 놓쳤다고 말했어. 모임이 늦을지도 몰라. (be, may, he, a little, for, late, the gathering)
→ He said he had missed the train. ______________________________

7 그녀가 네 아이디어를 받아들이지 않을지도 몰라. 그러니까 너는 2안을 준비해야 해.
(accept, she, your idea, not, might)
→ ______________________________ So you need to prepare plan B.

must (not), have to, don't have to

A 밑줄 친 부분에 유의하여 해석을 완성하시오.

1 You don't have to pick up the laundry. I already did.
→ 너는 세탁물을 ________________. 내가 이미 찾아왔어.

2 You must not take this medicine if you are pregnant.
→ 임신 중이면 이 약을 ________________.

3 You must follow the instructions when you operate this machine.
→ 이 기계를 작동할 때는 지시사항을 ________________.

4 She donated her kidney to a stranger. She must be an angel.
→ 그녀는 모르는 사람에게 신장을 기증했다. 그녀는 천사임이 ________________.

5 He threw up all night and had a high fever. He must have eaten spoiled food.
→ 그는 밤새 토하고 고열이 있었다. 그는 상한 음식을 ________________.

6 You will have to make a reservation at the restaurant because it is very popular.
→ 그 식당은 매우 인기가 있어서 ________________.

7 I texted her, but she didn't reply. She mustn't have checked the message.
→ 내가 그녀에게 문자를 보냈지만 그녀는 답을 하지 않았다. 내 메시지를 ________________.

B 문장의 의미가 통하도록 주어진 말을 이용하여 문장을 완성하시오.

1 You must finish the whole test within an hour. (have to)
→ You ________________________________ within an hour.

2 You cannot enter that room. It is for staff only. (must, not)
→ You ________________________________. It is for staff only.

3 It is necessary that you lose weight for your health. (must)
→ You ________________________________ for your health.

4 We don't have to hurry. We have enough time. (need, not)
→ We ________________________________. We have enough time.

5 You need to take the test in order to enter the college. (have to)
→ You ________________________________ in order to enter the college.

6 The train will leave at 9 o'clock sharp. So it is necessary that you not be late. (must)
→ The train will leave at 9 o'clock sharp. So you ________________.

C 우리말과 같은 뜻이 되도록 주어진 말과 must 또는 have to를 이용하여 문장을 완성하시오.

1 네가 해야 할 일은 결과를 기다리는 것뿐이다. (do)
→ All you ________ ________ ________ is wait for the result.

2 피부색으로 사람을 판단해서는 안 된다. (judge, people)
→ You ________ ________ ________ ________ on the basis of their skin color.

3 그 음식은 너무 매운 것이 틀림없어. 그가 땀을 엄청 흘리고 있어. (spicy)
→ The food ________ ________ ________ ________. He's sweating a lot.

4 너 정말 행복해 보여. 휴가를 즐겁게 보낸 모양이구나. (have)
→ You look so happy. You ________ ________ ________ an enjoyable holiday.

5 바다에서 수영을 할 때는 구명조끼를 입어야 한다. (wear, life jacket)
→ You ________ ________ ________ ________ ________ when you swim in the sea.

6 내일은 일요일이니까 일찍 일어날 필요가 없다. (get up)
→ I ________ ________ ________ ________ ________ early tomorrow because it is Sunday.

7 Lisa는 아파서 수업 중간에 조퇴를 해야 했다. (go, home)
→ Lisa ________ ________ ________ ________ in the middle of the class because she was sick.

D 우리말과 같은 뜻이 되도록 주어진 단어를 배열하시오.

1 우리는 표를 구입하지 않아도 되었다. (buy, we, have, didn't, the tickets, to)
→ ________________________________

2 너는 감기에 쉽게 걸려. 몸이 약한 게 틀림없어. (be, you, weak, very, must)
→ You catch colds easily. ________________________________

3 열쇠를 못 찾겠어. 어딘가 떨어뜨린 게 분명해. (it, must, I, somewhere, dropped, have)
→ I can't find my key. ________________________________

4 13세 이하의 어린이들은 롤러코스터를 타면 안 된다. (not, a roller coaster, must, ride)
→ Children aged thirteen and under ________________________________.

5 그것을 사용한 뒤에는 뚜껑을 반드시 닫아야 한다. (put, after, must, the lid, back on, you, it, use)
→ You ________________________________.

6 내가 표 두 장을 미리 예약했으니 우리는 줄 서서 기다릴 필요가 없어. (wait, we, in line, have to, don't)
→ I booked two tickets in advance, so ________________________________.

7 내가 초인종을 울렸지만 아무도 대답하지 않았다. 그들은 집에 없는 것이 틀림없다. (must, home, they, be, not)
→ I rang the doorbell, but nobody answered. ________________________________

should, ought to, had better

A 밑줄 친 부분에 유의하여 해석을 완성하시오.

1 You should stay within the speed limit.
→ 너는 제한 속도를 ____________________.

2 You really ought to start exercising.
→ 너는 정말로 운동을 ____________________.

3 You had better apologize to her right away.
→ 지금 당장 그녀에게 ____________________.

4 You should listen to your teacher during the class.
→ 수업 중에는 선생님 말씀을 ____________________.

5 You should not bother your brother when he is studying.
→ 네 형이 공부하고 있을 때 형을 ____________________.

6 They believe their country ought not to take part in the war.
→ 그들은 자신들의 나라가 그 전쟁에 ____________________ 믿고 있다.

7 When I drink something cold, my teeth ache. I had better go to the dentist.
→ 차가운 것을 마시면 이가 아프다. 치과에 ____________________.

B 보기 에서 알맞은 말을 골라 should (not) 또는 should (not) have p.p.를 이용하여 대화를 완성하시오.

보기	reserve	turn off	study	be	call	joke

1 A The movie is about to start.
B Yes. I ____________________ my cell phone right now.

2 A Mark is very angry with me. He won't talk to me at all.
B You ____________________ about that sensitive matter.

3 A I stayed up all night studying for the exam.
B Cramming is not effective at all. You ____________________ earlier.

4 A Excuse me. Can I talk to Mr. Brown?
B He's not in the office now. But he ____________________ back in half an hour.

5 A I can't visit my parents during the holidays. All the tickets are sold out.
B You ____________________ one in advance.

6 A Has Peter called?
B Not, yet. But he ____________________ me soon because he said he would call before he left.

C 우리말과 같은 뜻이 되도록 주어진 단어와 should 또는 ought to를 이용하여 문장을 완성하시오.

1 노인에게 자리를 양보해야 한다. (offer your seat)
→ You ______ ______ ______ ______ ______ to the elderly.

2 나 큰일 났어. 뭘 해야 좋을지 모르겠어. (do)
→ I'm in big trouble. I don't know what ______ ______ ______.

3 미안해. 그런 식으로 네게 말하지 말았어야 했는데. (tell)
→ I'm sorry. I ______ ______ ______ ______ like that.

4 너 창백해 보여. 하루 쉬어야 할 것 같아. (take a day off)
→ You look pale. I think you ______ ______ ______ ______ ______.

5 그 장난감이 다 팔렸어. 더 빨리 왔었어야 했는데. (come earlier)
→ The toys are all sold out. You ______ ______ ______ ______.

6 많이 연습했으니까 그녀는 경기에서 이길 것이다. (win the game)
→ She practiced a lot, so she ______ ______ ______ ______.

7 이렇게 중요한 문제에 대해 성급한 결정을 내리면 안 된다. (make a quick decision)
→ You ______ ______ ______ ______ ______ ______
about this important matter.

D 우리말과 같은 뜻이 되도록 주어진 단어를 배열하시오.

1 우리 서두르는 게 좋겠어. 기차를 놓칠지도 몰라. (better, hurry up, had, we)
→ ______________________ We might miss the train.

2 나 지금 약간 어지러워. 운전하지 않는 게 좋겠어. (not, I, drive, better, had)
→ I feel a bit dizzy now. ______________________

3 돼지꿈을 꿨을 때 복권을 샀어야 했는데. (should, a lottery ticket, I, bought, have)
→ ______________________ right after I dreamed about pigs.

4 가족과 좀 더 많은 시간을 보내도록 노력해야 한다. (spend, you, more time, try to, should)
→ ______________________ with your family.

5 나는 그의 조언을 따른 것이 후회된다. 그의 말을 듣지 말았어야 했는데. (shouldn't, him, I, listened to, have)
→ I regret following his advice. ______________________

6 사업상 중요한 부분이므로 그 회의를 미루지 않아야 한다. (to, the meeting, you, not, postpone, ought)
→ ______________________ because it's an important part of business.

7 그가 그 얘기를 다른 사람에게 듣기 전에 사실대로 이야기하는 게 좋을 거야. (tell, better, the truth, you, him, had)
→ ______________________ before he hears it from another person.

will, would, used to

A 보기 에서 알맞은 동사를 골라 would like to 또는 would rather (not)를 사용하여 대화를 완성하시오.

보기 go be sit talk drink

1 A Where would you like to be seated?
B I ________________ in the non-smoking section.

2 A Why don't you discuss it with Emma?
B I don't want her to know this problem. I ________________ to her.

3 A Would you like some milk?
B I ________________ some coffee.

4 A ________________ to Cindy's housewarming party? I'll pick you up at six.
B I'm sorry. I would rather not. I'm not feeling good today.

5 A Let's go shopping together tomorrow.
B I ________________ at home than go shopping in the crowd.

B 빈칸에 would 또는 used to를 써넣으시오. [둘 다 가능한 경우 would를 쓸 것]

1 My father ________________ read bedtime stories when I was little.

2 There ________________ be a park here, but now there are apartment buildings.

3 Brad ________________ be a troublemaker, but now he's one of the best students.

4 Lisa ________________ tease me a lot. Whenever she teased me, I ________________ cry.

5 There ________________ be a traditional market across the street.

C 우리말과 같은 뜻이 되도록 주어진 단어를 이용하여 문장을 완성하시오.

1 그 문제에 대해 지금 이야기하지 않는 게 낫겠어. (talk about)
→ I ________ ________ ________ ________ ________ the matter now.

2 나는 사람들 앞에서 이야기하는 것이 익숙하지 않다. (be, speak)
→ I ________ ________ ________ ________ ________ in front of people.

3 그는 젓가락을 사용하는 데 익숙하지 않다. (be, use)
→ He ________ ________ ________ ________ ________ chopsticks.

4 저 쇼핑몰은 쇼핑객으로 붐볐었다. (used, be crowded with, shoppers)
→ That mall ________ ________ ________ ________ ________ ________.

D 밑줄 친 부분에 유의하여 해석을 완성하시오.

1 Would you like to go to a movie?
→ 영화 보러 __________?

2 What type of room would you like?
→ 어떤 종류의 방을 __________?

3 Will you wait for a minute? Let me get my car key.
→ 잠시만 __________? 자동차 키 좀 가져올게.

4 Would you call a taxi for me, please?
→ 저를 위해 택시 좀 __________?

5 I would rather not answer the question right now.
→ 지금 당장은 그 질문에 __________.

6 My father used to be a math teacher, but he is retired now.
→ 우리 아빠는 예전에 수학 선생님 __________ 지금은 은퇴하셨다.

7 When my grandmother was sick, I would visit her every other week.
→ 우리 할머니가 아프셨을 때, 나는 2주에 한 번씩 할머니를 __________.

E 우리말과 같은 뜻이 되도록 주어진 단어를 알맞게 배열하시오.

1 그는 어렸을 때 온갖 종류의 책을 다 읽곤 했다. (all sorts of, read, would, books)
→ He __________ when he was young.

2 그녀는 규칙적인 생활을 하는 데 익숙하지 않다. (having, not, a regular lifestyle, she, used to, is)
→ __________

3 예전에는 이 주변에 사람들이 불법 주차를 하곤 했다. (people, around here, park, used to, illegally)
→ __________

4 오늘 나는 학교에 가지 않는 것이 낫겠어. 너무 아파. (not, school, rather, I, go to, today, would)
→ __________ I feel really ill.

5 새로운 직원인 Smith 씨를 소개하고 싶습니다. (introduce, I, like, would, to, our new employee)
→ __________ Mr. Smith.

6 이런 날씨에는 집에 있는 것보다 도보 여행을 가는 것이 낫겠어. (would rather, home, go, stay, than, hiking)
→ I __________ in this weather.

7 나의 여동생은 지금은 단 것을 좋아하지만, 어렸을 때는 단 것을 좋아하지 않았다. (like, she, use to, didn't, them)
→ My sister loves sweets now, but __________
when she was little.

Unit 44 추측의 정도

A 보기 에서 알맞은 말을 고르고 must 또는 may, might, could를 이용하여 대화를 완성하시오.

보기 be taking a test be intelligent be sick be my mother be tired be living

1 A Why isn't Tommy in tennis class?
 B I don't know. He ____________________.

2 A Sally got a perfect score on the math test again.
 B Wow. She ____________________.

3 A I stayed up all night because my dog was sick.
 B Yeah, I saw you dozing off in classes. You ____________________.

4 A Jack isn't answering his phone.
 B I'm not sure, but he ____________________ now.

5 A I talked to Lisa on the phone, and she sounded very happy.
 B Oh, she ____________________ a happy life in Vancouver.

6 A The windows of your house are wide open, and the lights are on.
 B Someone must be at home. It ____________________.

B 두 문장의 의미가 통하도록 문장을 완성하시오.

1 I am sure that she didn't buy a pet dog.
 → She _________________________ a pet dog.

2 I am sure that he forgot his wife's birthday.
 → He _________________________ his wife's birthday.

3 I am sure that I lost my wallet on the way home.
 → I _________________________ my wallet on the way home.

4 I am sure that she enjoys riding her horse.
 → She _________________________ riding her horse.

5 I am sure that he didn't visit his grandparents last weekend.
 → He _________________________ his grandparents last weekend.

6 I am not sure, but it is possible that she was late for school today.
 → She _________________________ late for school today.

7 I am not sure, but it is possible that she doesn't know your situation exactly.
 → She _________________________ your situation exactly.

C 우리말과 같은 뜻이 되도록 주어진 말을 이용하여 문장을 완성하시오.

1 그녀는 분명 회의에 늦을 거야. 기차를 놓쳤거든. (be late for)
→ She ________ ________ ________ ________ the meeting. She missed the train.

2 그 비행편은 취소됐을 리가 없어. 내가 이미 확인했어. (cancel)
→ The flight ________ ________ ________ ________. I've already checked it.

3 그는 수학여행을 가지 않을지도 몰라. 감기에 걸렸거든. (go on)
→ He ________ ________ ________ ________ the school trip. He caught a cold.

4 그는 공부를 열심히 한 게 틀림없어. 만점을 받았어. (study, hard)
→ He ________ ________ ________ ________. He got a perfect score.

5 그녀는 털 알레르기가 있을지도 몰라. 재채기를 몇 번 했어. (be allergic to)
→ She ________ ________ ________ ________ pet fur. She sneezed several times.

6 Nancy는 뉴욕에 있을 리가 없어. 내가 그녀를 오늘 아침에 봤거든. (be, in New York)
→ Nancy ________ ________ ________ ________ ________. I saw her this morning.

7 그는 다른 학교로 전학을 갔을지도 몰라. 한동안 그를 보지 못했어. (transfer)
→ He ________ ________ ________ to another school. I haven't seen him for a while.

D 우리말과 같은 뜻이 되도록 주어진 단어를 알맞게 배열하시오.

1 잘은 모르겠지만 그녀는 다른 도시로 이사 갈지도 몰라. (another city, she, to, move, may)
→ I'm not sure, but ____.

2 그는 오늘 커피를 네 잔이나 마셨어. 커피를 좋아하는 것이 틀림없어. (like, he, must, coffee)
→ He drank four cups of coffee today. ________________________________

3 토요일이었으니 그날 가게가 문을 닫았을지도 모른다. (may, closed, the shop, been, have)
→ It was Saturday, so ________________________________ on that day.

4 Henry는 흠뻑 젖었다. 우산을 깜빡하고 가져오지 않은 것이 틀림없다.
(to bring, he, forgotten, his umbrella, have, must)
→ Henry got all wet. ____

5 그녀가 그때 자고 있었을 리 없어. 그녀는 언제나 일찍 일어나거든. (asleep, she, have, couldn't, been)
→ ________________________________ then because she always gets up early.

6 그는 파티에 가지 않았을지도 몰라. 그는 사람이 많은 곳을 좋아하지 않아.
(gone, to the party, he, have, not, might)
→ ________________________________ He doesn't like crowded places.

7 그녀는 그의 사무실 근처에 살았었어. 그의 사무실이 어딘지 알지도 몰라. (it, she, where, might, is, know)
→ She used to live near his office. ________________________________

정중한 부탁이나 허가

A 보기 에서 동사를 어법에 맞게 바꿔 대화를 완성하시오.

보기	take	open	exchange	wait	use	ask

1 A Would you mind ___________ seats with me?
  B Of course not.

2 A Would you mind if I ___________ the window?
  B No, not at all. It feels stuffy in here.

3 A Would you mind if I ___________ your cell phone?
  B I'm sorry. I'm expecting a call.

4 A Would you mind if I ___________ you a personal question?
  B That depends.

5 A Would you mind ___________ a picture of us in front of this tower?
  B No problem at all. Give me your camera.

6 A Would you mind ___________ for a while? He will be back in a minute.
  B No problem.

B 상황을 읽고, 주어진 단어를 이용하여 허가를 구하거나 부탁을 하는 문장을 만드시오.

1 You want to check out the book in the library. You can ask:
(I, can) → ______________________________

2 You want to turn on the air conditioner. You can ask:
(I, could) → ______________________________

3 You want your friend to show you around the town. You can ask:
(you, will) → ______________________________

4 You want a waiter to get you a glass of iced water. You can ask:
(you, could) → ______________________________

5 You're a waiter. You want to take the customer's order. You can ask:
(I, may) → ______________________________

6 You want your teacher to explain the problem in detail. You can ask:
(you, would) → ______________________________

7 You want your friend to tell you how to get to the train station. You can ask:
(you, can) → ______________________________

C 우리말과 같은 뜻이 되도록 주어진 말을 이용하여 문장을 완성하시오.

1 거실 전등 좀 꺼줄래? (will, turn off, the light)

→ ___________ ___________ ___________ ___________ ___________ ___________ in the living room?

2 저를 집까지 태워주시겠어요? (would, mind, give)

→ ___________ ___________ ___________ ___________ me a ride home?

3 엄마, 책 사게 돈 좀 주실래요? (can, have, some money)

→ Mom, ___________ ___________ ___________ ___________ ___________ to buy a book?

4 당신 옆자리에 제가 앉아도 될까요? (would, mind)

→ ___________ ___________ ___________ if I took the seat next to you?

5 그는 사무실에 안 계십니다. 메모 남겨드릴까요? (take, a message)

→ He's not in the office. ___________ ___________ ___________ ___________ ___________?

6 창가 쪽 테이블에 앉는 것이 괜찮으신가요? (would, mind, get)

→ ___________ ___________ ___________ ___________ a table by the window?

7 그에게 오늘은 사무실에 돌아오지 않을 것이라고 전해 주시겠어요? (could, tell)

→ ___________ ___________ ___________ ___________ I won't be back to the office today?

D 우리말과 같은 뜻이 되도록 주어진 단어를 알맞게 배열하시오.

1 나 좀 혼자 내버려둘래? 나 시험공부 해야 해. (leave, will, alone, me, you)

→ ______________________________ I have to study for the exam.

2 오늘 좀 더 일찍 퇴근해도 될까요? (work earlier, you, mind, would, if, left, I)

→ ______________________________ today?

3 여권과 탑승권을 보여주시겠어요? (your passport, I, and, boarding pass, can, see)

→ ______________________________, please?

4 제가 내일 당신을 제 사무실에서 만날 수 있을까요? (meet, could, at my office, I, you, tomorrow)

→ ______________________________

5 자리를 한 칸 더 옆으로 옮겨주시겠어요? (mind, one more seat, would, moving over, you)

→ ______________________________

6 저를 국립 박물관에 데려다주시겠어요? (the National Museum, you, to, would, me, take)

→ ______________________________

7 제한 속도를 위반하셨습니다. 운전 면허증을 보여주시겠어요? (see, may, I, your, driver's license)

→ You broke the speed limit. ______________________________

Unit 46 제안하기

A 보기 에서 알맞은 표현을 골라 대화를 완성하시오.

보기			
	why don't you give	let's go out	let's turn
	why don't we have	shall I call	shall we shop

1 A If you are busy now, ______________ you back later?
  B Well, I'd better call you later.

2 A They offered me the job, but I think I'd better not take it.
  B ______________ it a try? I'm sure you can do it well.

3 A I failed the test. I'm very depressed. I don't want to stay home.
  B ______________ for a change.

4 A Marcy's department store is having a sale today.
  B ______________ for shoes there? You said you need new shoes.

5 A ______________ some snacks on the way home?
  B I'd love to, but I have to go. My mother told me to come home early.

6 A Now, ______________ to the topic about environmental pollution.
  B I think there are a lot of things we can do to stop environmental pollution.

B 보기 에서 알맞은 것을 골라 주어진 표현을 이용하여 문장을 완성하시오.

[1-4] Let's ~.

보기	keep	put	have	hurry up

1 ______________ this table in the living room.

2 ______________ some food delivered or eat out.

3 We don't have enough time. ______________

4 Even though you will be living a long way from here, ______________ in touch.

[5-8] Why don't we ~?

보기	order	participate	take	exercise

5 ______________________________ in the workshop?

6 ______________________________ regularly for our health?

7 ______________________________ pizza instead of eating out?

8 ______________________________ a walk and get some fresh air?

C 우리말과 같은 뜻이 되도록 주어진 단어를 이용하여 문장을 완성하시오.

1 우리 회의를 하루만 연기하면 어때요? (put off)

→ ______ ______ ______ ______ ______ the meeting for a day?

2 이제 잡담은 그만하고 일 합시다. (get down to)

→ Now, stop chatting, and ______ ______ ______ ______ work.

3 그 사고에 대해서는 잊지 맙시다. (forget about)

→ ______ ______ ______ ______ the incident.

4 그가 집에 왔을지도 몰라. 네가 그에게 다시 전화해보는 게 어때? (call)

→ He might have come home. ______ ______ ______ ______ him again?

5 제가 내일 당신의 아침 식사를 방으로 가져다 드릴까요? (bring, breakfast)

→ ______ ______ ______ ______ ______ to your room tomorrow?

6 우리 바다로 수영하러 갈까 아니면 그냥 리조트 안에서 놀까? (go swimming)

→ ______ ______ ______ ______ in the sea or just spend time within the resort?

7 내가 그에게 우리가 프로젝트 하는 것을 도와달라고 부탁해 볼까? (shall, ask, to help)

→ ______ ______ ______ ______ ______ ______ us do our project?

D 우리말과 같은 뜻이 되도록 주어진 단어를 알맞게 배열하시오.

1 우리 먼저 마실 것을 좀 주문할까요? (something, to drink, we, order, shall)

→ ______ first?

2 오늘 저녁 여섯 시에 내가 너를 데리러 갈까? (pick, shall, up, you, I, at six)

→ ______ this evening?

3 그의 앞에서 그 문제에 대해 이야기하지 말자. (the issue, let's, talk about, not)

→ ______ in front of him.

4 운동을 시작하기 전에 안전을 위해 준비 운동부터 하자. (we, warm up, exercising, let's, first, start, before)

→ ______ for safety.

5 엄마 생일을 위해 우리가 직접 저녁을 만드는 것이 어때? (make, why, by ourselves, don't, we, dinner)

→ ______ for mom's birthday?

6 이 질문은 너무 어려워. 건너뛰고 나중에 다시 해결해 보자. (skip, and, let's, it, it, tackle)

→ This question is too difficult. ______ later again.

7 다가오는 휴가 동안에 가족과 함께 좀 더 많은 시간을 보내는 것은 어때요?
(with your family, you, why, more time, don't, spend)

→ ______ during the upcoming holiday?

형용사의 종류와 어순

A 상황을 읽고, 주어진 단어를 '–ing' 또는 '–ed'로 바꿔 문장을 완성하시오.

1 Living in the country bores me. (bore)
→ I am ____________ with living in the country.
→ Living in the country is ____________ to me.

2 Traveling to a new country interests him. (interest)
→ Rick is ____________ in traveling to a new country.
→ Traveling to a new country is ____________ to Rick.

3 Studying until late every night exhausted him. (exhaust)
→ He was ____________ from studying until late every night.
→ Studying until late every night was ____________ to him.

4 The idea that human life is too short depresses him. (depress)
→ He is ____________ to think that human life is too short.
→ It is ____________ to think that human life is too short.

5 Jack was speaking ill of me behind my back. That really shocked me. (shock)
→ I was ____________ by the fact that Jack was speaking ill of me behind my back.
→ The fact that Jack was speaking ill of me behind my back was ____________ to me.

B 밑줄 친 부분을 바르게 고치시오. 틀리지 않았다면 ○표 하시오.

1 They always have alike hairstyles like twins. ____________
2 It seemed that he wanted to be left alone in the classroom. ____________
3 We found it excited to go on a backpacking trip to Europe. ____________
4 Injuring people were carried away to the hospital right after the accident. ____________
5 He does his best to make his customers feel satisfying with his service. ____________
6 My cell phone rang loudly in the theater. It was very embarrassed to me. ____________
7 She is afraid of trying new things, so she always does things she is familiar with. ____________
8 I know that exercising regularly is good for my health, but sometimes it is too tired. ____________

C **우리말과 같은 뜻이 되도록 주어진 단어를 이용하여 문장을 완성하시오.**

1 Kelvin은 기말 고사가 걱정된다. (be, worry, about)

→ Kelvin __________ __________ __________ the final exams.

2 많은 사람 앞에서 얼음 판 위에서 넘어진 것은 창피하다. (be, embarrass)

→ Falling on the ice in front of many people __________ __________.

3 방에 불을 끄지 마세요. 나는 천둥소리가 너무 무서워서요. (feel, frighten)

→ Please leave the lights on in the room because __________ __________ __________ by the thunder.

4 나는 그녀가 우리의 대화를 듣고 있었다는 것을 알고 깜짝 놀랐다. (be, surprise)

→ __________ __________ __________ to know she was listening to our conversation.

5 그녀는 자신의 우는 아기를 달래기 위해 아기의 등을 두드렸다. (soothe, cry, baby)

→ __________ __________ __________ __________ __________, she patted it on the back.

6 나는 열심히 공부했지만 결과는 매우 실망스러웠다. (the result, be, disappoint)

→ I studied hard, but __________ __________ __________ __________ __________.

7 이 표현은 구어체에서는 사용되지만 문어체에서는 적절하지 않다. (speak, write, language)

→ This expression is used in __________ __________, but it's not appropriate for __________ __________.

D **우리말과 같은 뜻이 되도록 주어진 단어를 배열하시오.**

1 그녀는 멋진 새 갈색 코트를 입고 있었다. (coat, new, nice, a, brown)

→ She was wearing ______________________________.

2 나는 정원에 아름답고 키가 큰 녹색 나무를 심고 싶다. (tree, a, green, tall, beautiful)

→ I want to plant ______________________________ in my garden.

3 탁자 위에 있는 큰 갈색 가죽 가방 좀 내게 건네주세요. (brown, bag, the, leather, large)

→ Please pass me ______________________________ on the table.

4 그녀는 파란 큰 눈에 아름다운 긴 금발 머리를 하고 있다. (long, blond, beautiful, blue, big, hair, eyes)

→ She has ____________________ with ____________________.

5 많은 사람이 문제를 인식하고 있지만 아무도 상황을 개선하려고 하지 않는다.
(the problem, aware of, lots of, are, people)

→ ______________________________, but nobody tries to improve the situation.

6 지난주에 눈이 많이 왔을 때 나는 우리 집의 낡은 파란 지붕이 매우 걱정되었다.
(worried about, of my house, I, the old, roof, very, blue, was)

→ ______________________________ when it snowed a lot last week.

부사의 종류와 위치

A **보기** 에서 알맞은 빈도부사를 골라 문장을 완성하시오. [중복 사용 가능]

보기 always usually often sometimes seldom never

1 나는 방과 후에 대개 친구들과 농구를 한다.

→ I ____________ play basketball with my friends after school.

2 인생에서 뭔가를 포기하는 것은 때로는 어려운 일이다.

→ It is ____________ hard to give up something in your life.

3 우리 부모님은 언제나 내가 새로운 것에 도전하도록 격려해 주셨다.

→ My parents have ____________ encouraged me to try challenging new things.

4 Diana는 사적인 것들에 대해서는 좀처럼 이야기를 하지 않는다.

→ Diana ____________ talks about personal things.

5 이 지역의 날씨는 빈번하게 바뀌어서, 항상 우산을 가지고 다녀야 한다.

→ The weather in this region changes frequently, so you ____________ need to carry your umbrella.

6 우리 아버지께서는 종종 반찬투정을 하시는데 어머니께서는 그것에 대해 아무 말씀도 하지 않으신다.

→ My father ____________ complains about food, and my mother ____________ says anything about it.

B 주어진 부사를 알맞은 위치에 넣어 문장을 다시 쓰시오.

1 My mother cleans my room. (often)

→ ____

2 His concert begins. (at 7:30 p.m., on December 24th)

→ ____

3 I studied English. (very hard, in the library, yesterday)

→ ____

4 My mother says children should go to bed. (always, early)

→ ____

5 My father has obtained a driver's license, so he tends to drive. (just, very carefully)

→ ____

C 보기 에서 알맞은 부사를 골라 문장을 완성하시오.

보기	already	almost	here	there	later	carefully	terribly	enthusiastically

1 우리 반 학생들은 우리 축구팀을 열정적으로 응원했다.
→ My classmates cheered our soccer team ____________.

2 나는 지금 출장 중이니까 나중에 네 메일을 확인할게.
→ I'm away on a business trip now, so I'll check your email ____________.

3 이 시간에 전화 드려 정말 죄송합니다만 급한 일이라서요.
→ I am ____________ sorry to call you at this hour, but it's an emergency.

4 무척 깨지기 쉬우니 이 꽃병을 조심해서 다루어야 합니다.
→ You need to handle this vase ____________ because it is very fragile.

5 내가 집에 도착했을 때, 그들은 이미 저녁 식사를 끝낸 뒤였다.
→ When I got home, they had ____________ finished dinner.

6 나는 거리를 건너던 개를 거의 칠 뻔해서 무척 놀랐다.
→ I was very surprised because I ____________ hit the dog crossing the street.

7 너 거기서 뭐 하고 있니? 여기로 와서 우리랑 함께 이야기하는 게 어때?
→ What are you doing ____________? Why don't you come ____________ and talk with us?

D 우리말과 같은 뜻이 되도록 주어진 단어를 배열하시오.

1 내가 역에 도착했을 때 기차는 이미 떠나버렸다. (already, the train, left, had)
→ When I arrived at the station, ________________________________.

2 그는 자신의 성공을 완전히 확신하고 있었다. (completely, was, he, sure)
→ ________________________________ of his success.

3 나는 파리의 에펠탑을 정말로 직접 보고 싶다. (to see, the Eiffel Tower, want, really, in Paris)
→ I ________________________________ in person.

4 저는 이미 숙제를 끝냈는데 이제 나가서 놀아도 되나요? (my homework, I've, finished, already)
→ ________________________________, so can I go out to play now?

5 우리는 가끔 서로 다툴 때도 있지만 여전히 좋은 친구 사이이다.
(each other, still, sometimes, argue with, good friends)
→ We ____________________, but we are ____________________.

6 그는 정중하게 공항 가는 길을 내게 물었고, 나는 방향을 알려주었다.
(how to, asked, he, get to, me, politely, the airport)
→ ________________________________, so I gave directions.

7 그녀는 그 당시에 대기실에서 자신의 차례를 초조하게 기다리고 있었다.
(nervously waiting, at that time, was, in the waiting room, her turn)
→ She ________________________________.

주의해야 할 형용사와 부사

A **보기** 에서 알맞은 것을 골라 우리말과 같은 뜻이 되도록 빈칸에 써넣으시오. [중복 사용 가능]

보기	enough	too	very

1 괜찮아요. 이미 충분히 먹었습니다.
→ No, thanks. I've already had ____________.

2 그녀는 자신의 승리에 대해 대단히 자신 있어 보였다.
→ She looked ____________ confident of her victory.

3 그는 맨 위쪽 선반에 손이 닿을 만큼 키가 크지 않다.
→ He is not tall ____________ to reach the top shelf.

4 그 수프는 너무 뜨거워서 나는 손도 대지 못했다.
→ The soup was ____________ hot, so I couldn't even touch it.

5 삼촌께서 내게 결혼할 만큼 충분한 나이가 되었다고 말씀하셨다.
→ My uncle told me that I'm old ____________ to get married.

6 그 코트는 너무 비싸서 나는 사지 않기로 결정했다.
→ The coat was ____________ expensive, so I decided not to buy it.

B **밑줄 친 부분에 유의하여 해석을 완성하시오.**

1 (1) Certain people have trouble eating flour-based food.
→ ____________________ 밀가루로 된 음식을 먹는 데 어려움이 있다.
(2) I'm certain that he won't be able to finish his work in time.
→ 나는 그가 제시간에 일을 끝낼 수 없을 거라고 ____________________.

2 (1) There are a few solutions to the present situation.
→ ____________________에 대한 몇 가지 해결책이 있다.
(2) The CEO is going to be present at the opening ceremony of New Year.
→ 그 최고경영자는 신년 행사에 ____________________.

3 (1) My wife repeatedly asked me not to be late for the family reunion.
→ 나의 아내는 내게 가족 모임에 ____________________ 신신당부했다.
(2) The organization was founded in the late 1980s and the late founder was one of the most respected people.
→ 그 단체는 ____________________ 설립되었고, ____________________는 가장 존경받는 사람들 중 한 명이었다.

C 보기 에서 단어를 고르고 주어진 말을 이용하여 문장을 완성하시오.

[1-3] 보기 such nearly so

1 나는 학교 가는 길에 트럭에 거의 치일 뻔했다. (be run over)
→ I ____________ ____________ ____________ ____________ by a truck on my way to school.

2 그곳은 대단히 아름다운 도시여서 돌아오고 싶지 않을 정도였다. (beautiful, city)
→ It was ____________ ____________ ____________ ____________ that I didn't want to come back.

3 남편과 나는 평일에 출근을 하기 때문에 우리 집은 보통 정말 조용하다. (quiet)
→ My husband and I go to work on weekdays, so our house is usually ____________ ____________.

[4-6] 보기 hardly highly late

4 거리 아래쪽에 있는 이탈리아 식당을 강력히 추천합니다. (be recommended)
→ The Italian restaurant down the street ____________ ____________ ____________.

5 최근에 깨달은 것은 인생에서 배움에 너무 늦은 때란 없다는 것이다. (too)
→ I've realized lately that it's not ____________ ____________ to learn in life.

6 나는 그 말썽꾸러기가 하버드에 합격했다는 것을 거의 믿을 수 없었다! (believe)
→ I could ____________ ____________ that the troublemaker had been accepted to Harvard!

D 우리말과 같은 뜻이 되도록 주어진 단어를 배열하시오.

1 그가 제시간에 오는 것은 거의 불가능하다. (that, is, unlikely, it, highly)
→ ________________________________ he will make it on time.

2 이번 시험에는 어려운 문제가 너무 많았다. (in this exam, too, questions, hard, many)
→ There were ________________________________.

3 마늘은 거의 모든 한국 음식에 사용된다. (all, is used, nearly, garlic, in, Korean food)
→ ________________________________

4 그녀는 그가 경기에서 또 이길 것이라고 확신했다. (would win, was, that, she, he, certain)
→ ________________________________ the game again.

5 그녀의 작고한 남편은 그녀와 아이들에게 막대한 유산을 남겼다. (late, a large fortune, her, left, husband)
→ ________________________________ to her and her children.

6 나는 새해 결심을 세웠지만 그것이 오래가지 못할 것이라는 것을 안다. (know, last, they, I, won't, long)
→ I made New Year's resolutions, but ________________________________.

7 그는 빨리 배우는 편이라 그것을 마스터하는 데 많은 시간이 필요하지 않았다. (he, learner, a, because, was, fast)
→ He didn't need much time to master it ________________________________.

원급을 이용한 비교 구문

A 보기 에서 알맞은 것을 골라 as ~ as를 사용하여 문장을 완성하시오.

보기	great	quickly	slowly	tall
	long	expensive	soon	

1 ____________ you are satisfied with it, I'm happy.

2 I think no love is ____________ a mother's love.

3 This camera is twice ____________ that one.

4 She ran ____________ she could to catch the last bus.

5 Turn right ____________ you pass the post office and keep going.

6 I didn't use to be taller than my sister. But now I am ____________ her.

7 I want you to speak ____________ possible because I'm not good at English.

B 문장의 의미가 통하도록 문장을 완성하시오.

1 Try to hold your breath as long as you can.
→ Try to hold your breath ____________.

2 This book looks less difficult than that one.
→ This book doesn't look ____________ that one.

3 The class was less interesting than I expected.
→ The class was not ____________ I expected.

4 She fell asleep as soon as she lay in her bed.
→ No ____________ in her bed ____________ she fell asleep.

5 You should have some rest as frequently as possible.
→ You should have some rest ____________.

6 He tried to arrive at the meeting place as early as possible.
→ He tried to arrive at the meeting place ____________.

7 A good personality is the most important thing when you make friends with someone.
→ Nothing is ____________ a good personality when you make friends with someone.

C 우리말과 같은 뜻이 되도록 주어진 단어를 이용하여 문장을 완성하시오.

1 이 컴퓨터는 저것보다 좋아 보이지 않는다. (look, good)
→ This computer ____ ____ ____ ____ ____ that one.

2 그의 두 번째 책은 첫 번째 책만큼 잘 팔린다. (sell, well)
→ His second book ____ ____ ____ ____ his first book.

3 우리 언니네 집은 우리 집보다 두 배는 더 크다. (twice, large)
→ My sister's house is ____ ____ ____ ____ mine.

4 네가 조용이 있기만 하면, 여기 있어도 좋다. (long, keep quiet)
→ You can stay here ____ ____ ____ ____ ____
____.

5 그는 지금까지 없었던 가장 훌륭한 소설가다. (great, novelist, ever)
→ He is ____ ____ ____ ____ ____ ____ lived.

6 그녀가 무대에 등장하자마자 열렬한 박수를 받았다. (no sooner, appear)
→ ____ ____ ____ ____ ____ on the stage
____ she got enthusiastic applause.

7 우리 반에서 어느 누구도 Sarah만큼 똑똑하지 않다. (no one, smart)
→ I think ____ ____ in my class is ____ ____ ____
Sarah.

D 우리말과 같은 뜻이 되도록 주어진 단어를 배열하시오.

1 이 도로가 저 도로보다 덜 미끄럽다. (that one, less, than, is, slippery)
→ This road ____.

2 공을 가능한 한 멀리 던지도록 해라. (the ball, possible, throw, far, as, as)
→ Try to ____.

3 그녀는 나이가 들었지만, 여전히 아름다웠다. (as, was, ever, as, she, beautiful)
→ Even though she got older, ____.

4 내일은 일요일이니까 내가 원하는 만큼 잘 수 있다. (sleep, I, much, as, want, I, can, as)
→ Tomorrow is Sunday, so ____.

5 그의 학교는 내가 생각했던 것만큼 여기서 멀지 않았다. (I, far, was, from here, thought, not, as, so)
→ His school ____.

6 그가 이야기를 마치자마자 방 안의 사람들은 모두 조용해졌다. (he, than, no sooner, finished, had, talking)
→ ____ everyone in the room went silent.

비교급을 이용한 비교 구문

A 빈칸에 than과 to 중 알맞은 것을 써넣으시오.

1 Every candidate will take written tests prior ___________ the interview.

2 She looks younger ___________ she actually is after she getting her haircut.

3 The idea that Western culture is superior ___________ Eastern culture is wrong.

4 This hotel offers much better service ___________ others, so it's very expensive.

5 The exam was less difficult ___________ I expected, so I was able to finish it in time.

6 She felt inferior ___________ her brother when it came to appearance and educational background.

7 He and I are in the same year at college, but he is junior ___________ me by two years.

8 My mother is three years senior ___________ my father but she looks younger ___________ him.

9 This sofa is more comfortable ___________ that one even though it is the cheaper of the two.

10 Today's temperature is the same as yesterday's, but it feels much hotter ___________ yesterday.

B 문장의 의미가 통하도록 문장을 완성하시오.

1 As I make more money, I feel less happy.

→ ___________ ___________ money I make, ___________ ___________ ___________ I feel.

2 The subway was not as crowded as yesterday.

→ The subway was ___________ ___________ ___________ yesterday.

3 I do not go to church as frequently as I used to.

→ I go to church ___________ ___________ ___________ I used to.

4 He was rich, and he has made much more money this year.

→ He got ___________ and ___________.

5 As it becomes more expensive, more people want to buy it.

→ ___________ ___________ expensive it becomes, ___________ ___________ people want to buy it.

6 Our product is not as competitive as theirs when it comes to price.

→ Our product is ___________ ___________ ___________ theirs when it comes to price.

C 다음 밑줄 친 부분을 바르게 고쳐 쓰시오.

1 More I talk to him, more I like him. __________
2 I think that car is the more expensive than the two. __________
3 It tastes more like barley tea to coffee, so it tastes delicious. __________
4 The salesperson told me that this camera is very better than that one. __________
5 She is junior than all of us in the club. __________

D 우리말과 같은 뜻이 되도록 주어진 단어를 이용하여 문장을 완성하시오.

1 그는 나이가 들면 들수록 아빠를 점점 더 닮아간다. (old, much)
→ ________ ________ he gets, ________ ________ he looks like his father.

2 조깅을 시작한 뒤로 그는 전보다 훨씬 더 건강해졌다. (much, healthy)
→ Since he began jogging, he has become ________ ________ ________ before.

3 그는 현재 받는 월급보다 더 높은 월급을 받기를 기대하고 있다. (high, pay)
→ He expects to receive ________ ________ ________ he is currently receiving.

4 우리 학교의 축구팀은 그의 학교 축구팀보다 체력적으로 훨씬 열등하다. (far, inferior)
→ The soccer team of my school is physically ________ ________ ________ ________ of his school.

5 내일 눈이 올 것이므로 내일은 평소보다 더 일찍 나가야 한다. (leave, early, usual)
→ It'll snow tomorrow, so you need to ________ ________ ________ ________.

E 우리말과 같은 뜻이 되도록 주어진 단어를 배열하시오.

1 운동을 많이 하면 할수록, 건강해진다. (the, the, healthier, get, more, you, exercise)
→ ________________ you do, ________________.

2 시간이 지날수록 그의 호흡은 점점 더 가빠졌다. (became, and, harder, his breathing, harder)
→ As time went by, ________________.

3 문제가 어려우면 어려울수록 나는 더욱더 집중하게 된다.
(difficult, concentrate, the, the, more, more, I)
→ ________________ the questions are, ________________.

4 네가 더 빨리 결정을 내리면 내릴수록 우리는 프로젝트를 더 빨리 끝낼 수 있을 것이다.
(the, the, make, sooner, more, you, quickly)
→ ________________ your decision, ________________ we'll be able to finish the project.

최상급을 이용한 비교 구문

A 보기 에서 알맞은 것을 골라 최상급으로 바꿔 문장을 완성하시오.

보기 thin far long late cold difficult high

1 English is ____________ ____________ ____________ subject to me.
2 Last Sunday was ____________ ____________ day of the year.
3 Mount Everest is ____________ ____________ mountain in the world.
4 Do you know what ____________ ____________ river in the world is?
5 You need to upgrade the software to ____________ ____________ version.
6 The company made ____________ ____________ cell phone in the world.
7 My uncle lives ____________ away from Seoul.

B 최상급 의미가 되도록 문장을 완성하시오.

1 He is the luckiest man in the world.
→ He is ________________________________ in the world. (비교급, any other)
→ ____________ other man in the world is ____________________ him. (no, 비교급)
→ ____________ other man in the world is ____________________ him. (no, 원급)

2 Today is the coldest day of this winter.
→ Today is ________________________________ of this winter. (비교급, any other)
→ ____________ day this winter is ____________________ today. (no, 비교급)
→ ____________ day this winter is ____________________ today. (no, 원급)

3 She is the most intelligent employee in my company.
→ She is ________________________________ in my company. (비교급, any other)
→ ____________ one in my company is ____________________ her. (no, 비교급)
→ ____________ one in my company is ____________________ her. (no, 원급)

4 That town is the most dangerous in the country.
→ That town is ________________________________ in the country. (비교급, any other)
→ ____________ town in the country is ____________________ that town. (no, 비교급)
→ ____________ town in the country is ____________________ that town. (no, 원급)

C 우리말과 같은 뜻이 되도록 주어진 단어를 이용하여 문장을 완성하시오.

1 우리 아버지는 다섯 남매 중 첫째다. (old)
→ My father is ___________ ___________ ___________ five children.

2 그는 1990년대에 가장 유명한 가수였다. (famous)
→ He was ___________ ___________ ___________ ___________ of the 1990s.

3 이것이 그 수학 문제를 푸는 가장 쉬운 방법이다. (easy, way)
→ This is ___________ ___________ ___________ to solve that math question.

4 우리가 이 기회를 최대한 이용하는 것이 중요하다. (make, most)
→ It is important for us to ___________ ___________ ___________ ___________ this chance.

5 그는 한국에서 가장 존경받는 최고경영자 중 한 사람이다. (respected, CEO)
→ He is ___________ ___________ ___________ ___________ ___________ ___________ in Korea.

6 이것이 회사로서는 최악의 상황이라는 것을 모두가 알고 있다. (bad, situation)
→ Everyone knows this is ___________ ___________ ___________ for the company ever.

7 내가 알기로는, 그녀는 결코 다른 사람을 속일만한 사람이 아니다. (late, person, deceive)
→ As far as I know, she would be ___________ ___________ ___________ ___________ ___________ others.

D 우리말과 같은 뜻이 되도록 주어진 단어를 배열하시오.

1 나는 그 소식을 듣고 전혀 놀라지 않았다. (surprised, in the least, at the news, not)
→ I was ___________________________________.

2 그녀는 대부분의 시간을 애완동물과 집에서 보낸다. (her time, spends, most of, at home)
→ She ___________________________________ with her pets.

3 나는 다른 어떤 악기 소리보다 기타 소리가 좋다. (musical instrument's, than, better, any other)
→ I like the sound of the guitar ___________________________________.

4 그가 추천해 준 호텔은 기껏해야 평균적인 수준이었다. (best, at, was, he, average, recommended)
→ The hotel that ___________________________________.

5 사람을 겉만 보고 판단하는 것만큼 위험한 것도 없다. (judging, nothing, people, is, as dangerous as)
→ ___________________________________ by their appearance.

6 나는 한국어가 가장 배우기 어려운 언어 중 하나라고 생각한다. (the hardest, to learn, one of, languages)
→ I think that Korean is ___________________________________.

7 사람들은 그가 농구 역사상 가장 훌륭한 선수였다고 말한다. (the history, the greatest, in, of basketball, player)
→ People say he was ___________________________________.

형용사를 이용한 기타 비교 구문

A **우리말과 같은 뜻이 되도록 the same as, similar to, different from 중에서 알맞은 말을 골라 문장을 완성하시오.**

1 내 여동생은 나와 똑같은 가방을 샀다.
→ My sister bought ____________ bag ____________ mine.

2 러시아의 기후는 한국의 기후와는 다르다.
→ The climate of Russia is ____________ ____________ that of Korea.

3 그 과학자는 지구와 매우 유사한 행성을 발견했다.
→ The scientist found a planet that is very ____________ ____________ Earth.

4 저는 그 문제에 관해서 당신과 다른 의견을 가지고 있습니다.
→ I don't have ____________ opinion ____________ yours on the issue.

5 나는 그의 목소리가 그의 아버지의 목소리와 매우 비슷하다고 생각했다.
→ I thought that his voice was very ____________ ____________ his father's.

6 어떤 사람들은 다른 사람들과 다른 생각을 말하는 것을 두려워한다.
→ Some people are afraid of expressing ideas ____________ ____________ others.

B **다음 두 문장이 같은 의미가 되도록 문장을 완성하시오.**

1 My birthday and my mother's birthday are the same.
→ My birthday is ____________ my mother's.

2 The bus that you and I have to take is the same.
→ I have to get on ____________ bus ____________ you have to.

3 Humans and animals are different in many ways.
→ Humans are ____________ animals in many ways.

4 The ukulele and the guitar look similar, but the ukulele is far smaller in size.
→ The ukulele looks ____________ the guitar, but it's far smaller in size.

5 It was found that the genes of gorillas and humans are similar.
→ It was found that the genes of gorillas are ____________ those of humans.

6 I found that the delivered goods and the sample are very different.
→ I found that the delivered goods are very ____________ the sample.

7 The new product from our rival company and our product are very similar.
→ The new product from our rival company is very ____________ ours.

C 우리말과 같은 뜻이 되도록 주어진 단어를 이용하여 문장을 완성하시오.

1 나는 Brian과 같은 반이다. (class)
→ I am in ________ ________ ________ ________ Brian.

2 네 전화번호는 예전이랑 똑같니? (before)
→ Is your phone number ________ ________ ________ ________?

3 두 자매는 너무 닮아서 구별하기가 무척 힘들다. (look)
→ The sisters ________ so ________ that it's very hard to tell them apart.

4 비올라는 크기와 모양 면에서 바이올린과 비슷하다. (violin)
→ The viola is ________ ________ ________ ________ in size and shape.

5 형사는 내게 그의 태도가 평소와 달랐었는지 물었다. (usual)
→ The detective asked me if his attitude was ________ ________ ________.

6 작업 환경이 내가 기대한 것과 달라서 나는 매우 실망했다. (my expectations)
→ I was very disappointed that the work environment was ________ ________ ________ ________.

7 우리의 DNA가 침팬지의 DNA와 매우 유사하다는 것은 잘 알려져 있다. (chimpanzees)
→ It is well known that our DNA is very ________ ________ ________ ________ ________.

D 우리말과 같은 뜻이 되도록 주어진 단어를 배열하시오.

1 우리 언니 식성과 나의 식성은 매우 비슷하다. (to, very, is, similar, mine)
→ My sister's taste in food ________________________.

2 영화는 그녀의 설명과는 차이가 있었다. (was, her descriptions, different, from)
→ The movie ________________________.

3 미국의 추수감사절은 한국의 추석과 유사하다. (similar, in Korea, is, Chuseok, to)
→ Thanksgiving in the United States ________________________.

4 유럽의 문화와 관습은 우리나라의 것과 매우 달랐다. (from, were, ours, different, very)
→ The culture and customs in Europe ________________________.

5 전에 만났던 그 장소에서 만나는 것이 어때요? (the same, before, meet, as, at, place)
→ Why don't we ________________________?

6 그 마을의 집은 내게는 모두 똑같아 보였다. (in the town, to me, all the houses, alike, looked)
→ ________________________

7 어린아이들에게 놀이는 배움과 같다고 전문가는 말했다. (the same, playing, learning, as, is)
→ The expert said ________________________ for children.

현재분사와 과거분사

A 보기 에서 알맞은 것을 골라 현재분사나 과거분사로 바꿔 문장을 완성하시오.

보기 fall break burn bark miss shake lean

1 그들은 없어진 아이를 아직 찾지 못했다.
→ They haven't found the ___________ child yet.

2 그녀는 떨리는 손으로 수화기를 들었다.
→ She picked up the phone with ___________ hands.

3 그 꼬마 아이는 낙엽을 밟으며 걷고 있었다.
→ The little boy was walking on the ___________ leaves.

4 그는 불에 탄 목재의 잿더미를 치우고 있었다.
→ He was cleaning up the ashes of ___________ wood.

5 저쪽에 나무에 기대어 서 있는 여자 아이는 누구니?
→ Who is the girl ___________ against the tree over there?

6 짖는 개는 좀처럼 물지 않는다.
→ ___________ dogs seldom bite.

7 우리 아버지는 마당에서 부러진 탁자를 고치고 있다.
→ My father is fixing the ___________ table in the yard.

B 주어진 단어를 문맥에 맞게 현재분사나 과거분사로 바꿔 문장을 완성하시오.

1 (annoy) My father's snoring was very ___________.
I was very ___________ by my father's snoring.

2 (interest) He is ___________ in learning foreign languages.
Learning foreign languages is ___________ to him.

3 (amaze) The gift my father bought for me was ___________.
I was ___________ at the gift my father bought for me.

4 (excite) Shopping is not as ___________ to men as to women.
Men are not as ___________ about shopping as women.

5 (terrify) My grandfather's ghost stories were ___________ to me.
I was ___________ of my grandfather's ghost stories.

6 (surprise) She was ___________ by his sudden and unexpected visit.
His sudden and unexpected visit was ___________ to her.

C 두 문장을 한 문장으로 만들 때 빈칸에 알맞은 말을 쓰시오.

1 I have a cat. It is called Cathy.
→ I have a cat ____________________.

2 My parents bought me a piano. It was made in Italy.
→ My parents bought me a piano ____________________.

3 I had to use a torn umbrella. It was very embarrassing.
→ I was ____________________ to use a torn umbrella.

4 The girl is chatting with someone in the classroom. She is my best friend.
→ The girl ____________________ in the classroom is my best friend.

5 I want to read a book during this summer vacation. It is written in English.
→ I want to read a book ____________________ during this summer vacation.

6 A man will be waiting for you at the airport. He will be wearing a blue shirt.
→ A man ____________________ will be waiting for you at the airport.

7 My family picture was taken two years ago. It is hanging on the wall in the living room.
→ My family picture ____________________ in the living room was taken two years ago.

D 우리말과 같은 뜻이 되도록 주어진 단어를 배열하시오.

1 내 휴대 전화는 붐비는 버스 안에서 도난당했다. (my cell phone, was, stolen)
→ ____________________ on the crowded bus.

2 무너진 건물로 인해 많은 사람들이 죽었다. (killed, building, were, by, the collapsed)
→ Many people ____________________.

3 그녀는 부은 눈을 선글라스로 가려야 했다. (with sunglasses, cover, swollen, her, eyes)
→ She had to ____________________.

4 우리 회사는 창립 이래 놀라운 속도로 성장하고 있다. (has grown, an alarming, is, at, rate)
→ Our company ____________________ since its foundation.

5 그녀는 잠든 아기 옆에서 책을 읽고 있었다. (next to, was reading, her, a book, sleeping baby)
→ She ____________________.

6 롤러코스터가 빠른 속도로 하강하자 나는 무서웠다.
(the roller coaster, frightened, very fast, when, went down, was)
→ I ____________________.

7 그는 소리 지르고 식당을 이리저리 뛰어다니는 아이들 때문에 짜증이 났다.
(and running, by the kids, annoyed, screaming)
→ He was very ____________________ around the restaurant.

분사의 쓰임

A 보기 에서 알맞은 것을 골라 현재분사나 과거분사로 바꿔 문장을 완성하시오.

[1-4] 보기 crawl burn lose bore

1 The students found the lecture so ____________.
2 She smelled something ____________ in the kitchen.
3 I decided to appear on TV to find my ____________ brother.
4 I was surprised to feel something ____________ up my leg.

[5-8] 보기 climb miss find shock

5 I found the ____________ piece of the jigsaw puzzle under the bed.
6 The newly ____________ painting is worth two hundred million dollars.
7 She was ____________ to hear that her grandmother passed away.
8 He saw the thief ____________ over the fence in the middle of the night.

B 두 문장을 한 문장으로 만들 때 빈칸에 알맞은 말을 쓰시오.

1 A kid was hit by a bicycle. He is my friend's son.
→ The kid ________________________ is my friend's son.
2 The man is wearing blue jeans. He is my brother.
→ The man ________________________ is my brother.
3 The window was broken. The pieces were all over the floor.
→ The pieces of the ________________________ were all over the floor.
4 The girl is singing and dancing on the stage. She is my daughter.
→ The girl ________________________ is my daughter.
5 My father is working for a company. The company makes computers.
→ My father is working for a ________________________.
6 Many people were invited to the wedding. They filled the wedding hall.
→ Many people ________________________ filled the wedding hall.

C 우리말과 같은 뜻이 되도록 분사와 주어진 단어를 이용하여 문장을 완성하시오.

1 그는 경기에서 져서 실망스러웠다. (be, disappoint)
→ He ____________ ____________ that he had lost the competition.

2 그녀는 금으로 만든 목걸이를 하고 있었다. (make of, gold)
→ She was wearing a necklace ____________ ____________ ____________.

3 여러분은 빈칸에 빠진 단어를 써 넣어야 합니다. (miss, words)
→ You have to write the ____________ ____________ in the blanks.

4 그녀는 내게 고장 난 컴퓨터를 고쳐 달라고 부탁했다. (break, computer)
→ She asked me to fix her ____________ ____________.

5 나는 그가 교실에서 그녀의 지갑을 훔치는 장면을 목격했다. (steal, purse)
→ I watched him ____________ ____________ ____________ in the classroom.

6 교실 밖에서 기다리고 있는 남자가 Sarah의 아버지이다. (wait, outside, the classroom)
→ The man ____________ ____________ ____________ ____________ is Sarah's father.

7 나는 시상식에서 내 이름이 불리는 것을 들었을 때 무척 기뻤다. (delight, hear, name, call)
→ I was very ____________ when I ____________ ____________ ____________ ____________ in the awards.

D 우리말과 같은 뜻이 되도록 주어진 말을 알맞게 배열하시오.

1 Emma는 기분 전환을 위해 머리를 잘랐다. (for a change, her, had, cut, hair)
→ Emma ____.

2 설명서가 영어로 쓰여 있어서 나는 읽을 수 없었다. (written, it, in English, was)
→ I couldn't read the instruction because ____.

3 나는 밤에 누가 피아노를 치는 소리를 들었다. (someone, the piano, heard, playing)
→ I ____ at night.

4 나는 부엌에서 깨진 유리 조각들을 치워야 했다. (pieces of, remove, glass, the broken)
→ I had to ____ in the kitchen.

5 실망한 관객들이 극장을 떠났다. (the audiences, disappointed, left)
→ ____ the theater.

6 티켓을 사려고 줄 서서 기다리는 많은 사람들이 있다. (waiting, many people, tickets, to buy, in line)
→ There are ____.

7 시험 결과는 이미 나와 있지만, 나는 그것을 알고 싶지 않다. (the exam result, been, released, has already)
→ ____, but I don't want to know it.

분사 구문

A 문장의 의미가 통하도록 분사구문을 이용하여 문장을 완성하시오.

1 Because she was sick, she took a few days off.
→ ______________________, she took a few days off.

2 He took a hot bath and drank a glass of cold beer.
→ He took a hot bath, ______________________.

3 While she was watching TV, she fell asleep on the sofa.
→ ______________________, she fell asleep on the sofa.

4 If you are confident to pass the exam, why don't you take it?
→ ______________________, why don't you take it?

5 After I graduated from college, I could enter the world-famous company.
→ ______________________, I could enter the world-famous company.

6 Although she is very thin, she still tries not to eat after 6 p.m. to lose weight.
→ ______________________, she still tries not to eat after 6 p.m. to lose weight.

7 Since she is allergic to some food, she needs to be careful when she eats out.
→ ______________________, she needs to be careful when she eats out.

B 주어진 접속사를 이용하여 문장의 의미가 통하도록 부사절을 완성하시오.

1 Crossing the road, you have to look both ways. (when)
→ ______________________, you have to look both ways.

2 My father had breakfast, reading the newspaper. (while)
→ My father had breakfast ______________________.

3 Finishing her homework, she went out to meet her friends. (after)
→ ______________________, she went out to meet her friends.

4 Asking her for advice, you will be able to receive help from her. (if)
→ ______________________, you will be able to receive help from her.

5 Being very old, he still travels around lots of countries. (even though)
→ ______________________, he still travels around lots of countries.

6 Having bought a new computer, he gave his old one to his brother. (because)
→ ______________________, he gave his old one to his brother.

C 우리말과 같은 뜻이 되도록 주어진 단어와 분사구문을 이용하여 문장을 완성하시오.

1 그녀는 심하게 다쳐서 수술을 받아야 했다. (be, seriously injured)

→ ________ ________ ________, she had to have an operation.

2 할 말이 없어서 나는 그냥 전화를 끊었다. (have, anything to say)

→ ________ ________ ________ ________ ________, I just hung up the phone.

3 그는 나를 가볍게 포옹해 준 후 기차에 올라탔다. (give, a light hug)

→ ________ ________ ________ ________ ________, he got on the train.

4 파티에 초대되지 못해서 그는 약간 실망스러워한다. (invite, to the party)

→ ________ ________ ________ ________ ________, he is a bit disappointed.

5 돈을 다 써버려서, 나는 걸어서 집으로 가야 했다. (spend, all my money)

→ ________ ________ ________ ________ ________, I had to walk home.

6 그녀는 그 영화를 세 번 넘게 봤기 때문에, 더 이상 보고 싶지 않았다. (see)

→ ________ ________ ________ ________ more than three times, she didn't want to see it again.

7 그 거대한 괴물을 직접 보고도, 나는 내 눈을 믿을 수가 없었다. (see, the giant monster)

→ ________ ________ ________ ________ in person, I couldn't still believe my eyes.

D 우리말과 같은 뜻이 되도록 주어진 말을 알맞게 배열하시오.

1 그는 시험에 떨어졌기 때문에 재시험을 봐야 했다. (the test, failed, he, take, had to, having)

→ ________________, ________________ a make-up test.

2 그는 지갑을 잃어버린 후, 그것을 소파 밑에서 찾았다. (lost, having, found it, he, his wallet)

→ ________________, ________________ under the sofa.

3 한 블록만 더 가면 우체국을 찾을 수 있을 겁니다. (will, going, find, one more block, you)

→ ________________, ________________ the post office.

4 그녀는 가난한 집에서 태어났지만 희망을 포기해 본 적이 없다. (a poor family, never, she, born to, has, given up)

→ ________________, ________________ hope.

5 그녀는 책을 읽다가 좋은 구절을 적어 놓았다. (noted, a book, she, reading, its good passages)

→ ________________, ________________.

6 할 일이 너무 많아서 그녀는 밤늦게까지 잠을 잘 수 없었다. (so much work, stay up, having, she, to do, had to)

→ ________________, ________________ until late at night.

7 그녀는 이제 미성년자가 아니므로 스스로 선택할 권리가 있다. (has, being, anymore, she, not, a minor, a right)

→ ________________, ________________ to make her own choices.

Unit 57 등위 접속사

A 보기 에서 알맞은 접속사를 골라 문장을 완성하시오.

[1-4] 보기 and but or [중복 사용 가능]

1 Is Daniel sick, __________ is he just sleeping?
2 We had dinner __________ had some dessert with coffee.
3 I studied English very hard, __________ I failed the English test again.
4 I wanted to see the show, __________ the tickets were already sold out.

[5-8] 보기 so for yet nor

5 I didn't tell anyone about it, __________ did she.
6 We decided to stay home, __________ it had been raining a lot.
7 She doesn't speak Korean, __________ she does seem to get our message.
8 You have been helping me a lot, __________ I want to treat you to dinner.

B 주어진 문장을 접속사를 이용하여 한 문장으로 만드시오.

1 The book was written in French. I couldn't read it at all. (for)
→ ______________________________

2 Are you still a college student? Did you already graduate? (or)
→ ______________________________

3 She speaks English well. She's afraid of speaking with foreigners. (yet)
→ ______________________________

4 She didn't come to school. She didn't come to the English academy. (nor)
→ ______________________________

5 He doesn't have much experience. He is doing well in the company. (but)
→ ______________________________

6 There were too many people in the shopping mall. I couldn't find my friend. (so)
→ ______________________________

7 I like being friends with Susan. I don't want to share a room with her. (but)
→ ______________________________

C 우리말과 같은 뜻이 되도록 주어진 단어를 이용하여 문장을 완성하시오.

1 그녀는 꿈을 이루었고 많은 돈을 벌었다. (make, money)

→ Her dreams came true, ________ she ________ ________ ________ ________ ________.

2 Victor는 시험에서 부정행위를 하지 않았고, 나도 마찬가지다. (nor)

→ Victor didn't cheat in the exam, ________ ________ ________.

3 방을 치워. 안 그러면 너의 어머니가 화낼 거야. (or, will, be)

→ Clean your room, ________ ________ ________ ________ ________ upset.

4 오늘 아침에 눈이 너무 많이 와서, 학생들은 학교에 가지 않았다. (so, go to school)

→ It snowed too much this morning, ________ ________ ________ ________ ________ ________.

5 나는 매일 아침 채소와 과일을 많이 먹는다. 왜냐하면 그것들은 건강에 좋기 때문이다. (for, healthy)

→ I eat lots of vegetables and fruits every morning, ________ ________ ________ ________.

6 어머니가 집에 오는 길에 우유와 달걀, 사과를 사오라고 내게 부탁했다. (some milk, eggs, apples)

→ Mom asked me to buy ________ ________, ________, ________ ________ on my way home.

7 그들은 재정적으로 그를 도와주고 싶었으나 그는 다른 사람들에게 어떠한 도움도 받지 않으려 했다. (yet, would, take, any help)

→ They wanted to help him financially, ________ ________ ________ ________ ________ ________ from others.

D 우리말과 같은 뜻이 되도록 주어진 말을 알맞게 배열하시오.

1 나는 행사에 초대를 받았지만 가고 싶지 않다. (don't, go, but, want, I, to)

→ I am invited to the ceremony, ________________________.

2 차를 드시겠어요, 아니면 커피를 드시겠어요? (or, some tea, would, like, coffee, you)

→ ________________________

3 그녀는 아들이 자신에게 거짓말을 했기 때문에 아들을 꾸짖었다. (to her, for, a lie, he, told)

→ She scolded her son, ________________________.

4 그는 외국어를 배워본 적이 없고, 나도 마찬가지이다. (a foreign language, have, has, nor, never learned, I)

→ He ________________________.

5 건물에서 화재가 발생했고, 곧 소방차 여러 대가 현장에 도착했다. (at the scene, fire trucks, several, soon arrived, and)

→ The fire broke out in the building, ________________________.

6 그녀는 동물을 좋아해서 개 두 마리, 고양이 세 마리를 키운다. (she, and, has, so, three cats, two dogs)

→ She likes animals, ________________________.

Unit 58 상관 접속사

A 주어진 동사를 어법에 맞게 바꿔 쓰시오.

1 Both Nick and I ____________ watching horror movies. (like)
2 Either Mike or I ____________ to work overtime today. (have)
3 Neither my sisters nor my mom ____________ my story. (believe)
4 Not only the players but also the coach ____________ to increase their amount of training. (want)

B 문장의 의미가 통하도록 주어진 상관 접속사를 이용하여 문장을 완성하시오.

1 You can study at home, or you can study at the library. (either ~ or)
→ You can study ______________________________.
2 The food she made was tasty. And it was healthy, too. (both ~ and)
→ The food she made was ______________________________.
3 Clair is very diligent, and she is smart, too. (not only ~ but also, as well as)
→ Clair is ______________________________.
→ Clair is ______________________________.
4 The lecture was not interesting, and it was not useful, either. (neither ~ nor)
→ The lecture was ______________________________.
5 My mother was upset with me. And she was disappointed with me.
(not only ~ but also / as well as)
→ My mother was ______________________________.
→ My mother was ______________________________.

C 밑줄 친 부분을 어법에 맞게 고쳐 쓰시오.

1 Both the bus and the subway <u>was</u> crowded with people. ____________
2 She as well as her kids <u>were</u> excited about the new house. ____________
3 Neither my brother nor my sister <u>like</u> watching baseball games. ____________
4 Either Lisa's father or her sister <u>help</u> her to do her homework after school. ____________

D **우리말과 같은 뜻이 되도록 주어진 단어와 상관 접속사를 이용하여 문장을 완성하시오.**

1 그 상점은 신발을 디자인하고 판매도 한다. (the shop, design, sell)

→ ______ ______ ______ ______ ______ ______ shoes.

2 회의는 목요일이나 금요일에 열릴 것이다. (on Thursday, on Friday)

→ The meeting will be held ______ ______ ______ ______
______ ______.

3 아버지와 나는 둘 다 매운 음식을 좋아한다. (my father, I, like)

→ ______ ______ ______ ______ ______ ______ spicy
food.

4 우리 집에 오려면 지하철을 타거나 버스를 타면 된다. (the subway, a bus)

→ You can take ______ ______ ______ ______ ______
______ to come to my house.

5 너도 그녀도 실수하지 않았으니 걱정 말아라. (you, she, make, any mistakes)

→ ______ ______ ______ ______ ______ ______
______, so don't worry.

6 그 수영장에는 안전시설도 없었고 안전요원도 없었다. (safety facilities, lifeguards)

→ The swimming pool had ______ ______ ______ ______ ______.

E **우리말과 같은 뜻이 되도록 주어진 말을 알맞게 배열하시오.**

1 그는 방어와 득점 둘 다 할 수 있다. (both, and, score, defend, goals)

→ He is able to ______________________________.

2 Jerry와 Maggie 둘 다 팀장 자격이 있다. (both, Jerry, Maggie, and, qualified, to be the team leader, are)

→ ______________________________

3 Alice도 나도 이번 주 토요일에 그 파티에 가지 않을 것이다. (the party, Alice, nor, am going to, neither, I)

→ ______________________________ this Saturday.

4 그는 독일은 물론 스위스에도 가본 적이 있다. (he, but also, not only, Germany, has been to, Switzerland)

→ ______________________________

5 Brian이나 Nick 중 한 사람이 오늘 설거지를 하기로 되어있다.
(Nick, the dishes, either, or, Brian, wash, is supposed to)

→ ______________________________ today.

6 Jones 씨는 애완동물로 커다란 뱀은 물론 두 마리의 호랑이를 키우고 있다.
(a giant snake, keeps, as well as, a couple of tigers)

→ Mr. Jones ______________________________ as pets.

Unit 59 명사절을 이끄는 종속 접속사

A 보기 에서 알맞은 접속사를 골라 써넣으시오. [중복 사용 가능]

보기 that whether if

1 The problem is ___________ there's a lot of traffic now.
2 ___________ the project will succeed or not is up to you.
3 I heard ___________ eating regularly and slowly is good for health.
4 The fact ___________ she got all A's surprised my classmates.
5 I realized ___________ making a lot of money doesn't ensure happiness.
6 We don't know ___________ or not he will be able to make it on time.
7 Many students wondered ___________ he would be punished according to the school rules.

B 주어진 문장을 「it ~ that」 구문을 사용하여 다시 쓰시오.

1 That he died of cancer is a rumor.
→ ___________________________

2 That the company shut down is true.
→ ___________________________

3 That she will advance to the final round is unlikely.
→ ___________________________

4 The fact that he will end up in jail eventually is obvious.
→ ___________________________

5 The fact that he can speak three languages is surprising.
→ ___________________________

6 That she refused the job offer from the big company is strange.
→ ___________________________

7 That the earth is suffering from environmental pollution is a fact.
→ ___________________________

C 두 문장을 한 문장의 간접의문문으로 바꿔 쓰시오.

1 I don't know. + Where do I have to get off?

→ ____________________

2 I wonder. + Who stole my laptop computer?

→ ____________________

3 Do you know? + What caused the building to catch fire?

→ ____________________

4 I don't remember. + Where did I put my student ID card?

→ ____________________

5 Could you tell me? + Why were you crying in the classroom?

→ ____________________

6 Let's ask him. What time do we have to gather in front of the main gate?

→ ____________________

7 I'd like to know. + Where can I get accurate information about backpacking?

→ ____________________

D 우리말과 같은 뜻이 되도록 주어진 말을 알맞게 배열하시오.

1 우리 할아버지께서 곧 회복되실지 잘 모르겠어. (will, if, soon, my grandfather, recover)

→ I am not sure ____________________.

2 나는 이번에는 누가 대상을 받을지 궁금하다. (is, win, wonder, going to, I, the top prize, who)

→ ____________________ this time.

3 더 나은 점수를 받기 위해 그가 최선을 다한 것은 사실이다. (he, true, that, his best, it, did, is)

→ ____________________ to get better grades.

4 그가 선거에서 이길 수 있을지는 확실하지 않다. (the election, he, whether, will, win, be able to)

→ ____________________ is uncertain.

5 나는 시험에서 떨어지면 그에게 뭐라고 말해야 할지 모르겠어. (tell, don't know, I, him, I what, should)

→ ____________________ if I fail the test tomorrow.

6 그 유명 배우가 그녀의 사촌이라는 사실은 믿기 어렵다. (her cousin, the famous actor, the fact, is, that)

→ ____________________ is unbelievable.

7 이 버스가 지금 어디로 가고 있는지 모르겠어. 우리는 엉뚱한 버스에 탔어!
(heading, I, this bus, don't, where, know, is)

→ ____________________ We are on the wrong bus!

부사절을 이끄는 종속 접속사 I

A 보기 에서 알맞은 접속사를 골라 써넣으시오.

[1-4] 보기 after while since before

1 ____________ my mother was peeling apples, I did the dishes.
2 He will understand you ____________ he is an open-minded person.
3 ____________ winter comes, my friends and I are going to visit Europe.
4 ____________ he had dinner, he had an upset stomach and felt like throwing up.

[5-8] 보기 in order that when until because

5 I will never forgive him ____________ he apologizes to me first.
6 I saw Sam crossing the street ____________ I was waiting at the traffic light.
7 You have to clean the toilet after school ____________ you were late.
8 I sat at the front of the classroom ____________ I could concentrate on the lecture.

B 보기 와 같이 두 문장을 접속사를 이용한 문장으로 바꿔 쓰시오.

보기
She was about to leave home. Her kid started to cry. (when)
→ When she was about to leave home, her kid started to cry.
→ Her kid started to cry when she was about to leave home.

1 I couldn't fall asleep easily. I drank too much coffee. (as)
→ ____________
→ ____________

2 She airs out the house. And then she cleans the house. (before)
→ ____________
→ ____________

3 I became a college student. I have never had my hair cut short since then. (since)
→ ____________
→ ____________

4 She heard that her son had a traffic accident. She fainted. (as soon as)
→ ____________
→ ____________

C 보기 와 같이 so that ~ can[could]을 이용하여 한 문장으로 만드시오.

보기	I left home early. I wanted to catch the bus. → I left home early so that I could catch the bus.

1 He made way for an ambulance. He wanted to let it pass quickly.

→ ______________________________

2 My sister helped me. She wanted me to finish my homework on time.

→ ______________________________

3 Try to spend some time in the sun. You can get enough vitamin D.

→ ______________________________

4 She will learn French. She wants to go to culinary school in France.

→ ______________________________

5 Please show us your membership card. You will receive the discounted rate.

→ ______________________________

D 우리말과 같은 뜻이 되도록 주어진 말을 알맞게 배열하시오.

1 그녀는 그것이 너무 비싸서 사지 않기로 했다. (too, because, was, expensive, it)

→ She decided not to buy it ______________________________.

2 우리 아버지께서는 집에 오시자마자 텔레비전을 켜신다. (comes, he, as soon as, home)

→ My father turns on the TV ______________________________.

3 그가 막 잠이 들려는 데 누군가 문을 두드렸다. (was, fall, he, when, about to, asleep)

→ ______________________________, somebody knocked on the door.

4 오늘 오후에 비가 올지도 모르니까 우산을 가져가세요. (might, this afternoon, since, it, rain)

→ You should take an umbrella ______________________________.

5 그녀는 프랑스를 여행하는 동안 이모를 방문했다. (was, France, while, traveling around, she)

→ She visited her aunt ______________________________.

6 나는 해외에 나가도록 허락해 주실 때까지 부모님께 조를 것이다. (they, me, go abroad, until, allow, to)

→ I will keep nagging at my parents ______________________________.

7 그는 이제 아르바이트를 구했으니 부모님에게 용돈을 받을 필요가 없다. (he, that, a part-time job, has, now)

→ ______________________________, he won't need to get allowance from his parents.

8 나는 그 문제에 관해 그와 이야기를 하다가 좋은 아이디어가 떠올랐다. (I, the issue, discussed, as, with him)

→ ______________________________, I came up with a good idea.

9 나는 이 집으로 이사를 온 후로 잠을 깊이 자지 못한다. (this house I, moved to, since)

→ I can't sleep deeply ______________________________.

부사절을 이끄는 종속 접속사 II

A 보기 에서 알맞은 접속사를 골라 써넣으시오.

[1-5] 보기 even though while if as long as unless

1 I like spicy food __________ my sister likes sweet food.
2 __________ you reveal the secret, everything will be fine.
3 __________ you do your best, the result will be good.
4 __________ my mother allows me to stay over, I will have a slumber party with my friends.
5 __________ he is physically challenged, he keeps trying to help others in need.

[6-10] 보기 even if whereas if ~ not such … that ~ so … that ~

6 He has ________ a big dog ________ I don't want to go to his house.
7 My parents want me to be a doctor ________ I want to be a teacher.
8 The map was ________ complicated ________ we couldn't find the gallery easily.
9 ________ he does ________ arrive on time, we have no choice but to leave without him.
10 ________ she doesn't win a medal, her participation in the competition will be meaningful in itself.

B 주어진 문장을 unless 또는 if ~ not을 이용하여 바꿔 쓰시오.

1 If it doesn't rain, I will drive to work tomorrow.
→ ______________________________

2 Unless it is soaked in the water, it can last up to five years.
→ ______________________________

3 If you don't have anything to say, I will end the meeting now.
→ ______________________________

4 Unless you give up, you will be able to achieve your dream someday
→ ______________________________

5 If you don't buy tickets in advance, you won't be able to see the concert.
→ ______________________________

C 주어진 문장을 「such … that ~」 또는 「so … that ~」을 이용하여 바꿔 쓰시오.

1 The food was very greasy. I left some on my plate.
→ ______________________________

2 She is a very attractive person. Everyone likes her.
→ ______________________________

3 His eyesight is very poor. He can't see anything without glasses.
→ ______________________________

4 I had a very light breakfast. I felt very hungry before lunchtime.
→ ______________________________

5 The restaurant is very popular. You have to book a table in advance.
→ ______________________________

6 Both of them were very furious. Nobody dared to end their argument.
→ ______________________________

7 The forest was a very dangerous place. My mother wouldn't let me go there.
→ ______________________________

D 우리말과 같은 뜻이 되도록 주어진 말을 알맞게 배열하시오.

1 그녀는 영어는 잘하는 반면 수학은 못한다. (is, math, while, she, poor at)
→ She is good at English ______________________________.

2 그렇게 비싸지만 않으면 우리는 그것을 살 것이다. (it's, expensive, as long as, that, not)
→ ______________________________, we will buy it.

3 만약 피자를 좋아하지 않는다면 네게 다른 음식을 만들어 줄게. (like, unless, pizza, you)
→ ______________________________, I will make some other food for you.

4 아이를 잃어버릴 경우를 대비해서 나는 아이에게 이름표를 붙여주었다. (lose, I, child, in case, my)
→ ______________________________, I put a name tag on him.

5 비록 그는 약하게 태어났지만 나중에 유명한 태권도 선수가 되었다. (born, although, weak, was, he)
→ ______________________________, he became a famous taekwondo athlete later.

6 공원이 무척 넓어서 우리는 잔디 위에서 축구를 할 수 있었다. (soccer, so, we, large, could, play, that)
→ The park was ______________________________ on the grass.

7 그는 집에 멋진 정원이 있어서 토요일마다 사람들을 초대한다. (in his house, such, that, garden, nice, a)
→ He has ______________________________ he invites people every Saturday.

관계대명사 I

A 보기 에서 알맞은 관계대명사를 골라 문장을 완성하시오. [중복 사용 가능]

보기 who whom which whose

1 Have you found the books ____________ you lost yesterday?
2 I became friends with a man ____________ wife is an actress.
3 The person ____________ you want to speak to has just stepped out.
4 The new employees ____________ we recruited last month were all enthusiastic.
5 This day care center mainly takes care of children ____________ parents both work.
6 I saw a girl ____________ was crying in the amusement park.
7 During this vacation, my family is going to stay in the island ____________ is located in the Pacific Ocean.

B 보기 와 같이 주어진 문장을 두 문장으로 나눠 쓰시오.

보기 This is something that can happen to everybody.
→ This is something. It can happen to everybody.

1 The subject in which I am interested is psychology.
→ ____________________

2 Have you had the milk that was in the refrigerator?
→ ____________________

3 People whom I met at the party were generally nice.
→ ____________________

4 The employees who work for the bank are all kind.
→ ____________________

5 What is the name of the girl whose father is a police officer?
→ ____________________

6 Catherine works for a company which handles wood furniture.
→ ____________________

C 두 문장을 주어진 관계대명사를 이용하여 한 문장으로 만드시오.

1 The movie was not recommendable. I saw it yesterday. (which)

→ ____________________

2 Walter has won the lottery. His dream was to be rich. (, whose)

→ ____________________

3 I teach students. Their goal is to enter Harvard University. (whose)

→ ____________________

4 The police finally arrested the thief. They were looking for the thief. (whom)

→ ____________________

5 Are you the person? I spoke to the person on the phone yesterday. (whom)

→ ____________________

6 We are going to have dinner at the restaurant. Lena recommended it to us. (which)

→ ____________________

7 The man teaches English in a middle school. He is going to get married this March. (who)

→ ____________________

D 우리말과 같은 뜻이 되도록 주어진 말을 알맞게 배열하시오.

1 내가 앉았던 그 좌석은 매우 불편했다. (I, very uncomfortable, sat on, was, which)

→ The seat ____________________.

2 시골에 살았던 Rita가 뉴욕으로 와서 모델이 되었다. (in the country, used to, who, live)

→ Rita, ____________________, moved to New York and became a model.

3 그녀가 이야기하고 있던 그 남자가 그 회사의 CEO이다. (talking to, whom, she, the man, was)

→ ____________________ is the CEO of the company.

4 Jake는 그 영화를 흥행작으로 만든 감독이다. (the movie, the director, a big hit, has made, who)

→ Jake is ____________________.

5 네가 지난번에 내게 사달라고 부탁했던 그 책 여기 있어. (which, to buy, the book, you, me, asked)

→ Here is ____________________ last time.

6 나는 10년 동안 만나지 못했던 옛 친구를 우연히 만났다.
(for ten years, whom, haven't seen, an old friend, I)

→ I ran into ____________________.

7 한국어가 모국어가 아닌 사람을 위해 통역사가 준비되어 있습니다. (Korean, language, is, whose, native, not)

→ We have an interpreter for people ____________________.

관계대명사 II - that, what

A 빈칸에 that과 what 중 알맞은 것을 골라 써넣으시오.

1 She is the last person ___________ would tell a lie.
2 I couldn't forget ___________ they did for me.
3 He asked me ___________ I wanted for my birthday.
4 ___________ I want to tell you is that he is not a reliable person.
5 The teacher asked me ___________ I really wanted to know.
6 You have the things ___________ I really need at the moment.
7 He said that it is the only chance ___________ he can give me.
8 The hotel ___________ I spent a few days in was very expensive.
9 I'm not sure ___________ I have to do next after I finish this work.
10 You finally bought ___________ I wanted to buy but couldn't afford.

B 밑줄 친 부분을 어법에 맞게 고쳐 문장을 다시 쓰시오.

1 Incheon, <u>that</u> I was born in, has changed a lot.
→ ___________________________

2 The man <u>which</u> lives next door was arrested last night.
→ ___________________________

3 She was wearing <u>that</u> I was thinking of buying.
→ ___________________________

4 They just ignored <u>the thing what</u> she warned them about.
→ ___________________________

5 The pictures <u>at that</u> you are looking were taken with a Polaroid camera.
→ ___________________________

6 <u>That</u> I can't tell you is why he left you without a word.
→ ___________________________

7 The museum <u>what</u> was burned down a year ago will be reopened next month.
→ ___________________________

C 우리말과 같은 뜻이 되도록 주어진 단어를 이용하여 문장을 완성하시오.

1 그녀는 지난밤에 먹은 것을 토했다. (eat)
→ She threw up ___________ ___________ ___________ last night.

2 그들은 우리가 요청한 것을 해줄 수 없다고 말했다. (ask for)
→ They said they couldn't do ___________ ___________ ___________ ___________.

3 나에게 가장 중요한 것은 정직함이다. (be, most important to me)
→ ___________ ___________ ___________ ___________ ___________ ___________ is honesty.

4 네게 지하실을 열 수 있는 열쇠를 가져다줄게. (open, the basement)
→ I will get you the key ___________ ___________ ___________ ___________.

5 우리가 이번 주 금요일까지 끝내야 하는 일은 많지 않다. (much work, have to, finish)
→ There isn't ___________ ___________ ___________ ___________ ___________ ___________ ___________ ___________ ___________ ___________.

6 나는 배송된 물건이 주문한 것과 달라서 고객 서비스센터에 전화했다. (order)
→ I called customer service because the delivered goods were different from ___________ ___________ ___________.

7 이 책들은 대부분 내가 가지고 있는 책과 똑같다. (the same books, have)
→ These are mostly ___________ ___________ ___________ ___________ ___________ ___________.

D 우리말과 같은 뜻이 되도록 주어진 말을 알맞게 배열하시오.

1 그것은 당신이 신경 쓸 일이 아닙니다. (care about, that, you, something, should)
→ That is not ___________________________.

2 당신이 무엇을 해야 하는지 말씀 드릴게요. (are supposed to, let me, you, do, tell you, what)
→ ___________________________

3 이번에는 네가 그를 이길 것이라고 나는 확신한다. (you, beat him, I'm sure, are going to, that)
→ ___________________________ this time.

4 그 웹사이트에는 내가 알고 싶은 모든 것이 있다. (know, everything, the website, I, has, that, want to)
→ ___________________________

5 나는 지난번에 네가 한 말이 맞았다는 것을 깨달았다. (last time, right, realized, you said, was, I, what)
→ ___________________________

6 나는 우리에게 대화가 더 필요하다는 너의 의견에 동의한다. (we, your opinion, more conversation, that, need)
→ I agree with ___________________________.

7 당신의 의견은 우리가 하려고 계획하고 있는 것과는 아무런 관계가 없습니다. (are planning, what, to do, we)
→ Your opinion has nothing to do with ___________________________.

관계부사와 복합관계사

A 빈칸에 보기 에서 알맞은 것을 골라 써넣으시오.

보기 when where why how

1 I want to know __________ I can speak English well.
2 We didn't know the reason __________ she was so upset.
3 We promised to meet again at the place __________ we first met.
4 Everyone will remember the year __________ the World Cup was held.

B 문장의 의미가 통하도록 주어진 문장을 복합관계사를 이용한 문장으로 바꿔 쓰시오.

1 Anyone who finds it first will be the winner.
→ ______________________________ will be the winner.
2 I don't believe anything that you say about him.
→ I don't believe ______________________________.
3 No matter which you choose, you will never regret your choice.
→ ______________________________, you will never regret your choice.
4 Every time when I have to study until late at night, I drink at least three cups of coffee.
→ ______________________________, I drink at least three cups of coffee.
5 No matter how expensive the tuition fees are, parents will send their kids to private institutes.
→ ______________________________, parents will send their kids to private institutes.

C 밑줄 친 부분을 어법에 맞게 고쳐 문장을 다시 쓰시오.

1 This is the studio why he spends most of his time.
→ ______________________________
2 This is the restaurant when I often have dinner with my friends.
→ ______________________________
3 He couldn't forget the day where he released his debut album.
→ ______________________________
4 I will tell you several ways how you can upgrade your navigation system.
→ ______________________________
5 His fans wanted to know the reason where he refused all the interviews.
→ ______________________________

D 두 문장을 관계부사를 이용하여 한 문장으로 만드시오.

1 The city was beautiful. We spent a week in the city.
→ ______________________________

2 This is the file. I keep lots of important data in it.
→ ______________________________

3 I know the way. I can bake cakes without an oven in that way.
→ ______________________________

4 I can't forget the day. I got on a plane for the first time that day.
→ ______________________________

5 Please tell me the reason. You didn't come to the event for that reason.
→ ______________________________

6 I will remember the summer vacation. I stayed with my grandmother on that vacation.
→ ______________________________

7 I want to know the reason. My best friend transferred to another school for that reason.
→ ______________________________

E 우리말과 같은 뜻이 되도록 관계부사와 복합관계사를 이용하여 문장을 완성하시오.

1 나는 슬플 때면 언제나 이 장소를 찾는다. (feel, sad)
→ ______ ______ ______ ______, I come to this place.

2 내 여동생은 내가 가는 곳이면 어디든지 따라가려고 한다. (go)
→ My sister tries to tag along with me ______ ______ ______.

3 이것들이 바로 그들이 암을 이겨냈던 방법이다. (overcome, cancer)
→ These are ______ ______ ______ ______.

4 내가 휴대 전화 번호를 바꾸어야 했던 이유가 있어. (have to, change)
→ There's a ______ ______ ______ ______ ______ ______
my cell phone number.

5 그 일자리를 원하는 사람은 누구나 지원할 수 있습니다. (want, the job)
→ ______ ______ ______ ______ can apply.

6 네가 효과적으로 발표할 수 있는 방법을 알려줄게. (can, give, a presentation)
→ Let me tell you ______ ______ ______ ______ ______
______ effectively.

7 기회가 또 있으므로 우리는 실망할 이유가 전혀 없다. (there, be, no)
→ We have another chance, so ______ ______ ______ ______
______ we should feel disappointed.

가정법 과거

A 주어진 단어를 이용하여 가정법 문장을 완성하시오.

1 If I ____________ you, I would accept his offer. (be)
2 If I ____________ an only child, I would be very lonely. (be)
3 If I ____________ a cell phone with me, I would call her now. (have)
4 If it ____________, we could go to the amusement park. (not, rain)
5 If you ____________ regularly, you would be very healthy. (exercise)
6 If I ____________ a fortune, I would buy a big house for my parents. (have)
7 If I ____________ the teacher, I would never give students homework. (be)

B 두 문장의 의미가 통하도록 가정법 문장을 완성하시오.

1 As I am not tall, I can't reach the top shelf.
→ ____

2 As I am full, I can't eat more cake.
→ ____

3 As I don't have enough money, I can't travel around Europe.
→ ____

4 As tomorrow isn't my grandfather's birthday, I won't visit him.
→ ____

5 As Jack and I don't go to the same school, we don't see each other often.
→ ____

6 As I don't have a camera with me now, I can't take a picture of the movie star.
→ ____

7 As the tall building blocks my house, I can't get enough warmth from the sun.
→ ____

8 As I don't know her phone number, I can't invite her to go to the movies with me.
→ ____

9 As I have many things to do, I can't spend more time with my children.
→ ____

C 우리말과 같은 뜻이 되도록 주어진 단어를 이용하여 문장을 완성하시오.

1 그녀가 20분 안에 도착하면 기차를 탈 수 있을 것이다. (arrive, can, get on)
→ If she ________ within twenty minutes, she ________ ________ ________ ________ ________.

2 내게 시간이 충분하다면 네 숙제를 도와줄 텐데. (have, enough time, help)
→ If I ________ ________ ________, I ________ ________ ________ with your homework.

3 우리 형이 차를 빌려주면, 내가 내일 6시에 너를 데리러 갈게. (lend, pick you up)
→ If my brother ________ ________ his car, I ________ ________ ________ ________ at six tomorrow.

4 내가 내일 학교에서 Greg을 만나면 네게 전화를 하라고 그에게 전해 줄게. (meet, tell)
→ If I ________ ________ in school tomorrow, I ________ ________ ________ to call you.

5 그녀는 조금만 더 열심히 공부한다면, 반에서 1등을 할 수 있을 텐데. (study, can, get, first place)
→ If she ________ a little harder, she ________ ________ ________ ________ in her class.

6 네가 중국 음식이 싫다면 이탈리아 음식이나 한국 음식을 먹어도 돼. (like, Chinese food, can, eat)
→ If you ________ ________ ________ ________, we ________ ________ Italian or Korean food instead.

D 우리말과 같은 뜻이 되도록 주어진 단어를 배열하시오.

1 시간을 되돌릴 수 있다면 무엇을 하시겠어요? (were able to, the clock, if, turn back, you)
→ What would you do ________________?

2 네가 만약 내 이삿짐 싸는 것을 도와준다면 너에게 저녁을 사 줄게. (for the move, help, if, pack, me, you)
→ ________________, I will buy you dinner.

3 내일 아침 일찍 일어나면, 나는 조깅을 갈 것이다. (tomorrow morning, go jogging, early, I'll, get up)
→ If I ________________, ________________.

4 오늘이 휴일이라면 할머니를 뵈러 갈 텐데. (my grandmother, would, were, visit, a holiday)
→ If today ________________, I ________________.

5 햇빛에 민감하지만 않다면 해변에서 일광욕을 할 텐데.
(sunbathe, were, would, not, on the beach, sensitive to sunlight)
→ If I ________________, I ________________.

6 그가 진심으로 뉘우치고 있다면 내가 그를 용서해 줄 텐데.
(forgive, he, would, genuinely, regretful, were, I, him)
→ If ________________, ________________.

가정법 과거완료 & 혼합 가정법

A 두 문장의 의미가 통하도록 가정법 과거완료 문장을 완성하시오.

1 As I didn't study hard, I couldn't go to college.
→ ______________________________

2 As she didn't take his advice, she didn't win the contest.
→ ______________________________

3 As he overslept this morning, he couldn't take the school bus.
→ ______________________________

4 As it rained a lot, the construction hasn't been finished yet.
→ ______________________________

5 As I took the wrong bus, I was late for the gathering.
→ ______________________________

6 As my computer broke down, I couldn't finish my homework earlier.
→ ______________________________

7 As I didn't know that she would transfer to another school, I didn't say goodbye to her.
→ ______________________________

B 두 문장의 의미가 통하도록 혼합 가정법 문장을 완성하시오.

1 As I hurt my leg, I can't go with you now.
→ ______________________________

2 As I didn't get a driver's license, I can't drive now.
→ ______________________________

3 As I have gained weight, this dress doesn't fit me now.
→ ______________________________

4 As I didn't sleep enough last night, I am sleepy now.
→ ______________________________

5 As I didn't get up early this morning, I am not in the classroom now.
→ ______________________________

6 As I didn't buy the tickets in advance, I am not enjoying the show now.
→ ______________________________

C 주어진 동사를 이용하여 후회, 유감을 나타내는 문장을 완성하시오.

1 네 이메일에 답장을 했어야 했는데 깜빡 했어. (respond)
→ I ____________________ to your email, but I forgot.

2 감기가 더 심해졌어. 너 병원에 갔어야 했는데. (see)
→ Your cold is getting worse. You ____________________ a doctor.

3 결정을 내리기 전에 너의 의견을 물어봤어야 했는데. (ask for)
→ I ____________________ your opinion before I made the decision.

4 나는 경기에서 또 졌다. 연습을 많이 했어야 했는데. (practice)
→ I lost the game again. I ____________________ a lot.

5 나는 또 혼이 났다. 학교에 지각하지 말았어야 했는데. (be)
→ I got a scolding from my teacher again. I ____________________ late for school.

6 싸움을 말리려고 하지 말았어야 했는데. 나 때문에 상황이 더 나빠졌다. (try)
→ I ____________________ to stop the fight. Things got worse because of me.

7 그녀는 엄마에게 그렇게 무례하게 말하지 말았어야 했는데. 그녀의 엄마는 정말로 화가 났다. (talk)
→ She ____________________ to her mother so rudely. Her mother was really upset.

8 임대료가 그렇게 비싸지 않았다면, 나는 다른 학생과 방을 나눠 쓰지 않아도 됐을 텐데. (be)
→ If the rent ____________________ that expensive, I wouldn't have shared a room with another student.

D 우리말과 같은 뜻이 되도록 주어진 단어를 배열하시오.

1 의사는 잘 먹고 잘 자라고 조언했다. (and, advised, I, that, eat, sleep, well)
→ The doctor ____.

2 매일 30분만 조깅을 해보라고 권하고 싶다. (go, recommend, jogging, you, that)
→ I ____ only half an hour every day.

3 세상이 내일 끝난다면, 나는 가족과 함께 있을 거야. (end, the world, if, tomorrow, should)
→ ____, I would be with my family.

4 가능한 한 빨리 그가 수술을 받는 것이 중요하다. (have, imperative, an operation, he, that)
→ It is ____ as soon as possible.

5 그들은 즉각적인 입장료의 환불을 요구했다. (the admission fee, demanded, be, that, should)
→ They ____ immediately refunded.

6 정기적으로 건강 검진을 받는 것이 바람직하다. (a medical checkup, desirable, you, that, get)
→ It is ____ regularly.

7 내가 어린 시절로 돌아간다면, 나는 미술을 공부할 것이다. (would, go back to, study, if, were to, I, art)
→ ____________________ when I was young, I ____________________.

Unit 67 기타 가정법

A 주어진 상황에 맞게 I wish 가정법 문장을 완성하시오.

1 I'm sorry I didn't learn how to play the piano.
→ I wish ______________________________.

2 I'm sorry you can't go to the English summer camp with us.
→ I wish ______________________________.

3 I'm sorry you didn't see the movie with us. It was very touching.
→ I wish ______________________________. It was very touching.

4 I'm sorry there are not more daycare centers for working parents.
→ I wish ______________________________.

5 This coffee shop is a bit cold. I'm sorry they don't turn up the heat.
→ This coffee shop is a bit cold. I wish ______________________________.

B 상황에 맞게 as if 가정법 문장을 완성하시오.

1 She talks ______________________________. In fact, she isn't a little kid.

2 They act ______________________________. In fact, they have seen me before.

3 Andrea acts ______________________________. In fact, Andrea isn't a millionaire.

4 He acts ______________________________. In fact, he didn't own the company.

5 He talks ______________________________ in front of others. In fact, I am not his girlfriend.

C 우리말과 같은 뜻이 되도록 주어진 단어를 이용하여 가정법 문장을 완성하시오.

1 너는 공항으로 떠나야 할 시간이다. (leave for)
→ It's time ______ ______ ______ ______ ______.

2 커피가 없다면 나는 불행할 것이다. (be, unhappy)
→ But for coffee, I ______ ______ ______.

3 어렸을 때 우유를 많이 마셨어야 했는데. (drink)
→ I wish I ______ ______ lots of milk when I was young.

4 그녀는 나에 대해 모든 것을 아는 것처럼 말한다. (know)
→ She talks ______ ______ ______ ______ ______ about me.

5 그의 도움이 아니었다면 나는 그 대회에 참가할 수 없었을 것이다. (participate in)
→ Without his help, I ______ ______ ______ ______ the contest.

D 주어진 문장을 but for, without 가정법 문장으로 바꿔 쓰시오.

1 If it were not for peace, the world would be miserable.

→ ______

→ ______

2 If it had not been for the life vest, she would have died.

→ ______

→ ______

3 If it had not been for his letter, I wouldn't have known the truth.

→ ______

→ ______

4 If it were not for the Internet, our lives would be very inconvenient.

→ ______

→ ______

5 If it had not been for my parents, I couldn't have graduated from college.

→ ______

→ ______

E 주어진 문장을 If를 생략한 가정법 문장으로 바꿔 쓰시오.

1 If I were not busy, I could help you clean up the house.

→ ______

2 If I were tall enough, I would enter the modeling competition.

→ ______

3 If you had told me about it earlier, I would have visited him in the hospital.

→ ______

4 If my car hadn't broken down, I would have gone to the airport to pick you up.

→ ______

5 If the department store were close to my house, I would go shopping every day.

→ ______

6 If my parents had let me travel by myself, I would have gone backpacking overseas.

→ ______

전치사의 역할

A 두 문장에 공통으로 들어갈 전치사를 쓰시오.

1 • I couldn't easily fall asleep owing ____________ the hot weather.
  • He had to quit his job due ____________ his illness.

2 • In addition ____________ regular exercise, healthy diet is very important.
  • Thanks ____________ your encouragement, I could overcome my difficulties.

3 • I tend not to skip breakfast for the sake ____________ my health.
  • I decided to try out for another audition instead ____________ being discouraged and doing nothing.

4 • This building is equipped with fire extinguishers in case ____________ a fire.
  • The staff always tries to be nice to customers in spite ____________ frequent complaints from them.

5 • She is afraid ____________ water, so she has never gone swimming.
  • They were ashamed of themselves for fighting in front ____________ their children.

B 밑줄 친 부분을 어법에 맞게 고쳐 쓰시오.

1 <u>In case</u> fire, you need to call 911 first. ____________
2 I like cats, but I am not fond <u>with</u> dogs. ____________
3 <u>Despite</u> she is still young, she is very thoughtful. ____________
4 Peter was arrested for <u>steal</u> an old lady's money. ____________
5 He canceled our appointment without <u>ask</u> me first. ____________
6 My mother made some snacks for me <u>during</u> I was studying. ____________
7 You should answer the easier questions first <u>without</u> there's much time left. ____________
8 She decided to take a rest <u>because of</u> she worked overtime for three days. ____________
9 Sometimes I can't concentrate on my studies <u>because</u> the habit of biting my fingernails. ____________

C 우리말과 같은 뜻이 되도록 주어진 단어를 이용하여 문장을 완성하시오.

1 우리는 나가는 대신 실내에 있기로 했다. (go out)
→ We decided to stay indoors ______ ______ ______ ______.

2 우리는 도서관 앞에서 만나기로 했다. (the library)
→ We're supposed to meet ______ ______ ______ ______ ______.

3 안전벨트 덕분에 그는 교통사고에서 살아남았다. (the seat belt)
→ He survived the car accident ______ ______ ______ ______ ______.

4 부모님의 반대에도 불구하고 그들은 결혼했다. (the opposition)
→ They got married ______ ______ ______ ______ ______ from their parents.

5 시차 때문에 그는 전화를 받을 수 없을 것이다. (due, the time difference)
→ He won't be able to answer the phone ______ ______ ______ ______ ______.

6 새로운 연구에 따르면 약간의 커피를 마시는 것은 건강에 좋다. (a new study)
→ ______ ______ ______ ______ ______, drinking some coffee is good for health.

7 크리스마스 시즌 동안 많은 상점이 대대적인 세일을 제공한다. (the Christmas season)
→ Lots of shops offer huge sales ______ ______ ______ ______.

D 우리말과 같은 뜻이 되도록 주어진 단어를 배열하시오.

1 심한 안개 때문에 차들이 서행을 하고 있다. (account, fog, on, of, heavy)
→ Cars are crawling ______________________.

2 엄청난 폭풍우로 그녀의 비행기가 연착되었다. (storms, because, huge, of)
→ Her plane was delayed ______________________.

3 그는 아기를 목욕 시킨 후 소파에서 잠이 들었다. (giving, a bath, after, his baby)
→ He fell asleep on the sofa ______________________.

4 나는 그 새 프로그램의 장점이 의심스러웠다. (doubtful, the benefits, of the new program, of, was)
→ I ______________________.

5 그녀의 도움이 없었다면 나는 그 프로젝트를 포기했을 것이다. (help, without, her, the project, given up)
→ I would have ______________________.

6 그를 통제할 수 있는 유일한 사람은 그의 할머니이다. (is, controlling, the only person, capable, him, of, who)
→ His grandmother is ______________________.

7 그 배우는 자신에 대한 소문 때문에 외출할 수 없었다. (couldn't, rumors, go out, because of, about him)
→ The actor ______________________.

Unit 69 전치사의 활용

A 주어진 단어를 어법에 맞게 바꿔 문장을 완성하시오.

1 Sam grew up to ____________ his grandfather. (resemble)
2 She said she wanted to ____________ him on Christmas Day. (marry)
3 The CEO contributed to ____________ the company. (expand)
4 We are going to ____________ a meeting tomorrow morning. (have)
5 My father told me that I would be used to ____________ by myself soon. (drive)
6 I'm not accustomed to ____________ early and ____________ breakfast. (get up, have)
7 Many young people tend to ____________ their marriage these days. (postpone)
8 I'm looking forward to ____________ a nice birthday present from my parents. (receive)

B 밑줄 친 부분을 어법에 맞게 고쳐 문장을 다시 쓰시오.

1 She knows that she always lacks of confidence.
→ ____

2 I wondered why she didn't answer to my question.
→ ____

3 My sister and I don't resemble with each other at all.
→ ____

4 I just wanted them to explain about why it happened.
→ ____

5 We had to wait in a long line to enter into the theater.
→ ____

6 I am going to ask her to marry with me on her birthday.
→ ____

7 He told me that we couldn't discuss about this matter on the phone.
→ ____

8 I agree with his opinion that we need to approach to the problem differently.
→ ____

C 우리말과 같은 뜻이 되도록 주어진 단어를 이용하여 문장을 완성하시오.

1 그녀의 최대 약점은 융통성이 부족하다는 것이다. (lack, flexibility)

→ Her weakest point is that ___________ ___________ ___________.

2 나의 사촌은 유명한 배우와 결혼을 해서 딸을 낳았다. (get married, a famous actor, give birth)

→ My cousin ___________ ___________ ___________ ___________ ___________ ___________

and ___________ ___________ ___________ a daughter.

3 그 단체는 빈곤 가정을 돕는 데 헌신하고 있다. (be dedicated to, help, poor families)

→ The organization ___________ ___________ ___________ ___________ ___________ ___________.

4 상담 선생님은 내가 그들에게 먼저 다가가는 것이 중요하다고 말했다. (approach, first)

→ My counselor said it is important for me ___________ ___________ ___________ ___________.

5 그녀는 내게 자신이 외출한 동안 전화를 좀 받아달라고 부탁했다. (answer, the phones)

→ She asked me ___________ ___________ ___________ ___________ while she's out.

6 적절히 먹는 것뿐 아니라 운동을 하는 것이 중요하다. (addition, eat, properly)

→ ___________ ___________ ___________ ___________ ___________, exercising is important.

7 우리는 우리의 계획에 대해 토의하기 위해 모임을 갖기로 했다. (discuss, plan)

→ We are supposed to have a meeting ___________ ___________ ___________ ___________.

D 우리말과 같은 뜻이 되도록 주어진 단어를 배열하시오.

1 많은 사람들이 세금 인상을 반대한다. (tax increases, lots of, object, people, to)

→ ____

2 나는 그녀가 왜 오늘 수업을 빠졌는지 궁금하다. (the classes, she, today, missed, why)

→ I wonder ____.

3 그는 다음 주 월요일에 하루 휴가를 낼 것이다. (to, a day off, Monday, take, next, is going)

→ He ____.

4 저희는 당신과 곧 일하게 될 것을 기대하고 있습니다. (with you, looking forward to, are, working)

→ We ____ soon.

5 이곳은 여성을 위한 곳이므로 남자는 그 방에 들어갈 수 없습니다. (enter, men, the room, cannot)

→ This is only for women, so ____.

6 그녀는 공개적으로 그 문제를 토의하고 싶어 하지 않는 것 같았다. (the matter, discuss, publicly, to)

→ She seemed unwilling ____.

7 주의 깊게 듣고 제한된 시간 안에 문제를 다 풀어야 합니다. (in, answer, a limited time, the questions)

→ You need to listen carefully and ____.

Unit 70 전치사와 기타 관용 표현

A 보기 에서 알맞은 것을 골라 빈칸에 써넣으시오. [중복 사용 가능]

보기 out at into for on

1 I cleaned ____________ my room while Mom was cooking.
2 I can't concentrate ____________ my studies with the radio on.
3 She didn't catch ____________ to the meaning of what he said.
4 She was angry ____________ herself for making such a silly mistake.
5 Please stop staring ____________ me like that. I'm a bit embarrassed.
6 I ran ____________ an old friend while I was traveling around the city.
7 She apologized ____________ having to leave before the event finished.
8 We need to divide ourselves ____________ two teams to play this game.
9 The brothers came to Korea to search ____________ their biological mother.
10 They didn't rule ____________ the possibility of failing to advance to the semi-finals.

B 보기 의 (A)와 (B)에서 각각 알맞은 것을 골라 빈칸에 써넣으시오.

보기					
	(A) depended	change	pay	figure	yelled
	(B) out	at	into	for	on

1 I'll ____________________ dinner since you helped me do my project.
2 The program is showing how caterpillars ____________________ butterflies.
3 We need to ____________________ the local markets before expanding overseas.
4 The spectators at the soccer game ____________________ the player after he failed to score.
5 He ____________________ his parents when he was young, but now he is living on his own.

C 보기 에서 알맞은 것을 고르고 적절한 전치사를 함께 사용하여 문장을 완성하시오.

보기 jumped insisting act look

1 She will ____________________ the main character in the play tonight.
2 The CEO had the team ____________________ the cause of the delay.
3 He likes her, so he ____________________ the chance to go with her.
4 Could you help me ____________________ my cell phone? I can't find it.
5 He kept ____________________ his innocence, but nobody believed him.

D 우리말과 같은 뜻이 되도록 주어진 단어를 이용하여 문장을 완성하시오.

1 과거는 그냥 잊어버리고, 너의 미래에 집중해. (focus, future)
→ Just forget about the past, and ________ ________ ________ ________.

2 그는 해외 취업 정보를 찾고 있는 중이다. (look, information)
→ He ________ ________ ________ ________ about working abroad.

3 그 TV광고는 젊은 세대를 겨냥한 것이다. (aim, the young generation)
→ The TV commercial ________ ________ ________ ________ ________.

4 그녀는 그의 농담을 이해할 수 없어서 웃을 수 없었다. (laugh, his joke)
→ She ________ ________ ________ ________ ________ because it was difficult to understand.

5 만약 성급한 결정을 내리면, 너는 나중에 후회할지도 몰라. (rush, a decision)
→ If you ________ ________ ________ ________, you may later regret it.

6 나는 오디션에서 그 영화의 몇몇 장면들을 연기했다. (act, a couple of scenes)
→ I ________ ________ ________ ________ ________ ________ from the movie in the audition.

7 나는 다음 학기에 교환학생프로그램에 지원할 것이다. (apply, a student exchange program)
→ I'll ________ ________ ________ ________ ________ ________ next semester.

E 우리말과 같은 뜻이 되도록 주어진 단어를 배열하시오.

1 내 신발이 낡아서 어머니께서는 새 신발을 사주셨다. (out, are, shoes, worn, my)
→ ________________________________ so Mom bought me new ones.

2 고객 서비스센터의 모든 직원은 방문객에게 미소를 건넸다. (the visitors, at, smiled)
→ All the employees in the customer service center ________________________________.

3 주차 요금으로 얼마를 지불해야 하나요? (have to, parking, do, how much, I, pay, for)
→ ________________________________

4 그녀가 외출할 때마다 그녀의 아이들은 같이 가겠다고 고집을 피운다. (with, insist, going, on, her)
→ Whenever she goes out, her children ________________________________.

5 Sam 삼촌은 마흔 살이지만, 그는 결혼을 서두르고 싶어 하지 않는다. (into, doesn't, rush, want, marriage, to)
→ Uncle Sam is 40 years old, but he ________________________________.

6 나는 그녀가 우리의 비밀을 누설했다는 것을 믿을 수가 없었다. (our secret, she, out, let)
→ I couldn't believe that ________________________________.

7 사회가 과정보다 결과에 중점을 둔다는 것은 문제이다.
(puts, over process, society, on, emphasis, results)
→ It is a problem that ________________________________.

화법

A 직접 화법을 간접 화법으로 바꿔 문장을 완성하시오.

1 Clair said, "Have you finished your homework?"
→ Clair asked me ______________________.

2 He said to me, "Why didn't you call me yesterday?"
→ He asked me ______________________.

3 My father said, "I'm going on a business trip next week."
→ My father said that ______________________.

4 Brian said, "What are you going to do on New Year's Day?"
→ Brian asked me ______________________.

5 She said, "Let's put off our trip until we save enough money."
→ She suggested that ______________________.

6 She said to me, "I'm going to buy Jason Michael's new album."
→ She told me that ______________________.

7 My father said to me, "Do you want me to drive you to school tomorrow?"
→ My father asked me ______________________.

B 간접 화법을 직접 화법으로 바꿔 문장을 완성하시오.

1 My mother asked me if I had had dinner.
→ My mother said to me, ______________________

2 He asked me if I knew when he would be back.
→ He said to me, ______________________

3 He asked me where we should meet the next day.
→ He said to me, ______________________

4 She told me not to eat instant noodles late at night.
→ She said, ______________________

5 Kelly asked me when I had graduated from college.
→ Kelly said to me, ______________________

6 Edward said that he wants to be an actor when he grows up.
→ Edward said, ______________________

C 우리말과 같은 뜻이 되도록 주어진 단어를 이용하여 간접 화법 문장을 완성하시오.

1 그는 그날 물어볼 것들이 많다고 말했다. (say, have)
→ He ________ ________ ________ lots of things to ask that day.

2 그녀는 우리에게 거기서 하루 더 머무르라고 말했다. (tell, stay)
→ She ________ ________ ________ ________ there one more day.

3 그는 내게 그 영화를 본 적이 있냐고 물었다. (ask, see, the movie)
→ He ________ me ________ ________ ________ ________ ________ ________.

4 Jessica 내게 어디서 목걸이를 샀냐고 물었다. (ask, buy, the necklace)
→ Jessica ________ me ________ ________ ________ ________ ________ ________.

5 그는 자신의 반에서 일 등을 했다고 엄마에게 말했다. (tell, get, first place)
→ He ________ his mom ________ ________ ________ ________ in ________ class.

6 그는 자신의 부모님이 3년 전에 돌아가셨다고 말했다. (say, parents, pass away)
→ He ________ ________ ________ ________ ________ three years ago.

7 우리 어머니는 나에게 저녁을 먹기 전에 손을 씻으라고 말했다. (tell, wash one's hands)
→ My mother ________ ________ ________ ________ ________ ________ before I have dinner.

D 우리말과 같은 뜻이 되도록 주어진 단어를 배열하시오.

1 그녀는 내게 그 차를 살 돈이 있냐고 물었다. (buy, if, money, the car, to, had, I)
→ She asked me ________________________________.

2 그는 식당에 자리를 예약하는 게 좋겠다고 제안했다. (at the restaurant, should, a table, we, book)
→ He suggested that ________________________________.

3 학생들은 선생님에게 언제 시험 결과가 발표되느냐고 물었다. (would, when, announced, the exam results, be)
→ The students asked the teacher ________________________________.

4 의사는 내게 며칠 동안 휴식을 취하는 것이 좋겠다고 말했다. (take a rest, me, I, for a few days, should, that, told)
→ The doctor ________________________________.

5 나는 그녀에게 그날 집안일 하는 것을 도울 수 있다고 말했다.
(her, that day, help, told her, I, do the housework, could)
→ I ________________________________.

6 Ben은 그녀에게 다음 날 자신의 생일 파티에 올 수 있느냐고 물었다.
(to his birthday party, could, if, come, she, the following day)
→ Ben asked her ________________________________.

일치

A 주어진 동사를 알맞게 바꿔 문장을 완성하시오.

1 We learned in class that the Earth __________ round. (be)
2 We all felt that she __________ hiding something from us. (be)
3 My parents believe that I __________ __________ someday. (will, succeed)
4 He realized that he __________ __________ his cell phone in the classroom. (leave)
5 I heard that you often __________ a walk after having breakfast. (take)
6 My grandfather said heaven __________ those who help themselves. (help)
7 I heard that he __________ __________ in Italy for three years before moving to Korea. (live)

B 주어진 문장을 과거 시제로 바꿔 다시 쓰시오.

1 He doesn't believe I am good at English.
→ He didn't believe ________________________________.
2 My mother says that I am too picky about food.
→ My mother said that ________________________________.
3 She says that somebody has stolen her cell phone.
→ She said that ________________________________.
4 She says that she has been looking forward to seeing me.
→ She said that ________________________________.
5 She thinks that Henry is the only person to solve the problem.
→ She thought that ________________________________.
6 Many people think that South Korea and North Korea will be unified soon.
→ Many people thought that ________________________________.
7 We learn in the Geography class that Australia has opposite seasons to Korea.
→ We learned in the Geography class that ________________________________.

C 우리말과 같은 뜻이 되도록 주어진 이용하여 문장을 완성하시오.

1 그녀는 일요일마다 교회에 간다고 말한다. (say, go, to church)

→ She ____________ that she ____________ ____________ ____________ every Sunday.

2 그는 어려울 때 친구가 진짜 친구라고 말했다. (say, be, a friend indeed)

→ He ____________ that a friend in need ____________ ____________ ____________ ____________.

3 그들은 그가 성공할 거라고 믿었지만 성공하지 못했다. (believe, will, succeed)

→ They ____________ that he ____________ ____________, but he didn't.

4 나는 그녀가 오랜 시간 동안 내게 거짓말을 해왔음을 알지 못했다. (know, lie)

→ I ____________ ____________ that she ____________ ____________ ____________ to me for a long time.

5 길거리에서 싸우고 있던 남자들이 한 시간 전에 체포되었다. (fight, be arrested)

→ The men who ____________ ____________ on the street ____________ ____________ an hour ago.

6 그녀는 내가 전에 캐나다에 가본 적이 있다는 것을 안다. (know, be, to Canada)

→ She ____________ that I ____________ ____________ ____________ ____________ before.

7 나는 제2차 세계대전이 1939년에 일어났다는 것을 안다. (know, break out, in 1939)

→ I ____________ that World War II ____________ ____________ ____________ ____________.

D 우리말과 같은 뜻이 되도록 주어진 단어를 배열하시오.

1 그는 내게 무소식이 희소식이라고 말했다. (is, no, good, news, news)

→ He told me that ____.

2 너 그들의 결혼식에 간다고 하지 않았었니? (go, wedding, you, to, would, their)

→ Didn't you say that ____?

3 그들은 결혼한 지 10년이 되었다고 말했다. (been married, for, they, ten years, had)

→ They said ____.

4 그녀는 2주마다 집안 대청소를 한다고 말했다. (her whole house, cleans, every two weeks, she)

→ She said ____.

5 한국은 1945년에 광복을 맞이했다고 선생님이 말했다. (independence, Korea, in 1945, regained)

→ The teacher said ____.

6 그녀는 내게 자기가 대학원에 합격했다고 말했다. (accepted, she, graduate school, been, to, had)

→ She told me that ____.

7 지금 무대에서 노래하고 춤추는 학생들은 우리 반이다.
(singing and dancing, are, are, who, on the stage now)

→ The students ____ my classmates.

도치

A **보기** 와 같이 밑줄 친 단어를 강조하는 문장으로 바꿔 쓰시오.

보기	A cat was under the car. → Under the car _____was a cat_____.

1 Only a few books were in the box.
→ In the box ____.

2 She could hardly believe what had happened to her.
→ Hardly ____.

3 I have never experienced hot weather like this before.
→ Never ____.

4 She seldom puts on her makeup when she goes out.
→ Seldom ____.

5 I knew little that he had been helping the poor secretly.
→ Little ____.

6 He had no sooner finished his work than he breathed a sigh of relief.
→ No sooner ____.

B 빈칸에 알맞은 대답을 넣어 대화를 완성하시오.

1 A Did you and Mike go to the seminar?
B I didn't go to the seminar, nor ________________.

2 A I was busy doing my homework at that time.
B So ________________. That's why I couldn't go to church.

3 A I liked the movie. The ending was especially good.
B So ________________.

4 A I don't know why I have to learn science.
B Neither ________________. I don't want to learn science or math.

5 A I can't go to the movies tonight.
B Neither ________________. I have to finish my report by tomorrow.

6 A The room feels very stuffy. I want to go outside for some fresh air.
B So ________________. Why don't we take a walk?

C 우리말과 같은 뜻이 되도록 주어진 단어를 이용하여 도치 문장을 완성하시오.

1 기차가 온다. (come, the train)
→ Here ___________ ___________ ___________.

2 출입문 입구에 어린 소년이 서 있었다. (stand, a little boy)
→ In the doorway ___________ ___________ ___________ ___________.

3 나는 지금까지 그렇게 아름다운 건물을 본 적이 없다. (see)
→ Never ___________ ___________ ___________ such a beautiful building.

4 나는 오늘 오후가 되어서야 그 사고에 대해 들었다. (hear about)
→ Not until this afternoon ___________ ___________ ___________ ___________ the accident.

5 어떠한 경우에도 그와 같은 일이 벌어지도록 내버려두지 않겠다. (will, let)
→ Under no circumstances ___________ ___________ ___________ such a thing happen.

6 그는 좀처럼 다른 사람들에게 자신의 개인적인 문제를 이야기하지 않는다. (talk about)
→ Rarely ___________ ___________ ___________ ___________ his personal matters to others.

7 그는 거짓말을 많이 해왔기 때문에 그녀는 그가 한 말을 거의 믿지 않을 것이다. (would, believe)
→ Scarcely ___________ ___________ ___________ what he said because he has lied a lot.

D 우리말과 같은 뜻이 되도록 주어진 단어를 배열하시오.

1 모퉁이에 큰 개가 서 있었다. (dog, a, stood, big)
→ At the corner ____.

2 그녀는 그의 글씨를 거의 알아볼 수 없었다. (his handwriting, read, she, could)
→ Hardly ____.

3 무대 뒤에 배우들이 사용하는 방이 하나 있다. (the actors, that, use, a room, is)
→ Behind the stage ____.

4 그녀는 지금까지 학교에 지각한 적이 없다. (late, so far, has, for school, she, been)
→ Never ____.

5 그가 집을 나서자마자 비가 오기 시작했다. (he, than, had, to rain, home, started, it, left)
→ No sooner ____.

6 그녀는 카페인 때문에 밤에는 좀처럼 커피를 마시지 않는다. (drink, does, at night, coffee, she)
→ Seldom ___________________________________ because of the caffeine.

7 월요일이 되어서야 나는 발표 자료에서 실수를 발견했다. (in the presentation materials, the error, find, did, I)
→ Not until Monday ____.

it의 특별 용법

A 주어진 문장을 가주어 it을 사용한 문장으로 바꿔 쓰시오.

1 Why he suddenly quit the job is not clear.
→ ______________________

2 To drive without wearing a seat belt is dangerous.
→ ______________________

3 That you need to study hard to enter college is true.
→ ______________________

4 That you can't come to his birthday party is too bad.
→ ______________________

5 To swim in the river without a life vest is dangerous.
→ ______________________

6 To make a mistake in front of many people is very embarrassing.
→ ______________________

7 To find someone who is fluent in both English and French won't be easy.
→ ______________________

B 보기 와 같이 밑줄 친 부분을 강조하는 문장으로 바꿔 쓰시오.

보기	English is my favorite subject. → It is English that is my favorite subject.

1 You need warm clothes for the camp.
→ ______________________

2 Her husband is waiting for her in the restaurant now.
→ ______________________

3 Mike caused the car accident on his way home.
→ ______________________

4 She watched the baseball game on TV with her friends yesterday.
→ ______________________

5 Ann will meet her mother in front of the department store today.
→ ______________________

C 우리말과 같은 뜻이 되도록 주어진 단어를 이용하여 문장을 완성하시오.

1 그가 결국에는 벌을 받게 될 것이 분명하다. (obvious)
→ It ______ ______ ______ he will be punished in the end.

2 Jeff와 내가 처음 만난 것은 그 파티에서였다. (at the party)
→ It ______ ______ ______ ______ ______ Jeff and I first met.

3 도서관에 책을 반납해야 했던 것은 지난주였다. (last week)
→ It ______ ______ ______ ______ I had to return the book to the library.

4 그녀가 그의 사무실을 찾는 데 한 시간이 걸렸다. (take, hour, find)
→ It ______ ______ ______ ______ ______ ______ his office.

5 그녀는 많은 사람들 앞에서 발표하는 것을 정말로 싫어한다. (hate)
→ She ______ ______ to make a presentation in front of many people.

6 그가 그렇게 어린 나이에 피아노를 치기 시작했다니 믿을 수 없는 일이었다. (unbelievable)
→ It ______ ______ ______ he started to play the piano at such a young age.

7 나는 우리와 함께 일하도록 그를 설득하는 것이 어렵다는 것을 알았다. (find, hard, persuade)
→ I ______ ______ ______ ______ ______ him to work with us.

D 우리말과 같은 뜻이 되도록 주어진 단어를 배열하시오.

1 옛 친구와 우연히 마주친 것은 극장에서였다. (ran into, I, it, that, in the theater, was)
→ ______________________________ my old friend.

2 내가 피자를 주문한 것은 30분 전이었다. (I, was, that, ordered, it, half an hour ago)
→ ______________________________ a pizza.

3 과거의 일을 후회하는 것은 소용없는 일이다. (what I did, regret, it, to, was, useless)
→ ______________________________ in the past.

4 그녀가 쿠키를 굽는 데는 30분밖에 걸리지 않았다. (only, it, to bake, half an hour, took, for her)
→ ______________________________ the cookies.

5 프로젝트 실패의 책임이 있는 것은 바로 그녀이다. (she, is responsible for, it, the failure, that, is)
→ ______________________________ of the project.

6 나는 가족과 외식하는 것을 정말 좋아하지만 오늘은 그러고 싶은 기분은 아니다.
(like, I, eating out, do, with my family)
→ ______________________________, but I don't feel like it today.

THIS IS GRAMMAR

이것이 진화하는 New This Is Grammar다!

- 판에 박힌 형식적인 표현보다 **원어민이 실제 일상 생활에서 바로 쓰는** 생활 영문법
- 문어체뿐만 아니라 **구어체 문법을 강조한 회화, 독해, 영작을 위한** 실용 영문법
- 현지에서 더는 사용하지 않는 낡은 영문법 대신 **시대의 흐름에 맞춘** 현대 영문법

이 책의 특징

★ 실생활에서 쓰는 문장과 대화, 지문으로 구성된 예문 수록
★ 핵심 문법 포인트를 보기 쉽게 도식화 · 도표화하여 구성
★ 다양하고 유용한 연습문제 및 리뷰, 리뷰 플러스 문제 수록
★ 중 · 고등 내신에 꼭 등장하는 어법 포인트의 철저한 분석 및 총정리
★ 회화 · 독해 · 영작 실력 향상의 토대인 문법 지식의 체계적 설명

This Is Grammar (최신개정판)시리즈

초급 1, 2 — **기초 문법 강화 + 내신 대비**
예비 중학생과 초급자를 위해 영어의 기본적 구조인 형태, 의미, 용법 등을 소개하고, 다양한 연습문제를 제공하고 있다. Key Point에 문법의 핵심 사항을 한눈에 보기 쉽게 도식화·도표화하여 정리하였다.

중급 1, 2 — **문법 요약(Key Point) + 체계적 설명**
중·고등 내신에 꼭 등장하는 문법 포인트를 철저히 분석하여 이해 및 암기가 쉽도록 예문과 함께 문법을 요약해 놓았다. 중급자들이 체계적으로 영문법을 학습할 수 있도록 충분한 콘텐츠를 제공하고 있다.

고급 1, 2 — **핵심 문법 설명 + 각종 수험 대비**
중·고급 영어 학습자들을 대상으로 내신, 토익, 토플, 텝스 등 각종 시험을 완벽 대비할 수 있도록 중요 문법 포인트를 분석, 정리하였다. 다양하고 진정성 있는 지문들을 통해 풍부한 배경지식을 함께 쌓을 수 있다.

www.nexusEDU.kr
넥서스 초·중·고등 사이트

www.nexusbook.com
넥서스 홈페이지

책에 대해 궁금한 사항은 넥서스에듀 홈페이지 1:1 고객상담 게시판을 이용하세요.

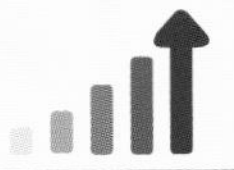

NEXUS Edu

LEVEL CHART

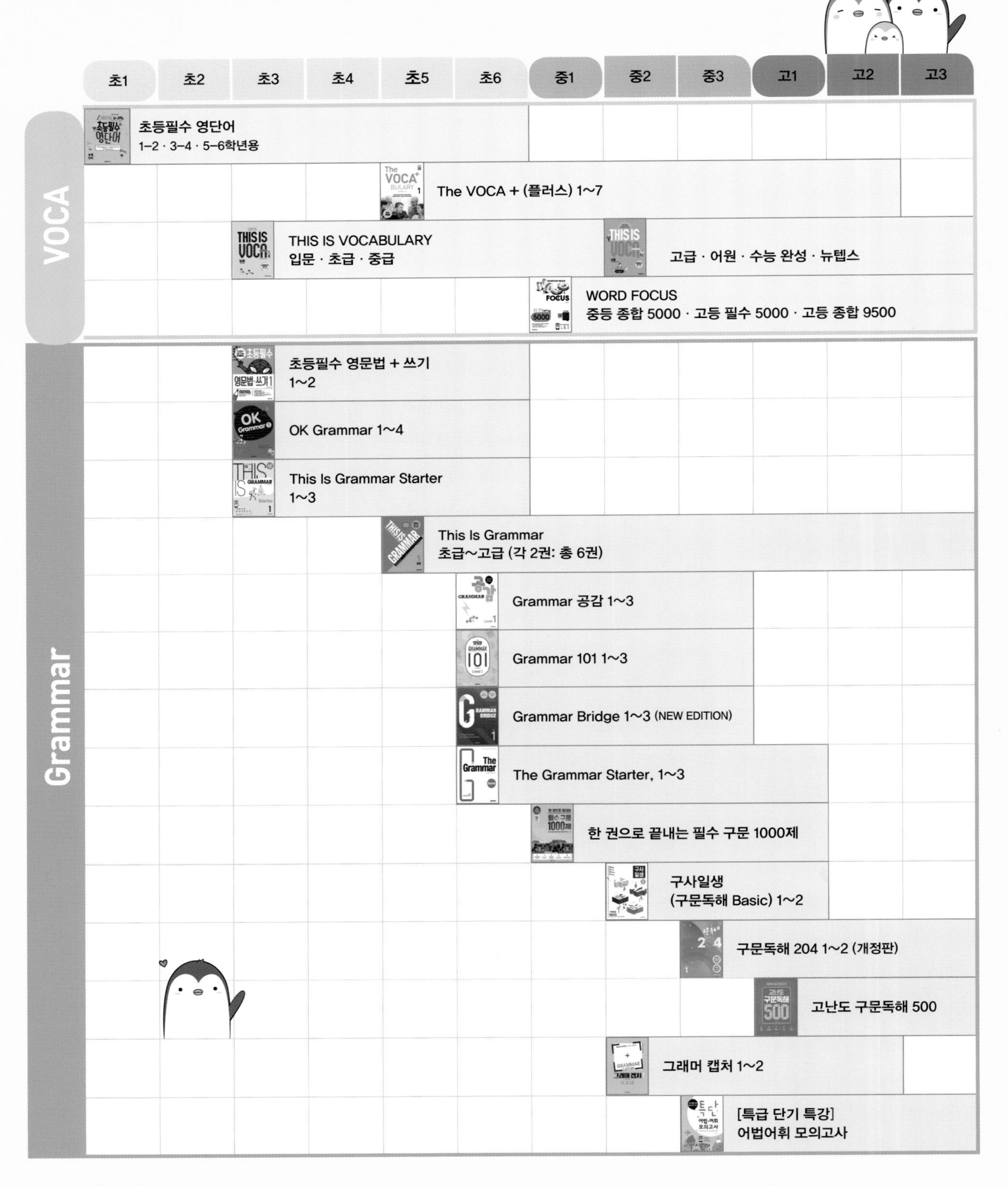

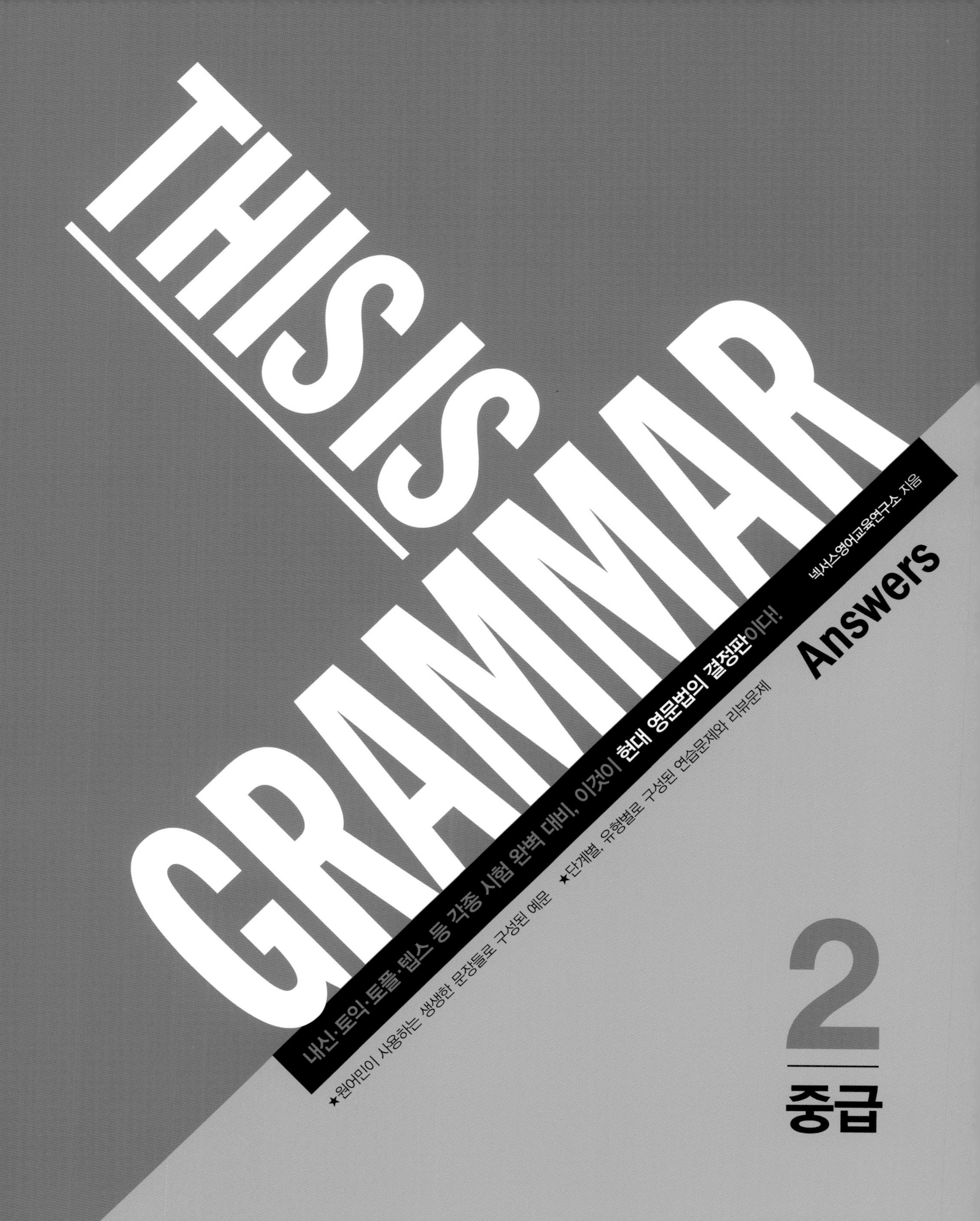
THIS IS GRAMMAR
Answers
넥서스영어교육연구소 지음
내신·토익·토플·텝스 등 각종 시험 완벽 대비, 이것이 현대 영문법의 결정판이다!
★원어민이 사용하는 생생한 문장들로 구성된 예문
★단계별, 유형별로 구성된 연습문제와 리뷰문제
2
중급

NEXUS Edu

REPLAY

p. 8~9

1 CHECK-UP

1 You should take notes.
2 He must get up early.
3 My brother will ride a bicycle.
4 She can translate Latin into English.
5 Ben might travel around South Africa.
6 The children had better go to bed early.
7 I must finish my homework by tonight.
8 You should watch the film.
9 Amy may buy a new laptop computer today.
10 He can jump seven meters in the long jump.

2 CHECK-UP

1 I can not[can't/cannot] find my cell phone.
2 You had better not leave.
3 She should not[shouldn't] do it again.
4 He must not[mustn't] take this bag.

3 CHECK-UP

1 May I have some sugar?
2 Can she check out this book?
3 Would you drink something cold?
4 Could he spend time with you this weekend?

Unit 39 EXERCISES

p. 12~13

A

1 be able to
2 be able to
3 Can
4 be able to
5 Can
6 can[is able to]
7 can[is able to]

해석

1 우리 아기는 몇 주 후면 걸을 수 있을 것이다.
2 우리는 네가 토요일에 우리와 함께할 수 있기를 바란다.
3 여기서 버스표를 살 수 있을까요? 시내로 나가고 싶은데요.
4 내가 그녀와 통화를 할 수 있을지도 몰라. 그녀가 괜찮아야 할 텐데.
5 나를 위해 이 편지 좀 부쳐 줄 수 있니? 나는 바로 회의가 있어.
6 우리 언니는 피아노와 기타를 칠 수 있다. 나는 언니가 정말로 부럽다.
7 월터는 야외에서 생활하는 데 노련한 사람이다. 그는 야생에서 혼자 살 수 있다.

B

1 can play
2 can't think
3 can relieve
4 can mimic
5 can't believe
6 can't travel

해석

1 나는 네가 원한다면 너를 위해 바이올린을 연주할 수 있다.
2 미안하지만 그 노래의 제목이 생각나지 않아.
3 초콜릿이나 커피 한 잔이 당신의 스트레스를 덜어줄 수 있습니다. 먹어 보세요.
4 어떤 새들은 인간을 흉내 낼 수 있다. 하지만 말을 할 수는 없다.
5 여름 방학이 벌써 끝났다니 믿을 수 없다!
6 우리는 올해 해외로 여행을 갈 수 없다. 항공료가 너무 비싸다.

C

1 ⓐ 2 ⓒ 3 ⓑ 4 ⓑ 5 ⓐ 6 ⓐ 7 ⓒ

해석

1 너는 이 사용 설명서를 이해할 수 있니?
2 그는 진심일 리 없어. 그는 그냥 널 놀리는 거야.
3 저 맛있는 케이크를 조금만 더 먹어도 되나요?
4 장거리 전화 거는 방법 좀 알려줄래요?
5 나는 퇴근 후에 쇼핑하러 갈 수 없었어. 너무 피곤했어.
6 우리는 환경을 살릴 수 있지만, 혼자서는 할 수 없다.
7 그녀는 교수일 리 없어. 그녀는 너무 어려 보여.

D

1 can[could], Can[Could]
2 couldn't
3 couldn't
4 Can[Could]
5 can't
6 couldn't, Can

해석

1 A: 죄송하지만, 문을 좀 잡아 주시겠어요?
B: 물론이죠.
2 A: 너 매우 피곤해 보여. 어젯밤에 충분히 못 잤니?
B: 응, 못 잤어. 잠을 잘 잘 수 없었어.
3 A: 집에 일찍 왔구나. 무슨 일 있었니?
B: 도서관이 너무 시끄러워서 집중할 수가 없었어요.
4 A: 소리를 좀 키워주시겠어요? 뒤에는 들리지 않아요.
B: 네, 잠시만요. 이제 어떠세요?
5 A: 저 여자가 차고 있는 시계의 브랜드를 아니?
B: 여기서 분간하긴 어렵지만 비싸 보여.
6 A: 미나가 처음에 캐나다로 갔을 때는 영어를 한마디도 못했어.
B: 놀라운데. 이제 그녀는 의사소통이 가능하니?

E

1 could have played
2 could come over
3 could have bought
4 could teach
5 could have asked
6 could have warned

해석

1 A: 존과 켈리는 주말에 아무것도 하지 않았어.
B: 정말? 우리랑 같이 놀 수 있었을 텐데.
2 A: 우리 내일 뭐 할까? 휴일이잖아.
B: 내가 너의 집에 놀러 갈 수도 있어.
3 A: 왜 그녀는 우리에게 이번 주말에 할인을 한다고 말하지 않았지?
B: 더 저렴한 가격에 물건을 살 수도 있었는데.
4 A: 토스트 말고 다른 것도 요리하는 법을 알면 좋겠는데.
B: 네가 원한다면 내가 가르쳐 줄 수도 있어.
5 A: 내게 도움을 요청할 수도 있었잖아. 나는 한가했는데.

B: 맞아. 혼자서 하기엔 너무 많은 일이었어.

6 A: 메리가 오늘 기분이 별로네. 네가 나한테 그 애를 놀리지 말라고 주의를 줄 수도 있었잖아.

B: 말하지 않은 건 미안해. 하지만 네가 메리를 놀릴 거라고 내가 어떻게 알았겠니?

Unit 40 EXERCISES

p. 15

A

1 추측 2 추측 3 허가 4 허가 5 허가 6 추측

해석

1 나는 다른 도시로 이사 가야 할지도 모른다고 생각했다.
2 모퉁이를 돌면 좋은 식당이 좀 있을지도 모른다.
3 너는 지금 가도 돼. 나가는 길에 문을 닫아 줘.
4 실례합니다. 인터뷰를 테이프에 녹음해도 될까요?
5 수업 끝나고 네 공책을 빌릴 수 있을까? 오늘은 집중할 수가 없었어.
6 소피아는 뮤지컬 보는 것을 좋아하니까 우리와 함께 가기를 원할지도 몰라.

B

1 He may[might] not believe your story.
2 Ken may[might] not be feeling well right now.
3 Ms. Kim may[might] be in the teachers' room.
4 She may[might] be the girl who Tom told you about.

해석

1 그는 너의 이야기를 믿지 않을지도 모른다.
2 켄은 지금 몸이 안 좋을지도 모른다.
3 김 선생님은 교무실에 있을지도 모른다.
4 그녀는 톰이 너에게 말한 그 소녀일지도 모른다.

C

1 may[might] as well walk 2 may[might] as well tell
3 may[might] as well watch 4 may[might] as well go

해석

1 당신은 버스를 막 놓쳤다. 버스는 한 시간에 한 대밖에 오지 않는다. 당신은 "나는 한 시간 동안 기다리고 싶지 않아. 나는 걸어가는 게 좋겠어."라고 말한다.
2 당신의 친구가 자신의 여자 친구에게 거짓말을 했다. 당신은 그에게 조언을 해 주길 원한다. 당신은 "너는 그녀에게 진실을 말하는 게 좋겠어. 그녀가 조만간 다 알아낼 거야."라고 말한다.
3 당신은 특별한 계획이 없고 지루하다. 몇 분 후에 텔레비전에서 영화가 시작한다. 당신은 "우리는 영화를 보는 게 좋겠어. 다른 할 일이 없어."라고 말한다.
4 당신은 콘서트 표가 있다. 그 밴드의 팬은 아니지만 다른 계획이 없어서 가기로 한다. 당신은 "나는 콘서트에 가는 게 좋겠어. 더 나은 할 일이 없거든."이라고 말한다.

Unit 41 EXERCISES

p. 18~19

A

1 don't have to 2 don't have to
3 mustn't 4 don't have to
5 doesn't have to 6 mustn't

해석

1 우리는 늦지 않았으므로 서두를 필요가 없다.
2 내일은 일요일이다. 그래서 나는 일찍 일어날 필요가 없다.
3 외국인에게 나이를 물어서는 안 된다. 그것은 예의가 없는 것이다.
4 성공하기 위해서 잘생기거나 똑똑할 필요는 없다.
5 메리는 내일 일하러 갈 필요가 없어서 늦잠 잘 수 있다.
6 조용히 해 주세요. 당신은 공부방에서 웃고 깔깔거리면 안 됩니다.

B

1 must not 2 must not 3 must
4 must not 5 must 6 must 7 must

해석

1 나는 디저트를 더 먹으면 안 돼. 다이어트 중이야.
2 저 교통 표지판은 시속 80km 이상으로 운전하면 안 된다는 뜻이야.
3 샌디는 나에게 온종일 한마디도 하지 않았어. 아직도 화가 나 있는 게 틀림없어.
4 신호가 빨간색일 때 길을 건너면 안 된다. 그것은 위험하다.
5 너는 저 부츠에 많은 돈을 지불했다. 품질이 좋은 게 틀림없다.
6 새로운 태국 식당은 항상 만원이다. 음식이 훌륭한 게 틀림없다.
7 너는 이 프로젝트가 5월 말까지 끝나야 한다는 것을 명심해야 한다.

C

1 must[have to] be 2 must[have to] hang up
3 must[has to] wear 4 must[have to] buy
5 must[has to] study 6 must[have to] remember
7 must[have to] repeat

해석

1 나는 내일 아침 8시에 시험 장소에 있어야만 한다.
2 너는 빨래를 당장 널어야만 한다. 그렇지 않으면 구겨질 것이다.
3 그녀는 시력이 매우 나빠서 안경을 써야만 한다.
4 우리는 주혁이와 지혜에게 그들의 결혼식을 위해 뭔가를 사 줘야 한다.
5 지섭이는 영어를 공부해야만 한다. 내일이 바로 기말고사다.
6 너는 마이크에게 전화해서 생일 축하한다고 말하는 것을 잊지 말아야 한다.
7 너는 배운 것을 잊지 않도록 반복해야 한다.

D

1 mustn't open 2 mustn't let
3 doesn't have to wear 4 doesn't have to shave
5 mustn't give up 6 mustn't eat
7 mustn't tell 8 don't have to decide

해석

1 네 생일 때까지 이 상자를 열어서는 안 된다.
2 너는 아이들이 하고 싶은 대로 하게 내버려 두어서는 안 된다.
3 짐은 일하러 갈 때 넥타이를 맬 필요가 없지만, 종종 매고 간다.
4 우리 할아버지께서는 턱수염을 기르신다. 그래서 면도할 필요가 없다.
5 승리가 불가능해 보여도 포기하면 안 된다.
6 너는 조개를 날로 먹으면 안 된다. 조개에는 해로운 박테리아가 있다.
7 내가 지갑을 잃어버렸다는 것을 아빠가 아시게 되는 걸 원치 않는다. 절대로 말해서는 안 된다.

8 미술을 공부할지 과학을 공부할지 아직 결정할 필요 없다. 너는 아직 그것에 대해 생각할 시간이 많다.

E

1 must have been
2 must have been
3 must have moved
4 must have been
5 must have mistaken
6 must have seen
7 must have been

해석

1 A: 나는 작년에 호주에서 여름 캠프에 참가했어.
B: 재미있었겠다.
2 A: 데이지가 오늘 아침에 버스에서 잠들어서 내릴 정류장을 놓쳤어.
B: 그녀는 매우 피곤했던 게 틀림없어.
3 A: 나는 최근에 미국인 선생님인 루이스를 못 봤어.
B: 나도 못 봤어. 그는 미국으로 돌아간 게 틀림없어.
4 A: 그들은 길 건너에 있는 아파트 건물을 헐고 있었어.
B: 매우 시끄러웠을 게 틀림없어.
5 A: 실례합니다만, 당신의 이름이 폴이죠, 그렇지 않나요?
B: 죄송합니다만, 다른 사람과 저를 착각하신 게 틀림없어요.
6 A: 수지와 뭘 해야 하지? 그녀와 제임스 카메론의 새 영화를 보는 것이 좋을까?
B: 그것은 좋은 생각이 아닌 것 같아. 그녀는 분명 이미 그것을 보았을 거야.
7 A: 나는 모든 문제를 다 틀렸어.
B: 퀴즈가 정말 쉬웠어. 너는 분명 수업 시간에 졸고 있을 거야.

Unit 42 EXERCISES

p. 22~23

1 should[ought to] protect
2 shouldn't[ought not to] break
3 should[ought to] respect
4 shouldn't[ought not to] stay
5 shouldn't[ought not to] work
6 should[ought to] make
7 shouldn't[ought not to] cause
8 should[ought to] read

해석

1 우리는 자연을 보호해야 한다.
2 사람들은 법을 어겨서는 안 된다.
3 너는 부모님을 존경해야 한다.
4 나는 더 오래 머무르면 안 돼. 우리 아이들이 나를 기다리고 있어.
5 내 생각에 너는 그와 일하면 안 될 것 같아. 그는 믿을만한 사람이 아니야.
6 주저할 시간이 없어. 그는 결정을 내려야 해.
7 그는 말썽꾸러기이다. 그는 수업 중에 그렇게 많은 말썽을 일으키지 말아야 한다.
8 영어 실력을 향상시키려면 더 많은 영어책을 읽어야 한다.

B

1 should have called
2 should have taken
3 should go
4 should have come
5 shouldn't have said
6 shouldn't complain

해석

1 늦어서 미안해. 내가 전화했어야 했는데.
2 지금 되돌아보면, 너의 충고를 받아들였어야 했는데.
3 너는 휴식이 필요해. 며칠 동안 여행을 가는 게 좋겠어.
4 어젯밤 댄스파티는 정말 재미있었어. 너도 왔어야 했는데.
5 너는 그렇게 말하지 말았어야 해. 그가 매우 당황한 것처럼 보였어.
6 너는 그렇게 불평하지 말아야 한다. 좀 더 긍정적인 사람이 되도록 노력해 봐.

C

1 should have invested
2 should have bought
3 should ask
4 should have won
5 should have sent
6 should get

해석

1 나는 주가가 폭락한 이후에 증권 시장에 투자했어야 했다.
2 오렌지가 할인 판매 중이었으니 너는 더 많이 샀어야 했다.
3 대량으로 물건을 살 때는 할인을 요구해야 한다.
4 우리 팀이 게임에서 이겼어야 했어. 심판의 판정이 공정하지 않았어.
5 나는 편지를 보냈지만 그는 그것을 받지 못했다. 좀 더 빨리 보냈어야 했는데.
6 친구네 집에서 하룻밤 자고 싶으면 너는 부모님의 허락을 받아야 한다.

D

1 had better put
2 had better put on
3 had better take
4 had better not drive
5 had better stay
6 had better not go out

해석

1 당신 친구가 방금 손가락을 베었다. 당신은 그녀에게 이렇게 말한다.
→ 너는 손가락에 반창고를 붙이는 게 좋겠어.
2 당신 친구가 해변에 갈 것이다. 밖은 햇빛이 쨍쨍하다. 당신은 그에게 이렇게 말한다. → 선크림을 충분히 바르는 게 좋겠다. 그렇지 않으면 햇볕에 탈지도 몰라.
3 당신은 톰과 산책하러 나갈 것이다. 비가 올 것 같다. 당신은 톰에게 이렇게 말한다. → 우리는 우산을 가져가는 게 좋겠어.
4 눈이 많이 내리고 있지만 아버지께서는 차로 출근을 하고 싶어 하신다. 당신은 아버지께 이렇게 말한다. → 오늘 차로 출근하지 않는 게 좋겠어요. 눈이 많이 오고 있어요.
5 당신 남동생은 심한 감기에 걸렸지만 나가고 싶어 한다. 당신은 그에게 이렇게 말한다. → 너는 나을 때까지 안에 있는 게 좋겠어.
6 톰이 자기와 함께 밖에 나가자고 했지만, 당신은 내일 시험이 있다. 당신은 그에게 이렇게 말한다. → 나는 밖에 나가지 않는 게 좋겠어.

1 should
2 should
3 had better
4 had better
5 shouldn't
6 shouldn't
7 had better not

해석

1 A: 마감일이 언제예요?
B: 지원서는 1월 11일 전에 발송되어야 합니다.
2 A: 이 케이크는 맛있어. 너도 한 조각 먹어 봐야 해.
B: 나도 그러고 싶어. 내가 사용할 수 있는 다른 접시가 있니?

3 A: 아, 안 돼. 바지에 스파게티 소스를 엎질렀어.
B: 얼룩이 지기 전에 지금 당장 그걸 씻는 게 좋겠어.

4 A: 이제 연습을 마무리하는 게 좋겠다. 좀 늦어졌어.
B: 그래. 오늘은 그만하자. 하지만 대회가 이제 일주일밖에 안 남았다는 걸 기억해.

5 A: 내 전화기 좀 건네줄래? 리오에게 전화하고 싶어.
B: 벌써 11시가 넘었어. 이렇게 늦게 그에게 전화하면 안 돼.

6 A: 개를 그렇게 괴롭히면 안 돼. 먹이나 주렴.
B: 죄송해요, 엄마.

7 A: 몇 분 후에 박 교수님과의 약속이 있어.
B: 늦지 않는 게 좋을 거야. 요즘 많이 바쁘시거든.

Unit 43 EXERCISES

p. 26~27

1 will 2 won't 3 will
4 Will, Would 5 Will, Would 6 won't

해석

1 줄이 곧 움직일 거야. 좀 더 참을성을 가져봐.
2 김 선생님, 늦어서 죄송해요. 다시는 이런 일이 없을 거예요. 약속해요.
3 아버지는 올해 51세이시다. 그는 내년에 52세가 될 것이다.
4 우리 집에 와서 내가 시험공부 하는 것 좀 도와줄래?
5 나는 이번 주 토요일에 팝 콘서트에 갈 거야. 나랑 같이 갈래?
6 커피를 더 마시지 마. 오늘 밤에 잠들지 못할 거야.

B

1 would rather buy 2 would rather exercise
3 would rather not tell 4 would rather stay
5 would rather come 6 would rather not get

해석

1 나는 차라리 파란색을 사겠어요. 그게 훨씬 더 좋아요.
2 그는 다이어트를 하느니 차라리 규칙적으로 운동하고 싶어 한다.
3 아빠한테 말하지 않는 게 낫겠어. 나에게 화를 내실 거야.
4 집에 있는 게 낫겠어. 밖에 나가기에는 너무 추워.
5 오늘 밤 표는 매진이야. 내일 다시 오는 게 좋겠어.
6 그 프로젝트에 참여하지 않는 게 낫겠어. 쉬운 일이 아니야.

C

1 make 2 queuing
3 go 4 drive
5 used to 6 was used to working
7 used to be 8 got used to

해석

1 콩은 두부를 만드는 데 사용된다.
2 우리는 택시를 타려고 줄을 서는 데 익숙하다.
3 우리 아빠는 주말마다 낚시를 가곤 했다.
4 나는 오래된 도요타를 운전했었지만 지금은 렉서스를 운전한다.
5 우리는 어렸을 때 여기서 농구를 하곤 했다.
6 지민이는 어려운 과제를 하는 데 익숙하다.
7 샘은 말썽꾸러기였지만 많이 변했다.
8 그는 처음에는 긴장했지만 곧 많은 사람들 앞에서 말하는 것에 익숙해졌다.

D

1 used to, used to/would
2 used to, used to/would
3 used to, used to/would
4 used to/would, used to/would
5 used to/would, used to
6 used to, used to/would
7 used to/would, used to/would

해석

1 내 여동생은 정말 머리가 길었다. 그녀는 매주 다른 색으로 머리를 염색하곤 했다.
2 그 강은 매우 깨끗했었다. 그래서 나는 어렸을 때 친구들과 그 강에서 수영을 하곤 했다.
3 나는 매우 조용했었다. 집에 손님이 올 때마다, 나는 질문을 받을 때까지 조용히 앉아 있곤 했다.
4 클라라는 용돈을 모두 음악 CD를 사는 데 써버리곤 했다. 그녀는 매주 동네 음반 가게로 달려가곤 했다.
5 나는 아이였을 때 채소를 절대 먹지 않았다. 채소를 냅킨에 숨겨서 나중에 개에게 주곤 했다. 개는 그걸 참 좋아했다.
6 니나는 간호사가 되기 전에 자유 시간이 많이 있었다. 그녀는 남자 친구와 공원에서 산책을 오래 하곤 했다.
7 우리 아버지와 나는 주말에 많은 시간을 함께 보내곤 했다. 그는 나를 낚시하는 데나 때때로 사냥하는 데 데려가곤 했다.

1 to have 2 rather
3 to read 4 is not used to making
5 used to be 6 would rather not have
7 used to wear 8 would rather see
9 used to travel 10 used to live

해석

1 디저트를 좀 드시겠어요? 아이스크림은 어때요?
2 나가서 먹는 것보다 차라리 집에서 뭔가 요리하는 게 더 낫겠어.
3 지루해 보여요. 만화책 좀 읽을래요?
4 카렌은 매우 수줍음이 많다. 그녀는 사람들 앞에서 이야기하는 것이 익숙하지 않다.
5 모퉁이에 편의점이 하나 있었는데, 지금은 없어졌다.
6 댄은 올해 자신의 생일에 큰 파티를 열지 않는 게 좋겠다고 말했다.
7 그녀는 안경을 쓰곤 했다. 하지만 수술하고 나서는 안경 없이도 선명하게 볼 수 있다.
8 나는 에펠탑을 보는 게 낫겠어. 너는 어때? 너는 무엇을 보고 싶니?
9 그레그는 여행을 상당히 많이 하곤 했다. 이제 그는 일이 너무 바빠서 그럴 수 없다.
10 제니는 도시의 작은 아파트에서 살았었지만, 작년에 시골로 이사했다.

REVIEW

p. 28~29

1 ⓔ 2 ⓑ 3 ⓕ 4 ⓐ 5 ⓐ 6 ⓖ
7 ⓕ 8 ⓓ 9 ⓒ 10 ⓖ 11 ⓒ

해설/해석

1 잘 들을 수 있기 때문에 소리를 지를 필요가 없다는 의미의 불필요를 나타냄
너는 소리를 지를 필요가 없어. 나는 네 말이 잘 들려.

2 충고가 필요하기 때문에 이야기하러 가도 되는지 묻는 표현으로 허가를 나타냄
나는 충고가 필요해. 내가 이야기하러 가도 돼?

3 물건을 샀어야 했으나 사지 않은 것에 대한 후회를 나타냄
나는 지난주 할인 판매 때 그것을 샀어야 했다.

4 맑은 날 북두칠성을 볼 수 있다는 의미로 능력 · 가능을 나타냄
맑은 날 밤에 하늘에 있는 북두칠성을 볼 수 있다.

5 기념품을 살 수 있다는 의미이므로 능력 · 가능을 나타냄
서울에 온 방문객들은 이태원에서 비싸지 않은 기념품들을 살 수 있다.

6 다른 사람들의 감정에 대해 더 이해심을 가져야 한다고 상대방에게 하는 충고임
너는 다른 사람들의 감정을 더욱 배려해야 한다.

7 그의 사무실에 들렀어야 했다는 후회를 나타냄
우리는 집에 오는 길에 그의 사무실에 들렀어야 했다.

8 내가 어렸을 때 아버지가 나를 무릎으로 들어 올렸다 내렸다 했다는 의미로 과거의 행동 · 습관을 나타냄
내가 어렸을 때 아버지가 무릎 위에서 나를 들어 올렸다 내렸다 했다.

9 아침에 차가 서리로 덮인 것을 보고 어젯밤의 일을 추측
어젯밤에 추웠던 게 틀림없다. 차가 서리로 덮여 있다.

10 케이티에게 사과하라고 말하고 있으므로 충고를 나타냄
케이티에게 사과하는 게 좋겠어. 그렇지 않으면 너를 절대 용서하지 않을 거야.

11 문장의 뒷부분에서 100% 확신을 할 수 없다고 말하는 것으로 미루어 보아 '추측'임을 알 수 있음
이 길이 원더랜드로 가는 방향이 맞을 수도 있지만, 100% 확신은 못 하겠다.

B

1 to help
2 could
3 had better not buy
4 had better have
5 should[ought to] buy
6 had to visit
7 may open
8 must clean out
9 used to have
10 would rather see
11 used to be

해설/해석

1 '~하고 싶다'라는 의미를 가진 would like는 뒤에 명사나 to부정사를 취하므로 to help가 적절
오늘 쿠키를 좀 구울지도 몰라요. 나를 도와주실래요?

2 고등학교 때 누구든지 웃게 만들 수 있었다는 의미로, 과거의 능력을 나타내는 could가 적절
제이미는 고등학교 때 누구든 웃게 할 수 있었다.

3 had better의 부정문은 「had better not+동사원형」
너는 이 수영복을 사지 않는 것이 좋겠다. 이건 네게 너무 작다.

4 「had better+동사원형」
그 문제에 대해서 너의 선생님과 이야기를 나눠 보는 게 좋겠다.

5 조언이나 충고를 나타내는 조동사에는 should와 ought to가 있다. should[ought to] buy가 적절
너는 내가 리즈를 위해 이 책을 사야 한다고 생각해? 그녀가 좋아하지 않으면 어쩌지?

6 어제 병원에 친구 병문안을 가야 했다는 의미로, 과거의 의무를 나타내는 had to visit가 적절
내 친구가 병원에 입원했다. 나는 어제 친구 병문안을 가야 했다.

7 「may+have+p.p.」는 '~했을지도 모른다'는 의미로, 과거에 대한 추측을 나타낸다. 하지만 해당 문장은 통장을 개설해도 된다고 허가를 해주는 표현이 되어야 하므로 may open이 적절
여기서 은행 계좌를 개설해도 됩니다만 신분증 두 종류가 필요합니다.

8 학생들이 사물함을 반드시 비워야 한다는 의미이므로, 강한 의무를 뜻하는 must clean out이 적절
모든 학생들은 학교가 끝나기 전에 자신의 사물함을 비워야 한다.

9 「used to+동사원형」은 '~하곤 했다', 「be used to -ing」는 '~하는 데 익숙하다'는 의미. CD를 많이 수집하곤 했다는 과거의 행동이나 습관을 의미하므로 used to have가 적절
나는 CD를 많이 수집하곤 했다. 하지만 이제는 그냥 인터넷에서 MP3 파일을 내려 받는다.

10 「would rather+동사원형」은 '차라리 ~하는 편이 낫겠다'라는 의미로, would rather see가 적절
내 친구는 영화를 보고 싶어 하지만, 나는 '캣츠'나 '맘마미아' 같은 라이브 공연을 보는 게 낫겠다.

11 과거의 반복적인 행동이나 습관을 나타낼 때는 would와 used to를 모두 쓸 수 있지만, 과거의 상태를 나타낼 때는 used to를 써야 함
우리 할머니 집 앞에 큰 나무가 있었다. 하지만 어느 날 나무가 벼락에 맞아 쓰러졌다.

C

1 will
2 must
3 be able to
4 could
5 don't have to
6 had to

해설/해석

1 next year(내년)로 보아 미래에 있을 일에 대해 말하는 것이므로 will이 적절
우리는 내년부터 전자책을 사용할 것이다.

2 히터를 반드시 꺼야 한다는 것은 강한 의무를 나타내므로 must가 적절
잠자리에 들기 전에 너는 반드시 히터를 꺼야 한다.

3 조동사는 함께 연달아 쓸 수 없고, 조동사 뒤에는 동사원형이 와야 하므로 be able to가 적절
제이가 너를 도와줄 수 있을지도 몰라. 그에게 부탁해 보는 게 어때?

4 작년에 LA에서 공부한 후 영어 능력이 향상되었다는 의미로 과거의 능력을 나타내므로 could가 적절
나는 작년에 LA에서 공부한 후로 영어를 더 잘 말할 수 있었다.

5 'Just help yourself.(마음껏 먹어.)'라는 표현으로 보아, 무언가를 먹을 때마다 물어보지 않아도 된다는 의미로, don't have to(~할 필요가 없다)가 적절
냉장고에서 먹고 싶은 것이 있을 때마다 나에게 물어볼 필요 없어. 그냥 마음껏 먹어.

6 '돈을 더 달라고 부탁해야 했다'라는 의미이며, 뒤 문장에서 과거 시제가 쓰였으므로 had to(~해야만 했다)가 적절
나는 집에 전화를 걸어 부모님에게 돈을 더 달라고 부탁해야 했다. 그들은 탐탁해 하지 않으셨다.

D

1 will	2 couldn't
3 used to	4 should
5 should	6 will have to
7 have to	8 must
9 May, would like to	10 should
11 would rather	

해설/해석

1 뒤에서 빠르게 회복하고 있다고 하는 것으로 보아 다시 축구를 할 수 있을 것이라는 긍정의 추측이 와야 하므로 will이 적절
그는 다시 축구를 할 수 있을 것이다. 그는 매우 빠르게 회복하고 있다.

2 늦게까지 일해서 만날 수 없었다는 의미가 되어야 하므로, 과거를 나타내는 couldn't가 적절
나는 늦게까지 일해야 했기 때문에 공항에서 몰리를 만날 수 없었다.

3 '~하곤 했다'라는 의미로 과거의 습관적인 행동을 나타낼 때는 used to와 would 둘 다 사용할 수 있지만, 상태를 나타낼 때는 used to만 사용할 수 있다. 아빠가 건강했다는 것은 과거의 행동이 아닌 상태를 설명하고 있는 것이므로 used to가 적절
우리 아빠는 건강했었다. 그는 윗몸 일으키기 220개를 쉽게 할 수 있었다!

4 상대방에게 조언이나 충고할 때 '~해야 한다'라는 의미로 쓰는 조동사는 should와 ought to가 있다. ought 뒤에 to가 빠져 있으므로 should가 적절
당신은 우리가 광고를 좀 더 많은 신문에 실어야 한다고 생각하나요?

5 「should have+p.p.」는 '~했어야 했다'라는 의미로 과거의 일에 대한 후회를, 「must have+p.p.」는 ~했음이 틀림없다'라는 의미로 과거에 대한 강한 추측을 나타낸다. 어젯밤에 즐거운 시간을 보냈다는 이야기를 듣고, 파티에 가지 않은 것에 대해 후회하는 것이므로 should가 적절
어젯밤에 너와 함께 파티에 갔어야 했는데. 넌 정말 재미있는 시간을 보낸 것 같구나.

6 조동사 will 뒤에는 동사원형이 와야 하므로 will have to가 적절
우리 엄마는 새로 산 컴퓨터를 사용하는 법을 모른다. 그래서 내가 가르쳐 드려야만 할 것이다.

7 엄마에게 돈을 달라는 것이 부끄러워 직업을 구해야 한다 또는 구하고 싶다는 내용이다. 의미상으로는 have to(~해야 한다)나 would like(~하고 싶다) 둘 다 가능해 보이지만, 「would like to+동사원형」이 되어야 하므로, have to가 적절
나는 직업을 구해야 한다. 엄마에게 매주 돈을 달라고 하는 데 지쳐버렸다. 정말 부끄럽다.

8 must는 '~해야 한다'라는 강한 의무나 필요성을, must not은 '~해서는 안 된다'는 금지를 나타낸다. 아침에 새가 지저귀는 소리에 깨고 싶지 않다면 새장을 덮어 두어야 한다는 필요성을 나타내므로 must가 적절
새를 기른다면, 잠자리에 들기 전에 새장을 덮어 두어야 해. 그렇지 않으면, 해가 뜰 때 지저귀며 깨어날 거야.

9 May I는 '제가 ~해도 될까요?', Should I는 '제가 ~해야 하나요?'라는 의미. 시간을 잠시 내어달라고 허락을 구하는 문장이므로 May I가 적절. used to는 '~하곤 했다', would like to는 '~하고 싶다'라는 의미. 과제에 대해 질문을 하고 싶다는 자신의 바람을 말하고 있으므로 would like to가 적절
죄송하지만, 김 교수님. 시간 좀 내주시겠어요? 기말 과제에 대해 질문하고 싶은데요.

10 표가 매진되어 영화를 보러 갈 수 없게 되자, 더 전에 예약을 해놓았어야 한다고 후회하고 있는 것이므로 should have made가 적절
A: 우리는 오늘 저녁에 영화 보러 갈 수 없어. 표가 매진되었어.
B: 정말? 좀 더 일찍 예약을 해야 했는데.

11 「would like to+동사원형」 ~하고 싶다, 「would rather+동사원형」 ~하는 편이 낫겠다
A: 방과 후에 나와 도서관에서 공부할래?
B: 미안, 나는 오늘 집에 일찍 가는 게 낫겠어.

REVIEW PLUS

p. 30

②

해설/해석

(A) 도움이 필요하다는 것으로 보아, 영어를 잘하지 못한다는 의미이므로 can't가 적절 (B) 선생님이 금색 별을 주곤 했다는 뜻이므로 과거의 행동이나 습관에는 used to가 적절 (C) 장식들이 나타나는 것을 보고 크리스마스가 가까워지고 있는 것에 대한 강한 확신을 보이므로 must가 적절

- 죄송하지만, 저는 영어를 못해요. 도움이 필요해요.
- 내가 초등학생이었을 때, 선생님은 우리에게 금색 별을 주시곤 했다.
- 크리스마스에 가까워진 것이 틀림없다. 장식들이 곳곳에서 보인다.

1 may　　2 must　　3 had better

해설/해석

1 도와줄 수 있을지도 모른다고 추측하며, 문제를 말해 보라는 것이므로 may가 적절
A: 네 문제를 말해 봐. 너를 도와줄 수 있을지도 몰라.
B: 그러지 않는 게 좋겠어. 너무 창피해.

2 법학 대학원에 합격한 것에 대해 가족들이 자랑스러워할 것이라는 강한 추측이므로 must가 적절
A: 나는 우리나라에서 최고의 법학 대학원 중 하나에 합격했어.
B: 너의 가족이 너를 매우 자랑스러워할 게 틀림없어.

3 전화번호를 적어 두지 않으면 잊어버릴 수 있으므로 적어두는 것이 좋겠다고 말하는 것이므로 bad better가 적절
A: 나는 당신의 번호를 적어두는 것이 좋겠어요. 그렇지 않으면 잊어버릴지도 몰라요.
B: 좋아요. 다시 한 번 말씀 드릴게요. 1457-9836입니다.

②

해설/해석

(A) English 201을 듣기 위해 필수적으로 English 101을 이수했어

야 함을 나타내므로 must가 적절 (B) 대학교에서 학습 과제로 요구될 수도 있다는 추측의 의미이므로 may가 적절 (C) 수업에 참가하는 학생들이 다른 학생들과 협동적으로 공부해야 한다는 의무를 나타내므로 should가 적절

English 201은 현재 브라운 대학에 다니는 ESL 학생들을 위한 중급 수준의 말하기 수업입니다. 이 수업에 등록하기 전에 English 101을 성공적으로 마쳐야 합니다. 이 수업에서 학생들은 짧은 연설을 준비하고 발표하는 방법을 배우게 되는데, 이는 대학교에서 학습 과제로 요구될 수 있는 부분입니다. 참가자들은 그 반의 다른 학생들과 협동적으로 학습할 준비가 되어 있어야 합니다. 출석이 요구되고, 모든 학생은 기말고사를 통과해야만 합니다.

PART 12

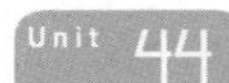

Unit 44 EXERCISES

p. 34~35

A

1 must 2 might 3 must 4 can't
5 can't 6 may

해석

1 봐! 모두 가방을 싸서 나가고 있어. 수업이 끝난 것이 틀림없어.
2 샘이 오늘 수업에 오지 않았어. 확실하지 않지만 그는 몸이 좋지 않을 수도 있어.
3 마이크의 팀이 가장 강한 것이 틀림없어. 그들은 이번 시즌에 한 번도 지지 않았어.
4 너랑 네 여동생은 방금 밥을 먹었잖아. 또 배가 고플 리가 없어!
5 우리는 청바지와 티셔츠를 입는 것이 허용되지 않기 때문에 학교에 청바지와 티셔츠를 입고 갈 수 없다.
6 그 식당을 예약하는 게 어때? 확실하지는 않지만 그 식당은 빨리 예약이 찰지도 몰라.

B

1 must have dropped
2 may hang out
3 must have stolen, may have left
4 can't have made up
5 could have run over
6 may have gone
7 can't have seen

해석

1 A: 너 뭘 찾고 있니?
B: 내 안경을 못 찾겠어. 어딘가에 떨어뜨린 게 틀림없어.
2 A: 안녕, 찰리. 너 봄 방학에 뭐 할 거니?
B: 모르겠어. 멕시코에 있는 해변에서 보낼지도 몰라.
3 A: 내 자전거가 사라졌어요. 누군가 훔쳐 간 게 틀림없어요.
B: 정말입니까? 다른 곳에 놓아두셨을 수도 있죠.
4 A: 루이스가 진에게 사과했다고 들었어. 그리고 다시 친해졌다면서.
B: 그들이 화해를 했을 리가 없어. 그들은 하루 종일 서로 말도 안 했어.
5 A: 길을 건너기 전에 양쪽을 살펴봤어야 했어. 차가 너를 칠 수도 있었잖아.
B: 앞으로 주의할게.
6 A: 마이크는 어디 있니? 그에게 줄 것이 있어.
B: 그는 집에 갔을지도 몰라. 가방을 챙겨서 삼십 분 전에 나갔어.
7 A: 에이미에게 무슨 일이 있는 거지? 오늘 복도에서 그녀를 지나쳐 갔는데, 나를 못 본 척했어.
B: 그녀가 너를 봤을 리가 없어. 너를 봤다면 인사를 했겠지.

C

1 may be 2 may not be 3 must be 4 must be

해석

1 A: 톰이 어디 있니? 나는 그와 이야기를 해야 해.
B: 잘은 모르지만 음악실에 있을지도 몰라.
2 A: 일본으로 여행가는 데 얼마가 필요할까? 100만원이면 충분할까?
B: 잘은 모르지만 충분하지 않을지도 몰라. 그곳은 물가가 매우 비싸다고 들었어.
3 A: 그는 성공한 남자임이 틀림이 없어. 그는 도심에 있는 건물을 소유하고 있고, 많은 직원들이 그의 회사에서 일해.
B: 맞아. 그의 사업은 매우 빨리 성장하고 있어.
4 A: 그는 여자 아이들에게 매우 인기가 있음이 틀림없어. 그는 여자 아이들에게 초콜릿을 많이 받았어.
B: 맞아. 그는 우리 학교에서 가장 잘생겼어.

D

1 can't have been 2 can't have taken
3 can't be 4 can't have heard
5 can't be 6 can't have been
7 can't have made

해석

1 A: 누가 찬장에서 과일 통조림을 꺼냈지? 마이크였니?
B: 마이크였을 리 없어. 그는 집에 없었어.
2 A: 피터가 내 태블릿 PC를 훔쳐간 게 틀림없어.
B: 그가 가져갔을 리 없어. 그는 나와 하루 종일 함께 있었는 걸.
3 A: 저 소년이 제니가 좋아하는 마이크니?
B: 저 사람이 마이크 일리가 없어. 제니가 말하길 그는 매우 날씬하다고 했는데 저 소년은 통통한 걸.
4 A: 제이크 봤어? 그가 내 전화를 안 받았어.
B: 그는 전화가 울리는 것을 들었을 리가 없어. 내가 그의 전화기가 거실에 있는 것을 봤는데, 그는 방에서 자고 있었거든.
5 A: 나는 문제를 다 풀었어.
B: 벌써? 그것이 가능할 리 없어. 그냥 문제를 읽기만 해도 최소한 5분은 걸려.
6 A: 실례합니다, 브라운 씨? 불평하게 되어 죄송하지만 댁의 개 때문에 어젯밤에도 또 잠을 잘 수 없었어요. 너무 시끄럽더군요.
B: 저희 개였을 리가 없어요. 맥스는 동물 병원에 있거든요.
7 A: 야, 이 보고서 혼자서 검토했어? 숫자에 많은 실수가 있어.
B: 아니, 필립이 했어. 하지만 그가 그런 실수를 했을 리가 없어. 그는 매우 주의 깊은 사람이거든.

Unit 45 EXERCISES

p. 38~39

A

1 Can I turn on the radio?
2 Could I turn up the volume?
3 Could I use the recipe book?

4 May I get some help to move the heavy boxes?
5 Could I borrow the notebook for the statistics exam?

해석

1 당신은 라디오를 켜기를 원한다. 당신은 이렇게 물을 수 있다.
→ 라디오를 좀 켜도 되니?
2 당신은 볼륨을 올리고 싶다. 당신은 이렇게 물을 수 있다.
→ 제가 볼륨을 올려도 될까요?
3 당신은 요리책을 사용하고 싶다. 당신은 이렇게 물을 수 있다.
→ 제가 요리책을 사용해도 될까요?
4 당신은 무거운 상자들을 나르는 데 도움을 받고 싶다. 당신은 이렇게 물을 수 있다.
→ 무거운 상자들을 나르는 데 도움을 좀 받을 수 있을까요?
5 당신은 통계학 시험을 위해 노트를 빌리고 싶다. 당신은 이렇게 물을 수 있다.
→ 통계학 시험을 위해 노트를 빌릴 수 있을까요?

B

1 had 2 turned 3 handing 4 leaned
5 giving 6 called 7 waiting

해석

1 A: 제가 창가 쪽 자리에 앉아도 될까요?
B: 그러세요.
2 A: 라디오를 켜도 될까요? 여기 너무 조용해서요.
B: 그럼요.
3 A: 이 서류를 선생님께 전해줄래?
B: 물론이지. 다른 건 없고?
4 A: 실례합니다. 제가 의자를 좀 뒤로 눕혀도 될까요?
B: 그럼요. 그렇게 하세요.
5 A: 이 가방을 위층으로 옮기는 데 도움을 주실 수 있나요?
B: 그럼요.
6 A: 조금 뒤에 전화를 다시 드려도 될까요? 지금은 이야기를 할 수 없어서요.
B: 네, 괜찮아요.
7 A: 20분 더 기다려주시겠어요? 지금은 자리가 다 차서요.
B: 음, 그러면 나중에 올게요.

C

1 Can you hold 2 Can I ask
3 Can I have 4 Can I use
5 Can you look after 6 Can you get
7 Can you help

해석

1 A: 잠깐만요, 엘리베이터 좀 잡아주시겠어요?
B: 네, 물론이죠.
2 A: 길을 좀 물어볼 수 있을까요?
B: 사실, 저도 여기 처음이라서요.
3 A: 오늘 너무 더워. 차가운 음료를 좀 줄래?
B: 그래. 오렌지 주스 괜찮아?
4 A: 네 휴대 전화를 잠깐만 사용할 수 있을까? 내 것을 집에 두고 왔어.
B: 물론이지, 여기 있어.
5 A: 내가 없는 며칠 동안 우리 개를 좀 돌봐줄 수 있어?
B: 물론이지. 내가 개 좋아하는 거 알잖아.
6 A: 수! 전화 좀 받아줄래? 지금 설거지 중이라서.
B: 알았어요.
7 A: 학교 축제 준비하는 것 도와줄 수 있어?
B: 그러고 싶은데 나는 할 일이 있어.

D

1 emptying 2 rode
3 taking 4 asked
5 proofreading 6 used
7 keeping

해석

1 A: 재활용 쓰레기통 좀 비워 줄래요?
B: 그럴게요. 버리는 곳만 잘 알려주세요.
2 A: 가게에 가는데 네 자전거를 타고 가도 될까?
B: 물론이야. 하지만 조심해. 브레이크가 약간 닳았어.
3 A: 나와 내 친구의 사진을 좀 찍어 줄래요?
B: 그래요. 카메라 사용하는 법만 알려주세요.
4 A: 우리가 질문을 좀 해도 될까요?
B: 그러렴. 무엇을 알고 싶니?
5 A: 내 수필을 교정해 주시겠어요? 큰 도움이 될 거예요.
B: 그러고 싶지만, 지금은 조금 바빠. 주말 이후까지 기다려줄 수 있니?
6 A: 이 의자를 사용해도 될까요? 의자 하나가 필요해요.
B: 그럼요.
7 A: 개를 마당에 둘래요? 제가 개에 알레르기가 있어서요.
B: 그럼요.

Unit 46 EXERCISES

p. 41

Why don't we go, Let's not go, Let's spend, Shall I call, Why don't you have

해석

A: 오늘 아침 날씨가 아주 좋네. 아침 식사 후에 바로 해변으로 가는 게 어때?
B: 나는 시내에 가서 가게들을 좀 둘러보는 게 좋겠어.
A: 벌써 쇼핑하려고? 우리가 피지에 온 첫날이야. 쇼핑하러 가지 말자.
B: 네 말이 맞아. 아침에는 해변에서 시간을 보내고 오후에 쇼핑을 가자.
A: 그래. 나가기 전에 아침을 먹자. 호텔에 있는 식당에 갈까?
B: 음, 그냥 룸서비스로 식사를 좀 주문하는 게 어때?
A: 그거 좋겠다. 내가 룸서비스에 전화할까?
B: 괜찮아. 내가 할게. 뭘 먹을래? 나는 아메리칸 브렉퍼스트를 주문할래. 나랑 같은 걸 먹는 게 어때?

1 Shall we go, Why don't we write, Let's start
2 Why don't you come over, Shall we try, Why don't you order

해석

1 A: 이번 여름에 샐리가 우리를 방문하면 캠핑 갈까?
B: 그녀가 캠핑 가는 걸 원할 거라고 생각해? 편지를 써서 물어보는 게 어떨까?
A: 아니. 나는 깜짝 캠핑이었으면 해. 매우 재미있을 거야! 지금 계획을 짜보자.
B: 좋아. 네가 그렇게 생각한다면.
2 A: 이 호텔 방 아름답다! 여기 와서 창밖을 좀 보는 게 어때?

B: 와! 정말 시내가 멋지게 보이네.
A: 그리고 좀 봐! 여행 책자를 보니 1층에 온천이 있대. 한번 가 볼까?
B: 그래. 하지만 우선 나는 룸서비스로 뭘 좀 주문할래.
A: 좋아. 그럼 내가 짐을 푸는 동안 네가 먹을 것을 주문하는 게 어때?

REVIEW

p. 42~43

1 ⓒ	2 ⓐ	3 ⓐ	4 ⓐ	5 ⓐ
6 ⓑ	7 ⓒ	8 ⓒ	9 ⓑ	10 ⓑ

해설/해석

1 '~하는 게 어때?'라는 뜻의 Why don't we ~?는 제안을 의미
루브르 박물관을 방문하는 게 어때?

2 '몇 달러만 빌릴 수 있을까요?'라는 의미의 Could I ~?는 허가를 구하는 표현
월급날까지 몇 달러만 빌릴 수 있을까요?

3 '가방 좀 지켜 줄래?'라는 의미의 Can you ~?는 부탁을 나타냄
내가 화장실에 간 동안 가방 좀 지켜 줄래?

4 '여권과 탑승권을 보여주시겠어요?'라는 의미의 May I ~?는 부탁을 나타냄
여권과 탑승권을 보여주시겠어요?

5 커피숍에 개를 데리고 들어가도 되는지 묻는 표현으로 Would you mind ~?는 허가를 나타냄
커피숍에 개를 데리고 들어가도 될까요?

6 데니스가 곧 올지도 모른다는 의미의 might는 추측을 나타냄
데니스가 곧 올지도 모르니까 서둘러 준비해.

7 '우리가 헌혈을 하는 것이 어때?'라는 의미의 제안을 나타냄
우리 헌혈하는 것이 어떨까? 많은 생명을 구할 수 있잖아.

8 '다른 옷을 사는 게 어때?'라는 의미의 Why don't you ~?는 제안을 나타냄
다른 옷을 사는 게 어때? 그게 너한테 훨씬 더 귀여워 보였어.

9 '바쁜 것이 틀림없다'라는 의미의 must는 추측을 나타냄
줄리엣은 오늘 밤에 우리와 스시 먹는 것을 원하지 않았어. 그녀는 바쁜 것이 틀림없어.

10 아팠을지도 모른다는 의미로서 might는 추측을 나타냄
제인이 어제 학교를 결석했니? 그녀는 아팠을지도 몰라.

1 may, help	2 must have
3 may be	4 must be
5 must be	6 may, be
7 may go, may be	

해설/해석

1 '무엇을 도와드릴까요?'라는 의미가 되어야 하므로 How may I help you?가 적절
A: 안녕하세요, 부인. 무엇을 도와드릴까요?
B: 소고기 2kg 주세요.

2 A가 동생에게 책을 주었으므로 동생이 분명히 가지고 있을 것이라는 확신의 의미로 must have가 적절
A: 너는 내가 어제 네 남동생에게 준 책을 받았니?
B: 아니, 아직. 하지만 그가 분명히 가지고 있을 거야.

3 상대방이 한 말이 맞을 수도 있다는 약한 추측을 나타내는 may be가 적절
A: 오늘 오후에 비가 올 것 같아.
B: 네 말이 맞을지도 몰라. 일단 기다려 봐야 할 것 같아.

4 크리스와 닮아서 그의 아들임을 확신하는 것이므로 must be가 적절
A: 크리스가 데리고 가고 있는 남자 아이 보이니?
B: 응. 크리스와 꼭 닮았어. 아들이 틀림없어.

5 저스틴의 이름이 문에 있는 것을 근거로 하여 집을 맞게 찾아왔음을 확신하고 있으므로 현재 상황에 대한 강한 추측을 나타내는 must be가 적절
A: 이 아파트가 맞는 게 틀림없어. 저스틴의 이름이 문에 쓰여 있잖아.
B: 네 말이 맞는 것 같아. 노크해 보는 게 어때?

6 샐러드가 신선한지 아닌지 확신을 가지고 있지 않으므로 현재 상황에 대한 약한 추측을 나타내는 may be가 적절
A: 점심으로 무엇을 먹어야 할까? 샐러드가 괜찮아 보여, 그렇지 않니?
B: 글쎄. 신선하지 않을지도 몰라. 언제 준비된 건지 점원에게 물어보자.

7 A에서 내일 날씨에 따라 하이킹을 갈 수도, 안 갈 수도 있으므로 확실하게 정해지지 않은 것임을 알 수 있다. 그러므로 미래의 일에 대한 약한 추측인 may go가 적절. B에서 일정을 확인해 봐야 해서 확실하지 않으므로 may be가 적절
A: 우리는 내일 소풍을 갈지도 몰라. 하지만 소풍 가는 것은 날씨에 달렸어. 너도 가고 싶니?
B: 그러고 싶지만, 바쁠지도 몰라. 일정을 확인해 볼게.

1 Let's eat out
2 Can I have
3 Would you mind if I closed
4 Can you help
5 Shall we meet
6 Would you mind picking up
7 Why don't you go

해설/해석

1 Let's ~는 '~하자'라는 뜻으로 제안할 때 사용
당신은 친구와 점심을 나가서 먹고 싶다. 당신은 이렇게 말할 수 있다.
→ 나가서 점심 먹자. 나는 태국 음식을 먹고 싶어.

2 Can I~?는 상대방의 허가를 구하는 표현
당신은 피자를 먹고 싶다. 당신은 이렇게 물을 수 있다.
→ 피자를 먹어도 될까요? 저는 약간 배가 고파요.

3 Would you mind if~?는 '~해도 될까요?'라는 의미로 상대방에게 허가를 구할 때 쓰는 표현
당신은 커튼을 치고 싶다. 당신은 이렇게 물을 수 있다.
→ 커튼을 쳐도 될까요? 여기 너무 밝아요.

4 Can you~?는 상대방에게 부탁을 하는 표현
당신은 남동생이 상 차리는 것을 도와주었으면 한다. 당신은 이렇게 물을 수 있다. → 내가 상 차리는 것을 도와줄 수 있니?

5 Shall we~?는 '~하자'라는 뜻으로 제안할 때 사용
당신은 6시에 은행 앞에서 그녀를 만나고 싶다. 당신은 이렇게 물을 수

있다. → 6시에 은행 앞에서 만날까?

6 Would you mind -ing~?는 '~해주시겠어요?'라는 의미로 상대방에게 부탁할 때 사용
당신은 네 여동생이 세탁물을 찾아오기를 원한다. 당신은 이렇게 물을 수 있다. → 집에 오는 길에 세탁물 좀 찾아올래?

7 Why don't you ~?는 '~하는 게 어때?'라는 뜻으로 제안할 때 사용
당신은 친구가 의사에게 진찰을 받으러 갔으면 한다. 당신은 이렇게 말할 수 있다. → 의사한테 가보는 게 어때? 훨씬 나아질 거야.

D

1 can't be a cat lover
2 He may have had lunch
3 He could be home late
4 That can't be Tina
5 She must be in the library
6 can't have behaved rudely
7 There might be a big event

해설

1 「can't+동사원형」은 거의 불가능하다고 생각되는 현재 일에 대한 부정적인 추측을 나타냄
2 may have p.p.는 '~했을지도 모른다'는 의미로 과거 사실에 대한 추측을 나타냄
3 could는 '~일 수도 있다'는 의미로 현재 사실에 대한 약한 추측에 사용
4 「can't+동사원형」은 거의 불가능하다고 생각되는 현재 일에 대한 부정적인 추측을 나타냄
5 must는 '~임이 틀림이 없다'는 의미로 현재 사실에 대한 강한 추측에 사용
6 can't have p.p.는 '~했을 리가 없다'는 의미로 과거 일에 대한 부정적인 추측을 나타냄
7 might는 '~일지도 모른다'는 의미로 현재 사실의 약한 추측에 사용

REVIEW PLUS

p. 44

1 ①　　　2 ③

해설/해석

1 (A) 멋진 식당을 보고 음식을 먹어 보자고 제안하는 의미의 Let's가 적절 (B) 두 개의 다른 음식을 시켜서 함께 먹자고 제안하는 것이므로 Shall we가 적절 (C) A가 자신의 메뉴를 정하고, B에게 또 다른 메뉴를 제안하는 것이므로 Why don't you가 적절
A: 이 레스토랑 멋지다! 새로운 것을 먹어 보자.
B: 두 개의 다른 음식을 시켜서 나눠 먹는 게 어때?
A: 그래. 나는 미트볼 스파게티를 먹으려고 해. 너는 비프 웰링턴을 주문하는 게 어때?
B: 좋아. 웨이터를 불러서 주문하자.

2 (A) 초콜릿 무스를 먹을 수도 있다는 의미가 되어야 하므로 가능성을 나타내는 could가 적절 (B) 고맙지만 더는 못 먹겠다는 의미가 되어야 하므로 can't가 적절 (C) 조금만 먹어 달라고 부탁하는 문장이 나와 있으므로 혼자서 먹기는 힘들 것 같다는 의미가 되어야 한다. might have가 적절
A: 정말 훌륭한 식사였어. 배불러!
B: 디저트로 뭘 좀 먹는 게 어때? 우리는 초콜릿 무스를 주문할 수 있어.
A: 아니, 됐어. 더는 못 먹겠어. 하지만 네가 먹고 싶으면 먹어.
B: 음, 내가 혼자서 다 먹긴 힘들 것 같아. 몇 입만 먹어 줄래?
A: 좋아. 하지만 딱 한 입만 먹을게.

① might ② had to

해설/해석

① 「might+have+p.p.」는 '~했을지도 모른다'라는 의미로 과거 사실에 대한 추측을, 「should+have+p.p.」는 '~했어야 했는데 그렇게 하지 못했다'라는 의미로 과거에 대한 후회를 나타낸다. 공룡이 온혈 동물이었을지도 모른다는 과거의 사실에 대한 추측을 나타내는 might가 적절 ② 공룡의 체온이 공기보다 높아야만 했다는 의미가 되어야 하므로 과거를 나타내는 had to(~했어야 했다)가 적절
학교에서 우리는 모두 공룡들이 느릿한 냉혈 파충류라고 배웠다. 하지만 그 반대가 사실일 수도 있다. 새로운 과학적 증거는 공룡이 파충류보다 포유류처럼 행동하는 온혈 동물이었을지도 모른다는 것을 보여준다. 이러한 결론은 다음의 두 가지 사실에서 이끌어낼 수 있다. 하나는 공룡의 성장 패턴으로, 이것은 온혈 포유류의 성장 패턴에 더 가깝다. 다른 한 가지는 알을 부화하기 위해 공기보다 공룡의 체온이 더 높아야 했다는 사실이다.

PART 13

REPLAY

p. 46~47

1 CHECK-UP

1 You look tired today.
2 The news made him sad.
3 The soup smells delicious.
4 My sister's bedroom is pink.
5 We saw many wild animals in the forest.

2 CHECK-UP

1 easily, easy
2 quiet, quietly
3 beautiful, beautifully
4 fluently, fluent
5 honest, honestly

3 CHECK-UP

1 two fifths
2 one third
3 twelve point six seven
4 one fourth[one quarter]
5 three fifths
6 five ninths
7 (zero) point seven two
8 eleven point eight eight

Unit 47 EXERCISES

p. 50~51

A

1 welcoming	2 motivated
3 excited	4 damaged
5 convincing	6 amazing
7 tiring	8 confusing

해석

1 리사는 항상 환영의 미소를 짓는다.
2 우리는 이 직책에 고도로 동기 부여된 젊은이를 찾고 있다.
3 그는 처음으로 그 연극을 공연하는 것에 대해 매우 신이 났다.
4 홍수로 불어난 물이 빠지고 난 후, 몇 개의 훼손된 다리가 발견되었다.
5 복제를 반대하는 당신의 주장이 전적으로 설득력이 있는 것은 아니에요. 제가 그 이유를 설명해 보겠어요.
6 유아들은 놀랍다. 그들은 겉보기에 노력 없이 새로운 단어를 습득한다.
7 지난 인도 여행은 좀 피곤했지만 좋은 추억이 많다.
8 나는 그의 강연 대부분은 이해하고 즐겼지만 그 중 일부는 약간 헷갈렸다.

1 embarrassed, embarrassing	2 confused, confusing
3 delighted, delighting	4 alarmed, alarming

해석

1 어리석은 실수가 그를 부끄럽게 했다.
→ 그는 어리석은 실수에 부끄러웠다.
→ 어리석은 실수가 그를 부끄럽게 했다.
2 자동 응답기의 메시지가 나를 혼란스럽게 했다.
→ 나는 자동 응답기의 메시지로 혼란스러움을 느꼈다.
→ 자동 응답기의 메시지가 나를 혼란스럽게 했다.
3 오늘 저녁 앙코르 공연이 관객들을 기쁘게 했다.
→ 관객들은 오늘 저녁 앙코르 공연에 기쁨을 느꼈다.
→ 오늘 저녁 앙코르 공연이 관객들을 기쁘게 했다.
4 그 지역에 조류 독감이 퍼질 가능성이 우리를 불안하게 했다.
→ 우리는 그 지역에 조류 독감이 퍼질 수 있다는 소식에 불안했다.
→ 그 지역에 조류 독감이 퍼질 수 있다는 가능성이 우리를 불안하게 했다.

1 sleeping	2 disappointing
3 interesting	4 a shy
5 틀린 것 없음	6 틀린 것 없음
7 embarrassing	8 astonishing
9 틀린 것 없음	10 틀린 것 없음

해석

1 그는 잠자는 아이에게 담요를 덮어 주었다.
2 올해의 판매 수치는 매우 실망스러웠다.
3 아, 당신이 한국 사람인지 몰랐어요. 흥미롭군요.
4 유니스는 그를 올려다보며 그에게 수줍은 미소를 지었다.
5 나는 강아지가 걱정되어 팔에 안고 집에 갔다.
6 나는 그 잡지의 내용과 정보에 매우 만족한다.
7 리즈는 자전거를 타다가 떨어졌다. 그것은 매우 창피했다.
8 신문은 대통령에 대한 놀라운 소문을 계속 보도해 왔다.
9 솔직히 말해서, 당신을 여기서 보게 되어 놀랐어요. 당신이 나타날 거라고 생각하지 못했거든요.
10 우리는 그 문제를 매우 잘 알고 있지만, 유감스럽게도 해결책이 없다.

D

1 Please hand me the large plastic bowl in the sink.
2 Hanbok is an example of traditional Korean clothing.
3 I'm so jealous of Jackie's beautiful long straight black hair.
4 Ben replaced the ugly big brown wooden desk with a new one.
5 They're an exciting new British band.
6 I can't find my small red sleeping bag.
7 David received two interesting new video games for Christmas.
8 Serry and Yumi are wearing the same blue cotton work clothing.

해석

1 저에게 싱크대에 있는 커다란 플라스틱 그릇을 건네주세요.
2 한복은 전통적인 한국 의복의 한 예이다.
3 나는 재키의 아름답고 긴 검은색 생머리가 매우 부럽다.
4 벤은 볼품없고, 큰 갈색 목재로 된 책상을 새것으로 바꿨다.
5 그들은 흥미로운 새 영국 밴드이다. 너는 가서 그들이 연주하는 것을 봐야 한다.
6 나의 작은 빨간색 침낭을 찾을 수가 없어. 너는 그것을 본 적이 있니?
7 데이비드는 크리스마스 때 두 개의 흥미로운 새 비디오 게임을 받았다.
8 세리와 유미는 같은 파란색 면 작업복을 입고 있다.

Unit 48 EXERCISES

p. 54~55

1 before	2 this month
3 ahead of	4 there
5 later	6 almost

해석

1 나는 전에 이곳에 왔던 것 같다.
2 나는 이달 말 쯤 한국에 돌아갈 것이다.
3 피자 배달원이 경찰차 앞에 차를 세웠다.
4 제니와 나는 킹 스트리트 그릴에서 만나 점심을 먹었다.
5 내가 뭘 하던 중인데, 나중에 다시 전화해도 될까?
6 우리 어머니는 출근하는 길에 언 도로에서 넘어질 뻔했다.

1 Do you √take the subway to work?
2 Mr. and Ms. Kim have √been to Australia.
3 Gwen is a nice student, so she √makes trouble in school.
4 My friend and I √have salad for lunch at the cafeteria these days.
5 Tim and I √do everything together. We're the best of friends.

6 My mother √drinks coffee, but my father √drinks coffee.

해석

1 당신은 대개 회사에 지하철을 타고 옵니까?
2 김 씨 부부는 호주에 가본 적이 한 번도 없다.
3 그웬은 착한 학생이라 학교에서 좀처럼 말썽을 피우지 않는다.
4 요즘 내 친구와 나는 종종 카페테리아에서 점심으로 샐러드를 먹는다.
5 팀과 나는 항상 모든 일을 함께한다. 우리는 친구들 중에서 가장 친하다.
6 우리 어머니는 가끔 커피를 마시지만 우리 아버지는 절대 커피를 마시지 않는다.

C

1 hard
2 Embarrassingly
3 soon
4 yet
5 carefully
6 easily
7 already
8 aggressively

해석

1 거의 온종일 비가 몹시 심하게 내리고 있다.
2 부끄럽게도 리즈는 자전거 타는 법을 몰랐다.
3 수전은 잠자리에 들자마자 곧 잠이 들었다.
4 샘은 UCLA에서 아직 어떤 대답도 듣지 못했다.
5 제출하기 전에 당신의 최종본을 신중하게 검토해 주세요.
6 한국의 축구팀은 일본 팀을 쉽게 이겼다.
7 그녀가 이미 공항에 도착했을 것 같아. 서두르자.
8 루디는 공격적으로 뛰었다. 그는 상대팀의 일부 선수들을 다치게 했다.

D

1 I'll go to the library by bus tomorrow to return these books.
2 The concert tickets sold out quickly at the box office this afternoon.
3 I saw someone running away from the jewelry shop at 11:30 last night.
4 He expressed his opinion confidently in front of many people yesterday.
5 Chris lived happily in Korea for twelve years before he moved back to Canada.
6 I bought a roll of film at a photography shop yesterday to photograph the carnival.
7 We were all waiting eagerly outside the studio at 7 o'clock to catch a glimpse of Alex.

해석

1 나는 이 책들을 반납하기 위해 내일 버스를 타고 도서관에 갈 것이다.
2 그 콘서트 표가 오늘 오후에 매표소에서 빠르게 매진되었다.
3 나는 어젯밤 11시 30분에 누군가가 보석 가게에서 도망치는 것을 보았다.
4 그는 어제 많은 사람들 앞에서 자신 있게 자신의 의견을 발표했다.
5 크리스는 캐나다로 돌아가기 전에 한국에서 12년 동안 행복하게 살았다.
6 나는 카니발을 찍으려고 어제 사진 가게에서 필름 한 통을 샀다.
7 우리 모두 알렉스를 잠깐이라도 보려고 7시에 스튜디오 밖에서 간절히 기다리고 있었다.

1 always, At night, excitedly, loudly
2 ever, quickly, rarely, just

해석

1 항상 뭔가 재미있는 일이 일어나고 있었다. 밤에 가족들이 인근 공원에 모이곤 했다. 어른들이 수다를 떨고, 농담을 하며 크게 웃는 동안 아이들은 신이 나서 이리저리 뛰어다니곤 했다. 분위기는 항상 즐겁고 활기찼다.
2 지금까지 거의 아무 일도 일어나지 않는다! 해가 지자마자, 모든 사람이 집 안으로 재빨리 달려 들어가 문을 닫는다. 길을 따라 조용히 걸어가면 사람들의 집 안에서 나오는 텔레비전 화면의 깜박거림뿐, 거의 아무도 볼 수 없다.

Unit 49 EXERCISES

p. 58~59

1 형용사
2 형용사
3 부사
4 부사
5 부사
6 형용사

해석

1 그는 어리석은 실수를 많이 했다.
2 나는 혼자 살지만 전혀 외롭지 않다.
3 요즘 아이들은 아주 빨리 자란다.
4 그 미술관은 화요일을 빼고 매일 연다.
5 우리는 다른 사람들의 말을 주의 깊게 들어야 한다.
6 그는 그것이 매우 돈이 많이 드는 사업임을 깨달았다.

1 ① ⓑ ② ⓐ
2 ① ⓓ ② ⓒ
3 ① ⓕ ② ⓔ

해석

〈보기〉
ⓐ 배심원 중 어떤 사람들은 피고인에게 유죄 선고하기를 거절했다.
ⓑ 오늘 아침 사고로 그 아이들에게 상담이 필요하다는 것은 확실하다.
ⓒ 당신의 현재 거주 국가와 직업을 말하시오.
ⓓ 참석해 있는 어린이들이 없어서 도서관은 조용했다.
ⓔ 내 친구는 항상 늦는다. 그것이 나를 언짢게 한다.
ⓕ 자금성은 20세기 후반 세계 문화유산으로 선언되었다.

1 ① 우리 팀이 경기에서 이길 것이라는 것이 거의 확실해 보인다.
② 우리가 즉시 논의해야 할 어떤 사항들이 있다.
2 ① 너는 내일 졸업식에 참석할 거니?
② 현재 학생회장과 달리 저는 학생 여러분에게 봉사하는 것을 신조로 하고 있습니다.
3 ① 너는 제임스가 몇 살인지 아니? 내 생각에 그는 20대 후반인 것 같아.
② 기차가 또 늦었다. 나는 회의를 놓치면 큰 곤경에 처할 것이다.

1 such
2 such
3 so
4 so
5 such
6 so

해석

1 그것들은 정말 훌륭한 공연이었어. DVD로 출시되는 게 몹시 기다려져.
2 아주 화창한 날이네요! 공원으로 소풍을 갑시다.
3 나는 정말 어리석었어요! 그렇게 행동하지 않았어야 했는데.

4 우리 선생님은 말을 너무 빨리 하셔서 이해하기 어렵다.
5 그가 그렇게 어린 나이에 성공하게 되었다니 놀라웠다.
6 왜 하루 종일 내 전화를 안 받았니? 네 걱정을 많이 했어.

D

1 enough
2 very
3 enough
4 very
5 enough
6 enough
7 too
8 very, too / very
9 very, too / very
10 too / very

해석

1 그녀는 대학생으로 보일 만큼 충분히 나이가 들어 보인다.
2 지하철역에 아주 가까이 사는 것은 매우 편리하다.
3 우리가 탈 자리가 충분히 있나요? 아마도 우리는 대형 택시를 불러야 할 것 같아요.
4 팀은 수가 어젯밤 파티에 오지 않아서 매우 화가 났다.
5 나는 우리가 화면에 충분히 가까이 있다고 생각해. 더 가까이 다가가지 말자.
6 박 선생님이 우리가 시험을 끝낼 만한 충분한 시간을 주지 않았기 때문에 불공평했다.
7 내 남동생은 세계에서 가장 높은 롤러코스터인 킹다 카를 타기에는 키가 너무 작았다.
8 당신의 아들은 매우 똑똑한 아이지만, 그는 다른 것들에 의해 너무 쉽게 산만해집니다.
9 나는 그녀가 말하는 것을 알아들으려면 매우 집중해서 들어야 했다. 그녀는 너무 조용히 말하고 있었다.
10 나는 내 여동생에게 생일 선물로 노트북 컴퓨터를 정말로 사 주고 싶었지만, 그것은 너무 비쌌다. 그래서 나는 아름다운 옷을 대신 주었다.

E

1 형용사, swimmer 수식, 빠른
2 부사, won't take 수식, 오래
3 형용사, summer 수식, 이른
4 형용사, course 수식, 어려운
5 부사, got up 수식, 늦게
6 형용사, marriage 수식, 긴
7 부사, study 수식, 열심히
8 부사, arrived 수식, 일찍
9 형용사, grandma 수식, 작고한
10 부사, dangerous 수식, 매우

해석

1 마이클은 빠른 수영 선수이다.
2 지금 이메일을 쓰고 있는데, 오래 걸리지는 않을 것이다.
3 식물은 초여름에 더 두드러지게 자란다.
4 고급 작문은 네게는 매우 어려운 과목이다.
5 나는 오늘 늦게 일어났지만 정시에 교실에 도착할 수 있었다.
6 우리 부모님은 길고 행복한 결혼생활을 해왔다.
7 나는 나중에 과학자가 될 수 있도록 열심히 공부해야 한다.
8 제이는 아침에 일찍 도착해서 지금은 약간 피곤해하고 있다.
9 우리는 돌아가신 할머니의 가구를 자선 단체에 기부할 것이다.
10 이 화학제품은 대단히 위험하므로 주의할 필요가 있다.

REVIEW

p. 60~61

1 bored
2 shocked
3 frightened
4 satisfying
5 pleasing
6 alarmed
7 depressing
8 delighted
9 tiring
10 embarrassing

해설/해석

1 내(I)가 지루하다고 느끼므로 bored가 적절
나는 그의 끝없는 불평이 상당히 지겨워지고 있다.

2 사람들(Most people)이 강도 사건에 대해 충격을 받았으므로 shocked가 적절
대부분의 사람들은 그 강도 사건에 대해 알고 충격을 받았다.

3 동물들(The animals)이 무서움을 느낀 것임, frightened가 적절
동물들은 공연하는 동안 무서움을 느꼈다.

4 식사(The meal)가 나를 만족스럽게 만든 것이므로 satisfying이 적절
내가 어젯밤에 럭키 가든에서 먹은 식사는 만족스러웠다.

5 힙합 음악이 10대의 귀를 즐겁게 하는 것이므로 pleasing이 적절
대부분의 10대들은 힙합 음악이 듣기에 좋다고 생각한다.

6 사람들(people)이 놀라움을 느꼈으므로 alarmed가 적절
그 사고는 심각하지 않았지만 사람들은 놀랐다.

7 영화가 나(I)를 우울하게 만드는 원인, depressing이 적절
나는 집에 혼자 있을 때 우울한 영화를 보지 않으려고 노력한다.

8 직원들(Workers)은 기쁨을 느끼는 주체이므로 delighted가 적절
그 회사 직원들은 회사 광고에 대한 반응에 기뻤다.

9 그날(day)이 제니를 피곤하게 하는 원인이므로 tiring이 적절
제니는 너무나 피곤한 하루를 보내서 콘택트렌즈도 빼지 않고 잠자리에 들었다.

10 그녀의 이야기가 나를 민망하게 하는 원인, embarrassing이 적절
그녀는 자신의 새 남자 친구가 얼마나 멋진지 계속 이야기했다. 너무나도 민망했다.

1 She gave me a small metal jewelry box.
2 There was a wonderful woolen rug on the floor.
3 I've just bought a beautiful wooden coffee table.
4 My father will be in Germany next month on business.
5 The puppies played excitedly in the park by the river all afternoon.
6 I gave my mother these two beautiful pink cotton table cloths.
7 Who knocked over the big new green plastic flower pot in the living room?

해설/해석

1 「한정사+크기+재료+목적+명사」
그녀가 나에게 작은 금속 보석 상자를 주었다.

2 「한정사+의견+재료+명사」
바닥에 멋진 울로 된 양탄자 깔개가 있었다.

3 「한정사+의견+재료+목적+명사」
나는 방금 아름다운 목재로 된 커피 테이블을 샀다.

4 부사(구)의 어순은 「장소+시간」
우리 아빠는 다음 달에 사업차 독일에 갈 것이다.

5 부사(구)의 어순은 「정도/양태+장소(작은, 큰)+시간」
강아지들이 오후 내내 강가의 공원에서 신나게 놀았다.

6 「한정사+수사+의견+색깔+재료+명사」
나는 엄마께 이 두 개의 아름다운 핑크색 면 테이블보를 드렸다.

7 「한정사+크기+신구+색깔+재료+명사」
누가 거실에 있는 커다란 새 녹색 플라스틱 꽃병을 넘어뜨렸니?

C

1 ① late ② lately
2 ① hard ② hardly
3 ① highly ② high
4 ① nearly ② near
5 ① mostly ② Most

해설/해석

1 ① after the usual time은 '평소 시간보다 후에', late은 '늦게'라는 의미 ② recently, lately는 '최근에'라는 의미
① 그녀가 늦게 도착했다.
② 나는 최근에 집 청소를 하지 않았다

2 ① not easy는 '쉽지 않은', hard는 '어려운, 힘든'이라는 의미 ② not at all는 '전혀 ~않은', hardly는 '거의 ~않은'이라는 의미
① 그녀의 결정을 받아들이는 것은 쉽지 않았다.
② 그들이 이겼지만, 그 결과는 전혀 놀랍지 않았다.

3 ① very, highly는 '매우, 몹시'라는 의미 ② a long way from the ground는 '땅에서 먼 거리', high는 '높이'라는 의미
① 윌리엄은 경쟁심이 매우 강한 선수이다.
② 독수리가 땅으로부터 멀리 하늘로 솟구쳐 날아올랐다.

4 ① almost, nearly는 '거의'라는 의미 ② close, near는 '가까운, 가까이에'라는 의미
① 이 소프트웨어를 내려 받는 데 거의 6시간이 걸렸다.
② 한 그룹의 학생들이 출입구 가까이에 서 있었다.

5 ① mainly, mostly는 '주로', '대체로'라는 의미 ② nearly, most는 '거의', '대부분의'라는 의미
① 이 회사의 직원들은 주로 여성이다.
② 회의실에 있는 사람들 대부분이 그의 아이디어에 반대했다.

D

1 five languages fluently
2 such a lovely face
3 enough food
4 틀린 것 없음
5 had never been
6 remarkably
7 too
8 completely exhausted
9 comfortable enough
10 틀린 것 없음

해설/해석

1 모양이나 태도를 나타내는 부사(fluently)는 목적어가 있을 때 목적어의 뒤쪽에 위치하므로 five languages fluently가 적절
그는 5개 국어를 유창하게 말한다.

2 '정말 사랑스러운 얼굴'이라는 의미로 face를 앞에서 수식해 주기 위해서는 형용사가 와야 하므로 lovely가 적절
너의 조카는 정말 사랑스러운 얼굴을 가지고 있다.

3 enough가 '충분한'이라는 뜻의 형용사로 명사를 수식할 때는 명사 앞에 위치하므로 enough food가 적절
매일 충분한 음식을 반드시 먹도록 해라.

4 빈도부사(always)는 일반동사 앞에 위치하므로 틀린 것 없음
존은 샤워할 때 항상 노래를 한다.

5 빈도부사(never)는 조동사 뒤에 위치한다. 완료시제에서 have동사는 조동사의 역할을 하므로 had never been이 적절
내 여동생은 전에 런던을 가본 적이 한 번도 없었다.

6 '뛰어나게 잘'이라는 의미가 되며, 부사 well(잘)을 강조하기 위해서는 또 다른 부사가 와야 하므로 remarkably가 적절
그는 나이에 비해 뛰어나게 기타를 잘 친다.

7 너무 작아서 넣을 수 없다는 의미의 「too+형용사+to+동사원형」의 형태가 와야 하므로 too가 적절
그 여행 가방은 너무 작아서 그의 옷을 모두 넣을 수 없었다.

8 켈리가 피곤함을 느끼는 것이므로 exhausted가 적절
켈리는 완전히 피곤해서 곧 잠이 들었다.

9 enough가 부사로 쓰여 형용사나 다른 부사를 수식할 때는 형용사/부사 뒤에 위치하고, 형용사로 쓰여 명사를 수식할 때는 명사 앞에 위치한다. comfortable은 형용사이므로 comfortable enough가 적절
그 집은 충분히 편안했지만, 사치스럽지는 않았다.

10 present가 한정적 용법으로 쓰일 때에는 '현재의'라는 의미가 되므로 틀린 것 없음.
그 식당의 현재 주인은 우리 할머니이다.

REVIEW PLUS

p. 62

1 ⑤
2 ③
3 ⑤
4 ① successfully ② safely ③ frightened

해설/해석

1 ⑤ 주어(you)가 화가 난 것이므로 annoying이 아니라 annoyed가 적절
① 그는 정말 훌륭한 선수이다.
② 나는 그렇게 맛없는 음식을 먹어 본 적이 없다.
③ 나는 너무 피곤해. 집에 갈 수 있으면 좋겠어.
④ 내가 그것을 그때까지 끝낸다는 것은 거의 불가능했다.
⑤ 너는 아직도 나에게 화가 나 있니? 나를 용서해 줘.

2 ① 최근에 어디 있었니?'가 의미상 자연스러우므로 late이 아니라 lately가 적절 ② 「신구+재료(목적)」 steel new가 아니라 new steel 이 적절 ④ 주어(I)를 보충 설명하는 주격보어이므로 curiously가 아니라 형용사 curious가 적절 ⑤ 빈도부사(sometimes)는 일반동사 앞에 위치하므로 visit something이 아니라 sometimes visit가 적절
① 너는 최근에 어디에 있었니?
② 나는 엄마에게 새 칼을 사 주었다.
③ 최근 나에 대한 그녀의 태도가 다소 차가워졌다.
④ 이 영화 몇 번이나 봤어요? 궁금해요.
⑤ 나는 때때로 일이 없는 한가한 시간에 서울에 있는 형을 방문한다.

3 ⑤ 「too+형용사+to+동사원형」은 '너무 ~해서 …할 수 없다', 「형용사+enough to+동사원형」은 '~할 수 있을 만큼 충분히 …하

다'라는 의미, 키가 충분히 커서 의자 없이 전구를 간다는 것이 문맥상 자연스러우므로 too tall이 아니라 tall enough가 적절

① A: 너는 전에 제니를 만난 적이 있니?
B: 응. 나는 여섯 달 전에 그녀를 만났어.
② A: 얼마나 자주 머리를 자르니?
B: 한 달에 한 번 잘라.
③ A: 너는 언제 숙제를 끝냈니?
B: 어제 끝냈어.
④ A: 나는 그가 졸업식 날 우리에게 해준 말을 잊을 수 없을 거야.
B: 나도 그래. 킹 박사님은 매우 영감을 주는 연설가야.
⑤ A: 제이슨에게 의자를 갖다 주는 게 어때?
B: 괜찮아. 그는 의자 없이도 전구를 갈아 끼울 수 있을 만큼 충분히 커.

4 ① '성공적으로 조종했다'라는 의미가 되어야 하므로 동사 steered를 수식하는 것은 부사 successfully가 적절 ② '무사히 구출되었다'라는 의미가 되어야 하므로 동사 rescued를 수식하는 safely가 적절 ③ passenger(승객)가 겁을 먹은 것이므로 frightened가 적절

"허드슨 강의 영웅"

조종사 체슬린 설렌버거가 비행기의 엔진이 모두 정지되었음을 알렸을 때는 US 항공 1549편이 뉴욕시의 라구아디아 공항을 막 출발한 뒤였다. 꾸물거릴 시간도 없이 숙련된 조종사는 훼손된 비행기로는 공항으로 회항할 수 없다는 것을 재빨리 깨달았다. 그 대신에 그는 허드슨 강으로 성공적으로 비행기의 방향을 돌려 물 위로 천천히 착륙했다. 155명의 승객과 승무원 모두 무사히 구조되었고, 지금 이 조종사는 영웅으로 불리고 있다. 겁에 질린 한 승객은 "우리가 모두 살아 있는 것은 정말 행운이에요."라고 말했다. "우리는 설렌버거 기장에게 우리의 생명을 빚졌어요."라고 또 다른 승객이 말했다.

REPLAY

p. 64~65

1 CHECK-UP

1 wiser, wisest
2 more, most
3 cheaper, cheapest
4 prettier, prettiest
5 younger, youngest
6 better, best
7 hotter, hottest
8 easier, easiest
9 warmer, warmest
10 earlier, earliest
11 larger, largest
12 harder, hardest
13 bigger, biggest
14 less, least
15 heavier, heaviest
16 more popular, most popular
17 worse, worst
18 weaker, weakest
19 more important, most important
20 sadder, saddest
21 longer, longest
22 more difficult, most difficult
23 more slowly, most slowly
24 worse, worst
25 better, best
26 more, most

2 CHECK-UP

1 better 2 heavier 3 sweeter
4 more quietly 5 bigger

3 CHECK-UP

1 hottest 2 busiest 3 most beautiful
4 cleanest 5 most slowly

Unit 50 EXERCISES

p. 68~69

A

1 as hard as 2 as difficult as
3 as white as 4 as pretty as
5 as strong, as 6 as much, as
7 as many, as 8 as tough as

해석

1 수진이는 민진이만큼 영어를 열심히 공부한다.
2 기말시험은 내가 생각한 것만큼 어렵지 않았다.
3 내 흰 티셔츠가 눈처럼 새하얗게 될까?
4 당신의 딸이 저 드레스를 입으니 공주처럼 예뻐 보이네요.
5 제니는 베스만큼 강한 장거리 달리기 선수이다.
6 사라는 내가 가진 돈의 세 배만큼 많은 돈을 가지고 있다.
7 당신이 원하는 만큼 많은 토핑을 피자에 추가할 수 있습니다.
8 스테이크가 가죽처럼 질겨서 전혀 먹을 수 없었다.

B

1 No, sooner, than 2 five, times, as, as
3 as, soon, as, possible 4 As, soon, as
5 as, much, as, we, can 6 twice, as, as

해석

1 내가 잠자리에 들자마자, 누군가가 초인종을 눌렀다.
2 너는 네가 먹은 것의 다섯 배 더 많은 칼로리를 먹을 수 있다.
3 너의 도움이 필요해! 가능한 한 빨리 우리 집으로 와줘.
4 비가 그치자마자 태양이 구름을 뚫고 나타났다.
5 우리는 영어 말하기 연습을 가능한 한 많이 해야 한다.
6 그녀의 컴퓨터 메모리는 나의 컴퓨터보다 두 배 더 크다.

C

1 Sugar is as sweet as honey.
2 A lake isn't as big as a sea.
3 My photocopy isn't as clear as hers.
4 Pearls aren't as rare as black diamonds.
5 Jieun has visited Europe as many times as you.

6 A koala isn't as dangerous as a grizzly bear.
7 The Thompsons have as many children as the Browns.
8 Winter in Canada is as cold and bitter as winter in Russia.
9 John doesn't eat as much junk food as his brother Peter.
10 Ice hockey players are as superstitious as basketball players.
11 Romantic comedies are as interesting as horror movies.
12 The waiters at this restaurant aren't as kind as the waiters at that restaurant

해석

1 설탕은 꿀만큼 달다.
2 호수는 바다만큼 크지 않다.
3 내 복사본은 그녀의 것만큼 뚜렷하지 않다.
4 진주는 검은 다이아몬드만큼 진귀하지는 않다.
5 지은이는 너만큼 여러 번 유럽을 가봤다.
6 코알라는 큰 회색 곰만큼 위험하지 않다.
7 톰슨 씨 가족은 브라운 씨 가족만큼 많은 자녀가 있다.
8 캐나다의 겨울은 러시아의 겨울만큼 춥고 매섭다.
9 존은 그의 남동생 피터만큼 정크푸드를 많이 먹지 않는다.
10 아이스하키 선수들은 농구 선수들만큼 미신에 사로잡혀 있다.
11 로맨틱 코미디는 공포 영화만큼 재미있다.
12 이 식당의 웨이터들은 저 식당의 웨이터들만큼 친절하지 않다.

Unit 51 EXERCISES

p. 72~73

1 of 2 than 3 to 4 of 5 of 6 than
7 than 8 to 9 than 10 to 11 than 12 to

해석

1 둘 중에서 이 수박이 더 달다.
2 당신은 확실히 나보다 더 용감한 사람입니다.
3 나는 발표에 앞서 그녀와 이야기를 해야 한다.
4 둘 중에서 이 전구가 더 효율적이다.
5 두 쌍의 스키 중에서 이것이 싸다
6 그 집보다 뒤뜰에 있는 느릅나무가 더 크다.
7 피터는 조보다 자신감이 없는 체스 선수이다.
8 에티오피아산 커피는 인도네시아산 커피보다 더 우수하다.
9 리즈는 런던이나 맨체스터보다 작은 도시이다.
10 이 제품들은 작년에 우리가 샀던 것들보다 품질이 떨어진다.
11 미셸은 여동생보다 더 많은 공포 영화를 봤다.
12 피트는 나보다 한 살 어리지만 우리는 오랫동안 친구로 지내왔다.

B

1 The older we grow, the wiser we get.
2 The faster the taxi driver drove, the more nervous I became.
3 The louder the band played, the more excited the crowd got.
4 The faster we get the classroom clean, the sooner we can all leave.
5 The higher Jeff rose in the balloon, the more he could see of the savanna.
6 The harder you practice the piano, the more quickly you will be a famous pianist.

해석

1 우리는 나이가 들면 들수록 더 현명해진다.
2 택시 운전사가 빠르게 운전하면 할수록 나는 더 겁이 났다.
3 그 밴드가 크게 연주하면 할수록 관객들은 더 흥분했다.
4 우리가 교실을 빨리 청소하면 할수록 우리는 모두 더 빨리 떠날 수 있다.
5 제프는 기구를 타고 높이 오르면 오를수록 사바나를 더 많이 볼 수 있었다.
6 네가 피아노를 더 열심히 연습할수록 더 빨리 유명한 피아니스트가 될 것이다.

1 yours 2 the sooner
3 than 4 of
5 틀린 것 없음 6 happy
7 very 생략 또는 even, much, far, still, a lot으로 변경
8 than 9 틀린 것 없음
10 that of Russia 11 those of Dickens
12 than

해석

1 그의 경험이 너의 것보다 더 다양하다.
2 네가 빨리 먹으면 먹을수록 나는 더 빨리 치울 수 있다.
3 엄마가 오늘은 과일보다 채소를 더 많이 샀다.
4 둘 중에서 이 영화가 더 재미있다.
5 나는 정확하게 네가 가진 돈의 두 배를 가지고 있다.
6 미셸은 그 여행에 대해 수보다 만족하지 못한다.
7 케빈은 나보다 훨씬 더 비싼 옷을 가지고 있다.
8 놀랍게도 버스가 지하철보다 덜 붐빈다.
9 경제학자들은 점점 더 낙관적이 되었다.
10 싱가포르의 기후는 러시아의 기후보다 훨씬 더 덥다.
11 트롤로프의 소설은 디킨스의 소설보다 더 재미있다.
12 시골 사람들은 대개 대도시 사람들보다 더 친절하다.

D

1 darker and darker 2 angrier and angrier
3 colder and colder 4 more and more dangerous
5 better and better 6 more and more expensive
7 more and more fluently 8 more and more tired
9 more and more anxious 10 heavier and heavier

해석

1 곧 비가 올 것 같다. 하늘이 점점 더 어두워지고 있다.
2 제이크의 이웃은 너무 시끄러웠다. 그는 점점 더 화가 났다.
3 나는 장갑을 끼지 않고 스키를 타고 있었다. 내 손이 점점 더 차가워졌다.
4 히치하이킹은 더는 안전하지 않다. 그것은 점점 더 위험해지고 있다.
5 베스는 학교 합창단에 가입했다. 그녀의 노래는 점점 더 좋아지고 있다.
6 물가가 점점 더 비싸지고 있어서 엄마가 걱정하고 있다.
7 그 소녀는 요즘 영어를 공부한다. 그녀는 점점 더 유창하게 말한다.

8 시간이 지남에 따라 그는 매일 같은 일을 하는 것에 점점 더 지루해졌다.
9 수가 시험을 보고 있었다. 시간이 너무 빨리 지나가는 것 같았다. 그녀는 점점 더 긴장되었다.
10 나는 혼자서 그 모든 짐을 운반해야만 했다. 시간이 갈수록 짐이 점점 더 무거워지는 것 같았다.

Unit 52 EXERCISES

p. 76~77

1 last　　2 farthest　　3 brightest　　4 worst

해석

1 이번이 너에게 알려주는 마지막이다.
2 지금까지 당신이 수영해서 가장 멀리 간 거리가 얼마나 됩니까?
3 그레그는 반에서 가장 똑똑한 학생이다. 그는 모든 과목에서 A를 받았다.
4 그것이 우리가 몇 해 만에 겪은 최악의 눈보라였다.

1 one of the most attractive cities
2 one of the biggest problems
3 one of the most famous cities
4 one of the greatest scientists

해석

1 퀘벡은 캐나다에서 가장 매력적인 도시 중 하나이다.
2 범죄는 현대 도시에서 가장 큰 문제 중 하나이다.
3 맨해탄은 미국에서 가장 유명한 도시 중 하나이다.
4 아인슈타인은 세상에서 가장 훌륭한 과학자 중 한 명이었다.

1 shorter than any other route / No, shorter than / No, as short as
2 hotter than any other day / No, hotter than / No, as hot as
3 cleaner than any other room / No, cleaner than / No, as clean as
4 more expensive than all the other cars / No, more expensive than / No, as expensive as

해석

1 이것이 시내로 가는 가장 가까운 길이다.
2 오늘이 올 여름 중 가장 더운 날이다.
3 내 방이 우리 집에서 가장 깨끗한 방이다.
4 이것은 세상에서 가장 비싼 차다.

D

1 the hardest, of　　2 the coldest, of
3 the tallest, in　　4 the oldest, in
5 the most respected, in　　6 the most delicious, in
7 the most influential, in　　8 the most famous, in
9 the most popular, of　　10 the newest, in
11 the most thrilling, of

해석

1 오늘은 내 인생에서 가장 힘든 날이었다.
2 오늘이 일 년 중 가장 추운 날이다.
3 너의 반에서 가장 키가 큰 학생은 누구니?
4 저 학교가 이 도시에서 가장 오래된 건물이다.
5 그는 세계에서 가장 존경받는 과학자이다.
6 페퍼로니는 이 식당에서 가장 맛있는 피자다.
7 브라운 씨는 세계에서 가장 영향력이 있는 작가이다.
8 톰 스미스는 자기 나라에서 가장 유명한 배우다.
9 이 노래는 100곡이 넘는 곡 가운데 가장 인기 있는 곡이다.
10 그 녹음실은 국내에서 가장 최신형의 사운드 기계를 가지고 있다.
11 그의 최신 추리 소설은 그가 쓴 책들 중 가장 스릴 있다.

E

1 more important　　2 the worst
3 clearer　　4 (the) farthest
5 as wasteful　　6 the last
7 more depressing

Unit 53 EXERCISES

p. 79

1 similar to　　2 similar to
3 similar to　　4 different from
5 the same as　　6 different from
7 the same as

해석

1 인간의 DNA와 침팬지의 DNA는 비슷하다.
2 나의 서체가 너의 서체와 비슷하다.
3 나의 새 인라인 스케이트는 스티브의 인라인 스케이트와 비슷해 보인다.
4 인간의 뇌와 침팬지의 뇌는 다르다.
5 내 기말 에세이 주제는 너의 기말 에세이 주제와 같다.
6 바다에서 사는 물고기는 호수에서 사는 물고기와 다르다.
7 콘서트의 날짜와 기말고사의 날짜가 똑같다.

B

1 to　　2 alike　　3 from　　4 as
5 as　　6 as　　7 from　　8 to
9 from　　10 to　　11 alike　　12 alike

해석

1 우리 언니는 우리 오빠와 비슷하게 생기지 않았다.
2 아이들이 모두 유니폼을 입으니 매우 비슷하게 보인다.
3 그 영화는 책과 완전히 달랐다.
4 이 빵은 저 빵과 완전히 똑같은 맛이 난다.
5 나의 일정은 너의 일정과 같다. 잘됐다!
6 그의 전화번호가 전과 같지 않은 것 같다.
7 새로운 소프트웨어가 옛날 것과 그렇게 다르지 않은 것 같다.
8 샐리는 성격 면에서 그녀의 어머니와 매우 비슷하다.
9 아프리카를 여행한 나의 경험은 그의 경험과 달랐다.
10 그 변명은 어제 네가 나에게 말했던 것과 비슷하다.
11 그 두 조각상은 비슷해 보여서 우리는 그들을 거의 분간할 수 없다.
12 훈련되지 않은 눈으로 보면 이 두 장의 사진은 똑같아 보이지만, 실제로는 매우 다르다.

REVIEW

p. 80~81

1 she	2 theirs
3 sooner	4 last
5 newest	6 more modern
7 animal	8 the best
9 places	10 hottest

해설/해석

1 괄호 뒤에 did가 왔으므로 주격이 적절
나는 그녀만큼 점심을 많이 먹지 않았다.

2 비교 대상이 내 남동생의 새 스포츠카와 그들의 스포츠카(their sports car)여야 하므로 theirs(그들의 것)가 적절
내 남동생의 새 스포츠카는 그들의 것만큼 빠르다.

3 「비교급+than」의 형태이므로 sooner가 적절
정말 빨랐어! 그는 내가 기대했던 것보다 더 일찍 도착했어.

4 「the last+사람」은 '~할 마지막 사람이다'라는 의미로 '~하지 않을 사람'이라는 뜻, latest는 '최근의, 최신의'라는 의미
너는 내가 이 헬스클럽에서 볼 거라 결코 예상하지 못했던 사람이다.

5 「the+최상급」이므로 newest가 적절
그것은 현재 구입할 수 있는 가장 최신형 모델이므로 비싸다.

6 「비교급+than」이므로 more modern이 적절
이 건물은 그 옆에 있는 것보다 더 오래되었지만 더 현대적이다.

7 「비교급+than any other+단수명사」이므로 animal이 적절
하마는 아프리카의 다른 어떤 동물보다도 더 위험하다.

8 make the best use of는 '~을 최대한 잘 이용하다'라는 의미
신입생들은 UCLA에서 공부하는 동안 시간을 최대한 잘 이용하는 방법을 배우게 될 것이다.

9 「one of the+최상급+복수명사」는 '가장 ~한 것 중 하나'라는 의미이므로 places가 적절
프랑스령 리비에라는 매우 아름답지만 물가가 비싼 곳이다. 사실 그곳은 세상에서 가장 물가가 비싼 곳 중 하나이다.

10 「one of the+최상급+복수명사」이므로 hottest가 적절
호주 동부 해안에 있는 케언즈는 남쪽에 있는 멜버른보다 더 덥다. 그곳은 호주에서 가장 더운 지역 중 한 곳에 위치해 있다.

B

1 Susan is much thinner now than last year.
2 She speaks English as well as Spanish.
3 It's much colder today than yesterday.
4 Seoul is more densely populated than any other city in Korea.
5 Jonathan studies English and math as hard as his brother.
6 Beijing has not been as successful as Tokyo at attracting tourists.
7 Joe has risen to the top because he trains harder now than before.

해설/해석

1 now와 last year를 비교하므로 than 뒤에 중복되는 주어와 동사(she was) 생략 가능
수잔은 작년보다 지금 훨씬 날씬하다.

2 English와 Spanish를 비교하므로 중복되는 주어와 동사(she speaks)는 생략 가능
그녀는 영어를 스페인어만큼 잘 한다.

3 today와 yesterday를 비교하므로 than 뒤에 중복되는 주어와 동사(it was) 생략 가능
어제보다 오늘이 훨씬 더 춥다.

4 Seoul과 any other city를 비교, 중복되는 동사는 생략 가능
서울은 한국의 어떤 다른 도시보다 인구가 더 밀집해 있다.

5 Jonathan과 his brother를 비교하므로 중복되는 동사 생략 가능
조나단은 그의 형만큼 열심히 영어와 수학을 공부한다.

6 Beijing과 Tokyo를 비교하므로 Tokyo 뒤에 중복되는 동사인 has 생략 가능
북경은 관광객을 유치하는 데 도쿄만큼 성공적이지는 않았다.

7 now와 before를 비교하므로 before 앞에 중복되는 동사인 did 생략 가능
조는 이전보다 더 열심히 훈련했기 때문에 정상의 자리에 올라섰다.

1 as fast as we could
2 as entertaining as
3 as many books as possible
4 more and more important
5 The less we spend, the richer we become

해설/해석

1 「as+형용사+as+주어+can/could」는 '가능한 한 ~하게'라는 의미
우리가 너무 늦어서 미안해요. 최대한 빨리 여기에 왔어요.

2 「A as+원급+as B」는 'A는 B만큼 ~하다'라는 의미로 두 대상의 정도가 동등함을 나타냄
나는 '스파이더맨 3'가 '스파이더맨' 시리즈의 이전 영화만큼 재미있는 것 같지 않았다.

3 「as+형용사+명사+as possible」은 '가능한 한 ~한 (+명사)'라는 의미
나는 수의사가 되려고 공부하고 있어서 동물 해부학에 관해 가능한 한 많은 책을 읽고 있다.

4 「more and more+원급」은 '점점 더 ~해지는'이라는 의미
요즘 온라인 연락처를 만드는 것이 구직자들에게 점점 더 중요해지고 있다.

5 「The 비교급+주어+동사, the 비교급+주어+동사」는 '~하면 할수록 더 ~하다'라는 의미
우리 아버지께서 가장 좋아하시는 속담은 '덜 쓸수록 더 부자가 된다.'이다.

1 small, smaller, more stunning
2 slow, worst, better
3 nicer, more playful, best
4 tallest, hardest
5 most energetic, faster, stronger

해설/해석

1 A에서 「as+원급+as」이므로 small이 적절, B에서 「비교급+than」이므로 smaller가 적절, -ing로 끝나는 형용사의 비교급은 more를 덧붙이므로 more stunning이 적절

A: 모나리자는 사람들이 말하는 것만큼 작니?

B: 응. 네가 생각하는 것보다 훨씬 더 작을걸. 하지만 네가 상상할 수 있는 것보다 더 놀라워. 볼 때마다 점점 더 아름다워지거든.

2 A에서 「as+원급+as」이므로 slow가 적절, 「the+최상급」이므로 bad의 최상급인 worst가 적절, B에서 이번 달과 다음 달이 비교 대상이므로 good의 비교급인 better가 적절

A: 이번 달의 경기가 지난달의 두 배만큼 둔하네요. 사실, 지금까지 우리가 겪은 최악의 달이 되어가고 있어요.

B: 나쁜 소식이군요, 조. 하지만, 다음 달에는 더 나아질 거라고 확신해요. 기운내세요!

3 A에서 「비교급+than」이므로 nicer가 적절, B에서 「비교급+than」이고, -ful로 끝나는 형용사의 비교급은 more를 덧붙이므로 more playful이 적절, 「the+최상급」이므로 good의 최상급인 best가 적절

A: 어떤 종류의 애완동물을 갖고 싶니? 내 생각엔 고양이보다는 개를 기르는 게 더 나을 것 같아.

B: 나는 반대야. 개는 고양이보다 더 명랑하기는 하지만, 고양이가 깨끗하고 조용하기 때문에 (고양이가) 최고의 애완동물이야.

4 A에서 「the+최상급」이므로 tallest와 hardest가 적절

A: 왜 모든 사람이 에베레스트 산에 오르는 것을 대단한 일이라고 생각하지? 에베레스트는 가장 높은 산일지 모르지만, 오르기에 가장 어렵지는 않아. K2가 에베레스트보다 기술적으로 훨씬 더 어려워.

B: 모르겠어. 하지만 솔직히 말하면 둘 다 내 능력 밖이야.

5 A에서 I've ever seen은 '내가 지금까지 본'이라는 의미로 「the+최상급」과 함께 사용되는 어구이므로 most energetic이 적절, B에서 「비교급+than」이므로 faster, stronger가 적절

A: 네 남동생은 내가 지금까지 본 사람 중에서 단연코 가장 활기 찬 소년이야.

B: 아마도 초등학교 때 축구 선수였기 때문일 거야. 내 동생은 팀의 모든 다른 선수들보다 더 빠르고 강했어.

REVIEW PLUS

p. 82

 A

1 ② 2 ③ 3 ④

해설/해석

1 weather balloons(기상 관측기구)와 commercial airliners(민간 항공기)가 비교 대상이므로 「as+원급+as」나 「비교급+than」이 가능, 따라서 higher than이나 as high as가 적절

많은 기상 관측기구들이 대부분의 민간 항공기보다 더 높이 난다.

2 올해 여름의 날씨와 작년의 여름의 날씨가 비교 대상이므로 「비교급+than」을 쓸 수 있다. bad의 비교급은 worse이고 비교급은 much, even, still, far, a lot을 써서 강조할 수 있으므로 even worse than이 적절

이번 여름의 날씨는 지난여름 날씨보다 훨씬 더 나쁘다.

3 이 스파게티와 수잔이 만든 파스타가 비교 대상이므로「as+원급+as」나 「비교급+than」이 가능, 감각동사 taste(~한 맛이 나다)는 뒤에는 형용사보어를 취하므로 as good as 또는 better than이 적절

이 스파게티는 수잔이 지난 주말에 우리에게 만들어 줬던 파스타만큼 맛이 좋다.

 B

⑤

해설/해석

⑤ 「비교급+than」이므로 shortest가 아니라 shorter가 적절

① 오토바이는 스쿠터보다 더 빠르다.

② 알프스는 유럽에서 가장 높은 산맥이다.

③ 존은 피터보다 겨우 두 달 어리다.

④ 중국은 세계에서 가장 많은 인구를 가지고 있다.

⑤ 중국의 양쯔 강은 아마존 강보다 짧다.

 C

① students ② programs ③ closer ④ strong

해설/해석

①, ② 「one of the+최상급+복수명사」는 '가장 ~한 …들 중 하나'라는 의미로 복수인 students, programs가 적절 ③ 「much(비교급 강조)+비교급+than」은 '~보다 훨씬 더 …한'이라는 의미로 closer가 적절 ④ Her wish와 her desire가 비교 대상이고 「as+원급+as」의 형태를 취하고 있으므로 strong이 적절

사라는 뉴욕 주에서 가장 똑똑한 학생 중 하나이다. 지금 그녀에게는 결정해야 할 중요한 것이 있다. 뉴햄프셔에 있는 다트머스 대학에 가야 하는지, 뉴욕에 있는 콜롬비아 대학에 가야 하는 지이다. 다트머스는 미국에서 가장 훌륭한 공학 프로그램 중 하나를 갖추고 있고, 사라는 언젠가 건축가가 되기를 간절히 원한다. 하지만 콜롬비아는 다트머스보다 사라의 고향에서 훨씬 더 가깝다. 가족과 함께 있고 싶은 그녀의 바람은 성공하고 싶은 그녀의 바람만큼이나 강하다. 당신이라면 어떻게 하겠는가?

PART 15

Unit 54 EXERCISES

p. 86~87

 A

1 building 2 made
3 talking 4 stealing
5 named 6 growing
7 broken 8 surrounded
9 singing 10 troubled

해석

1 나는 참새가 둥지를 짓는 것을 보았다.
2 그는 한국에서 만들어진 새 휴대폰을 샀다.
3 저기서 마이크와 이야기를 하고 있는 남자를 아니?
4 우리 아버지가 정원에서 사과를 훔치는 소년을 보았다.
5 이 서류를 티나 정이라는 이름의 여자에게 전해주세요.
6 우리나라에서 버려진 개들의 숫자가 증가하고 있다.
7 지진이 있고 나서 창문 하나와 유리 꽃병 하나가 깨졌다.
8 켈리는 자신을 동경하는 사진작가들의 무리에 의해 둘러싸여 있었다.
9 그녀는 한밤중에 누군가 큰 소리로 노래를 부르는 것을 들었다.

10 이렇게 혼란스러운 시기에 약간의 좋은 소식을 들으니 좋다.

B

1 disappointing, disappointed
2 satisfying, satisfied
3 amazing, amazed
4 touching, touched
5 shocked, shocking
6 confused, confusing
7 amusing, amused

해석

1 그 선물은 그녀를 실망스럽게 했다. 그녀는 그 선물에 실망했다.
2 너의 의견이 우리를 만족스럽게 했다. 우리는 너의 의견에 매우 만족했다.
3 그들의 뒷마당 크기가 나를 놀라게 했다. 나는 그들의 뒷마당 크기에 놀랐다.
4 내가 지난 주말에 본 영화는 감동적이었다. 나는 지난 주말에 본 영화에 감동했다.
5 사람들은 그 유명 인사부부의 이혼에 충격을 받았다. 그 유명 인사부부의 이혼은 사람들에게 충격을 주었다.
6 독자들은 복잡한 설명 때문에 혼란스러워했다. 그 복잡한 설명이 독자들에게 혼란을 주었다.
7 영화제에서 상영된 몇몇 단편 영화들은 재미있었다. 관객들은 영화제에서 상영한 단편 영화로 즐거웠다.

C

1 depressed
2 annoying
3 inspiring
4 interesting
5 excited
6 surprising

해석

1 민지는 자신의 애완용 앵무새가 죽었을 때 몹시 우울했다.
2 그녀는 말하면서 손톱을 물어뜯는 불쾌한 습관을 가지고 있다.
3 그 강의는 고무적이었다. 그것은 내 인생관을 완전히 바꿔 놓았다.
4 TV에서 아프리카 원숭이에 관한 흥미로운 프로그램을 방영했다.
5 에이미는 크리스마스이브에 너무나 신이 났다. 그녀는 잠을 잘 수가 없었다.
6 그는 온종일 정크푸드를 먹는다. 그래서 그가 그렇게 건강하지 않은 것은 놀라운 일이 아니다.

D

1 worried
2 embarrassing
3 bored
4 annoying
5 surprised
6 satisfied
7 disappointed

해석

1 나는 사고가 있었다는 것을 듣고 걱정되었다.
2 학생들은 새로 온 선생님에게 당황스러운 질문을 많이 했다.
3 오늘 교장 선생님의 훈화 말씀 동안 나는 너무나 지루했다. 나는 그냥 잠이 들었다.
4 수지가 의자를 가지고 끽끽거리는 소음을 내고 있다. 그것은 정말 짜증난다!
5 나는 네가 배가 아파서 학교를 조퇴했다고 해서 매우 놀랐어.
6 그 색깔이 마음에 드나요? 만약 마음에 들지 않는다면, 더 밝은 색조로 바꾸어 드릴 수 있어요.
7 하와이 여행이 취소되었다. 나는 정말로 가고 싶었기 때문에 매우 실망했다.

E

1 현재분사
2 동명사
3 동명사
4 현재분사
5 동명사
6 동명사
7 현재분사

해석

1 잠자는 아기를 좀 봐. 정말 귀여워!
2 치마를 입어보실 수 있어요. 탈의실은 저쪽입니다.
3 내 생각에 새 침낭을 사는 게 좋겠어. 이 침낭은 해졌어.
4 불쌍한 샘! 그는 폭발하는 폭죽에 손을 심하게 다쳤어.
5 대기실에 계세요. 의사 선생님께서 곧 진찰해 주실 겁니다.
6 아이들에게 더는 껌을 사 주지 마세요. 그들의 이가 썩을 거예요.
7 짖고 있는 개가 무서워서 그 꼬마는 집에 들어가기를 주저하고 있다.

Unit 55 EXERCISES

p. 90~91

A

1 The stolen artwork was recovered by chance.
2 Some fried potatoes and onions would taste good.
3 The boy sitting next to Ally is her new boyfriend, John.
4 They live in a renovated mansion originally built in 1890.
5 The teacher gave us a challenging assignment for homework.
6 The cancelation of the school trip was disappointing news to the students.
7 A lot of excited shoppers rushed to the grand opening of the new shopping mall.

해석

1 그 도둑맞은 미술 작품을 우연히 되찾았다.
2 약간의 튀긴 감자와 양파는 맛이 좋을 것이다.
3 앨리 옆에 앉아 있는 소년은 그녀의 새 남자 친구인 존이다.
4 그들은 1890년에 최초로 지어졌던 개조된 저택에 살고 있다.
5 선생님은 우리에게 숙제로 힘든 과제를 내주었다.
6 수학여행의 취소는 학생들에게 실망스러운 소식이었다.
7 많은 신이 난 쇼핑객들이 새로 개점된 쇼핑몰에 서둘러 갔다.

B

1 cheated
2 waiting
3 done
4 reading
5 walking
6 saying
7 having
8 confused
9 amazed
10 exhausted
11 beating
12 annoyed

해석

1 솔직히 말해서, 나는 그의 제안에 속은 것 같은 느낌이 들었다.
2 너무 오랫동안 기다리게 해서 미안해.
3 그는 그 보고서가 6시까지 완료되기를 원한다고 말했다.
4 우리 아버지는 신문을 읽으면서 아침을 드셨다.
5 페기는 카페에 앉아서 거리를 걸어가는 사람들을 바라보고 있었다.
6 네가 우리 가족에 대해 그런 말을 하는 것을 내버려 두지 않겠어!
7 어젯밤에 사람들이 싸우는 소리를 들었니?
8 혼란스러워 보이는구나. 내가 그것을 다시 한 번 설명해 주기를 바라니?
9 우리는 결혼식에 맛있는 음식이 많아서 놀랐다.

10 그는 10시간 이상 일한 뒤에 매우 지쳤다.
11 나는 달리기 선수들이 마지막 직선 코스에 들어왔을 때 내 심장이 몹시 뛰는 것을 느꼈다.
12 그는 학생들이 너무 많은 질문을 하자 약간 짜증이 나는 것 같았다.

1 having	2 swimming	3 seen
4 delayed	5 destroyed	6 thought
7 published	8 written	9 done
10 having	11 running	12 arrived

해석

1 너는 악몽을 꾸고 있었니?
2 아이들이 바다에서 수영하고 있다.
3 우리는 이미 그 영화를 봤다.
4 회의는 다음날로 연기되었다.
5 그 건물은 1886년에 화재로 파괴되었다.
6 해외여행 가는 것에 대해 생각해 본 적이 있니?
7 '뉴욕 타임스'는 1851년에 처음으로 발행되었다.
8 나는 고등학교 이후로 영어로 일기를 써왔다.
9 우리 집의 모든 그림들은 우리 어머니가 그린 것이었다.
10 학생들은 학교 규칙에 대한 토론을 하고 있다.
11 에릭은 학교에 늦지 않기 위해 가능한 한 빨리 뛰고 있었다.
12 버스가 막 도착했지만 매우 붐빈다. 다음 것을 타자.

D

1 stolen on the subway
2 performing in front of people
3 talking on the phone over there
4 The baby singing and dancing in the video
5 filled with bad odor
6 climbing a cliff without any safety equipment

해석

1 그는 그 지갑을 찾았다. 누군가 지하철에서 그의 지갑을 훔쳤다. → 그는 지하철에서 도난당한 지갑을 찾았다.
2 나는 원숭이를 보았다. 원숭이는 사람들 앞에서 공연을 하고 있었다. → 나는 사람들 앞에서 공연하는 원숭이를 보았다.
3 저 소녀가 보이니? 그녀는 저쪽에서 전화 통화를 하고 있어. → 저쪽에서 전화 통화를 하고 있는 소녀가 보이니?
4 아기가 나를 미소 짓게 했다. 그는 비디오에서 노래하고 춤추고 있었다. → 비디오에서 노래하고 춤추는 아기가 나를 미소 짓게 했다.
5 그는 방의 모든 창문을 열었다. 그 방은 나쁜 냄새로 가득했다. → 그는 나쁜 냄새로 가득한 방의 모든 창문을 열었다.
6 나는 한 남자를 보았다. 그는 어떤 안전 장비도 없이 절벽을 오르고 있었다. → 나는 어떤 안전 장비도 없이 절벽을 오르는 한 남자를 보았다.

Unit 56 EXERCISES

p. 94~95

1 (Although) (Being) Born into a poor family
2 (After) Listening to the song several times
3 (While) Playing baseball with his friends
4 (While) Trying to sleep last night
5 (When) Reaching into my bag for my wallet
6 (As) Winning first place in the contest
7 (As) Having lived in the USA as a child

해석

1 그녀는 가난한 가정에서 태어났지만 꿈을 절대 포기하지 않았다.
2 존은 그 노래를 몇 번 들은 후에, 그것을 완벽하게 부를 수 있었다.
3 알렉스는 친구들과 야구를 하던 중에 발목을 심하게 삐었다.
4 내가 어젯밤에 잠을 자려고 하는데 밖에서 발걸음 소리가 들렸다.
5 지갑을 꺼내려고 가방 안에 손을 넣었을 때, 나는 지갑을 도둑맞았다는 사실을 알았다.
6 그가 그 대회에서 1등을 하자, 그는 유명 인사가 되었다.
7 나는 어릴 때 미국에 살아서, 영어를 할 수 있다.

B

1 Being	2 틀린 것 없음
3 Recovering[Having recovered]	4 틀린 것 없음
5 Done	6 틀린 것 없음
7 틀린 것 없음	8 Scolded

해석

1 첼시는 배가 매우 고파서 스파게티를 만들어 먹었다.
2 그는 교통 체증에 갇혀서 정시에 회의에 도착할 수 없었다.
3 아람이는 독감이 나아서 병원에 갈 필요가 없었다.
4 하나는 외국에서 공부했음에도, 귀국 후 직장을 구할 수 없었다.
5 이 그림은 유명한 화가가 그린 것이라서 많은 돈이 들 것이다.
6 그 부상당한 여성은 구출되고 나서, 즉시 병원으로 이송되었다.
7 마크는 도시에서 길러져서 시골 생활의 소박함을 알지 못한다.
8 제이슨은 반 친구들 앞에서 꾸중을 들어서 수치스러움을 감출 수가 없었다.

1 When you pay a bill, you need to check if it is correct.
2 After he had had an operation, he began to recover.
3 Because I was hungry, I ate some bread between meals.
4 As soon as he gets up in the morning, he drinks a cup of water.
5 Though we hadn't booked tickets, we still could see the musical.
6 If I am promoted next year, I will treat you to a gorgeous dinner.

해석

1 계산을 할 때 그것이 맞는지 확인해야 한다.
2 그는 수술을 받은 후로 회복되기 시작했다.
3 나는 배가 고파서 간식으로 빵을 좀 먹었다.
4 그는 아침에 일어나자마자 물 한 컵을 마신다.
5 우리는 티켓을 예매하지 않았지만 여전히 뮤지컬을 볼 수 있었다.
6 내년에 승진을 한다면 네게 멋진 저녁을 대접할게.

1 listening to the radio
2 Having failed the exam

3 Having had a big lunch
4 Having so much work to do
5 Having the flu, I couldn't do
6 It raining tomorrow, we'll have to cancel
7 There being so many cars on the road

REVIEW

p. 96~97

1 embarrassing	2 parked
3 charming	4 cornered
5 injured	6 Fallen
7 disapproving	8 interested
9 excited	10 tempting
11 convincing	12 frightened

해설/해석

1 그의 행동(His behavior)이 창피하게 만드는 것이므로, embarrassing이 적절
그의 행동은 창피스러웠다.

2 자동차(The car)는 주차되는 것이므로 parked가 적절
저 밴 옆에 주차된 자동차가 내 것이다.

3 오래된 시골집(old cottage)이 사람을 매료시키는 것이므로 charming이 적절
나의 부모님은 현재 멋지고 오래된 시골집에서 살고 있다.

4 동물(animal)이 궁지에 몰리는 것이므로 cornered가 적절
궁지에 몰린 동물이 가장 위험하다.

5 그 남자(man)가 부상을 당하는 것(수동)이므로 injured가 적절
구급차가 그 부상당한 남자를 병원으로 실어갔다.

6 나무(trees)가 폭풍에 의해 이미 쓰러진 것이므로 완료형인 Fallen이 적절
폭풍이 끝나고 쓰러진 나무가 인근을 어지럽혔다.

7 선생님이 그 학급을 못마땅해 하여 그러한 시선을 보내는 것(능동)이므로 disapproving이 적절
선생님은 그 학급에 못마땅해 하는 시선을 보냈다.

8 그녀(she)가 흥미를 갖는 것이므로 interested가 적절
그녀는 그가 하는 이야기에 흥미를 갖는 듯 보였다.

9 팬들(fans)이 흥분하는 것이므로 excited가 적절
흥분한 팬들이 소리 지르고 환호하며 모두 일어섰다.

10 제안(your offer)이 구미가 당기는 것이므로 tempting이 적절
너의 제안은 구미가 당기지만 생각해 볼 시간이 좀 필요해.

11 주장(argument)이 설득력이 있는 것이므로 convincing이 적절
그녀는 토론 시간 동안 매우 설득력이 있는 주장을 펼쳤다.

12 개(dogs)가 놀라는 것이므로 frightened가 적절
폭풍이 부는 동안 깜짝 놀란 개들이 우리 안에서 낑낑거렸다.

1 annoying	2 confusing
3 closed	4 shocking
5 bored	6 surprising
7 disgusting	8 entertaining
9 introduced	10 fascinating
11 exciting	12 interested

해설/해석

1 소리 지르는 아기들(Screaming babies)이 다른 누군가를 짜증나게 하는 원인이므로 annoying이 적절
소리 지르며 우는 아기들은 다른 승객들을 짜증나게 할 수 있다.

2 도로 표지판(The road signs)이 보는 사람을 혼란스럽게 하는 원인이므로 confusing이 적절
이 주변의 도로 표지판은 아주 혼란스럽다.

3 닫힌 문(the door)이므로 완료의 의미인 closed가 적절
로봇은 닫힌 문을 통과하지 못했다.

4 마크가 운전시험에 떨어졌다는 사실이 듣는 사람에게 충격을 주는 원인이므로 shocking이 적절
마크가 운전 시험에 떨어졌다는 사실은 상당히 충격적이었다.

5 내가 게임에 지루함을 느끼는 것이므로 bored가 적절
나는 이 게임을 하는 것이 지루해. 밖에 나가자.

6 심판의 판정(The referee's decision)이 다른 누군가를 놀라게 하는 원인이므로 surprising이 적절
그 심판의 판정은 전혀 놀라운 것이 아니었다.

7 흡연 습관(habit)이 다른 사람을 역겹게 하는 원인이므로 disgusting이 적절
흡연은 아주 역겨운 습관이야! 나는 네가 금연하길 바라.

8 광대(clown)가 다른 누군가를 재미있게 해주는 것이므로 entertaining이 적절
그 광대는 재미있었고, 그 마술사는 굉장했다.

9 연사(speaker)가 소개되는 것이므로 수동인 introduced가 적절
그 회의에서 소개된 연사는 큰 환영을 받았다.

10 책의 이야기가 환상적인 것이므로 fascinating이 적절
히말라야 여행에 대한 책의 이야기는 환상적이었다.

11 돌아가는 바퀴(The spinning wheel)이 신나게 만들어 주는 것이므로 exciting이 적절
놀이공원의 돌아가는 바퀴는 정말 신난다.

12 제퍼슨 씨가 관심을 갖는 것이므로 interested가 적절
제퍼슨 씨는 이 교수님이 그에게 설명해 준 그 이론에 관심이 있는 듯 보였다.

1 repaired	2 틀린 것 없음
3 irritating	4 called
5 unopened	6 waiting
7 틀린 것 없음	8 disappointed
9 틀린 것 없음	10 틀린 것 없음
11 surprised	12 Not knowing

해설/해석

1 그녀의 자동차(her car)가 수리되는 것이므로 repaired가 적절
그녀는 자신의 자동차 수리를 맡겼다.

2 존(John)이 두려움을 느끼는 것이므로 terrified가 적절
존은 직장을 잃는 것을 두려워한다.

3 소음(That noise)이 짜증나게 하는 원인이므로 irritating이 적절
그 소음은 짜증이 난다. 제발 그만해!

4 내 이름(my name)이 불리는 것이므로 called가 적절
나는 이 선생님에 의해 내 이름이 불리는 것을 들었다.

5 그의 편지(his letter)가 개봉되지 않은 상태로 남아 있는 것이므로 unopened가 적절
그녀는 그의 편지를 개봉하지 않은 채로 상자 안에 남겨 두었다.

6 그(him)가 기다리는 것이므로 waiting이 적절
너는 그를 그렇게 오랫동안 기다리게 해서는 안 돼.

7 내(I)가 기쁨을 느끼는 것이므로 delighted가 적절
나는 너를 이렇게 빨리 다시 보게 되어 기쁘다.

8 내(I)가 실망을 느끼는 것이므로 disappointed가 적절
나는 너의 결정을 듣게 되어 실망스러웠다.

9 현대 미술(modern art)이 혼란스러움과 지겨움을 느끼게 하는 원인이므로 confusing과 boring이 적절
나는 현대 미술이 매우 혼란스럽고 지겹다고 생각한다.

10 제시카의 음식(her food)이 손대지 않은 상태로 남아 있는 것이므로 untouched가 적절
제시카는 자신의 음식을 손대지 않은 채로 접시 위에 남겨 두었다.

11 내가 놀라는 것이므로 surprised가 적절
나는 오늘 은행의 긴 줄을 보고 놀랐다.

12 분사구문의 부정은 앞에 not을 붙임
무엇을 해야 하는지 몰라서, 그 어린 소녀는 울기 시작했다.

D

1 Being an international city
2 (Being) Seen upside down
3 The sign being written in French
4 Having met him many times before
5 Not having enough money to take a taxi
6 (Before) Coming to class
7 Waiting for her nails to dry
8 Not knowing what to do

해설/해석

1 접속사(Because)와 주어(New York)를 생략하고, 동사를 -ing형으로 바꿈
뉴욕은 큰 국제도시이므로, 훌륭한 토속 음식점이 많다.

2 접속사(When)와 주어(the image)를 생략하고, 동사를 -ing형으로 바꾼다. 이때 분사구문의 being은 생략 가능
뒤집어보면 그 이미지는 웃는 얼굴 같이 보인다.

3 부사절의 주어인 the sign과 주절의 주어인 I가 같지 않아서 주어를 생략하고 분사구문을 만들 수 없다. 주어 the sign은 그대로 살리고 be동사를 -ing형으로 바꾸어 분사구문을 만듦
표지판이 프랑스어로 쓰여 있어서 나는 그것을 이해할 수 없었다.

4 접속사(As)와 주어(I)를 생략하고, 분사 구문의 시제(had met)가 주절의 시제(recognized)보다 앞서므로 「having+과거분사」가 적절
나는 전에 그를 여러 번 만났기 때문에, 그를 즉시 알아볼 수 있었다.

5 분사 구문의 부정은 분사 앞에 not을 붙임
나는 택시를 탈 만큼 충분한 돈이 없었기 때문에 집에 걸어갔다.

6 접속사(Before)와 주어(Jason)를 생략하고 동사를 -ing형으로 바꾼다. after, before, although 등 추측하기 어려운 접속사는 남겨 두기도 함
제이슨은 수업에 오기 전에, 대개 커피 한 잔을 마신다.

7 접속사(While)와 주어(Jini)를 생략하고 동사를 -ing형으로 바꿈
지니는 손톱이 마르기를 기다리는 동안, 잡지를 읽고 있었다.

8 접속사(Because)와 주어(the boy)를 생략하고, 동사를 -ing형으로 바꾼 뒤, 분사구문의 -ing 앞에 not을 붙임
그 소년은 무엇을 해야 할지 몰라서 울음을 터뜨렸다.

REVIEW PLUS

p. 98

1 ⑤ 2 ② 3 ②
4 Because(As/Since 등) Jiwoo grew up[has grown up] overseas, she enjoys eating foods from other countries.

해설/해석

1 ⑤ 빅토리아 폭포(The Victoria Falls)가 보는 사람을 놀라게 하므로 amazing이 적절
① 오늘의 퍼즐은 헷갈린다.
② '쏘우 II'는 정말 무서운 영화였다.
③ 사라는 게임에서 지자 매우 실망했다.
④ 최 씨의 사고에 관한 뉴스는 불쾌했다.
⑤ 빅토리아 폭포는 네가 보게 될 가장 놀라운 광경일 것이다.

2 ② 저녁을 먹은 것은 더는 먹고 싶지 않은 시점인 지금보다 먼저 일어난 일이므로 Having had a big dinner already가 적절
① 어젯밤 내가 TV를 보고 있을 때 전화가 왔다.
② 저녁을 이미 많이 먹어서 나는 더는 먹고 싶지 않다.
③ 켈리는 보고서를 끝마치려고 서두르다가 실수로 컴퓨터를 껐다.
④ 막대기가 공중으로 던져진 후에 개에 의해 잡혔다.
⑤ 내가 목욕을 하는 동안 물이 욕조 양옆으로 새어 나갔다.

3 ② 주어(I)가 창피스러움을 느끼는 것이므로 embarrassing이 아니라 embarrassed가 적절
① A: 나는 오늘 수업을 못 들었어. 수업은 재미있었니?
B: 응. 굉장했어.
② A: 오늘 지선이 앞에서 넘어진 것은 정말 창피스러웠어.
B: 그러게 말이야. 내가 다 창피했어.
③ A: 너는 알렉스가 나에게 관심이 있다고 생각하니?
B: 그럴 수도 있을 것 같아. 그는 네가 지나갈 때 항상 쳐다보고 미소를 지어.
④ A: 저것은 정말 재미있는 놀이 기구였어. 한 번 더 탈까?
B: 음, 나는 그렇게 재미있는 것 같지 않아. 대신 다른 거 타보자.
⑤ A: 비행은 어땠니? 나는 네가 홍콩에서 네 시간 경유를 했다고 들었어.
B: 응, 맞아. 피곤한 일이었어. 다음에는 직항을 타야겠어.

4 「having+p.p.」로 시작하는 분사 구문의 시제는 주절의 시제보다 앞선다는 뜻이므로, 과거 시제인 grew up이나 현재완료 has grown up이 적절. 이유나 원인의 부사절을 이끄는 접속사는 because, since, as 등이 있음
지우는 한국 여권을 가지고 있지만, 그녀는 자신을 세계 시민이라고 생각하기를 좋아한다. 그녀는 아버지가 외교관이어서 수년간 여러 나라에서 살며 공부했다. 당연히, 지우는 외국에서 자랐기 때문에 다른 나라의 음식을 먹는 것을 즐긴다. 그녀가 가장 좋아하는 음식 중에는 멕시코의 타코, 중국의 만두, 이탈리아 피자가 있다. 물론 그녀는 모국의 음식, 특히 잡채를 좋아한다.

PART 16

Unit 57 EXERCISES p. 101

A

1 or 2 and
3 but 4 and
5 but 6 or

해석

1 너는 97년 6월에 태어났니, 아니면 98년 6월에 태어났니?
2 아이들은 거대한 눈 요새를 만들고 눈덩이를 던졌다.
3 나는 밤새 숙제를 했지만, 끝내지 못했다.
4 한나의 아버지와 우리 삼촌은 대학 때 가장 친한 친구였다.
5 전자사전은 편리하지만 비싸다.
6 그녀가 전화를 받지 않았다. 그녀는 아마 자고 있었거나 샤워 중이었을 것이다.

B

1 yet 2 nor 3 so 4 for

해석

1 햇볕은 꽤 따뜻하지만, 공기는 서늘하다.
2 나는 회의에 가지 않았고, 그들도 가지 않았다.
3 비가 많이 와서, 나는 창문을 닫으려고 일어섰다.
4 날씨가 너무 더워서 나는 정말로 수영하러 가고 싶었다.

C

1 Jim stayed home all day, for he was feeling quite ill.
2 My knee started hurting again, so I stopped running.
3 John has a Ph.D. in engineering, yet he continues to work as a waiter.
4 Susan wasn't answering her phone, nor was she answering her email.
5 The customers didn't like its new product, nor did they like its services.
6 Erick was good at singing and dancing, yet he didn't want to be a singer.

해석

1 짐은 많이 아파서 온종일 집에 있었다.
2 내 무릎이 다시 아프기 시작해서, 나는 달리기를 멈췄다.
3 존은 공학 박사 학위가 있지만, 계속해서 웨이터로 일한다.
4 수잔은 전화를 받지 않았고, 이메일에 답장도 하지 않았다.
5 고객들은 새로운 상품을 좋아하지 않았고, 서비스도 마음에 들어 하지 않았다.
6 에릭은 노래를 잘하고 춤을 잘 췄지만 가수가 되고 싶어 하지 않았다.

Unit 58 EXERCISES p. 103

A

1 Tracy is not only clever but also hard-working.
2 We should either walk quickly or take a taxi.
3 Neither Mike nor his sisters like fast food.
4 The crowd at the stadium was both large and enthusiastic.
5 She as well as I was not invited to the party.

해석

1 트레이시는 똑똑할 뿐만 아니라 일도 열심히 한다.
2 우리는 빨리 걷거나 택시를 타야 한다.
3 마이크도, 그의 여동생들도 패스트푸드를 좋아하지 않는다.
4 경기장에 관중이 많았고 열광적이었다.
5 나뿐만 아니라 그녀도 파티에 초대받지 못했다.

B

1 enjoys 2 need
3 are 4 has
5 is 6 are
7 have

해석

1 캐시뿐만 아니라 데비도 음악 듣는 것을 좋아한다.
2 주방과 식당 모두 페인트칠이 필요하다.
3 우리 언니나 오빠들이 내게 운전하는 것을 가르쳐 줄 것이다.
4 LA 뿐만 아니라 샌프란시스코에도 많은 중국인 공동체가 있다.
5 이 간단한 식사를 준비하는 데는 시간과 노력이 들지 않는다.
6 팀과 제임스는 모두 이번 여름에 앙코르 와트를 방문할 계획이다.
7 리사 뿐만 아니라 그녀의 여동생들도 작년부터 LA에 살고 있다.

C

1 skiing, skating 2 nor
3 틀린 것 없음 4 or
5 틀린 것 없음 6 shouting
7 want

해석

1 나의 아버지는 스키, 스케이트, 수영을 좋아한다.
2 켈리도 너도 클럽에 가입할 수 없을 것이다.
3 너는 오른쪽으로도 왼쪽으로도 꺾어서는 안 돼. 똑바로 가.
4 나의 영국인 친구들은 오늘이나 내일 떠날 것이다.
5 톰이나 내가 공항에 샘을 데리러 갈 것이다.
6 안전 요원이 팔을 휘두르며 내게 소리치고 있었다.
7 우리 부모님과 우리 형은 산에서 휴가를 보내고 싶어 한다.

Unit 59 EXERCISES p. 106~107

A

1 Did you hear √he'll be leaving soon?
2 It was quite surprising √he passed the exam.
3 I think √the lawn in your backyard needs trimming.
4 The problem is √you aren't being honest enough with me.
5 It is obvious √computers makes our lives far more convenient.
6 The most important point is √nothing is impossible if

you try your best.

해석

1 그가 곧 떠날 거라는 소식을 들었니?
2 그가 시험을 통과했다는 것은 꽤 놀라운 일이었다.
3 내 생각에 너희 뒷마당의 잔디는 손질이 필요한 것 같다.
4 문제는 네가 내게 충분히 솔직하지 않다는 것이다.
5 컴퓨터가 우리의 삶을 훨씬 더 편리하게 만든다는 것은 분명하다.
6 가장 중요한 점은 네가 최선을 다한다면 불가능한 것은 없다는 것이다.

B

1 that
2 whether
3 whether
4 whether
5 Whether
6 that

해석

1 나는 수학이 꽤 재미있다고 생각한다.
2 그것은 모두 그녀가 시간이 충분한지 아닌지에 달렸다.
3 나는 지훈이가 우리 프로젝트에서 자신이 맡은 부분을 끝냈는지 아닌지 궁금하다.
4 메이는 존이 축제에 올 것인지 아닌지 물었다.
5 우리가 이길지 말지는 그 스타 선수의 컨디션에 달려있다.
6 길거리에 그렇게 많은 쓰레기가 있다는 것은 꽤 불쾌한 일이다.

C

1 It is a miracle that you weren't hurt in the accident.
2 It is a big problem that prices are currently going up.
3 It is wrong that you blame others for your own mistakes.
4 It is not surprising at all that Robert was late for school today.
5 It is clear that your audience didn't understand you well enough.

해석

1 네가 그 사고에서 다치지 않은 것은 기적이다.
2 최근에 가격이 계속 상승하고 있는 것은 큰 문제이다.
3 네 실수에 대해 다른 사람들을 비난하는 것은 잘못이다.
4 로버트가 오늘 학교에 늦었다는 것은 전혀 놀랍지 않다.
5 청중이 당신을 충분히 잘 이해하지 못했다는 것은 명백하다.

D

1 I don't know what the man said.
2 Tell me what you had for dinner.
3 We wonder when Yunho will show up.
4 I'd like to know what the teacher said.
5 I wonder where Sara and James went last night.
6 Do you know what Sam gave his best friend, Mike?
7 Could you please tell me where the nearest music shop is?
8 Do you know when Jin's parents will arrive from Melbourne?
9 Could you tell me what you were doing in front of my house?

해석

1 나는 그가 뭐라고 말했는지 모르겠어.
2 네가 저녁으로 무엇을 먹었는지 말해 줘.
3 우리는 윤호가 언제 나타날 것인지 궁금하다.
4 나는 선생님께서 뭐라고 말씀하셨는지 알고 싶다.
5 나는 사라와 제임스가 어젯밤에 어디에 갔었는지 궁금하다.
6 샘이 제일 친한 친구인 마이크에게 무엇을 주었는지 아니?
7 가장 가까운 음반 가게가 어디에 있는지 말해 주시겠어요?
8 진의 부모님이 언제 멜버른에서 도착할지 아니?
9 우리 집 앞에서 무엇을 하고 있었는지 말해 주시겠어요?

1 How do you think she will react
2 I wonder if I will fit in
3 Do you know who won the baseball game
4 He knew that she would overcome her difficulties

Unit 60 EXERCISES

p. 110~111

1 as soon as
2 while
3 because
4 since
5 When
6 since
7 As
8 so that

해석

1 평소와 마찬가지로, 달은 해가 지자마자 떠오를 것이다.
2 우리 아버지는 면도하면서 혼자 콧노래를 흥얼거리는 것을 좋아한다.
3 TV에 결함이 있어서 나는 환불을 요구해야 했다.
4 신디는 아프리카에서 돌아온 후로 매우 바빴다.
5 잭이 도착했을 때, 제이콥과 사라는 이미 커피를 마시고 있었다.
6 우리가 아이였을 때부터 나는 팀을 알아 왔다. 그는 나의 가장 친한 친구 중 한 명이다.
7 시간이 지남에 따라, 나는 한국 문화를 더 잘 이해하게 되었다.
8 그는 가능한 한 빨리 그 일을 끝낼 수 있도록 자신을 도와달라고 내게 말했다.

1 Since you paid for the concert tickets, I insist on paying for dinner.
2 As she was older than him, Greg let the lady take the taxi first.
3 When Jihu was living in Melbourne, he made several new Australian friends.
4 Before I had a chance to explain, he just angrily hung up the phone.
5 I turned the lights off in order that he could have a deep sleep.
6 I have to leave home early tomorrow so that I can catch the first train.
7 As soon as Nicole heard someone knocking at the door, she rushed to answer it.

해석

1 네가 콘서트 표 값을 냈으니까, 내가 저녁을 사야 한다.
2 그레그는 그 숙녀가 자신보다 나이가 들었기 때문에, 그녀가 먼저 택시를 타도록 했다.
3 지후는 멜버른에 살고 있었을 때 몇 명의 새로운 호주 친구들을 사귀었다.
4 내가 설명할 기회를 가지기도 전에 그는 화를 내며 그냥 전화를 끊었다.
5 나는 그가 깊은 잠을 잘 수 있게 전등을 껐다.
6 나는 첫 기차를 탈 수 있도록 내일 일찍 집을 나서야 한다.
7 니콜은 누군가가 문을 두드리는 것을 듣자마자 대답하기 위해 급히 달려 나갔다.

C

1 until	2 Before
3 when	4 after
5 Because	6 so that

해석

1 내 생각에 팀의 다른 사람들이 도착할 때까지 우리가 기다리는 것이 좋겠다.
2 자리에 앉기 전에 내게 물 한 잔을 더 가져다주세요.
3 나는 어제 집에 왔을 때 부모님께서 주무시고 계신 걸 보았다.
4 그는 대학을 졸업한 후 바로 은행에 취업했다.
5 어젯밤에는 너무 추워서 우리는 개를 안에서 자도록 했다.
6 아이스하키 선수들은 다치지 않으려고 많은 보호 장비를 착용한다.

D

1 leaves	2 finish
3 was	4 will look for
5 starts	6 apologizes

해석

1 나는 그가 기차가 떠나기 전에 올 수 있을지 잘 모르겠다.
2 나는 계약이 끝나면 너를 보러 시드니로 갈 것이다.
3 나는 그리스에 있는 동안 아테네에 있는 파르테논 신전을 보러 갔다.
4 그녀는 경영학 석사 과정을 마친 후 미국에서 일자리를 알아볼 것이다.
5 비가 오는 즉시, 우리는 짐을 싸서 집으로 갈 것이다.
6 그가 진심으로 내게 사과할 때까지 나는 그를 용서하지 않을 것이다.

E

1 Rock climbers use talc so that they can grasp slippery rocks.
2 I gave Sally my phone number so that she could contact me.
3 Please arrive early so that we can have lunch together before the meeting.
4 She took an English course so that she could talk with her foreign friends.

해석

1 암벽 등반가들은 미끄러운 바위를 붙잡으려고 활석을 사용한다.
2 나는 샐리가 내게 연락할 수 있도록 그녀에게 나의 연락처를 주었다.
3 우리가 회의를 시작하기 전에 점심을 먹을 수 있도록 일찍 도착해 주세요.
4 그녀는 외국인 친구들과 이야기하기 위해서 영어 강의를 들었다.

Unit 61 EXERCISES

p. 114~115

1 If	2 such
3 whereas	4 Though
5 although	6 Even though
7 in case	8 unless
9 as long as	10 While
11 In case	

해석

1 날씨가 충분히 따뜻하다면, 나는 재킷을 입지 않을 것이다.
2 그것은 너무 비싼 정장이어서 론은 그것을 사기 위해 돈을 빌려야 했다.
3 제이슨은 키가 크고 건장하지만, 그의 남동생인 샘은 키가 작고 말랐다.
4 거의 매일 비가 왔지만 우리는 발리에서의 휴가를 즐겼다.
5 킴은 위험하다는 것을 알았음에도, 집에 혼자 걸어왔다.
6 수의 스페인어는 완벽하지 않았지만, 그녀는 의사소통을 할 수 있다.
7 네가 나에게 연락할 필요가 있을 때를 대비해서 내 전화번호를 냉장고에 남겨 놓았어.
8 해적들은 배의 주인이 자신들이 요구한 것을 하지 않는다면 배를 침몰시키겠다고 협박했다.
9 스미스 부부는 제인의 보모를 구하기만 한다면 오늘 저녁 우리와 함께 할 것이다.
10 어떤 사람들은 대중 앞에서 노래하는 것을 좋아하지만, 다른 사람들은 그것을 꽤 창피하게 생각한다.
11 과제에 대해 너희가 질문이 있을 경우에 대비해서, 나는 내일 오후 내내 연구실에 있겠다.

1 We'll both be late for the concert unless you hurry up.
2 Unless we protect endangered species, many of them will soon disappear.
3 Unless you pay the correct postage in advance, your letter will not be mailed.
4 You cannot apply for a driver's license unless you are eighteen or older.
5 You won't be able to enter the museum unless you book the tickets in advance.

해석

1 네가 서두르지 않으면 우리 둘 다 콘서트에 늦을 것이다.
2 우리가 지금 멸종위기에 처한 종들을 보호하지 않는다면, 곧 그들 중 다수가 사라질 것이다.
3 네가 미리 정확한 우편 요금을 내지 않는다면 네 편지는 발송되지 않을 것이다.
4 네가 18세 이상이 아니라면 너는 운전면허에 응시할 수 없다.
5 티켓을 미리 예매하지 않는다면 너는 박물관에 입장할 수 없을 것이다.

1 ⓒ　2 ⓑ　3 ⓓ　4 ⓐ　5 ⓔ

해석

1 비록 그는 지팡이를 짚고 걷지만, 여전히 꽤 활동적이다.

2 나는 집에 있는 것을 선호하는 반면에, 여자 친구는 밖에 나가는 것을 좋아한다.
3 김 선생님은 여전히 아프지만, 오늘 수업을 할 것이다.
4 비록 나는 너에게 동의하지 않지만, 너의 의견을 존중한다.
5 네가 열심히 노력한다고 해도 짧은 시간에 그 문제를 풀 수는 없을 것이다.

D

1 in case
2 If
3 Whereas
4 unless
5 Although

해석

1 나중에 필요할 때를 대비해서 돈을 좀 저축하는 게 어때?
2 내일 비가 온다면 우리는 그냥 TV를 보면서 실내에 있을 것이다.
3 어떤 사람들은 자주 불평하지 않는 반면, 다른 사람들은 끊임없이 불평한다.
4 요즘은 충분히 열심히 노력하지 않는다면 괜찮은 직업을 가지기 어렵다.
5 미나는 여전히 몹시 목이 말랐음에도, 너무 수줍어서 스미스 부인에게 마실 것을 한 잔 더 부탁할 수 없었다.

E

1 The leather jacket was so expensive that I couldn't buy it.
2 It was so cold that I didn't want to go out without my car.
3 She is such a good student that all the teachers in her school like her.
4 He has such high marks that he has applied for a full scholarship to Oxford.
5 The weather was so beautiful that we decided to go for a swim after dinner.
6 There was such a strong wind that we decided to stay indoors and play cards.

해석

1 그 가죽 재킷은 너무 비싸서 살 수 없었다.
2 너무 추워서 나는 차 없이 나가고 싶지 않았다.
3 그녀는 매우 훌륭한 학생이어서 그녀의 학교 선생님들은 모두 그녀를 좋아한다.
4 그는 성적이 아주 좋아서 옥스퍼드 전액 장학금에 지원했다.
5 날씨가 너무나 좋아서 우리는 저녁을 먹고 나서 수영하러 가기로 결정했다.
6 바람이 너무 세게 불어서 우리는 집안에 머물면서 카드놀이를 하기로 결정했다.

REVIEW

p. 116~117

A

1 as
2 As soon as
3 until
4 before
5 As
6 As soon as
7 before
8 When
9 until
10 since
11 As
12 until

해설/해석

1 '나이가 들어감에 따라'라는 의미이므로 as가 적절
그는 나이가 들어감에 따라 더 현명해졌다.
2 '소식을 듣자마자'라는 의미이므로 As soon as가 적절
마이클은 그 소식을 듣자마자 웃음을 터뜨렸다.
3 '무서운 장면이 지나갈 때까지'라는 의미이므로 until이 적절
제니는 무서운 영화 장면이 지나갈 때까지 눈을 감았다.
4 '앉기 전에'라는 의미이므로 before가 적절
저녁 식사하러 앉기 전에 꼭 손을 깨끗이 하도록 해라.
5 '점점 늦어지기 때문에'라는 의미이므로 As가 적절
점점 늦어지니까 설거지는 내일까지 내버려 두자.
6 '기적이 울리자마자'라는 의미이므로 As soon as가 적절
차장이 기적을 울리자마자, 기차가 출발할 것이다.
7 '제출하기 전에'라는 의미이므로 before가 적절
점수를 받기 위해 과제를 제출하기 전에 항상 주의 깊게 확인해라.
8 '여덟 살 때'라는 의미이므로 When이 적절
마크는 여덟 살 때, 자전거 사고로 떨어져 다리가 부러졌다.
9 '해가 질 때까지'라는 의미이므로 until이 적절
캐롤은 해가 질 때까지 해변에 머물렀다.
10 '아이였을 때부터'라는 의미이므로 since가 적절
나는 앤이 아이였을 때부터 알아왔다. 그녀는 내 친구의 딸이다.
11 '위층에 다가감에 따라'라는 의미이므로 As가 적절
우리가 위층에 다가감에 따라 소음은 점점 더 커졌다.
12 '다음 달에 용돈을 받을 때까지'라는 의미이므로 until이 적절
미안하지만, 다음 달에 용돈을 받을 때까지 네게 저녁을 사줄 수 없어.

B

1 hear
2 lives with
3 enjoy
4 Since, As 등
5 had to
6 unless
7 dirty
8 Although, Though 등
9 drive
10 because, since, as 등
11 but, yet 등
12 while, whereas 등

해설/해석

1 '소식을 들을 때까지'라는 의미로, 시간 부사절에서는 현재가 미래를 대신하므로 hear가 적절
너에게 연락을 받을 때까지 기다릴게.
2 「neither A nor B」는 'A와 B 둘 다 아니다'라는 의미이고, B(Seho)에 동사의 수를 일치시키므로 lives with가 적절
지호와 세호 모두 더는 부모님과 함께 살지 않는다.
3 nor는 '~도 또한 아니다'라는 의미로 절과 절을 연결하는 접속사이다. 「nor does+주어+동사원형」이므로 enjoy가 적절
수하는 그림 그리는 것을 좋아하지 않고, 노래하는 것 또한 좋아하지 않는다.
4 '기차 시간보다 일찍 왔기 때문에'라는 의미가 되어야 하므로, 이유를 나타내는 Since나 As 등의 접속사가 적절
우리가 기차 시간보다 일찍 왔으니까, 커피 한 잔 마시자.
5 「so … that ~」은 '너무 …해서 그 결과 ~하다'라는 뜻으로, 과거

에 햇살이 밝았던 것이므로 선글라스를 '써야 했다'라는 의미가 되도록 had to가 적절
햇살이 너무나 밝아서 우리는 진한 선글라스를 써야만 했다.

6 '먹지 않으면 배가 고플 것이다'라는 의미가 되어야 자연스러우므로 if를 unless로 고쳐야 한다.
간식을 먹지 않으면 배구 연습을 하는 동안에 배가 고플 것이다.

7 「both A and B」는 'A와 B 둘 다'라는 의미의 상관 접속사로, A와 B는 병렬 구조를 가져야 하므로 dirty가 적절
우리가 지난주에 머물렀던 호텔방은 춥고 더러웠다.

8 '비록 대학을 중퇴했지만'이라는 의미가 되어야 하므로 Although나 Though 등이 적절
비록 그는 대학을 중퇴했지만, 용케도 부자가 되었다.

9 등위 접속사 and로 병렬 연결된 동사로 can(조동사) 뒤에 동사원형 vote와 get이 왔으므로 drive가 적절
이제 너는 열여덟 살이 지났으니까 투표할 수도, 결혼할 수도, 운전을 할 수도 있다.

10 '숙제가 있기 때문에 같이 못 간다'는 의미가 되어야 하므로 이유를 나타내는 접속사 because, since, as 등이 적절
나는 해야 할 숙제가 있어서 오늘밤 너와 함께 쇼를 보러 갈 수 없다.

11 '부탁했지만 주저했다'는 의미이므로 두 절이 상반된 의미를 나타내는 접속사 but 또는 yet 등이 적절
샘은 캐리에게 토론 클럽에 참여하라고 부탁했지만 그녀는 받아들이기를 주저했다.

12 '다른 나라에서는 모욕인 반면에'라는 의미이므로 양보절을 이끄는 접속사 while 또는 whereas 등이 적절
어떤 나라에서 'V' 표시는 '승리'를 상징하는 반면 다른 나라에서는 모욕의 의미로 사용된다.

C

1 is	2 will stay in
3 is	4 are
5 eat	6 don't
7 are	8 looks
9 wear	10 are
11 are	12 keep

해설/해석

1 「either A or B」는 B(work)에 동사의 수를 일치시키므로 is가 적절
공부나 일이 조쉬가 해야 할 일이다.

2 오늘 밤에 집에 있을 것이라는 미래의 의미이므로 will stay in이 적절
사라가 나를 초대하지 않으면 나는 오늘 밤에 그냥 집에 있을 거야.

3 「neither A nor B」는 B(German)에 동사의 수를 일치시키므로 is가 적절
스페인어도 독일어도 지금 한국에서 많이 배우지 않는다.

4 「not only A but also B」는 B(soccer players)에 동사의 수를 일치시키므로 are가 적절
야구 선수들뿐만 아니라 축구 선수들도 많은 돈을 받는다.

5 「neither A nor B」는 B(I)에 동사의 수를 일치시키므로 eat이 적절
우리 아버지와 나는 둘 다 생선회를 먹지 않아요. 우리는 스테이크를 먹겠어요. 고마워요.

6 조건 부사절에서는 현재 시제가 미래 시제를 대신하므로 don't가 적절
두 시까지 오지 못하면 예약이 취소될 것입니다.

7 「either A or B」는 B(his brothers)에 동사의 수를 일치시키므로 are가 적절
존이나 그의 남동생들이 이 방을 쓸 예정이다.

8 「B as well as A」는 'A뿐만 아니라 B도'의 뜻으로, 의미상 B를 더 강조, B(Tim)에 동사의 수를 일치시키므로 looks가 적절
그의 친구들뿐만 아니라 팀 또한 매년 스키 캠프를 기다린다.

9 '더 따뜻한 코트를 입지 않는다면'의 의미가 되어야 하고, unless는 'if ~ not'이라는 조건과 부정의 의미를 동시에 가지므로 wear가 적절, 조건 부사절에서는 현재가 미래를 대신함
만약 네가 더 따뜻한 코트를 입지 않는다면, 오늘 저녁에 너는 추울 것이다.

10 「both A and B」는 복수동사로 받으므로 are가 적절
캔버라와 오타와는 둘 다 수도 이름이다.

11 「not only A but also B」 B는 B에 동사의 수를 일치시키므로 are가 적절
코치뿐만 아니라 팀원들도 경기 결과에 만족하고 있다.

12 if 조건 부사절에서는 현재가 미래를 대신하므로 keep이 적절
양상추를 밀폐 용기에 담아 냉장고에 보관한다면, 양상추는 아삭아삭한 상태를 유지할 것이다.

1 Gary will	2 riding
3 such	4 sailing
5 patient	6 is
7 is	8 have
9 attends	10 nor
11 is	12 so

해설/해석

1 간접의문문은 「의문사+주어+동사」의 어순이므로 Gary will이 적절
나는 개리가 언제 도착할지 궁금하다.

2 「either A or B」에서 A와 B는 병렬 구조를 이루어야 하므로 riding이 적절
그는 수영도, 보트 타는 것도 좋아하지 않는다.

3 「such(+a/an)+형용사+명사」의 구문이 되어야 하므로 such가 적절
나는 그에게 그렇게 예쁜 딸이 있는 것을 보고 놀랐다.

4 「both A and B」에서 A와 B는 병렬 구조를 이루어야 하므로 sailing이 적절
나의 아버지는 여가에 낚시와 배 타는 것을 즐기신다.

5 「not only A but also B」의 상관 접속사 구문으로 A(kind)와 B(patience)가 형용사로 병렬 구조를 이루어야 하므로 patient가 적절
올해 나의 담임선생님은 친절할 뿐만 아니라 인내심도 많다.

6 「neither A nor B」는 B(their mother)에 동사의 수를 일치시키므로 is가 적절
아이들도 그들의 어머니도 지금 집에 없다.

7 「either A or B」는 B(Henry)에 동사의 수를 일치시키므로 is가 적절

오늘은 샐리나 헨리가 저녁을 준비하기로 되어 있다.

8 Unless는 'if ~ not'이라는 조건과 부정의 의미를 동시에 가지므로 따로 not이 필요 없다.

네가 여행 경비를 낼 충분한 돈이 없다면, 내가 좀 빌려 줄게.

9 「neither A nor B」는 'A와 B 둘 다 아니다'의 뜻으로 부정어 not을 따로 쓰지 않으므로 attends가 적절

그 코치와 인기 선수 모두 기자 회견에 참석하지 않는다.

10 「neither A nor B」는 상관 접속사이므로 nor가 적절

파멜라와 샬 모두 단것을 좋아하지 않기 때문에 굳이 디저트를 만들지 않아도 된다.

11 if 조건절에서는 현재가 미래를 대신하므로 is가 적절

내일 날씨가 좋다면, 내가 너와 네 남동생을 낚시에 데려갈게.

12 such는 형용사만을 수식할 수 없고, 「so … that ~」은 '너무 …해서 그 결과 ~하다'의 뜻으로, 명사 없이 「so+형용사/부사+that」으로 쓰므로 so가 적절

제프는 너무나 바빠서 지난주에 자신을 도울 조수를 고용해야 했다.

REVIEW PLUS

p. 118

1 ⑤ 2 ④

해설/해석

1 ⑤ '진실을 이야기해 주지 않는다면'이라는 의미가 되어야 하고 뒤에 not이 있으므로 if가 적절

이상하게도, 그 소년이나 그의 누나 모두 자신들에게 어떤 일이 일어났는지 경찰관에게 이야기하려 하지 않았다. 당황한 그 경찰관은 만약 그들이 자신에게 진실을 이야기해 주지 않는다면, 그들을 경찰서로 데리고 가야 할 것이라고 참을성 있게 설명했다.

2 ④ neither A nor B는 B(his sister)에 동사의 수를 일치시켜야 하므로 likes가 적절

제프와 그의 누나는 토요일에 우리와 함께 영화 보러 갈 것이다. 제프와 그의 누나 둘 다 공포 영화를 좋아하지 않기 때문에, 우리는 '런어웨이 브라이드' 같은 로맨틱 코미디나 '글래디에이터' 같은 드라마를 봐야 할 것이다.

③

해설/해석

(A) '좋게 들릴 수도 있지만'이라는 의미이므로 Even though가 적절 (B) '가격이 내려가기 시작할 때'라는 의미이므로, When이 적절 (C) 「both A and B」가 주어로 쓰였을 때는 복수동사를 취하므로 are가 적절

모든 사람은 상품이나 서비스의 가격 상승인 인플레이션에는 익숙하다. 하지만, "디플레이션"은 어떨까? 디플레이션은 상품의 가격이 점진적으로 떨어지는 것을 일컫는다. 이것이 좋게 들릴 수도 있겠지만, 사실은 그렇지 않다. 가격이 하락하기 시작하면 사람들은 좀 더 시간이 지나면 가격이 더 내려갈 것으로 생각하기 때문에 TV나 자동차, 옷 등과 같은 물건의 구매를 멈춘다. 가격이 너무나 빨리 내려가서 그 결과 회사들은 문을 닫거나 직원들을 해고한다. 실제로, 과도한 인플레이션과 디플레이션 모두는 경제에 해롭다.

Unit 62 EXERCISES

p. 122~123

1 was
2 are
3 are
4 which
5 whose
6 are
7 that
8 which
9 which

해석

1 우리가 지금을 맡긴 그 남자는 범죄자였다.
2 우리를 이 파티에 초대한 그 부부가 너의 뒤에 서 있다.
3 옆집에 사는 아이들은 매우 예의가 바르다.
4 그들이 마신 우유가 상한 것이어서 그들은 모두 아팠다.
5 네가 방금 이름을 부른 신사는 한 시간 전에 떠났다.
6 버스정류장으로 가는 길을 묻는 사람들은 노르웨이에서 온 사람들이다.
7 현대 영문학을 가르치는 그 교수는 훌륭한 강사다.
8 냉장고는 저온으로 음식을 보존하는 데 사용되는 주방 제품이다.
9 수백 마리의 박쥐가 발견된 그 동굴은 마을에서 겨우 몇 킬로미터 떨어져 있다.

1 ⓓ which you use to unlock a door
2 ⓒ who works in a coffee shop
3 ⓖ who is in charge of a museum, art gallery, or library
4 ⓑ which you use to play tennis
5 ⓗ who is famous, especially in the entertainment business
6 ⓐ who shops at a store
7 ⓔ which help you see better
8 ⓕ which you use to pick up and eat food

해석

1 열쇠는 문을 열 때 쓰는 것이다.
2 바리스타는 커피 전문점에서 일하는 사람이다.
3 큐레이터는 박물관이나 미술관, 도서관을 책임지는 사람이다.
4 라켓은 테니스를 할 때 사용하는 것이다.
5 유명 인사는 특히 연예계에서 유명한 사람이다.
6 고객은 가게에서 물건을 사는 사람이다.
7 안경은 더 잘 보게 도와주는 물건이다.
8 포크는 음식을 찍어 먹는 데 사용하는 것이다.

1 Did you see the postcard which came this morning?
2 The books which were written by Jane Austen are my favorite.
3 The people who live upstairs talk very loudly in the mornings.
4 Do you remember the girl who showed us the way to

the mall?

5 She changed her mind, which made us all pleased.

6 I was introduced to Mark's sister Jenny, who is a famous actress.

해석

1 오늘 아침에 온 우편엽서를 봤니?

2 제인 오스틴이 쓴 책들이 내가 가장 좋아하는 것이다.

3 위층에 사는 사람들은 아침마다 매우 크게 이야기한다.

4 우리에게 쇼핑몰로 가는 길을 알려준 그 소녀를 기억하니?

5 그녀는 마음을 바꾸었는데 그것이 우리 모두를 기쁘게 했다.

6 나는 마크의 여동생 제니에게 소개되었는데 그녀는 유명한 배우이다.

D

1 Where's the can of cola which I bought yesterday?

2 Here's the magazine which I told you about earlier.

3 The teacher whom I wanted to consult with was away on her honeymoon.

4 The pictures which Jim took on his trip to Australia were very impressive.

5 The man whom I worked with last week has become one of my closest friends.

6 The book which I misplaced last week was found in the first drawer of my desk.

해석

1 내가 어제 사온 콜라 어디 있니?

2 여기 내가 전에 너에게 말했던 잡지가 있다.

3 내가 상담하고 싶었던 선생님은 신혼여행을 떠났다.

4 짐이 호주 여행에서 찍은 사진들은 매우 인상적이었다.

5 지난주에 내가 함께 일했던 그 남자는 나의 가장 친한 친구 중 한 명이 되었다.

6 내가 지난주에 어디다 두고 찾지 못했던 그 책은 내 책상 첫 번째 서랍에서 발견되었다.

Unit 63 EXERCISES

p. 126~127

A

1 that/which	2 that/which
3 that/which	4 that
5 which	6 which
7 which	8 which
9 which	10 which
11 that/which	

해석

1 나의 오빠는 웹사이트를 디자인하는 회사에 다닌다.

2 나는 지난주에 온라인으로 산 신발을 엄마에게 보여주었다.

3 골다공증은 주로 나이가 많은 사람들이 잘 걸리는 질병이다.

4 그 팝스타는 퍼지고 있는 모든 소문을 부인했다.

5 그 건물은 1950년대에 지어졌고 지금은 박물관으로 사용되고 있다.

6 그 밴드는 그들의 최신 히트곡을 연주했는데, 그것은 모든 사람을 따라 부르게 했다.

7 우리는 파라다이스 호텔에 머물렀는데, 그곳은 내 친구가 추천한 곳이었다.

8 그가 보고 있던 그 그림은 유명 화가가 그린 것이었다.

9 집들이 있는 산 중턱이 비 때문에 약해지고 있다.

10 '24'의 마지막 편을 인터넷으로 내려 받아 봤는데, 정말 재미있었다.

11 네가 어제 빅마트에서 산 겨울 코트가 오늘은 50% 할인 판매를 한다.

B

1 what	2 what	3 that	4 that
5 that	6 What	7 that	8 What
9 that	10 what	11 that	

해석

1 너는 선생님께서 지금 하신 말씀을 들었니?

2 미안하지만 나는 네가 하려고 하는 말이 이해가 안 돼.

3 올해 그가 받은 성적은 작년보다 나았다.

4 런던을 방문 중인 내 친구들은 다음 달에 여기로 돌아올 것이다.

5 나는 파티에 초대되었던 사람들 중 누구도 알지 못했다.

6 우리를 정말로 걱정시킨 것은 그 아이들이 매우 건강해 보이지 않는다는 것이었다.

7 우리가 어제 본 농구 경기는 매우 재미있었다.

8 내가 알고 싶어 했던 것은 주문한 물건을 받는 데 얼마나 걸리느냐는 것이었다.

9 내가 아팠을 때, 네가 쓴 편지들은 내게 많은 위안을 주었다.

10 내가 그녀에게 몇 번을 부탁했음에도, 그녀는 그가 한 말을 내게 해주지 않았다.

11 나는 환경 보호의 중요성에 대해 쓰인 책을 읽고 있다.

C

1 C	2 R	3 R	4 C	5 C	6 C
7 R	8 R	9 R	10 R	11 C	12 C

해석

1 나는 지금 그녀가 파리에 살고 있을지도 모른다고 들었다.

2 코엑스 몰로 가는 버스를 어디서 탈 수 있나요?

3 그녀는 내가 너를 소개시켜 주고 싶은 여자다.

4 모든 사람들은 그들이 변화를 가져올 것이라고 굳게 믿었다.

5 폭발 사고에서 아무도 다치지 않았다는 것은 정말 기적이다.

6 나는 8시까지 집에 오겠다고 어머니께 약속했다.

7 우리는 내가 찾고 있던 정보를 인터넷에서 발견했다.

8 그 남자는 자신이 저지르지도 않은 범죄 때문에 교도소에 보내졌다.

9 내게 공항에 가는 길을 알려준 그 남자는 매우 친절했다.

10 너는 시내에 막 개업한 멕시코 식당에 가봤니?

11 너는 테플론이 지구에서 가장 미끄러운 물질이라는 것을 아니?

12 나는 수가 올해의 졸업생 대표로 뽑혔다는 소식을 들었다.

D

1 what	2 that	3 what	4 what
5 that	6 That	7 that	8 that
9 what	10 that	11 what	12 that

해석

1 솔직히 나는 다음에 무엇을 해야 할지 결정을 할 수 없다.

2 밤새 밖에 내버려 두었던 음식이 모두 상했다.

3 제니퍼에게 네가 학교 가는 길에 본 것을 정확하게 말해.

4 그날 밤 일어난 일에 대한 샘의 이야기는 믿기 어렵다.
5 나는 프랑스에서 우리가 방문했던 작은 마을의 이름을 잊어버렸다.
6 우리 팀이 그 경기에서 이길 것이라는 사실은 의심의 여지가 없었다.
7 네가 앉아 있는 의자는 우리 아버지께서 손수 만드신 것이다.
8 일기예보에 따르면 태풍이 일본으로 접근하고 있다.
9 그가 나를 오해했다. 그는 내가 실제로 하지 않은 것을 내가 했다고 그냥 믿어버렸다.
10 리처드가 자신의 깜짝 파티에 대해 알고 있다는 사실은 약간 실망스럽다.
11 나는 그가 자신이 하고 싶지 않은 것을 내게 하라고 시켜서 그가 싫었다.
12 나는 한국어로 번역된 더글러스 케네디의 책을 읽고 있다.

Unit 64 EXERCISES

p. 130~131

A

1 why	2 how	3 when	4 how
5 where	6 why	7 where	8 when

해석

1 나는 우리 개가 왜 계속 먹기를 거부하는지 모르겠다.
2 전문가들도 여전히 우주가 형성된 방법을 정확히 모른다.
3 1969년은 인류가 처음으로 달에 도달한 해이다.
4 그 스타 요리사는 TV에서 버터 없이 빵을 만드는 방법을 보여주었다.
5 이곳이 지난주에 그레그가 자신의 약혼녀에게 청혼한 식당이다.
6 너는 많은 한국 사람들이 영어를 배우는 이유를 아니?
7 자동차 사고가 일어난 곳에 경찰이 즉시 도착했다.
8 2001년 9월 11일은 테러리스트들이 뉴욕의 세계 무역 센터를 공격한 날이다.

1 I really like how she dresses.
2 Do you know the reason why Jay isn't in class today?
3 Edinburgh is the town where Alexander Graham Bell was born.
4 She didn't want to tell me the reason why she missed the class.
5 Jim asked his teacher how he could improve his pronunciation.
6 All the students look forward to the day when summer vacation begins.
7 Thanksgiving Day is the day when all the family members gather to celebrate the harvest.

해석

1 나는 그녀가 옷을 입는 방식이 좋다.
2 너는 제이가 오늘 수업에 오지 않은 이유를 아니?
3 에든버러는 알렉산더 그레이엄 벨이 태어난 마을이다.
4 그녀는 자신이 수업에 빠진 이유를 내게 말하고 싶어 하지 않았다.
5 짐은 어떻게 발음을 개선할 수 있는 방법을 선생님에게 물었다.
6 모든 학생들은 여름방학이 시작하는 날을 기다린다.
7 추수감사절은 모든 가족이 모여서 수확을 축하하는 날이다.

1 where	2 the way 또는 how 삭제
3 when	4 where
5 why	6 the way 또는 how 삭제
7 when	8 where
9 when	10 when
11 how	12 how 삭제

해석

1 이곳이 차가 버스와 충돌한 정확한 지점이다.
2 시간을 어떻게 보내려고 계획을 세웠는지 말해 줄래?
3 2005년은 지수가 프린스턴에서 경영학 석사를 받은 해였다.
4 도쿄에는 네가 저렴하게 식사를 할 수 있는 작은 식당들이 많다.
5 내가 네가 합격점을 받지 못했던 이유를 설명해 줄게.
6 우리 아버지는 내게 모형비행기를 조립하는 방법을 가르쳐주셨다.
7 네 엄마와 내가 결혼한 날은 춥고 비가 왔다.
8 내가 자란 마을의 그 지역은 완전히 재개발이 되었다.
9 다음 주 목요일이 수리 기사가 우리 집에 오는 날이다.
10 1988년은 한국이 서울에서 올림픽 경기를 개최한 해이다.
11 우리는 모두 그녀가 보안 직원들에 의해 어떤 취급을 받았는지 듣고는 매우 화가 났다.
12 나는 네게 영어를 빠르게 향상시킬 수 있는 쉬운 세 가지 방법을 알려 줄 것이다.

1 However	2 Whatever
3 whenever	4 wherever
5 whoever	6 whatever
7 whomever	8 wherever
9 whatever	10 However
11 Whoever	

해석

1 아무리 피곤하더라도 너는 그것을 해야만 한다.
2 네가 무슨 결정을 내리더라도 너의 부모님은 너를 지지해줄 것이다.
3 버터 대신에 가능하면 언제라도 올리브유를 사용하도록 해라.
4 휴가에 우리는 네가 가고 싶은 곳 어디든지 갈 수 있어. 제한이 없어!
5 헤일리의 푸들을 찾아서 돌려주는 사람은 누구라도 보상을 받을 것이다.
6 나는 무슨 일이 있어도 너를 응원하려고 여기 있는 거야. 그러니 최선을 다하기만 해라.
7 네가 원하는 누구에게든 여분의 콘서트 표를 주어도 좋다.
8 그레이엄 사령관은 영국 해군이 보내는 곳이면 어디든 가야 한다.
9 우리는 날씨가 어떻든 간에 내일 해변에서 배구를 할 것이다.
10 네가 아무리 똑똑하다고 생각해도 김 교수님의 수업이 쉽지 않다는 것을 알게 될 것이다.
11 내 책상에 콜라를 쏟고 그것을 닦지 않은 사람은 누구든 정말 나쁜 사람이다.

REVIEW

p. 132~133

1 why	2 with whom
3 that	4 who
5 Whatever	6 whatever
7 that	8 What

9 who	10 where
11 however	12 whom

해설/해석

1 reason이 선행사, for the reason을 대신하는 관계부사 why가 적절
우리의 계획이 성공 못할 이유가 없다.

2 The man이 선행사인데, 의미상 '지난 프로젝트를 함께 했던'이라는 의미가 되어야 하므로 with whom이 적절
내가 지난 프로젝트를 함께 했던 그 남자는 꽤 도움이 되었다.

3 The hat이 선행사, 목적격 관계대명사 that이 적절
네가 쓰고 있는 모자는 네 머리에 비해 다소 크다.

4 The woman이 선행사, 주격 관계대명사 who가 적절
너의 상태를 체크해 줬던 그 여자는 간호사이다.

5 '이유가 무엇이든지 간에'라는 의미의 Whatever가 적절
이유가 무엇이든 간에 요즘은 더 적은 수의 사람들이 쇼핑한다.

6 '네가 원하는 것이 무엇이든'이라는 의미의 whatever가 적절
스미스 씨나 아니면 그냥 스티브 중에 네 마음에 드는 것으로 날 불러도 좋다.

7 The computer가 선행사, 목적격 관계대명사 that이 적절
내가 일을 위해 사용하는 컴퓨터는 너무 낡았다.

8 did의 목적어가 되면서 선행사를 포함한 관계대명사인 what이 적절
팀이 한 일은 잘못된 것이었다. 이제 그는 그 결과에 직면해야 한다.

9 The child가 선행사, 주격 관계대명사 who가 적절
운동장을 가장 빨리 달려서 가로지르는 아이가 상을 받을 것이다.

10 The place가 선행사, 관계부사 where가 적절
내가 태어난 곳은 너무 작아서 너는 지도에서 그것을 찾을 수조차 없다.

11 '아무리 ~하더라도'라는 의미의 however가 적절
너는 오늘 허드렛일을 아무리 하고 싶지 않더라도 해야 한다.

12 The boy가 선행사, saw의 목적어가 되는 목적격 관계대명사 whom이 적절, we saw for the boy waiting이라는 문장은 성립하지 않으므로 for whom은 적절하지 않음
오늘 아침에 우리가 본 학교 밖에서 기다리던 그 소년은 제니의 남동생이다.

1 however	2 when
3 whom	4 Whatever
5 which	6 whose
7 What	8 whenever
9 that	

해설/해석

1 '그것의 가격이 얼마가 되든지'라는 의미의 however가 적절
만약 내가 무엇인가를 정말 좋아한다면, 그것의 가격이 얼마든 간에 나는 그것을 살 것이다.

2 선행사가 the month로 시간을 나타내므로 관계부사 when이 적절
7월은 대부분의 미국인들이 휴가를 가는 달이다.

3 the sales clerk이 선행사, to의 목적격 관계대명사인 whom이 적절
이 사람이 네가 저번에 이야기를 했던 판매원이니?

4 '네가 무슨 결정을 내리든지'라는 의미의 Whatever가 적절
네가 무슨 결정을 내리든지 나는 그것이 옳은 선택이 되리라 확신한다.

5 subject가 선행사, 전치사 about의 목적어가 되는 목적격 관계대명사 which가 적절
스포츠는 나의 아버지가 몇 시간이고 이야기할 수 있는 주제이다.

6 선행사가 the man, his window에서 his를 대신하는 소유격 관계대명사 whose가 적절
네가 이 사람의 유리창을 깼어. 이제 사과하렴.

7 선행사가 없고 find의 목적어가 되어야 하므로 선행사를 포함하는 관계대명사 What이 적절
내게 가장 소중한 것은 행복이다.

8 '원할 때면 언제든'이라는 의미의 whenever가 적절
24시간 현금 자동 입출금기가 있다. 네가 원할 때면 언제든지 돈을 찾을 수 있다.

9 선행사가 the only picture, 목적격 관계대명사 that이 적절
이것이 그 작가가 죽기 전에 팔았던 유일한 그림이다.

1 ⓐ what he told me
2 ⓕ that I borrowed from the library yesterday
3 ⓒ what she has to do next
4 ⓖ that I need to plug in the notebook computer
5 ⓓ what you saw at the museum
6 ⓗ that I want to wear to the graduation ceremony
7 ⓔ that gave a performance last night
8 ⓑ that you can offer

해설/해석

1 그가 나에게 말한 것을 믿을 수 없다는 의미이므로 what he told me가 적절, believe 다음에 선행사가 없으므로 선행사를 포함하면서 told의 직접목적어가 되는 관계대명사 what이 적절
나는 그가 나에게 말한 것을 믿을 수 없다. 그는 과장하는 경향이 있다.

2 the books가 선행사이므로 관계대명사 that이 적절
나는 어제 도서관에서 빌린 책들을 찾을 수 없다.

3 선행사가 없으므로 선행사를 포함하는 관계대명사 what이 적절
그녀는 다음에 무엇을 해야 할지 확신하지 못한다. 그녀는 조언이 필요하다.

4 the adapter가 선행사이므로 관계대명사 that이 적절
노트북 컴퓨터에 꽂는 데 필요한 어댑터가 어디 있니?

5 선행사가 없으므로 선행사를 포함하는 관계대명사 what이 적절
오늘 박물관은 어땠어? 네가 박물관에서 본 것에 대해 이야기해 줘.

6 the outfit이 선행사이므로 관계대명사 that이 적절
이것은 내가 졸업식에 입고 싶은 옷이다.

7 The hip-hop band가 선행사이므로 주격 관계대명사 that이 적절
어젯밤에 공연을 했던 힙합 밴드는 환상적이었다.

8 the best price가 선행사이고 offer the best price가 되므로 목적격 관계대명사 that이 적절

이것이 당신이 제공할 수 있는 최상의 가격인가요?

D

1 which[that]
2 who[that]
3 that[which]
4 which[that]
5 in which
6 What
7 whenever
8 whatever
9 the way 또는 how 삭제

해설/해석

1 The brown boots가 선행사, 주격 관계대명사로 which나 that이 적절
현관문 옆에 있는 갈색 부츠는 내 것이다.

2 The engineers가 선행사, 사람을 받는 주격 관계대명사 who나 that이 적절
그 건물을 디자인한 기술자들이 상을 받았다.

3 The book이 선행사, are reading의 목적어가 되는 관계대명사이면서 선행사를 포함하지 않는 that이나 which가 적절
네가 읽는 그 책이 그 작가가 쓴 최고의 책이다.

4 the rumors가 선행사, 주격 관계대명사 which[that]이 적절
신디에 대해 퍼지고 있는 그 소문들은 완전히 사실이 아니다.

5 I had all of my important contacts in my address book.이 되므로 in which가 적절
나는 나의 모든 중요한 연락처가 적힌 주소록을 잃어버렸다.

6 know의 목적어가 되면서 선행사를 포함한 관계대명사 What이 적절
내가 알고 싶은 것은 고장 난 히터를 고치는 데 얼마나 오래 걸리느냐는 것이다.

7 '~할 때마다'라는 의미의 whenever가 적절
나는 미국에 오려고 네덜란드를 떠나던 날을 생각할 때마다 운다.

8 '어떤 상황에서도'라는 의미의 whatever가 적절
이 재킷은 어떤 상황에서도 너를 멋져 보이고 돋보이게 해줄 것이다.

9 관계부사 how는 the way와 같이 쓸 수는 없으므로 the way나 how를 삭제해야 한다.
캠프 지도원이 어린이들에게 저녁으로 먹을 물고기를 잡는 방법을 가르쳐 주었다.

REVIEW PLUS

p. 134

1 ②
2 ①

해설/해석

1 (A) 선행사는 the town, your grandfather was born and raised there에서 there를 대신하는 where가 적절 (B) 선행사는 The street performance, feature의 주어가 되는 which가 적절, 계속적 용법이므로 that을 사용하지 않음
• 이곳이 너의 할아버지가 태어나고 자란 마을이다.
• 거리 공연은 노래와 악기 연주를 특징으로 하는데, 유럽에서 흔히 볼 수 있다.

2 (A) 선행사 the file은 사물, 전치사 on의 목적어이지만 전치사 바로 뒤에 온 것이 아니므로 which나 that이 적절 (B) 선행사는 My best friend, see의 목적어가 되는 계속적 용법의 관계대명사 whom이 적절
• 네가 작업하고 있던 파일에 무슨 일이 생긴 거니?
• 나는 학교에서 매일 가장 친한 친구들 만나는데 그는 항상 새롭고 재미있는 말할 거리를 가지고 있다.

②

해설/해석

① know의 목적어가 되는 선행사를 포함한 관계대명사 ② 무엇이라는 의미의 의문사 ③ saw의 목적어가 되는 선행사를 포함한 관계대명사 ④ planning의 목적어가 되는 선행사를 포함한 관계대명사 ⑤ had의 목적어가 되는 선행사를 포함한 관계대명사
① 그가 알고 싶어 하는 것은 너의 이름이다.
② 너의 아버지는 무슨 일을 하시니?
③ 배심원에게 당신이 본 것을 정확하게 말해주세요.
④ 이 편지는 그들이 계획하는 것을 명확하게 보여준다.
⑤ 나는 돈을 많이 갖고 있지는 않았지만, 내가 가지고 있던 것을 그에게 주었다.

① who ② that ③ where

해설/해석

① people이 선행사, rush의 주어가 되는 who가 적절 ② something이 선행사, have bought의 목적어가 되는 that이 적절 ③ a point가 선행사, General customers can afford them at this point.에서 at this point를 대신하므로 where가 적절
얼리어답터는 다른 누군가가 사기 전에 새로운 전자 기기를 사려고 서두르는 사람들이다. 그들이 최신 제품을 사려고 몇 시간씩 줄을 서서 기다리는 것을 쇼핑몰에서 볼 수 있다. 얼리어답터들은 약간 까다롭지만, 그들이 산 것이 마음에 들면 그들은 그것을 다른 사람에게 추천할 것이다. 시간이 지남에 따라, 이 기기들의 가격은 일반 소비자들도 살 수 있을 정도의 선까지 떨어진다.

PART 18

Unit 65 EXERCISES

p. 137

1 goes
2 doesn't arrive
3 spoke
4 were
5 can

해석

1 보은이는 일본에 가면, 일본어를 배울 것이다.
2 윌슨은 빨리 도착하지 않으면, 기차를 놓칠 것이다.
3 수지가 중국어를 한다면, 그녀는 북경을 더 쉽게 여행할 수 있을 텐데.
4 미리암의 시력이 더 좋다면, 그녀는 안경을 쓸 필요가 없을 텐데.
5 에이미는 공부를 열심히 한다면, 가고 싶은 학교에 입학할 수 있다.

1 If we were in Paris, we could see the Eiffel Tower.
2 If the weather were good, Jason would take his dogs for a walk.
3 If they had enough money, they could build the proposed tower.
4 If the trans-Korea railroad were completed, we could travel by rail to Europe.

해석

1 우리는 파리에 있지 않아서 에펠탑을 볼 수 없다.
→ 우리가 파리에 있다면 에펠탑을 볼 수 있을 텐데.
2 날씨가 좋지 않아서, 제이슨은 개를 산책시키지 않을 것이다.
→ 날씨가 좋다면 제이슨은 개를 산책시킬 텐데.
3 그들은 돈이 충분하지 않아서 제안한 타워를 지을 수 없다.
→ 그들에게 돈이 충분하다면 제안한 타워를 지을 수 있을 텐데.
4 한반도 종단 철도가 완성되지 않아서, 우리는 유럽까지 기차로 여행할 수 없다.
→ 한반도 종단 철도가 완성된다면 유럽까지 기차로 여행할 수 있을 텐데.

1 snowed
2 continues
3 were
4 were
5 decreases
6 want

해석

1 눈이 많이 온다면 우리는 밖에 나가서 눈사람을 만들 텐데.
2 지구 온난화가 계속된다면 해수면이 급격히 상승할지도 모른다.
3 경제가 나아진다면 우리 부모님께서는 용돈을 더 주실 수 있을 텐데.
4 서울에는 차가 너무 많다. 차가 더 적다면 교통은 그렇게 혼잡하지 않을 텐데.
5 남극의 어류의 수가 훨씬 더 많이 줄어든다면 펭귄은 먹이를 찾는 데 어려움을 겪을 것이다.
6 많은 나라들이 온실가스를 많이 배출한다. 우리가 지구 온난화를 통제하고 싶다면 우리는 온실가스 배출을 줄여야 한다.

EXERCISES

p. 140~141

1 If the judges had been fair, our team could have won the gold medal.
2 If our teammate Jinho hadn't been sick, we would have won the volleyball match.
3 If radar had been available, the Titanic wouldn't have struck the iceberg and sunk.
4 If we hadn't cut down so many trees, the bald eagle wouldn't have become endangered.
5 If he had saved enough money, he could have bought a car.
6 If I had known there were various kinds of scholarships, I would have applied for them.

해석

1 심판이 공정하지 않아서 우리 팀이 금메달을 딸 수 없었다.
→ 심판이 공정했더라면 우리 팀이 금메달을 땄을 텐데.
2 우리 팀의 진호가 아파서 배구 시합에서 이기지 못했다.
→ 우리 팀의 진호가 아프지 않았더라면 우리는 배구 경기에서 이겼을 텐데.
3 레이더를 사용할 수 없어서 타이타닉 호가 빙산에 충돌해 가라앉았다.
→ 레이더를 사용할 수 있었더라면 타이타닉 호가 빙산에 충돌해 가라앉지는 않았을 텐데.
4 우리가 나무를 너무 많이 잘라내서, 흰머리 독수리가 멸종 위기에 처했다.
→ 우리가 그렇게 많은 나무를 잘라내지 않았더라면 흰머리 독수리가 멸종 위기에 처하지 않았을 텐데.
5 그가 충분한 돈을 저축하지 않아서, 그는 차를 살 수 없었다.
→ 그가 충분한 돈을 저축했다면 그는 차를 살 수 있었을 텐데.
6 나는 다양한 장학금이 있다는 것을 몰라서 신청하지 못했다.
→ 나는 다양한 장학금이 있다는 것을 알았다면 신청했을 텐데.

B

1 If I had studied French, I wouldn't have a difficult time traveling in Africa now.
2 If my brother hadn't spilled milk over my computer, I wouldn't need to buy a new one.
3 If Bell hadn't invented the telephone, we couldn't live a comfortable life.
4 If Mom hadn't gone out to meet her friend, she could teach you how to knit.
5 If we had left home earlier, we could enter the musical theater now.
6 If I had turned on the alarm last night, I would be on the school bus now.

해석

1 나는 프랑스어를 공부하지 않아서 지금 아프리카를 여행하는 데 어려움이 있다. → 내가 프랑스어 공부를 했더라면 지금 아프리카를 여행하는 데 어려움이 없을 텐데.
2 내 동생이 내 컴퓨터에 우유를 쏟아서 새로 하나 사야 한다. → 내 동생이 내 컴퓨터에 우유를 쏟지 않았다면 새로 하나 사야 할 필요가 없을 텐데.
3 벨이 전화기를 발명해서, 우리는 편리한 삶을 살 수 있다. → 벨이 전화기를 발명하지 않았더라면 우리는 편리한 삶을 살 수 없을 텐데.
4 우리 엄마가 친구를 만나러 나갔기 때문에, 네게 바느질 하는 방법을 가르쳐 줄 수 없다. → 우리 엄마가 친구를 만나러 나가지 않았다면 네게 바느질 하는 방법을 가르쳐줄 수 있을 텐데.
5 우리가 집에서 일찍 나오지 않았기 때문에, 지금 뮤지컬 극장에 입장할 수 없다. → 우리가 집에서 일찍 나왔다면, 지금 뮤지컬 극장에 입장할 수 있을 텐데.
6 내가 어젯밤에 알람을 켜놓지 않았기 때문에, 지금 학교 버스를 타고 있지 않다. → 내가 어젯밤에 알람을 켜놨더라면 지금 학교 버스에 타고 있을 텐데.

1 be
2 have
3 hadn't gone
4 had known, have cleaned
5 had sung, have embarrassed
6 hadn't become

7 had defeated

해석

1 만약 네가 이 지름길로 오자고 우기지만 않았더라도 우리는 지금 길을 잃고 헤매지 않을 텐데.
2 그가 옷에 그렇게 많은 돈을 쓰지 않았더라면 지금 약간의 돈이 있을 텐데.
3 나는 숙제를 끝낼 수가 없다. 내가 파티에 가지 않았더라면 지금 걱정하지 않아도 될 텐데.
4 나는 네가 방문하는지 몰랐어. 내가 알았더라면 집을 치웠을 텐데.
5 내가 어젯밤 파티에서 노래를 더 잘 불렀다면 친구들 앞에서 망신당하지 않았을 텐데.
6 공룡은 거대한 소행성의 충돌에 의해 죽었다. 공룡이 멸종되지 않았더라면 인간은 결코 지구를 통치하지 못했을 텐데.
7 로마인들이 자마 전쟁에서 카르타고의 위대한 장군 한니발을 패배시켰다. 한니발이 로마인을 물리쳤더라면 유럽의 역사는 아주 달라졌을 텐데.

D

1 should have listened
2 should have gotten off
3 should have studied
4 should have worn
5 should have won
6 should have taken
7 should have bought

해석

1 모든 것이 잘못되었어. 내가 네 충고를 들었어야 했는데.
2 우리는 정류장을 놓쳤어. 우리는 전 정류장에서 내렸어야 했어.
3 프레드는 기말고사에서 낮은 점수를 받았다. 그는 좀 더 열심히 공부해야 했는데.
4 오늘은 내가 생각했던 것보다 더 추워. 나는 꽁꽁 얼 것 같아. 나는 더 두꺼운 코트를 입었어야 했는데.
5 산드라는 훌륭한 배우이다. 그녀는 '그레이 아나토미'에서 맡은 배역으로 에미 상을 받았어야 했는데.
6 빅토리아의 자연스러운 아름다움은 장관이다. 우리는 거기 있는 동안 더 많은 사진을 찍었어야 했는데.
7 우리는 표를 구하지 못해서 제시카의 콘서트를 놓쳤다. 우리는 표가 처음 판매되기 시작했을 때 샀어야 했는데.

Unit 67 EXERCISES

p. 144~145

1 I lived closer to school
2 our team had made it to the final
3 English weren't so difficult for me to learn
4 I had studied enough to get a good grade on the science exam
5 my family were here with me
6 my mother could spend enough quality time with me

해석

1 학교 가까이에 살지 않아서 유감이다.
→ 학교 가까이에 살면 좋을 텐데.
2 우리 팀이 결승전에 가지 못해서 유감이다.
→ 결승전에 갔더라면 좋았을 텐데.
3 내가 배우기에 영어는 너무 어려워서 유감이다.
→ 내가 배우기에 영어가 그렇게 어렵지 않다면 좋을 텐데.
4 과학 시험에서 좋은 성적을 받도록 충분히 공부를 하지 못해서 유감이다.
→ 과학 시험에서 좋은 성적을 받도록 충분히 공부를 했더라면 좋을 텐데.
5 우리 가족이 나와 함께 여기 오지 못해서 유감이다.
→ 우리 가족이 나와 함께 여기에 있다면 좋을 텐데.
6 나는 엄마가 나와 충분한 시간을 보낼 수 없어서 유감이다.
→ 엄마가 나와 충분한 시간을 보낼 수 있다면 좋을 텐데.

1 were
2 had seen
3 hadn't slept
4 were
5 were
6 were
7 helped
8 had been

해석

1 그는 마치 우리 아버지인 것처럼 말하지만, 사실 그는 우리 아버지가 아니다.
2 그는 귀신을 본 것처럼 말하지만, 사실은 귀신을 보지 않았다.
3 그녀는 어젯밤에 잠을 못 잔 것처럼 행동하지만, 사실은 어젯밤에 잠을 잤다.
4 그녀는 내가 유명한 스타인 것처럼 나를 바라보지만, 사실 아니다.
5 그는 그 주제에 대해 전문가처럼 말하지만, 사실 그는 전문가가 아니다.
6 그는 그 여배우가 자신의 친한 친구인 것처럼 말하지만, 사실 그 여배우는 그의 친구가 아니다.
7 그는 매일 어머니를 돕는 척하지만 사실, 그는 어머니를 전혀 돕지 않는다.
8 그 선수는 선수 인생에 마지막 게임인 것처럼 최선을 다 했다. 사실 마지막 게임은 아니었다.

1 Were it not for the Internet, our lives would be less convenient.
2 Were it not for the sun and water, no creature would exist on the earth.
3 Had it not been for the bad weather, the event would have been more successful.
4 Had it not been for the bravery of the firefighters, many lives might have been lost.
5 Had it not been for my mother's love, I wouldn't have become a successful business person.
6 Had it not been for great patriots like Ahn Junggeun Korea might never have become independent.

해석

1 인터넷이 없다면, 우리 삶은 덜 편리했을 거야.
2 태양과 물이 없다면, 어떠한 생물도 지구상에 존재하지 못할 거야.
3 악천후가 아니었다면, 그 행사는 좀 더 성공적이었을 거야.
4 소방관들의 용기가 아니었다면, 많은 사람이 목숨을 잃었을 거야.
5 우리 어머니의 사랑이 없었다면, 나는 성공적인 사업가가 되지 못했을 거야.
6 안중근과 같은 위대한 애국자가 없었더라면, 한국은 결코 독립할 수 없었을 거야.

D

1	Were	2	went
3	had	4	had finished
5	had had	6	knew
7	had spent	8	had not been

해석

1 음악과 예술이 없다면 우리 삶은 지루할 거야.
2 너는 다이어트를 할 때가 되었어. 너무 많이 살이 쪘어.
3 나는 그 코트를 사고 싶다. 그것을 살 돈이 있다면 좋을 텐데.
4 그는 마치 자신이 혼자 그 프로젝트를 끝낸 것처럼 이야기한다. 사실 많은 사람들이 그를 도왔다.
5 나는 어제 시험이 있었는데 완전히 망쳤다. 공부할 충분한 시간이 있었더라면 좋을 텐데.
6 그녀는 자신이 그에 대해 모든 것을 아는 것처럼 말한다. 사실 그녀는 그에 대해 아무것도 모른다.
7 그녀는 자신이 이탈리아에서 여름 방학을 보낸 것처럼 이야기한다. 사실 그녀는 그러지 않았다.
8 하워드 카터는 투탕카멘 왕의 무덤을 발견한 고고학자였다. 그가 아니었다면 우리는 투탕카멘의 시대에 대해 전혀 몰랐을지도 모른다.

REVIEW

p. 146~147

1	is	2	exercised
3	feel	4	goes
5	had not gone	6	be
7	had not been	8	hadn't eaten

해설/해석

1 우리가 내일 소풍을 갈 것(will go)이므로 미래를 의미, 조건절에서는 현재가 미래를 대신하므로 is가 적절
내일 날씨가 화창하면, 우리는 소풍을 갈 것이다.

2 '삶에 힘이 더 생길 텐데'라는 가정법 과거(would have)가 쓰였으므로 exercised가 적절
네가 운동을 더 하면, 삶에 더 많은 에너지가 생길 텐데.

3 '약을 먹었다면(가정법 과거완료: had taken), 지금 기분이 더 나을 텐데(가정법 과거)'라는 의미이므로 feel이 적절. 주절의 by now로 혼합 가정법이 쓰였음을 알 수 있음
젠이 그 약을 먹었다면, 지금쯤 훨씬 나을 텐데.

4 내가 수희를 그리워할 것(will miss)이므로 미래를 의미, 조건절에는 goes가 적절
수희가 뉴질랜드에 공부하러 가면, 나는 그녀를 아주 많이 그리워할 것이다.

5 '에이미가 머리가 젖은 채로 밖에 나가지 않았다면(가정법 과거완료), 지금 아프지 않았을 텐데(가정법 과거: wouldn't be sick now)'라는 의미이므로 가정법 과거완료인 had not gone이 적절
에이미가 머리가 젖은 채로 밖에 나가지 않았다면, 그녀는 아프지 않을 텐데.

6 '지진이 일어나지 않았다면(가정법 과거완료: had not happened), 지금 폐허로 남아 있지는 않을 텐데(가정법 과거)'라는 의미이므로 be가 적절. 주절의 now로 혼합 가정법임을 알 수 있음
지진이 일어나지 않았다면, 그 도시가 지금 폐허로 남아 있지는 않을 텐데.

7 '도움이 없었다면(가정법 과거완료), 마감 전에 마치지 못했을 텐데(가정법 과거완료: could not have finished)'라는 의미이므로 had not been이 적절
도움이 없었다면, 우리는 마감 전까지 이 일을 결코 마칠 수 없었을 거야.

8 '자러 가기 전에 간식을 먹지 않았다면'이라는 의미이고, 과거 사실에 대한 아쉬움을 나타낼 때 「I wish+주어+had+p.p.」를 사용하므로 hadn't eaten이 적절
내가 자기 전에 군것질하지 않았다면 좋을 텐데. 오늘 아침 속이 매우 불편해.

1 had gotten
2 would play
3 has
4 hadn't invented, have won
5 hadn't stayed up, have missed
6 hadn't practiced, be
7 hadn't broken, have to buy

해설/해석

1 '생일에 새 자전거를 받지 못해서 유감이다'라는 내용으로 과거 사실에 대한 유감을 표현하는 가정법 과거완료(had gotten)가 적절
내 생일에 새 자전거를 받지 못해서 유감이다.
→ 생일에 새 자전거를 받았으면 좋았을 텐데.

2 현재 사실의 반대를 나타내는 가정법 과거로 주절에 would play를 쓰는 것이 적절
그는 바이올린 연습을 충분히 하지 않는다. 그래서 그는 바이올린을 잘 켜지 못한다.
→ 그가 바이올린을 충분히 연습한다면, 그는 바이올린을 잘 켤 수 있을 텐데.

3 조셉이 바다에서 오래 놀아서 햇볕에 탔을지도 모른다(might have)는 추측의 의미이다. 현재 사실을 반대로 가정한 것이 아니고 현재 사실을 추측한 것이므로 '마치 ~처럼 보인다'라는 의미의 부사절(직설법)임을 알 수 있다. has가 적절
조셉은 오랜 시간을 바다에서 놀면서 보냈다. 그는 햇볕에 탔을지도 모른다.
→ 조셉은 햇볕에 탄 것처럼 보인다.

4 '이순신 장군이 거북선을 발명하지 않았다면'이라고 과거 사실의 반대(hadn't invented)를 가정하므로 가정법 과거완료(have won)가 와야 함
이순신 장군이 거북선을 고안했다. 그는 임진왜란의 많은 해전에서 승리를 거두었다.
→ 이순신 장군이 거북선을 고안하지 않았다면, 임진왜란의 많은 해전에서 승리하지 못했을 거야.

5 '밤새 시험공부를 하느라고 깨어 있지 않았다면'이라고 과거의 반대(hadn't stayed up)를 가정하므로 가정법 과거완료(have missed)가 적절
나는 밤새도록 시험공부를 하느라고 깨어 있어서, 학교로 가는 버스를 놓쳤다.
→ 밤새 시험공부를 하느라고 깨어 있지 않았다면 학교로 가는 버스를 놓치지 않았을 텐데.

6 if절에는 '조가 어려서부터 농구 연습을 하지 않았더라면'이라고 과거 사실의 반대(hadn't practiced)를 가정하고, 주절에는 '유명한 선수가 아닐 텐데'라고 현재 사실의 반대(wouldn't be)를 가정하므로 혼합 가정법이 사용됨

조는 어려서부터 농구를 연습했다. 그는 지금 유명한 선수이다.
→ 조가 어려서부터 농구 연습을 하지 않았다면, 그는 지금 유명한 선수가 아닐 거야.

7 '과거에 노트북이 고장 나지 않았다면(hadn't broken), 지금 새로 사지 않아도 될 텐데(would not have to buy)'라는 혼합 가정법이 사용됨

크리스틴의 노트북 컴퓨터가 고장 났다. 그래서 그녀는 지금 새것을 사야 한다.
→ 크리스틴의 노트북 컴퓨터가 고장 나지 않았다면, 지금 새것을 사지 않아도 될 텐데.

C

1 have drowned
2 run
3 feel
4 be
5 be
6 were
7 had had
8 had
9 keeps
10 attend
11 had gone

해설/해석

1 과거 사실의 반대(hadn't learned)를 나타내는 가정법 과거완료이므로 would have drowned가 적절

그가 수영을 배우지 않았다면, 익사했을 거야.

2 '기차를 탈 수 있을 것이다'라는 미래(will still make it)를 의미하므로 run이 적절

네가 빨리 뛰어 가면 아직 기차를 탈 수 있을 것이다.

3 현재 사실의 반대를 나타내는 가정법 과거이므로, 주절에 wouldn't feel이 적절

나는 애완동물이 없다. 애완동물이 있다면, 나는 외롭지 않을 텐데.

4 if절에 '더 열심히 연습한다면'이라고 현재 사실에 대한 반대(practiced)를 가정하므로 가정법 과거(would be)가 적절

켈리가 더 열심히 연습한다면, 그녀는 더 좋은 피아노 연주자가 될 텐데.

5 '친구들이 없다면'이라고 현재 사실의 반대(weren't)를 가정하므로 be가 적절

친구들이 없다면 삶은 정말 외로울 거야.

6 '내가 열 살인 것처럼'이라고 현재 사실의 반대를 가정하므로 가정법 과거인 were가 적절

나의 어머니는 항상 내가 아직도 열 살인 것처럼 대한다.

7 '축구 선수가 되었을 텐데'라고 과거 사실의 반대(would have become)를 가정하므로 had had가 적절

내가 재능이 있었다면, 축구 선수가 되었을 텐데.

8 '하와이에 갈 돈이 있으면'이라고 현재 사실의 반대를 가정하므로 had가 적절

하와이에 갈 돈이 있으면 좋을 텐데. 돈이 없어서 유감이다.

9 '폭우에 모래가 씻겨나갈 것이다'라는 미래를 의미하므로 if조건절에 현재 시제인 keeps가 적절

폭우가 계속 온다면, 해변에 더 많은 모래가 씻겨나갈 것이다.

10 if절에서 '선생님의 도움이 아니었다면'이라고 과거 사실의 반대(had not been)를 가정하지만, 주절의 now로 혼합 가정문임을 알 수 있으므로 wouldn't attend가 적절

선생님이 아니었더라면, 나는 이렇게 좋은 대학에 못 다닐 텐데.

11 '뉴욕에 갔었다면, 엘리스 섬과 자유의 여신상을 방문했을 텐데'라고 과거 사실의 반대(could have visited)를 가정하므로 had gone이 적절

우리가 뉴욕에 갔었다면, 엘리스 섬과 자유의 여신상을 방문할 수 있었을 텐데.

D

1 take
2 weren't
3 feel
4 continues
5 be
6 go
7 had known
8 hadn't come
9 keeps
10 be
11 had done

해설/해석

1 '내가 너라면'이라고 현재 사실의 반대(were)를 가정하므로 take가 적절

내가 너라면, 나는 결코 시험을 치지 않을 텐데.

2 '비행기가 이륙할 수 있을 텐데'라고 현재 사실의 반대(could take off)를 가정하므로 weren't가 적절

안개가 많이 끼지 않았다면, 비행기가 이륙할 수 있을 텐데.

3 '보니가 잠을 잘 잤다면 지금 기분이 상쾌할 텐데'라는 혼합 가정의 문장이므로 would have feel은 would feel이 되어야 함

보니가 잘 잤다면, 그녀는 지금 기분이 상쾌할 텐데.

4 '계속 공부하면 훌륭한 변호사가 될 것이다'는 의미로 미래(will become)를 나타내므로 조건절은 continues가 적절

수지가 공부를 계속한다면, 그녀는 훌륭한 변호사가 될 것이다.

5 if절에서 '아침을 거르지 않았다면'으로 과거 사실의 반대(Had I not skipped = If I hadn't skipped)를 가정하지만, 주절의 now로 혼합 가정문임을 알 수 있으므로 be가 적절

내가 아침을 거르지 않았다면, 지금 배가 고프지 않을 텐데.

6 if절에서 '강이 얼어 있다면'으로 현재 사실의 반대(were frozen)를 가정하므로 go가 적절

저 강이 얼어 있다면, 그들은 거기로 얼음낚시를 갈 텐데.

7 '너의 어머니가 병원에 계신 것을 알았다면'이라고 과거사실의 반대를 가정하는 가정법 과거완료인 had known이 적절

내가 너의 어머니께서 병원에 계신 것을 알았더라면 찾아뵈었을 텐데.

8 '다니엘이 한국에 오지 않았다면, 만나지 못했을 텐데'라는 과거 사실의 반대(wouldn't have met)를 가정하는 가정법 과거완료이므로 hadn't come이 적절

다니엘이 한국에 오지 않았다면, 그는 자신의 사랑스러운 아내를 만나지 못했을 거야.

9 '세계의 인구가 계속 증가하면, 식량 부족을 경험하게 될 것이다'라는 추측(may experience)을 나타내므로 조건의 부사절에는 keeps가 적절

세계 인구가 계속 증가한다면, 우리는 심각한 식량 부족을 겪게 될 것이다.

10 if절에서 '빙하 시대가 끝나지 않았다면'이라고 과거 사실의 반대

(had not ended)를 가정하지만, 주절의 still로 현재 사실의 반대를 가정하는 혼합 가정문임을 알 수 있으므로 be가 적절
마지막 빙하 시대가 끝나지 않았다면, 북반구 대부분은 아직도 얼음 아래에 덮여 있을 것이다.

11 주절은 '그녀가 원하는 대학에 지원했을 텐데(would have)'라는 의미로 과거 사실에 대한 반대를 가정하고 있으므로 if절은 had done이 적절
그녀가 시험을 잘 쳤다면, 그녀가 다니고 싶은 대학에 지원했을 텐데.

REVIEW PLUS

p. 148

1 ② 2 ⑤

해설/해석

1 현재에 이룰 수 없는 소망을 나타낼 때: 「I wish+가정법 과거」
우리에겐 마감 전까지 몇 시간밖에 없다. 우리에게 프로젝트를 끝내기 위한 시간이 더 있다면 좋을 텐데.

2 '과거에 화산이 폭발하지 않았다면, 오늘날 하와이가 존재하지 않을 것'이라는 의미로 과거의 사건이 현재에까지 영향을 미치는 혼합 가정문임
하와이 섬은 화산에 의해 형성되었다. 화산이 폭발하지 않았다면, 오늘날 하와이 섬은 존재하지 않을 텐데.

⑤

해설/해석

⑤ '박물관에 갔다면, 많은 아름다운 그림들을 볼 수 있었을 텐데'라는 가정법 과거완료를 만들려면 went를 had gone으로 바꿔야 함
① 내가 너라면, 매일 책을 읽으려고 노력할 텐데.
② 내가 부유한 사람이라면, 더 많은 돈을 자선 단체에 기부할 텐데.
③ 그가 충분히 키가 크다면, 우리 팀에서 농구를 할 텐데.
④ 짐이 더 똑똑하다면, 그는 기술자가 될 수 있을 텐데.
⑤ 박물관에 갔다면, 많은 아름다운 그림들을 볼 수 있었을 텐데.

④

해설/해석

(A) 앞 문장에서 여전히 이해하지 못한다고 했으므로 '이해한다면'이라고 하려면 현재 사실의 반대를 가정하는 가정법 과거(understood)가 적절 (B) '그들이 경고 시스템을 개발한다면, 많은 생명을 살릴 수 있다'는 현재 사실의 반대를 가정하므로 가정법 과거(could save)가 적절 (C) '쓰나미가 감지된다면, 경고가 영향을 받을 수 있는 모든 지역으로 보내질 것'이라는 현재 사실의 반대를 가정하므로 가정법 과거(would be)가 적절
수세기 동안, 우리는 쓰나미가 지진에 의해 발생한다고 알아 왔지만, 여전히 그것에 대해 잘 모르고 있다. 과학자들이 지진이 어떻게 작용하는지에 대해 더 잘 이해한다면, 지진을 예측할 수 있을 것이다. 그들이 조기 경고 시스템 같은 것을 구축할 수만 있다면 여러 생명을 구할 수 있을 것이다. 불행하게도, 예측 시스템은 여전히 우리의 지식 밖에 있다. 만약 쓰나미가 정확히 감지된다면 영향을 받을 수 있는 모든 지역에 경고가 보내질 것이다.

PART 19

REPLAY

p. 150~151

1 CHECK-UP

1 on 2 on, in
3 at, in 4 at, at
5 at

2 CHECK-UP

1 until 2 for
3 during 4 by
5 for

3 CHECK-UP

1 at 2 on
3 in 4 from
5 on 6 into
7 through

Unit 68 EXERCISES

p. 154~155

1 (1) P (2) C 2 (1) P (2) C
3 (1) P (2) C 4 (1) C (2) P

해석

1 (1) 크리스틴은 여섯 시 전에 파티에 도착하기를 원했다.
(2) 연어는 알을 낳기 전에 강을 거슬러 올라간다.
2 (1) 나는 수요일까지 출장 가 있을 것 같다.
(2) 우리는 너의 아버지가 집에 오실 때까지 저녁을 먹을 수 없다.
3 (1) 에이미의 할머니께서는 에이미가 태어난 후에 돌아가셨다.
(2) 그녀는 대학을 졸업한 뒤에 해외로 나갈 것이다.
4 (1) 그는 키가 제일 작지만 반에서 가장 빨리 달린다.
(2) 그는 불편함에도 불구하고 버스로 출근을 했다.

B

1 ⓐ 2 ⓑ
3 ⓑ 4 ⓐ

해석

1 우리 건물의 보안 요원은 아주 쾌활하다.
2 우리 부모님은 내가 태어나기 전에 작은 섬에서 살았다.
3 참가자들을 위한 사은품은 중앙 로비에 준비되어 있습니다.
4 거실 벽의 그림은 내가 그린 것이다.

1 during 2 while
3 because 4 unless
5 because of 6 without
7 in case of 8 in case

해석

1 나는 뉴욕에 머무르는 동안 많은 친구들을 사귀었다.
2 그녀는 아기가 자는 동안 샤워를 했다.
3 우리는 비행기가 지연되어 화가 났다.
4 미리 신청하지 않으면 너는 이 강좌를 수강할 수 없다.
5 그는 나의 생각 없는 말 때문에 깊은 상처를 받은 것 같았다.
6 인간은 물과 공기 없이는 단 하루도 살 수 없다.
7 선생님은 비상시에 대비하여 자신의 전화번호를 우리에게 알려주었다.
8 학생들은 지진이 발생할 것에 대비해서 정기적으로 지진 훈련을 받는다.

D

1 except	2 on
3 for	4 opposite
5 to	6 with
7 of	8 for
9 in	10 at

해석

1 나를 제외하고 아무도 그의 결정에 불평하지 않았다.
2 나는 제니의 책상 위에 있던 일기를 읽고 싶었지만 그러지 않았다.
3 너는 건강을 위해 정기적으로 운동을 해야 한다.
4 역 맞은편에 있는 집들은 수십 년 전에 지어졌다.
5 소피아는 어제 돌고래를 보러 수족관에 갔다.
6 그는 요리를 하는 동안 라디오에서 나오는 노래를 따라 불렀다.
7 이 마을의 거의 모든 집들은 벽돌로 지어졌다.
8 그는 병원에서 자신의 생각 없는 행동에 대해 사과했다.
9 군중 가운데 일부 난폭한 축구 팬들이 경기를 완전히 망쳤다.
10 버스 정류장에 있던 그 남자는 내게 지하철역으로 가는 길을 물었다.

E

1 to	2 in
3 of	4 to
5 of	6 to
7 to	8 of
9 of	10 For
11 of	12 on

해석

1 그는 시차 때문에 밤에 잠을 이룰 수 없었다.
2 나는 다비드상 앞에서 친구들을 향해 미소 지었다.
3 큰 변화를 두려워하는 것은 당연한 것이다.
4 그의 조언 덕분에 우리는 어려움을 극복할 수 있었다.
5 의사들은 붉은 육류 대신에 생선을 더 많이 먹으라고 사람들에게 제안한다.
6 영어 외에 그녀는 프랑스어와 일본어를 배우고 있다.
7 나의 세 살짜리 조카의 말에 따르면 외계인은 정말로 존재한다.
8 그녀는 혼자서 그 문제를 풀 수 있었다고 말했다.
9 너무 시끄러워서 나는 공부에 집중할 수 없었다.
10 아이들을 위해 교육이 우리의 최우선 순위가 되어야 한다.
11 그녀는 성공에도 불구하고 자신이 이룬 것에 만족하지 않는다.
12 강풍으로 실외 배드민턴 경기는 취소되었다.

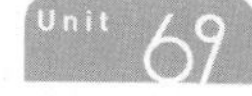

Unit 69 EXERCISES

p. 158~159

A

1 on	2 to
3 ×	4 ×
5 ×	6 ×
7 ×, ×	8 to, ×

해석

1 브리트니와 나는 월요일에 수영하러 갈 계획이다.
2 애슐리는 유명한 영화배우와 결혼할 것이다.
3 한국은 물이 부족하기 때문에 나는 물을 낭비하지 않으려고 노력한다.
4 비행기가 지금 JFK 국제공항에 접근하고 있습니다.
5 우리 팀은 ABC 대학과 다음 주 토요일에 축구 경기를 할 것이다.
6 선생님이 수학 문제를 푸는 간단한 방법을 설명해 주었다.
7 간호사가 토미의 병에 대해 의논하려고 의사의 사무실에 들어갔다.
8 우리는 당신을 만나서 파트너십에 대해 의논할 것을 정말 기대하고 있습니다.

B

1 am used	2 lacks
3 Today	4 getting married to
5 discuss	6 explained
7 answered	8 these days
9 approaching	10 carrying out
11 resemble	12 entered

해석

1 나는 요즘 아침 일찍 조깅을 하러 가는 데 익숙하다.
2 그는 인내심이 부족하지만 약점을 극복하려고 노력한다.
3 오늘, 학생들은 장애인을 돕는 방법을 배울 것이다.
4 우리 이모는 다음 주에 그녀의 오랜 남자 친구와 결혼을 한다.
5 우리는 언제 그리고 어떻게 학급 반장을 뽑을지 토의할 것이다.
6 과학 선생님이 공룡이 어떻게 멸종했는지 설명했다.
7 릴리는 모든 질문에 정확히 답했고 선생님은 그녀를 칭찬했다.
8 요즘 대부분의 아이들은 컴퓨터를 쉽고 빠르게 배운다.
9 그 기자는 거대한 소행성이 내년에 지구에 접근할 것이라고 말했다.
10 많은 수의 학생들과 학부모들은 그 새로운 정책을 시행하는 것에 반대하고 있다.
11 우리 언니와 나는 서로 닮아서 사람들이 종종 내게 우리가 쌍둥이인지 묻는다.
12 그 인기 있는 코미디언은 교실에 들어와서 학생들에게 열렬한 환영을 받았다.

C

1 going	2 studying
3 preserving	4 developing
5 turning	

해석

1 대부분의 학생들은 일본으로 수학여행을 가는 것에 반대했다.
2 학생들은 밤늦게까지 공부하는 것에 익숙해져 있다.
3 그 노인은 다음 세대를 위해 자연을 보호하는 것에 헌신했다.
4 내 꿈은 위대한 발명품을 만들어내어 기술 발전에 공헌하는 것이다.

5 모든 전등을 끄는 것 외에도 외출하기 전에 가스레인지를 잠갔는지 확인하는 것을 잊지 마세요.

1 dedicated, to, helping
2 object, to, accepting
3 looking, forward, to, watching
4 opposed, to, building
5 is, accustomed, to, getting, up
6 is, used, to, driving
7 contributed, to, developing
8 In, addition, to, receiving

Unit 70 EXERCISES

p. 162~163

A

1 on	2 into
3 at	4 for
5 at	6 out
7 on	8 on
9 into	10 out
11 into	12 out
13 for	14 of

해석

1 그는 아무 말도 하지 않고 그저 계속 공부만 했다.
2 김 선생님이 학급을 각각 다섯 개의 별개의 그룹으로 나누었다.
3 '월드 뉴스'라는 잡지는 한국의 10대를 대상으로 한다.
4 마이클과 제임스는 온종일 그들의 잃어버린 강아지를 찾았다.
5 너를 향해 미소를 짓는 저 잘생긴 남자애가 누구니? 내 생각에 그가 너를 좋아하는 것 같아!
6 아직 아무것도 배제하지 말자. 존, 우리에게 너의 의견을 말해 봐.
7 그 남자는 심문을 받기 전에 변호사를 만나겠다고 주장했다.
8 이 선생님의 학생들은 항상 도움이 되는 조언을 받으려고 그에게 의존한다.
9 나는 어떤 것도 성급하게 하고 싶지 않다. 기다리면서 무슨 일이 일어나는지 볼 것이다.
10 저 운동화는 약간 낡아 보인다. 바꾸는 게 어때?
11 레오는 마지막 학년을 놀라울 정도로 잘해냈다. 그는 심지어 옥스퍼드에 들어갔다.
12 매 학기 말에 학생들은 사물함을 비우도록 요청받는다.
13 나는 미국에서 호텔 경영을 공부하기 위해 장학금을 신청했다.
14 나는 어렸을 때 강에 빠진 이후로 물을 두려워한다.

1 divided into	2 concentrate on
3 worn out	4 ran into
5 apologize for	6 figure out
7 search for	8 targeted at

해석

1 한국은 두 나라로 나뉘어져 있다.
2 나는 네가 그렇게 시끄럽게 하면 일에 집중할 수가 없어.
3 내 낡은 신발의 굽이 닳아서 수리를 했다.
4 나는 어제 신디와 우연히 마주쳤어. 너에게 인사 전해 달래.
5 너는 지난주 수업 중에 제니에게 그렇게 형편없이 대한 것에 대해 사과해야 한다.
6 열 시간 후에 그녀는 포기했다. 그녀는 그 퍼즐을 풀 수 없었다.
7 나는 자주 인터넷을 이용해서 내가 필요한 정보를 찾는다.
8 이 광고는 초등학생들을 겨냥한 것이다.

1 at	2 into
3 out	4 for
5 on	6 of
7 on	

해석

1 (1) 나는 그 남자가 나를 왜 노려보고 있었는지 몰랐다.
(2) 그녀는 내가 무엇을 말하는지 이해하지 못하겠다고 말했다.
2 (1) 그는 어제 영화관에서 옛 친구를 우연히 만났다.
(2) 공주가 개구리에게 키스를 하자 그는 왕자로 변했다.
3 (1) 그는 내가 비밀을 누설했다고 의심했다.
(2) 그 영화배우는 은퇴 가능성을 배제하지 않았다.
4 (1) 아이들은 크리스마스이브에 '진짜' 산타클로스를 기다렸다.
(2) 그 매니저는 내게 물건을 잘못 보낸 것에 대해 사과했다.
5 (1) 처음에 나는 잘하지 못했지만 하면 할수록 나는 빨리 이해했다.
(2) 교실에 있던 학생들은 시험에 집중하고 있었다.
6 (1) 전 세계에서 많은 아이들이 배고픔으로 죽어가고 있다
(2) 너는 네 행동이 잘못되었기 때문에 그것을 부끄러워해야 한다.
7 (1) 그는 결과보다는 과정에 더 중점을 두었다.
(2) 십 대들은 부모보다 또래에 더 의존하는 경향이 있다.

1 insisted, on, going, out	2 pay, for
3 was, angry, at[with]	4 applied, for
5 laughed, at	6 got, into

REVIEW

p. 164~165

1 in	2 until
3 for	4 of
5 for	6 to
7 ×	8 at
9 to	10 about

해설/해석

1 연도 앞에는 in이 적절
제프는 1991년부터 여기에서 일하기 시작했다.

2 '깨어 있었다'는 의미로, 계속적인 동작이나 상태를 나타낼 때 until이 적절
나는 어젯밤에 세 시까지 깨어 있었다.

3 pay for는 '~의 값을 지불하다, 돈을 내다'라는 의미
그 콘서트 표를 사는 데 얼마를 지불했니?

4 be proud of는 '~을 자랑스러워하다'라는 의미

마크의 어머니는 그의 성과를 몹시 자랑스러워했다.

5 look for는 '~을 찾다'라는 의미
나는 차 열쇠를 찾고 있어요. 찾는 것 좀 도와줄래요?

6 look forward to -ing는 '~하기를 고대하다'라는 의미
나는 가까운 장래에 당신의 소식을 다시 듣기를 고대합니다.

7 「these+시간 표현」 앞에는 전치사를 주로 생략
우리 할아버지는 요즘에 매우 건강하고 튼튼해 보인다.

8 jump at은 '(기회에) 기꺼이 응하다'라는 의미
내 남동생은 작년에 월드 베스트에서 일하는 기회에 기꺼이 응했다.

9 get married to는 '~와 결혼하다'라는 의미
빌은 어제 아름다운 정원에서 내 여동생과 결혼했다.

10 complain about은 '~에 대해 불평하다'라는 의미
방금 일본에 다녀온 레오는 비싼 물가에 대해 불평했다.

B

1	in case of	2	during
3	in spite of	4	while
5	despite	6	while
7	because	8	because of
9	unless	10	because of

해설/해석

1 「in case+주어+동사」와 「in case of+(동)명사」는 '~의 경우에 대비하여'라는 의미, a fire는 명사이므로 in case of가 적절
우리는 화재에 대비해서 정기적으로 소방 훈련을 해야 한다.

2 「during+기간 명사」와 「while+주어+동사」는 '~ 동안에'라는 의미, the night은 기간 명사이므로 during이 적절
너는 밤에 이상하거나 특이한 소리를 들었니?

3 「although+주어+동사」와 「in spite of+(동)명사」는 '~에도 불구하고'라는 의미, their differences of opinion은 명사구이므로 in spite of가 적절
그들은 의견의 차이가 있음에도 그럭저럭 함께 일을 해나갔다.

4 「during+기간 명사」와 「while+주어+동사」는 '~ 동안에'라는 의미, 'he took a nap ~'은 주어와 동사가 있는 문장이므로 while이 적절
아빠가 소파에서 낮잠을 자는 동안, 우리는 아버지의 날 선물을 사러 나갔다.

5 「although+주어+동사」와 「despite+(동)명사」는 '~에도 불구하고'라는 의미, having a test는 동명사구이므로 despite가 적절
그들은 다음 날 시험이 있음에도 영화를 보러 시내에 갔다.

6 「during+기간 명사」와 「while+주어+동사」는 '~ 동안에'라는 의미, 'I change ~'는 주어와 동사가 있는 문장이므로 while이 적절
유니폼을 벗고 청바지로 갈아입는 동안 나를 기다려 줘.

7 「because+주어+동사」와 「because of+(동)명사」는 '~때문에'라는 의미, 'there was ~'는 주어와 동사가 있는 문장이므로 because가 적절
밖에서 공사를 해서 나는 숙제에 집중할 수 없었다.

8 「because+주어+동사」와 「because of+(동)명사」는 '~때문에'라는 의미, the hot weather and mosquitoes는 명사구이므로 because of가 적절
야영자들 모두 더운 날씨와 모기 때문에 피곤하고 짜증이 났다.

9 「without+-ing」와 「unless+주어+동사」는 '~하지 않으면'이라는 의미, 'you've got ~'은 주어와 동사가 있는 문장이므로 unless가 적절
대학 학위와 2년간의 경험이 없으면 그 일자리에 지원할 수 없다.

10 「because+주어+동사」와 「because of+(동)명사」는 '~때문에'라는 의미, the professor는 명사이므로 because of가 적절
내가 그 수업을 신청한 가장 큰 이유는 그 수업을 담당하는 교수님 때문이다. 그는 저명한 작가이고, 나는 그의 작품의 열렬한 팬이다.

C

1	living	2	eating
3	on 삭제	4	got married to
5	because of	6	approached
7	resembles, resemble	8	while
9	getting	10	discuss
11	on 삭제		

해설/해석

1 「get used to+(동)명사」 ~하는 데 익숙해지다
그는 집을 떠난 후로 혼자 사는 것에 익숙해졌다.

2 「instead of+(동)명사」 ~ 대신에
우리는 집에서 먹는 대신 외식을 하기로 했다.

3 last, next, every, each, today, tomorrow 등과 같은 시간 관련 어구 앞의 전치사는 주로 생략
우리 엄마와 나는 매주 일요일 교회에 간다.

4 「get married to」 ~와 결혼하다
우리 이모는 유명한 농구 선수와 결혼했다.

5 「because+주어+동사」와 「because of+(동)명사」는 '~때문에'라는 의미, sudden heavy rain은 명사구이므로 because of가 적절
갑작스러운 폭우 때문에 경기를 중단해야 했다.

6 approach가 '~에게 접근하다'라는 뜻일 때는 전치사를 쓰지 않음
낯선 사람이 그녀에게 접근하더니 자신을 그녀에게 소개했다.

7 resemble이 '~를 닮다'라는 뜻일 때는 전치사를 쓰지 않음
우리 언니는 엄마를 닮았고, 나는 아빠를 닮았다.

8 「during+기간 명사」와 「while+주어+동사」는 '~ 동안에'라는 의미, her mother was ~는 주어와 동사가 있는 문장이므로 여기서는 while이 적절
매기는 엄마가 저녁을 준비하는 동안 피아노를 연습했다.

9 for the sake of는 '~을 위하여'라는 의미로 전치사이므로 뒤에 (동)명사를 취함
단지 시험에서 좋은 성적을 받기 위해서 영어를 배워서는 안 된다.

10 discuss가 '~에 대해 의논하다'라는 뜻일 때는 전치사를 쓰지 않음
우리 가족은 할아버지의 칠순 잔치에 대해 이야기하기 위해 모였다.

11 last, next, every, each, today, tomorrow 등과 같은 시간 관련 어구 앞의 전치사는 주로 생략
우리는 다음 주 금요일에 소풍을 가기로 되어 있었지만 태풍이 오고 있었기 때문에 취소되었다.

D

1	yelled at	2	figured out

3 jumped at
4 looked for
5 worn out
6 depends on
7 went on
8 waiting for
9 rushed into
10 divided into

해설/해석

1 「yell at」 ~에 소리 지르다
그는 매우 화가 나서 내게 소리를 질렀다.

2 「figure out」 이해하다, 해결하다
그녀는 전자레인지가 왜 작동하지 않는지 알아냈다.

3 「jump at」 ~에 덤벼들다, 초대에 기꺼이 응하다
경찰은 용의자에게 달려들어 그를 체포했다.

4 「look for」 ~을 찾다
나는 잃어버린 지갑을 찾아보았으나 어디에서도 찾을 수 없었다.

5 「wear out」 닳아 없어지게 하다, 지치게 하다
아빠의 신발이 낡아서 나는 아빠께 새 신발을 사드리기로 했다.

6 「depend on」 ~에 의존하다, ~에 달려 있다
이번 주말에 우리가 낚시를 갈지 말지는 날씨에 달려있다.

7 「go on」 ~을 계속하다
그녀는 비록 아기를 돌보느라 바빴지만 일을 계속했다.

8 「wait for」 ~을 기다리다
가뭄이 여러 달 동안 계속되었고 우리는 비 오는 날을 기다리고 있다.

9 「rush into」 ~을 서둘러 하다, ~로 급하게 뛰어들다
소방관들이 화재가 난 건물에 뛰어 들어가 그 안의 사람들을 구출했다.

10 「divide into」 ~으로 나누다
학생들은 영어 능력에 따라서 네 그룹으로 나뉘었다.

REVIEW PLUS

p. 166

1 ⑤ 2 ④ 3 ⑤

해설/해석

1 '자극받지 않으면 공격하지 않는다'가 자연스러우므로 '~하지 않으면'의 뜻으로 사용될 수 있고 주어와 동사를 취할 수 있는 unless가 적절
야생 동물은 자극받지 않으면 공격하지 않는다.

2 「this+시간 표현」 앞에는 전치사를 주로 생략
알렉스는 오늘 아침에 학교에 오는 도중에 교통사고를 당했다.

3 be good at은 '~을 잘하다, ~에 능숙하다'라는 의미
미나는 매일 연습을 하기 때문에 피겨 스케이트를 잘 탄다.

1 ⑤ 2 ②

해설/해석

1 ⑤ 「resemble+사람」은 '~을 닮다'라는 의미이므로 resemble with가 아니라 resemble이 적절
① 로버트는 자신의 일에 집중해야 한다.
② 사라는 작년에 남자 친구와 결혼했다.
③ 윤하는 리아의 아름다움과 뛰어난 유머감각을 부러워했다.
④ 나는 자전거를 조심스럽게 벽에 기대어 세웠다.
⑤ 사람들 대부분은 내가 어머니를 닮았다고 말한다.

2 ② 「be used to+-ing」는 '~하는 데 익숙하다'라는 의미. 이때 to는 전치사로 뒤에 명사나 동명사를 써야 하므로 take가 아니라 taking이 적절
① 브라운 씨는 모퉁이에 있는 그 건물을 소유하고 있다.
② 나는 이제 내 여동생을 돌보는 데 익숙하다.
③ 민준이는 하나에게 발을 밟은 것에 대해 사과했다.
④ 우리는 인터넷을 사용해서 영어 실력을 향상시킬 수 있다.
⑤ 우리는 오늘 저녁에 은혜네 집에서 파티를 할 것이다.

① to ② next to ③ for ④ at

해설/해석

① 「be proud of+(동)명사」, 「be proud to+동사원형」'~을 자랑스러워하다'라는 의미, announce는 동사원형이므로 to가 적절 ② be located 뒤에는 장소 부사구가 위치, '산책길 옆에'라는 의미로 next to가 적절 ③ '아이들을 위한'이라는 의미로 for가 적절 ④ jump at은 '~에 기꺼이 응하다'라는 의미.
글렌 그로브 시 위원회는 우리 지역 사회 레크리에이션 센터의 개관을 알리게 되어 자랑스럽습니다. 이 센터는 레이크쇼어 대로에 있는 산책길 옆에 자리 잡고 있습니다. 그리고 이곳은 규정에 맞는 크기의 농구 코트 두 개, 스케이트보드 공원, 그리고 열두 살 이하의 어린이들을 위한 미술과 공예실을 특징으로 하고 있습니다. 많은 생각과 관심이 이 센터를 계획하는 데 쏟아 부어졌습니다. 저희는 글렌 그로브에 있는 모든 사람이 가까운 장래에 저희를 찾아오는 기회를 얻기를 희망합니다. 그곳에서 곧 만납시다!

PART 20

Unit 71 EXERCISES

p. 171

1 she was taking Biology 101 that week
2 she moved[had moved] to Tokyo the previous year
3 I was the most attractive girl in the class
4 she was sharing her room with her sister then
5 he was proud of me because I always tried my best
6 they would have a party for the new student that night

해석

1 줄리아는 그 주에 생물학 101을 들을 것이라고 말했다.
2 그녀는 나에게 그 이전 해에 도쿄로 이사했다고 말했다.
3 저스틴이 나에게 내가 반에서 가장 매력적인 소녀라고 말했다.
4 캐시는 그때 여동생과 방을 함께 쓰고 있다고 나에게 말했다.
5 아버지는 내가 항상 최선을 다하기 때문에 내가 자랑스럽다고 말했다.
6 그는 그날 밤 그들이 새로 온 학생을 위해 파티를 열 것이라고 내게 말했다.

B

1 what I wanted to eat
2 if[whether] I really liked studying English
3 what we were doing there
4 if[whether] I knew why she had skipped the class that day
5 if[whether] she was going to come to his photo exhibition
6 what time I was going to the English academy

B

1 내 친구는 나에게 무엇을 먹고 싶은지 물었다.
2 지아가 나에게 정말 영어 공부하는 것을 좋아하느냐고 물었다.
3 그 안전 요원이 우리에게 거기에서 무엇을 하느냐고 물었다.
4 그가 내게 그녀가 그날 왜 수업에 빠졌는지 아냐고 물었다.
5 그가 그녀에게 자신의 사진 전시회에 올 거냐고 물었다.
6 그녀가 내게 영어 학원에 몇 시에 갈 거냐고 물었다.

Unit 72 EXERCISES

p. 173

1	was	2	saw 또는 had seen
3	has	4	틀린 것 없음
5	(had) improved	6	bites
7	틀린 것 없음	8	틀린 것 없음
9	divided	10	틀린 것 없음
11	틀린 것 없음	12	entered

해석

1 그가 나를 만나서 매우 기쁘다고 말했다.
2 제임스는 이전에 여기에서 캐롤을 보았다고 믿었다.
3 그녀는 대개 7시에 저녁을 먹는다고 내게 말했다.
4 우리 엄마는 매주 월요일에 빨래한다고 말했다.
5 그는 학교 성적이 이번에 많이 올랐다고 생각했다.
6 그녀는 긴장할 때 손톱을 물어뜯는다고 내게 말했다.
7 기름은 물보다 밀도가 낮아서 물 위에 뜬다.
8 그는 점심을 먹으러 주로 이 식당에 온다고 말했다.
9 우리는 한국 전쟁이 우리나라를 두 국가로 분단시켰다는 것을 배울 것입니다.
10 우리는 혈액이 사람 몸무게의 7퍼센트를 차지한다고 배웠다.
11 그는 자신의 아들이 어려움을 극복하고 마침내 성공할 것이라는 사실을 믿었다.
12 나는 미국이 1941년 진주만 공격이 있은 직후 바로 제2차 세계 대전에 참전했다는 것을 안다.

1	is	2	is
3	is	4	is
5	belong	6	were
7	go	8	are
9	requires	10	have
11	is	12	seem

해석

1 우는 것은 스트레스에 대한 자연스러운 반응이다.
2 가죽 장갑을 낀 소녀가 내 여동생이다.
3 너무 많은 비타민을 먹는 것은 너의 건강에 좋지 않다.
4 가장 많은 골을 넣은 선수가 경기 후에 MVP가 될 것이다.
5 상자 안에 있는 옷은 나와 내 여동생의 것이다.
6 그는 자신의 학교 선생님들이 매우 좋다고 말했다.
7 피터와 로만은 형제이고, 같은 학교에 다닌다.
8 저기에서 농구하고 있는 소년들이 우리 반 아이들이다.
9 다섯 개의 볼링 핀으로 곡예를 부리는 것은 손과 눈의 훌륭한 조화를 필요로 한다.
10 수와 클라라는 배구팀 소속인데 오늘 연습이 있다.
11 통계학은 스미스 교수님이 강의하는데 이번 학기에는 개설되지 않는다.
12 배심원으로 뽑힌 사람들 대부분 성격이 좋아 보인다.

Unit 73 EXERCISES

p. 175

1 was a beautiful maple tree
2 stood a lost child crying
3 had a second passed before the lights turned on
4 can you blame him for being absent from work today
5 will I forget the foreign friends I met during my trip to London
6 had I reached the door than I realized I had forgotten my keys

해석

1 그의 정원에 아름다운 단풍나무 한 그루가 있었다.
2 큰 나무 옆에 길을 잃은 아이가 울면서 서 있었다.
3 1초도 지나지 않아 불이 켜졌다.
4 너는 결코 그가 오늘 결근한 것을 나무랄 입장이 아니다.
5 나는 런던을 여행하는 동안 만났던 외국 친구들을 결코 잊지 못할 것이다.
6 나는 문에 다다르자마자 열쇠를 깜빡했다는 것을 깨달았다.

1	am I	2	can he
3	do I	4	is she
5	is my brother	6	have I
7	do I		

해석

1 A: 나는 스웨덴에서 왔어요.
B: 나도 그래요. 만나서 정말 반가워요.
2 A: 너와 너의 형은 스키를 탈 수 있니?
B: 아니. 나는 스키를 잘 못 타고 우리 형도 못 타.
3 A: 난 공포 영화를 좋아하지 않아.
B: 나도 그래. 다른 거 보자.
4 A: 너와 네 여동생은 음악 캠프에 갈 거니?
B: 아니. 나는 음악 캠프에 가지 않을 거고, 내 동생도 안 갈 거야.
5 A: 너와 네 형은 유학을 갈 거니?
B: 아니. 나는 유학을 안 갈 것이고, 우리 형도 마찬가지야.
6 A: 우리 너무 오래 걸었나 봐. 발에 물집이 생겼어.

B: 나도 그래. 아프지, 그렇지 않니?

7 A: 나는 영어가 가장 좋아.
B: 나도 그래. 그래서 내가 영어를 공부하는 데 많은 시간을 쓰는 거야.

Unit 74 EXERCISES

p. 178~179

Ⓐ

1 It is important for me to prepare for the final exam.
2 It is still unclear where Nick will live next year.
3 It was completely untrue what Jerry said to Mary yesterday.
4 It is interesting that you grew up and got an education in Israel.
5 It is not decided yet when the Hollywood star will visit Korea.
6 It is not questionable that she is qualified to be the student representative.
7 It is clear that some computer games can have a bad influence on children.

해석

1 기말시험을 준비하는 것은 나에게 있어 중요한 일이다.
2 내년에 닉이 어디서 살지는 여전히 불분명하다.
3 제리가 어제 메리에게 말한 것은 전적으로 사실이 아니었다.
4 네가 이스라엘에서 자라고 교육 받았다는 사실은 흥미롭다.
5 그 할리우드 스타가 한국에 언제 올지는 아직 정해지지 않았다.
6 그녀가 학생 대표가 될 자질이 있다는 것은 의심의 여지가 없다.
7 일부 컴퓨터 게임들이 아이들에게 나쁜 영향을 줄 수 있다는 것은 분명하다.

Ⓑ

1 to help people in need
2 to get up early every day
3 to spank children in public
4 to explain myself repeatedly
5 not to eat anything after 6:00 p.m.
6 to keep a diary in English every day
7 to go to bed early before exams
8 to see an old man wandering alone around the park
9 to exchange text messages, images, and videos with people in different countries

해석

1 그들은 어려움에 처한 사람들을 돕는 것이 옳다고 믿는다.
2 나는 매일 일찍 일어나는 것이 매우 어렵다는 것을 알게 되었다.
3 많은 사람은 공개적으로 아이들을 때리는 것이 옳지 않다고 믿는다.
4 나는 내 행동을 계속해서 해명하는 것은 시간 낭비라고 생각한다.
5 니콜은 오후 여섯 시 이후로 아무것도 먹지 않기로 규칙을 정했다.
6 나는 매일 영어로 일기를 쓰는 것을 습관으로 만들 것이다.
7 우리 어머니는 시험 전에 내가 일찍 자는 것이 현명하다고 생각한다.
8 그는 그 노인이 공원 주변을 혼자 어슬렁거리는 것을 보고 이상하다고 생각했다.
9 이 애플리케이션은 다른 나라의 사람들과 문자와 이미지, 동영상을 교환하는 것을 가능하게 해준다.

Ⓒ

1 It was Mary that called you this morning.
2 It was a new mobile phone that Yunju wanted.
3 It is the plants on the balcony that need watering.
4 It is on shoes that Jenny spends most of her allowance.
5 It was in 2004 that Alex met his current girlfriend in London.
6 It was an animal shelter that our class visited for volunteering.
7 It was a fallen branch lying across the road that caused the accident.
8 It was on Elm Street that Michael crashed his new motorcycle last night.

해석

1 오늘 아침 네게 전화를 한 것은 바로 메리였다.
2 윤주가 원한 것은 바로 새로운 휴대폰이었다.
3 물을 줘야 하는 것은 바로 발코니의 식물들이다.
4 제니가 용돈의 대부분을 쓰는 데는 바로 신발이다.
5 알렉스가 현재의 여자 친구를 런던에서 만났던 때는 바로 2004년이었다.
6 우리 반이 자원봉사를 위해 방문한 곳은 바로 동물보호소였다.
7 그 사고를 일으켰던 것은 바로 도로를 가로질러 누워 있던 쓰러진 나뭇가지였다.
8 어젯밤에 마이클이 자신의 새 오토바이를 부순 곳은 바로 엘름가였다.

Ⓓ

1 He did tell me
2 It is fun to learn about
3 It takes twenty minutes for me to go
4 It took me half an hour to walk
5 It was yesterday that
6 considered it a mistake to hire Ryan

REVIEW

p. 180~181

Ⓐ

1 are	2 if
3 It	4 is
5 are	6 are
7 have	8 had I
9 is	10 does my brother
11 promise	12 was
13 is	14 listens

해설/해석

1 The CDs가 주어이므로 are가 적절
이 용기에 있는 CD들은 우리 형의 것이다.

2 '브리짓이 케빈을 초대했는지 아닌지를'이라는 의미가 되어야 하므로 if가 적절
내 친구가 나에게 브리짓이 케빈을 초대했는지 아닌지 물었다.

3 that 이하가 진주어이므로 가주어 It이 적절
오늘 가게가 모두 문을 닫았다는 것이 이상하다.

4 '세상이 둥글다'는 것은 일반적인 진리이므로 is가 적절
세상이 둥글다는 것이 항상 받아들여졌던 것은 아니었다.

5 The cookbooks가 주어이므로 are가 적절
냉장고 위에 있는 요리책들은 우리 어머니의 것이다.

6 부정어(At no time) 도치 구문으로 players가 주어이므로 are가 적절
선수들은 심판과 결코 다투어서는 안 된다.

7 The two cartons of milk가 주어이므로 have가 적절
냉장고에 있는 우유 두 팩이 상했다.

8 부정어(Nowhere)가 문장 앞으로 나가 주어 동사가 도치된 문장으로 had I가 적절
어디에서도 이보다 더 아름답게 장식된 방은 본적이 없다.

9 '태양에서부터 세 번째에 있는 행성이 지구'라는 것은 일반적인 진리이므로 is가 적절
우리는 지구가 태양에서부터 세 번째에 있는 행성이라고 배웠다.

10 nor 구문에서 주어 동사가 도치되므로 does my brother가 적절
나는 중국 음식을 좋아하지 않고, 우리 형도 마찬가지다.

11 동사를 강조하기 위해 「do/dose/did+동사원형」을 사용했으므로 promised가 아닌 promise가 적절
그녀는 같은 실수를 다시 저지르지 않겠다고 정말로 약속했다.

12 직접화법을 간접화법으로 전환할 때 전달동사의 시제가 과거(told)이고 부사구도 that day이므로 that절의 시제도 과거가 적절
그녀는 그날 스터디 그룹을 시작할 것이라고 내게 말했다.

13 동명사구(Washing your hands often)가 주어이므로 is가 적절
손을 자주 씻는 것은 감기에 걸리지 않는 가장 좋은 방법이다.

14 '스트레스를 받을 때 음악을 듣는다'는 현재의 습관(gets)을 이야기하므로 listens가 적절
마이클은 스트레스가 쌓이면 음악을 듣는다고 말했다.

1 was a box of candy
2 the window in the kitchen that was broken yesterday
3 the gold medal that she won at the Olympics last year
4 did try his best to get excellent results in all subjects
5 my brother that[who] graduated high school with honors last year
6 does he have breakfast because he has to go to school very early

해설/해석

1 부사구(on the top shelf)가 문장 앞으로 나가면서 주어와 동사가 도치
맨 꼭대기 선반에 사탕 한 박스가 있었다.

2 「it is/was ~ that …」 강조문을 이용하여 주어를 강조
어제 깨진 것은 바로 부엌의 창문이었다.

3 「it is/was ~ that …」 강조문을 이용하여 목적어를 강조
그녀가 작년 올림픽에서 딴 것은 바로 금메달이었다.

4 동사를 강조하기 위해 「do/dose/did+동사원형」을 사용
그는 모든 과목에서 좋은 결과를 얻기 위해 정말로 최선을 다했다.

5 「it is/was ~ that …」 강조문을 이용하여 주어를 강조
작년에 우수한 성적으로 고등학교를 졸업한 사람은 우리 형이었다.

6 부정어(Rarely)가 문장 앞으로 나가면서 주어와 동사가 도치되므로 「부정어+do[does, did]+주어+동사원형~」의 형태
그는 매우 일찍 학교를 가야 하기 때문에 아침을 거의 먹지 않는다.

C

1 comes the train
2 where I saw
3 said to, told 등
4 are going to
5 틀린 것 없음
6 she
7 did I
8 틀린 것 없음
9 have I seen
10 틀린 것 없음
11 stretch
12 틀린 것 없음
13 it a waste of time to wait in a long line to see the concert
14 do

해설/해석

1 부사 Here가 강조되어 문두에 오면 주어 동사의 어순이 바뀌므로 comes the train이 적절
기차가 온다!

2 간접화법은 「where+주어+동사」의 어순이므로 where I saw가 적절
그는 나에게 어디서 그 차를 보았느냐고 물었다.

3 said는 전치사 없이 목적어를 취하지 않으므로 said to나 told가 적절
그녀는 자신이 한국말을 못한다고 나에게 말했다.

4 The CEO and his brother가 주어이므로 are going to가 적절
최고 경영자와 그의 동생은 교도소에 갈 것이다.

5 still로 지금도 런던 남부에 살고 있느냐고 묻는 것임을 알 수 있으므로 live를 쓰는 것이 맞음
그는 나에게 아직도 런던의 남부에 살고 있느냐고 물었다.

6 She told us that she didn't need any help.에서 주어를 강조한 문장이므로 she가 적절
우리에게 어떠한 도움도 필요하지 않다고 말한 것은 바로 그녀였다.

7 Little이 문두에 쓰였으므로 주어와 동사가 도치된 did I가 적절
마크가 내게 사실을 말하고 있지 않았다는 것을 나는 전혀 몰랐다.

8 주절의 시제가 과거라도 종속절이 현재의 습관을 나타내면 주절의 동사가 종속절의 시제에 영향을 주지 않음
그녀는 대개 인형을 안고 잠을 잔다고 말했다.

9 부정어 Rarely가 문장의 앞에 왔으므로 주어 동사가 도치된 have I seen이 적절
나는 TV에서 그렇게 재미있는 크리켓 게임을 거의 본 적이 없다.

10 The kids가 주어이므로 are가 적절
그네 옆에서 노는 아이들이 나의 아이들이다.

11 '로키 산맥이 캐나다에서 미국까지 뻗쳐 있다'는 일반적인 진리에는 현재 시제를 쓰므로 stretch가 적절
나는 로키 산맥이 캐나다부터 미국까지 뻗어 있다고 배웠다.

12 「It ~ that」 구문으로 주어 Mr. Kim이 강조되었으므로 that과 who

둘 다 가능
방과 후 스포츠 프로그램을 관리하는 사람은 김 선생님이다.

13 가목적어 it을 활용해야 하는 문장으로 진목적어는 to wait in a long line to see the concert임
나는 콘서트를 보려고 길게 줄을 서는 것은 시간 낭비라고 생각한다.

14 「so+동사+주어」 구문으로 all of my friends가 주어이므로 do가 적절
나는 추운 날엔 정말 뜨겁고 매운 수프를 먹는 걸 좋아하고, 내 친구들도 모두 그래.

1 It is a mystery how this great pyramid was built.
2 It is exciting to do outdoor activities on a sunny day.
3 It is pleasant to see an old couple walking hand in hand.
4 It is dangerous to swim in the sea on a cold day like this.
5 It is surprising that such a young kid can communicate with foreigners without difficulties.

해설/해석

1 주어가 의문사절이 되어 길어진 경우로 가주어 It을 사용한 구문으로 바꿈
이 거대한 피라미드가 어떻게 지어졌는지는 미스터리다.

2 주어가 to부정사가 되어 길어진 경우로 가주어 It을 사용한 구문으로 바꿈
맑은 날에 실외활동을 하는 것은 신난다.

3 주어가 to부정사가 되어 길어진 경우로 가주어 It을 사용한 구문으로 바꿈
노부부가 손을 잡고 걷는 것을 보는 것은 유쾌한 일이다.

4 주어가 to부정사가 되어 길어진 경우로 가주어 It을 사용한 구문으로 바꿈
이렇게 추운 날에 바다에서 수영하는 것은 위험하다.

5 주어가 that절이 되어 길어진 경우로 가주어 It을 사용한 구문으로 바꿈
그렇게 어린 아이가 어려움 없이 외국인과 의사소통을 할 수 있다는 것은 놀라운 일이다.

REVIEW PLUS

p. 182

1 ④ 2 ②

해설/해석

1 ④ '신발이 어디 있었는지 몰랐다'라는 뜻으로 과거의 일을 이야기하고 있으므로 doesn't가 아니라 didn't가 적절
① 그녀는 동물을 만져 볼 수 있는 어린이 동물원이 어디인지 알고 싶어 한다.
② 스키와 같은 새로운 스포츠를 배우는 데는 시간이 걸린다.
③ 정시에 오고, 최선을 다하는 것이 중요하다.
④ 빌리는 자신의 신발이 어디 있는지 모르겠다고 했다.
⑤ 내가 인터넷에서 무엇인가를 찾는 데는 단 몇 초밖에 걸리지 않는다.

2 ② My neighbors가 주어이므로 has가 아니라 have가 적절
① 영양가 있는 샐러드를 만드는 데는 오랜 시간이 걸리지 않는다.
② 휴가 중인 우리 이웃은 두 마리의 개를 기른다.
③ 나는 삼 분 넘게 숨을 참을 수 있다. 제프도 그렇다.
④ 가게 점원이 나에게 내 치수를 찾는 것을 그녀가 도와줘도 되느냐고 물었다.
⑤ 나는 그에게 내 표를 보여 주어야만 했고, 그는 그제야 나를 들여보내 주었다.

③

해설/해석

③ She asked you, "Do you want something to drink?"를 간접화법으로 바꾼 것으로 의문사가 없는 의문문을 간접화법으로 바꾸려면 that이 아니라 if나 whether를 사용
① A: 뭐라고? 방금 뭐라고 했어?
B: "내가 내일 전화할게."라고 말했어.
② A: 그가 네가 영어를 할 수 있는지 물었어.
B: 응, 할 수는 있지만 조금밖에 못해.
③ A: 그녀가 뭐라고 말했니? 나는 못 들었어.
B: 그녀는 네게 뭔가 마시고 싶은지 물었어.
④ A: 김 선생님이 내게 연습을 더하러 오라고 충고하셨어.
B: 그래서 넌 어떻게 할 거야?
⑤ A: 방금 누가 전화했니?
B: 릴리였어. 그녀는 내가 레슬리를 파티에 초대했는지 물었어.

⑤

해설/해석

⑤ 부정어구 Never가 문두에 쓰였으므로 주어와 동사가 도치되어야 하므로 have we가 적절
"내가 너희에게 수수께끼를 낼게, 알았지?"라고 마크가 말했다. "너희가 이것을 풀 수 있는지 봐봐." 그가 계속했다. "카우보이가 여인숙에 on Friday에 가서 이틀 밤을 머무르고, on Friday에 떠났어. 어떻게 이게 가능할까?" "카우보이가 토요일에 떠났다고 했니?"라고 윤호가 마크에게 물었다. "아니, 나는 카우보이가 on Friday에 떠났다고 했어" 마크가 대답했다. "일요일에?"라고 윤호가 다시 물었다. "아니! 그 카우보이가 떠난 것은 바로 on Friday였어!"라고 마크가 소리쳤다. "난 모르겠어."라고 혜수가 말했다. "나도."라고 소희가 투덜거렸다. "잠깐만, 마크? 네가 "on"이라고 말할 때 그것이 on a horse를 말하는 거니, 아니면 on that day를 말하는 거니?"라고 바다가 물었다. "네가 맞췄어! 프라이데이는 카우보이의 말 이름이야." 라고 마크가 말했다. "그렇게 바보 같은 수수께끼는 처음 들어봐!"라고 반 친구들이 불평했다.

Workbook

PART 11

UNIT 39

A **1** can **2** can **3** Can **4** be able to **5** be able to

B **1** was able to handle the problem **2** am not able to hear **3** I can drive **4** couldn't concentrate on his work **5** wasn't able to see the mountains

C **1** 받을 수 있을까요 **2** 도와줄 수 있니 **3** 끝낼 수 있을 것이다 **4** 일 리가 없어 **5** 할 수가 없어서

D **1** Can you swim **2** could not help crying **3** can[could] lend **4** could have left **5** can[could] have **6** could have told **7** could get

E **1** It can't be true **2** Could you keep an eye on my bag **3** could be my friend **4** I cannot help smiling **5** was able to win the gold medal **6** can't comply with your request this time **7** You could have checked it once again

UNIT 40

A **1** may[might] reject **2** may[might] be **3** may[might], let **4** may[might] drop by

B **1** They may[might] be stuck in a traffic jam. **2** He may[might] not know how to solve this problem. **3** He may[might] be playing basketball with his friends. **4** She may[might] not want to participate in this project.

C **1** 생각하는 게 당연해 **2** 오지 않을지도 몰라 **3** 남겨 드릴까요 **4** 돌아가는 게 좋겠어

D **1** May I ask **2** may[might] be sick **3** may[might] be asleep **4** may[might] be canceled **5** might as well accept **6** may well be upset **7** may[might] be

E **1** May I close the windows? **2** You may well feel bored. **3** We may as well wait a little more. **4** He may be meeting a client **5** She might be in the hospital **6** He may be a little late for the gathering. **7** She might not accept your idea.

UNIT 41

A **1** 찾아올 필요 없어 **2** 복용해서는 안 된다 **3** 따라야 한다 **4** 틀림없다 **5** 먹은 것이 틀림없다 **6** 예약을 해야 할 것이다 **7** 확인하지 않은 것이 틀림없다

B **1** have to finish the whole test **2** must not enter that room **3** must lose weight **4** need not hurry **5** have to take the test **6** must not be late

C **1** have to do **2** must not judge people **3** must be too spicy **4** must have had **5** must wear a life jacket **6** don't have to get up **7** had to go home

D **1** We didn't have to buy the tickets. **2** You must be very weak. **3** I must have dropped it somewhere. **4** must not ride a roller coaster **5** must put the lid back on after you use it **6** we don't have to wait in line **7** They must not be home.

UNIT 42

A **1** 지켜야 한다 **2** 시작해야 한다 **3** 사과하는 게 좋겠다 **4** 들어야 한다 **5** 방해하지 않아야 한다 **6** 참여하지 말아야 한다고 **7** 가는 것이 좋겠다

B **1** should turn off **2** shouldn't have joked **3** should have studied **4** should be **5** should have reserved **6** should call

C **1** ought to offer your seat **2** I should do **3** shouldn't have told you **4** should take a day off **5** should have come earlier **6** should win the game **7** should not make a quick decision

D **1** We had better hurry up. **2** I had better not drive. **3** I should have bought a lottery ticket **4** You should try to spend more time **5** I shouldn't have listened to him. **6** You ought not to postpone the meeting **7** You had better tell him the truth

UNIT 43

A **1** would like to sit **2** would rather not talk **3** would rather drink **4** Would you like to go **5** would rather be

B **1** would **2** used to **3** used to **4** would, would **5** used to

C **1** would rather not talk about **2** am not used to speaking **3** is not used to using **4** used to be crowded with shoppers

D **1** 갈래 **2** 원하세요 **3** 기다려 줄래 **4** 불러 주시겠어요 **5** 답하지 않는 것이 낫겠다 **6** 이었지만 **7** 방문하곤 했다

E **1** would read all sorts of books **2** She is not used to having a regular lifestyle. **3** People used to park illegally around here. **4** I would rather not go to school today. **5** I would like to introduce our new employee **6** would rather go hiking than stay home **7** she didn't use to like them

PART 12

UNIT 44

A **1** may[might/could] be sick **2** must be intelligent **3** must be tired **4** may[might/could] be taking a test **5** must be living **6** may[might/could] be my mother

B **1** can't[couldn't] have bought **2** must have forgotten **3** must have lost **4** must enjoy **5** can't[couldn't] have visited **6** may[might/could] have been **7** may[might] not know

C **1** must be late for **2** can't[couldn't] have been canceled **3** may[might] not go on **4** must have studied hard **5** may[might/could] be allergic to **6** can't[couldn't] be in New York **7** may[might/could] have transferred

D **1** she may move to another city **2** He must like coffee. **3** the shop may have been closed **4** He must have forgotten to bring his umbrella. **5** She couldn't have been asleep **6** He might not have gone to the party. **7** She might know where it is.

UNIT 45

A **1** exchanging **2** opened **3** used **4** asked **5** taking **6** waiting

B **1** Can I check out the book? **2** Could I turn on the air conditioner? **3** Will you show me around the town? **4** Could you get me a glass of iced water? **5** May I take your order? **6** Would you explain the problem in detail? **7** Can you tell me how to get to the train station?

C **1** Will you turn off the light **2** Would you mind giving **3** can I have some money **4** Would you mind **5** May I take a message **6** Would you mind getting **7** Could you tell him

D **1** Will you leave me alone? **2** Would you mind if I left work earlier **3** Can I see your passport and boarding pass **4** Could I meet you at my office tomorrow? **5** Would you mind moving over one more seat? **6** Would you take me to the National Museum? **7** May I see your driver's license?

UNIT 46

A **1** shall I call **2** Why don't you give **3** Let's go out **4** Shall we shop **5** Why don't we have **6** let's turn

B **1** Let's put **2** Let's have **3** Let's hurry up. **4** let's keep **5** Why don't we participate **6** Why don't we exercise **7** Why don't we order **8** Why don't we take

C **1** Why don't we put off **2** let's get down to **3** Let's not forget about **4** Why don't you call **5** Shall I bring your breakfast **6** Shall we go swimming **7** Shall I ask him to help

D **1** Shall we order something to drink **2** Shall I pick you up at six **3** Let's not talk about the issue **4** Let's warm up first before we start exercising **5** Why don't we make dinner by ourselves **6** Let's skip it and tackle it **7** Why don't you spend more time with your family

PART 13

UNIT 47

A **1** bored, boring **2** interested, interesting **3** exhausted, exhausting **4** depressed, depressing **5** shocked, shocking

B **1** similar **2** ○ **3** exciting **4** Injured **5** satisfied **6** embarrassing **7** ○ **8** tiring

C **1** is worried about **2** is embarrassing **3** I feel frightened **4** I was surprised **5** To soothe her crying baby **6** the result was very disappointing **7** spoken language, written language

D **1** a nice new brown coat **2** a beautiful tall green tree **3** the large brown leather bag

4 beautiful long blond hair, big blue eyes **5** Lots of people are aware of the problem **6** I was very worried about the old blue roof of my house

UNIT 48

A **1** usually **2** sometimes **3** always **4** seldom **5** always **6** often, never

B **1** My mother often cleans my room. **2** His concert begins at 7:30 p.m. on December 24th. **3** I studied English very hard in the library yesterday. **4** My mother always says children should go to bed early. **5** My father has just obtained a driver's license, so he tends to drive very carefully.

C **1** enthusiastically **2** later **3** terribly **4** carefully **5** already **6** almost **7** there, here

D **1** the train had already left **2** He was completely sure **3** really want to see the Eiffel Tower in Paris **4** I've already finished my homework **5** sometimes argue with each other, still good friends **6** He politely asked me how to get to the airport **7** was nervously waiting her turn in the waiting room at that time

UNIT 49

A **1** enough **2** very **3** enough **4** too **5** enough **6** too

B **1** 어떤 사람들은, 확신한다 **2** 현재 상황, 참석할 예정이다 **3** 늦지 말라고, 1980년대 후반에, 작고한 설립자

C **1** was nearly run over **2** such a beautiful city **3** so quiet **4** is highly recommended **5** too late **6** hardly believe

D **1** It is highly unlikely that **2** too many hard questions in this exam **3** Garlic is used in nearly all Korean food. **4** She was certain that he would win **5** Her late husband left a large fortune **6** I know they won't last long **7** because he was a fast learner

PART 14

UNIT 50

A **1** As long as **2** as great as **3** as expensive as **4** as quickly as **5** as soon as **6** as tall as **7** as slowly as

B **1** as long as possible **2** as difficult as **3** as interesting as **4** sooner had she lain, than **5** as frequently as you can **6** as early as he could **7** as important as

C **1** doesn't look as good as **2** sells as well as **3** twice as large as **4** as long as you keep quiet **5** as great a novelist as ever **6** No sooner had she appeared, than **7** no one, as smart as

D **1** is less slippery than that one **2** throw the ball as far as possible **3** she was as beautiful as ever **4** I can sleep as much as I want **5** was not so far from here as I thought **6** No sooner had he finished talking than

UNIT 51

A **1** to **2** than **3** to **4** than **5** than **6** to **7** to **8** to, than **9** than **10** than

B **1** The more, the less happy **2** less crowded than **3** less frequently than **4** richer, richer **5** The more, the more **6** less competitive than

C **1** the more, the more **2** of **3** than **4** even, much, far, still, a lot 등 **5** to

D **1** The older, the more **2** much healthier than **3** higher pay than **4** far inferior to that **5** leave earlier than usual

E **1** The more exercise, the healthier you get **2** his breathing became harder and harder **3** The more difficult, the more I concentrate **4** The sooner you make, the more quickly

UNIT 52

A **1** the most difficult **2** the coldest **3** the highest **4** the longest **5** the latest **6** the thinnest **7** farthest

B **1** luckier than any other man / No, luckier than / No, as lucky as **2** colder than any other day / No, colder than / No, as cold as **3** more intelligent than any other employee / No, more intelligent than / No, as intelligent as **4** more dangerous than any other town / No, more dangerous than / No, as dangerous as

C **1** the eldest of **2** the most famous singer **3** the easiest way **4** make the most of **5** one of the most respected CEOs **6** the worst situation **7** the last person to deceive

D **1** not in the least surprised at the news **2** spends most of her time at home **3** better than any other musical instrument's **4** he recommended was at best average **5** Nothing is as dangerous as judging people **6** one of the hardest languages to learn **7** the greatest player in the history of basketball

UNIT 53

A **1** the same, as **2** different from **3** similar to **4** the same, as **5** similar to **6** different from

B **1** the same as **2** the same, as **3** different from **4** similar to **5** similar to **6** different from **7** similar to

C **1** the same class as **2** the same as before **3** look, alike **4** similar to the violin **5** different from usual **6** different from my expectations **7** similar to that of chimpanzees

D **1** is very similar to mine **2** was different from her descriptions **3** is similar to Chuseok in Korea **4** were very different from ours **5** meet at the same place as before **6** All the houses in the town looked alike to me. **7** playing is the same as learning

PART 15

UNIT 54

A **1** missing **2** shaking **3** fallen **4** burned **5** leaning **6** Barking **7** broken

B **1** annoying, annoyed **2** interested, interesting **3** amazing, amazed **4** exciting, excited **5** terrifying, terrified **6** surprised, surprising

C **1** called Cathy **2** made in Italy **3** embarrassed **4** chatting with someone **5** written in English **6** wearing a blue shirt **7** hanging on the wall

D **1** My cell phone was stolen **2** were killed by the collapsed building **3** cover her swollen eyes with sunglasses **4** has grown at an alarming rate **5** was reading a book next to her sleeping baby **6** was frightened when the roller coaster went down very fast **7** annoyed by the kids screaming and running

UNIT 55

A **1** boring **2** burning **3** lost **4** crawling **5** missing **6** found **7** shocked **8** climbing

B **1** hit by a bicycle **2** wearing blue jeans **3** broken window **4** singing and dancing on the stage **5** company making computers **6** invited to the wedding

C **1** was disappointed **2** made of gold **3** missing words **4** broken computer **5** stealing her purse **6** waiting outside the classroom **7** delighted, heard my name called

D **1** had her hair cut for a change **2** it was written in English **3** heard someone playing the piano **4** remove the broken pieces of glass **5** The disappointed audiences left **6** many people waiting in line to buy tickets **7** The exam result has already been released

UNIT 56

A **1** Being sick **2** drinking a glass of cold beer **3** Watching TV **4** Being confident to pass the exam **5** Graduating from college **6** Being very thin **7** Being allergic to some food

B **1** When you cross the road **2** while he was reading the newspaper **3** After she finished her homework **4** If you ask her for advice **5** Even though he is very old **6** Because he had bought a new computer

C **1** Being seriously injured **2** Not having anything to say **3** Giving me a light hug **4** Not invited to the party **5** Having spent all my money **6** Having seen the movie **7** Seeing the giant monster

D **1** Having failed the test, he had to take **2** Having lost his wallet, he found it **3** Going one more block, you will find **4** Born to a poor family, she has never given up **5** Reading a book, she noted its good passages **6** Having so much work to do, she had to stay up **7** Not being a minor anymore, she has a right

PART 16

UNIT 57

A **1** or **2** and **3** but **4** but **5** nor **6** for **7** yet **8** so

B **1** I couldn't read the book at all, for it was

written in French. **2** Are you still a college student, or did you already graduate? **3** She speaks English well, yet she's afraid of speaking with foreigners. **4** She didn't come to school, nor did she come to the English academy. **5** He doesn't have much experience, but he is doing well in the company. **6** There were too many people in the shopping mall, so I couldn't find my friend. **7** I like being friends with Susan, but I don't want to share a room with her.

C **1** and, made a lot of money **2** nor did I **3** or your mother will be **4** so students didn't go to school **5** for they are healthy **6** some milk, eggs, and apples **7** yet he wouldn't take any help

D **1** but I don't want to go **2** Would you like some tea or coffee? **3** for he told a lie to her **4** has never learned a foreign language, nor have I **5** and several fire trucks soon arrived at the scene **6** so she has two dogs and three cats

UNIT 58

A **1** like **2** have **3** believes **4** wants

B **1** either at home or at the library **2** both tasty and healthy **3** not only very diligent but also smart, smart as well as very diligent **4** neither interesting nor useful **5** not only upset, but also disappointed with me, disappointed as well as upset with me

C **1** were **2** was **3** likes **4** helps

D **1** The shop both designs and sells **2** either on Thursday or on Friday **3** Both my father and I like **4** either the subway or a bus **5** Neither you nor she made any mistakes **6** neither safety facilities nor lifeguards

E **1** both defend and score goals **2** Both Jerry and Maggie are qualified to be the team leader. **3** Neither Alice nor I am going to the party **4** He has been to not only Germany, but also Switzerland. **5** Either Brian or Nick is supposed to wash the dishes **6** keeps a couple of tigers as well as a giant snake

UNIT 59

A **1** that **2** Whether **3** that **4** that **5** that **6** whether **7** whether[if]

B **1** It is a rumor that he died of cancer. **2** It is true that the company shut down. **3** It is unlikely that she will advance to the final round. **4** It is obvious that he will end up in jail eventually. **5** It is surprising that he can speak three languages. **6** It is strange that she refused the job offer from the big company. **7** It is a fact that the earth is suffering from environmental pollution.

C **1** I don't know where I have to get off. **2** I wonder who stole my laptop computer. **3** Do you know what caused the building to catch fire? **4** I don't remember where I put my student ID card. **5** Could you tell me why you were crying in the classroom? **6** Let's ask him what time we have to gather in front of the main gate. **7** I'd like to know where I can get accurate information about backpacking.

D **1** if my grandfather will recover soon **2** I wonder who is going to win the top prize **3** It is true that he did his best **4** Whether he will be able to win the election **5** I don't know what I should tell him **6** The fact that the famous actor is her cousin **7** I don't know where this bus is heading.

UNIT 60

A **1** While **2** since **3** Before **4** After **5** until **6** when **7** because **8** in order that

B **1** I couldn't fall asleep easily as I drank too much coffee., As I drank too much coffee, I couldn't fall asleep easily. **2** Before she cleans the house, she airs it out., She airs out the house before she cleans it. **3** Since I became a college student, I have never had my hair cut short., I have never had my hair cut short since I became a college student. **4** As soon as she heard that her son had a traffic accident, she fainted., She fainted as soon as she heard that her son had a traffic accident.

C **1** He made way for an ambulance so that it could pass quickly. **2** My sister helped me so that I could finish my homework on time. **3** Try to spend some time in the sun so that you can get enough vitamin D. **4** She will learn French so that she can go to culinary school in France. **5** Please show us your membership card so that you can receive the discounted rate.

D **1** because it was too expensive **2** as soon as he comes home **3** When he was about to fall asleep **4** since it might rain this afternoon **5** while she was traveling around France **6** until they allow me to go abroad **7** Now that he has a part-time job **8** As I discussed the issue with him **9** since I moved to this house

UNIT 61

A **1** while **2** Unless **3** As long as **4** If **5** Even though **6** such, that **7** whereas **8** so, that **9** If, not **10** Even if

B **1** Unless it rains, I will drive to work tomorrow. **2** If it isn't[is not] soaked in the water, it can last up to five years. **3** Unless you have anything to say, I will end the meeting now. **4** If you don't give up, you will be able to achieve your dream someday. **5** Unless you buy tickets in advance, you won't be able to see the concert.

C **1** The food was so greasy that I left some on my plate. **2** She is such an attractive person that everyone likes her. **3** His eyesight is so poor that he can't see anything without glasses. **4** I had such a light breakfast that I felt very hungry before lunchtime. **5** The restaurant is so popular that you have to book a table in advance. **6** Both of them were so furious that nobody dared to end their argument. **7** The forest was such a dangerous place that my mother wouldn't let me go there.

D **1** while she is poor at math **2** As long as it's not that expensive **3** Unless you like pizza **4** In case I lose my child **5** Although he was born weak **6** so large that we could play soccer **7** such a nice garden in his house that

PART 17

UNIT 62

A **1** which **2** whose **3** who(m) **4** who(m) **5** whose **6** who **7** which

B **1** The subject is psychology. I am interested in it. **2** Have you had the milk? It was in the refrigerator. **3** People were generally nice. I met them at the party. **4** The employees are all kind. They work for the bank. **5** What is the name of the girl? Her father is a police officer. **6** Catherine works for a company. It handles wood furniture.

C **1** The movie which I saw yesterday was not recommendable. **2** Walter, whose dream was to be rich, has won the lottery. **3** I teach students whose goal is to enter Harvard University. **4** The police finally arrested the thief whom they were looking for. **5** Are you the person whom I spoke to on the phone yesterday? **6** We are going to have dinner at the restaurant which Lena recommended to us. **7** The man who is going to get married this March teaches English in a middle school.

D **1** which I sat on was very uncomfortable **2** who used to live in the country **3** The man whom she was talking to **4** the director who has made the movie a big hit **5** the book which you asked me to buy **6** an old friend whom I haven't seen for ten years **7** whose native language is not Korean

UNIT 63

A **1** that **2** what **3** what **4** What **5** what **6** that **7** that **8** that **9** what **10** what

B **1** Incheon, which I was born in, has changed a lot. **2** The man that[who] lives next door was arrested last night. **3** She was wearing what I was thinking of buying. **4** They just ignored what she warned them about. **5** The pictures at which you are looking were taken with a Polaroid camera. **6** What I can't tell you is why he left you without a word. **7** The museum that[which] was burned down a year ago will be reopened next month.

C **1** what she ate **2** what we asked for **3** What is most important to me **4** that[which] opens the basement **5** much work that[which] we have to finish by this Friday **6** what I ordered **7** the same books that I have

D **1** something that you should care about **2** Let me tell you what you are supposed to do. **3** I'm sure that you are going to beat him

4 The website has everything that I want to know. **5** I realized what you said last time was right. **6** your opinion that we need more conversation **7** what we are planning to do

UNIT 64

A **1** how **2** why **3** where **4** when

B **1** Whoever finds it first **2** whatever you say about him **3** Whichever you choose **4** Whenever I have to study until late at night **5** However expensive the tuition fees are

C **1** This is the studio where[in which] he spends most of his time. **2** This is the restaurant where[in which] I often have dinner with my friends. **3** He couldn't forget the day when[on which] he released his debut album. **4** I will tell you several ways you can upgrade your navigation system. **5** His fans wanted to know the reason why[for which] he refused all the interviews.

D **1** The city where we spent a week was beautiful. **2** This is the file where I keep lots of important data. **3** I know how I can bake cakes without an oven. **4** I can't forget the day when I got on a plane for the first time. **5** Please tell me the reason why you didn't come to the event. **6** I will remember the summer vacation when I stayed with my grandmother. **7** I want to know the reason why my best friend transferred to another school.

E **1** Whenever I feel sad **2** wherever I go. **3** how they overcame cancer **4** reason why I had to change **5** Whoever wants the job **6** how you can give a presentation **7** there is no reason why

PART 18

UNIT 65

A **1** were **2** were **3** had **4** didn't rain **5** exercised **6** had **7** were

B **1** If I were tall, I could reach the top shelf. **2** If I were not full, I could eat more cake. **3** If I had enough money, I could travel around Europe. **4** If tomorrow were my grandfather's birthday, I would visit him. **5** If Jack and I went to the same school, we would see each other often. **6** If I had a camera with me now, I could take a picture of the movie star. **7** If the tall building didn't block my house, I could get enough warmth from the sun. **8** If I knew her phone number, I could invite her to go to the movies with me. **9** If I didn't have many things to do, I could spend more time with my children.

C **1** arrives, can get on the train **2** had enough time, would help you **3** lends me, will pick you up **4** meet Greg, will tell him **5** studied, could get first place **6** don't like Chinese food, can eat

D **1** if you were able to turn back the clock **2** If you help me pack for the move **3** get up early tomorrow morning, I'll go jogging **4** were a holiday, would visit my grandmother **5** were not sensitive to sunlight, would sunbathe on the beach **6** he were genuinely regretful, I would forgive him

UNIT 66

A **1** If I had studied hard, I could have gone to college. **2** If she had taken his advice, she would have won the contest. **3** If he had not overslept this morning, he could have taken the school bus. **4** If it had not rained a lot, the construction would already have been finished. **5** If I hadn't taken the wrong bus, I wouldn't have been late for the gathering. **6** If my computer hadn't broken down, I could have finished my homework earlier. **7** If I had known that she would transfer to another school, I would have said goodbye to her.

B **1** If I hadn't hurt my leg, I could go with you now. **2** If I had got a driver's license, I could drive now. **3** If I hadn't gained weight, this dress would fit me now. **4** If I had slept enough last night, I wouldn't be sleepy now. **5** If I had got up early this morning, I would be in the classroom now. **6** If I had bought the tickets in advance, I would be enjoying the show now.

C **1** should have responded **2** should have seen **3** should have asked for **4** should have practiced **5** shouldn't have been **6** shouldn't have tried **7** shouldn't have talked **8** hadn't been

D **1** advised that I eat and sleep well **2** recommend that you go jogging **3** If the world should end tomorrow **4** imperative that he have an operation **5** demanded that the admission fee should be **6** desirable that you get a medical checkup **7** If I were to go back to, would study art

UNIT 67

A **1** I had learned how to play the piano **2** you could go to the English summer camp with us **3** you had seen the movie with us **4** there were more daycare centers for working parents **5** they would turn up the heat

B **1** as if she were a little kid **2** as if they hadn't seen me before **3** as if she were a millionaire **4** as if he had owned the company **5** as if I were his girlfriend

C **1** you left for the airport **2** would be unhappy **3** had drunk **4** as if she knew everything **5** couldn't have participated in

D **1** But for peace, the world would be miserable., Without peace, the world would be miserable. **2** But for the life vest, she would have died., Without the life vest, she would have died. **3** But for his letter, I wouldn't have known the truth., Without his letter, I wouldn't have known the truth. **4** But for the Internet, our lives would be very inconvenient., Without the Internet, our lives would be very inconvenient. **5** But for my parents, I couldn't have graduated from college., Without my parents, I couldn't have graduated from college.

E **1** Were I not busy, I could help you clean up the house. **2** Were I tall enough, I would enter the modeling competition. **3** Had you told me about it earlier, I would have visited him in the hospital. **4** Had my car not broken down, I would have gone to the airport to pick you up. **5** Were the department store close to my house, I would go shopping every day. **6** Had my parents let me travel by myself, I would have gone backpacking overseas.

PART 19

UNIT 68

A **1** to **2** to **3** of **4** of **5** of

B **1** In case of **2** of **3** Although[Even though/Though] **4** stealing **5** asking **6** while **7** unless **8** because **9** because of

C **1** instead of going out **2** in front of the library **3** thanks to the seat belt **4** in spite of the opposition **5** due to the time difference **6** According to a new study **7** during the Christmas season

D **1** on account of heavy fog **2** because of huge storms **3** after giving his baby a bath **4** was doubtful of the benefits of the new program **5** given up the project without her help **6** the only person who is capable of controlling him **7** couldn't go out because of rumors about him

UNIT 69

A **1** resemble **2** marry **3** expanding **4** have **5** driving **6** getting up, having **7** postpone **8** receiving

B **1** She knows that she always lacks confidence. **2** I wondered why she didn't answer my question. **3** My sister and I don't resemble each other at all. **4** I just wanted them to explain why it happened. **5** We had to wait in a long line to enter the theater. **6** I am going to ask her to marry me on her birthday. **7** He told me that we couldn't discuss this matter on the phone. **8** I agree with his opinion that we need to approach the problem differently.

C **1** she lacks flexibility **2** got married to a famous actor, gave birth to **3** is dedicated to helping poor families **4** to approach them first **5** to answer the phones **6** In addition to eating properly **7** to discuss our plan

D **1** Lots of people object to tax increases. **2** why she missed the classes today **3** is going to take a day off next Monday **4** are looking forward to working with you **5** men cannot enter the room **6** to discuss the matter publicly **7** answer the questions in a limited time

UNIT 70

A **1** out **2** on **3** on **4** at **5** at **6** into **7** for **8** into **9** for **10** out

B **1** pay for **2** change into **3** figure out **4** yelled at **5** depended on

C **1** act out **2** look into **3** jumped at **4** look for **5** insisting on

D **1** focus on your future **2** is looking for information **3** aims at the young generation **4** didn't laugh at his joke **5** rush into a decision **6** acted out a couple of scenes **7** apply for a student exchange program

E **1** My shoes are worn out **2** smiled at the visitors **3** How much do I have to pay for parking? **4** insist on going with her **5** doesn't want to rush into marriage **6** she let out our secret **7** society puts emphasis on results over process

PART 20

UNIT 71

A **1** if[whether] I had finished my homework **2** why I didn't call[hadn't called] him the previous day[the day before] **3** he was going on a business trip the following week **4** what I was going to do on New Year's Day **5** we (should) put off our trip until we save enough money **6** she was going to buy Jason Michael's new album **7** if[whether] I wanted him to drive me to school the next[following] day

B **1** "Have you had dinner?" **2** "Do you know when he will be back?" **3** "Where should we meet tomorrow?" **4** "Don't[Do not] eat instant noodles late at night." **5** "When did you graduate from college?" **6** "I want to be an actor when I grow up."

C **1** said he had **2** told us to stay **3** asked, if[whether] I had seen the movie **4** asked, where I had bought the necklace **5** told, he got first place, his **6** said his parents passed away **7** told me to wash my hands

D **1** if I had money to buy the car **2** we should book a table at the restaurant **3** when the exam results would be announced **4** told me that I should take a rest for a few days **5** told her I could help her do the housework that day **6** if she could come to his birthday party the following day

UNIT 72

A **1** is **2** was **3** will, succeed **4** had, left **5** take[took] **6** helps **7** had, lived

B **1** I was good at English **2** I was too picky about food **3** somebody had stolen her cell phone **4** she had been looking forward to seeing me **5** Henry was the only person to solve the problem **6** South Korea and North Korea would be unified soon **7** Australia has opposite seasons to Korea

C **1** says, goes to church **2** said, is a friend indeed **3** believed, would succeed **4** didn't know, had been lying **5** were fighting, were arrested **6** knows, have been to Canada **7** know, broke out in 1939

D **1** no news is good news **2** you would go to their wedding **3** they had been married for ten years **4** she cleans her whole house every two weeks **5** Korea regained independence in 1945 **6** she had been accepted to graduate school **7** who are singing and dancing on the stage now are

UNIT 73

A **1** were only a few books **2** could she believe what had happened to her **3** have I experienced hot weather like this before **4** does she put on her makeup when she goes out **5** did I know that he had been helping the poor secretly **6** had he finished his work than he breathed a sigh of relief

B **1** did he **2** was I **3** did I **4** do I **5** can I **6** do I

C **1** comes the train **2** stood a little boy **3** have I seen **4** did I hear about **5** will I let **6** does he talk about **7** would she believe

D **1** stood a big dog **2** could she read his handwriting **3** is a room that the actors use **4** has she been late for school so far **5** had he left home than it started to rain **6** does she drink coffee at night **7** did I find the error in the presentation materials

UNIT 74

A **1** It is not clear why he suddenly quit the job. **2** It is dangerous to drive without wearing a seat belt. **3** It is true that you need to study hard to enter college. **4** It is too bad that you can't come to his birthday party. **5** It is dangerous to swim in the river without a life vest. **6** It is very embarrassing to make a mistake in front of many people. **7** It won't be easy to find someone who is fluent in both English and French.

B **1** It is warm clothes that you need for the camp. **2** It is in the restaurant that her husband is waiting for her now. **3** It was Mike that caused the car accident on his way home. **4** It was yesterday that she watched the baseball game on TV with her friends. **5** It is Ann that will meet her mother in front of the department store today.

C **1** is obvious that **2** was at the party that **3** was last week that **4** took her an hour to find **5** does hate **6** was unbelievable that **7** found it hard to persuade

D **1** It was in the theater that I ran into **2** It was half an hour ago that I ordered **3** It was useless to regret what I did **4** It took only half an hour for her to bake **5** It is she that is responsible for the failure **6** I do like eating out with my family

THIS IS GRAMMAR

이것이 진화하는 New This Is Grammar다!

· 판에 박힌 형식적인 표현보다 **원어민이 실제 일상 생활에서 바로 쓰는** 생활 영문법
· 문어체뿐만 아니라 **구어체 문법을 강조한 회화, 독해, 영작을 위한** 실용 영문법
· 현지에서 더는 사용하지 않는 낡은 영문법 대신 **시대의 흐름에 맞춘** 현대 영문법

이 책의 특징

★ 실생활에서 쓰는 문장과 대화, 지문으로 구성된 예문 수록
★ 핵심 문법 포인트를 보기 쉽게 도식화 · 도표화하여 구성
★ 다양하고 유용한 연습문제 및 리뷰, 리뷰 플러스 문제 수록
★ 중 · 고등 내신에 꼭 등장하는 어법 포인트의 철저한 분석 및 총정리
★ 회화 · 독해 · 영작 실력 향상의 토대인 문법 지식의 체계적 설명

This Is Grammar (최신개정판) 시리즈

초급 1, 2 **기초 문법 강화 + 내신 대비**
예비 중학생과 초급자를 위해 영어의 기본적 구조인 형태, 의미, 용법 등을 소개하고, 다양한 연습문제를 제공하고 있다. Key Point에 문법의 핵심 사항을 한눈에 보기 쉽게 도식화·도표화하여 정리하였다.

중급 1, 2 **문법 요(Key Point) + 체계적 설명**
중·고등 내신에 꼭 등장하는 문법 포인트를 철저히 분석하여 이해 및 암기가 쉽도록 예문과 함께 문법을 요약해 놓았다. 중급자들이 체계적으로 영문법을 학습할 수 있도록 충분한 콘텐츠를 제공하고 있다.

고급 1, 2 **핵심 문법 설명 + 각종 수험 대비**
중·고급 영어 학습자들을 대상으로 내신, 토익, 토플, 텝스 등 각종 시험을 완벽 대비할 수 있도록 중요 문법 포인트를 분석, 정리하였다. 다양하고 진정성 있는 지문들을 통해 풍부한 배경지식을 함께 쌓을 수 있다.

www.nexusEDU.kr
넥서스 초·중·고등 사이트

www.nexusbook.com
넥서스 홈페이지

책에 대해 궁금한 사항은 넥서스에듀 홈페이지 1:1 고객상담 게시판을 이용하세요.

초1	초2	초3	초4	초5	초6	중1	중2	중3	고1	고2	고3

Writing

- 공감 영문법+쓰기 1~2
- 도전만점 중등내신 서술형 1~4
- 영어일기 영작패턴 1-A, B · 2-A, B
- Smart Writing 1~2

Reading

- Reading 101 1~3
- Reading 공감 1~3
- This Is Reading Starter 1~3
- This Is Reading 전면 개정판 1~4
- 원서 술술 읽는 Smart Reading Basic 1~2
- 원서 술술 읽는 Smart Reading 1~2
- [특급 단기 특강] 구문독해 · 독해유형
- [앱솔루트 수능대비 영어독해 기출분석] 2019~2021학년도

Listening

- Listening 공감 1~3
- The Listening 1~4
- 넥서스 중학 영어듣기 모의고사 25회 1~3
- 도전! 만점 중학 영어듣기 모의고사 1~3
- 만점 적중 수능 듣기 모의고사 20회 · 35회

TEPS

- NEW TEPS 입문편 실전 250+ 청해 · 문법 · 독해
- NEW TEPS 기본편 실전 300+ 청해 · 문법 · 독해
- NEW TEPS 실력편 실전 400+ 청해 · 문법 · 독해
- NEW TEPS 마스터편 실전 500+ 청해 · 문법 · 독해